THE
ROMAN CATHOLICS

**Recent Titles in
Denominations in America**

The Unitarians and the Universalists
David Robinson

The Baptists
William Henry Brackney

The Quakers
Hugh Barbour and J. William Frost

The Congregationalists
J. William T. Youngs

The Presbyterians
Randall Balmer and John R. Fitzmier

THE
ROMAN CATHOLICS

PATRICK W. CAREY

Denominations in America, Number 6
Henry Warner Bowden, *Series Editor*

Greenwood Press
Westport, Connecticut · London

Library of Congress Cataloging-in-Publication Data

Carey, Patrick W.
   The Roman Catholics / Patrick W. Carey.
      p.   cm.—(Denominations in America, ISSN 0193–6883 ; no. 6)
   Includes bibliographical references and index.
   ISBN 0–313–25439–7 (alk. paper)
   1. Catholic Church—United States—History.   2. Catholics—United
States—Biography.   3. United States—Church history.   I. Title.
II. Series.
BX1406.2.C346   1993
282'.73—dc20   93–20125

British Library Cataloguing in Publication Data is available.

Library of Congress Catalog Card Number: 93–20125
ISBN: 0–313–25439–7
ISSN: 0193–6883

First published in 1993

Greenwood Press, 88 Post Road West, Westport, CT 06881
An imprint of Greenwood Publishing Group, Inc.

Printed in the United States of America

∞™

The paper used in this book complies with the
Permanent Paper Standard issued by the National
Information Standards Organization (Z39.48–1984).

10 9 8 7 6 5 4 3 2 1

To our sons, Brian and Michael

Think back on the days of old, think over the years, down the ages. Ask of your father, let him teach you; of your elders, let them enlighten you.

Deuteronomy 32:7

CONTENTS

SERIES FOREWORD

The Greenwood Press Denominations in America Series follows a distinguished precedent. These current volumes improve on earlier works by including more churches than before and by looking at all of them in a wider cultural context. The prototype for this series appeared almost a century ago. Between 1893 and 1897, twenty-four scholars collaborated in publishing thirteen volumes known popularly as the American Church History Series. These scholars found twenty religious groups to be worthy of separate treatment, either as major sections of a volume or as whole books in themselves. Scholars in this current series have found that outline to be unrealistic, with regional subgroups no longer warranting separate status and others having declined to marginality. Twenty organizations in the earlier series survive as nine in this collection, and two churches and an interdenominational bureau have been omitted. The old series also excluded some important churches of that time; others have gained great strength since then. So today, a new list of denominations, rectifying imbalance and recognizing modern significance, features many groups not included a century ago. The solid core of the old series remains in this new one, and in the present case a wider range of topics makes the study of denominational life in America more inclusive.

Some recent denominational histories have improved with greater attention to primary sources and more rigorous scholarly standards. But they have too frequently pursued themes for internal consumption alone. Volumes in the Greenwood Press series strive to surmount such parochialism while remaining grounded in the specific materials of concrete ecclesiastical traditions. They avoid placing a single denomination above others in its distinctive truth claims, ethical norms, and liturgical patterns. Instead, they set the history of each church in the larger religious and social context that shaped the emergence of notable denominational features. In this way the authors in this series help us understand the interaction that has occurred between different churches and the broader aspects of American culture.

Each of the historical studies in this current series has a strong biographical focus, using the real-life experiences of men and women in church life to highlight significant elements of an unfolding sequence. The first part of every volume singles out important watershed issues that affected a denomination's outlook and discusses the roles of those who influenced the flow of events. The second part consists of biographical sketches, featuring those persons and many others who contributed to the vitality of their religious heritage. This format enables authors to emphasize the distinctive features of their chosen subject and at the same time recognize the sharp particularities of individual attributes in the cumulative richness that their denomination possesses.

The author of this volume has met the challenge of a daunting task and has acquitted himself well in the face of it. American Roman Catholics stem from one of the most ancient forms of Christianity, and Carey does a wonderful job in balancing its earlier precedents with distinctive features developed on these shores. For the past 150 years this church has also been the largest single denomination in the United States, and here too the author has dealt admirably with core values shared over the centuries as well as the diverse elements that helped Catholic adherents grow to such impressive statistical strength. He includes here the familiar themes of nativist anti-Catholicism, immigration, and urban dioceses as centers of ecclesiastical power. He pays due notice to ethnic diversity and is sensitive to both abuses of authority and the calls for justice expressed by German, Irish, Italian, and Polish peoples, clergy and laity alike. As Professor and Chair in the Department of Theology at Marquette University, Carey is advantageously situated to take readers deftly through doctrinal controversies, considerations of canon law, and the influence that Rome has exerted over the years with its Curia and Councils. And perhaps most importantly he explains contemporary problems and options with considerable skill and even-handedness. All these virtues combine to forge within the following pages the most succinct, thorough, and judicious coverage of American Catholics to date.

HENRY WARNER BOWDEN

PREFACE

Contemporary American Catholicism, like its earlier forms, appears to many outside the tradition as a monolithic unity because of its centralized forms of government and its reliance upon institutions as signs of its strength and authority. Yet within Catholicism there are movement and change, adaptation and renewal, a manifold and dizzying diversity, and an openness and freedom that challenges neat historical categories. Whether the historian focuses upon the elite articulators and institutional implementations of the Catholic tradition or upon the people's reception and the popular, or folk, amalgamative appropriations of that tradition, he or she is in constant danger of overlooking or minimizing something that is significant to the total historical experience. History is not an exact science, and that is nowhere more evident than in the attempts to describe religious traditions—and especially in my own attempts here to make sense of American Catholicism.

This reference work is divided into two sections, the first being a narrative of selected themes and the second a series of biographical essays. The narrative focuses upon the themes of continuity and change, unity and diversity, growth and decline, alienation and reconciliation, as these recur in the institutional, intellectual, spiritual, ethnic, and political or social developments of the church. The first section analyzes in particular how the American experience itself (with its predominantly Protestant and republican culture) has influenced the reception and modification of the Catholic tradition.

The second section of this book contains a series of biographical sketches of significant ecclesiastical and lay leaders in American Catholicism. I selected the persons to be included on the principle that they could not be left out of any list of persons who have made major and explicit contributions to the life and/or thought of American Catholicism. Because of the limits of space and available biographical studies, however, I have not included a number of persons who were also important to the church's development. The biographies follow the pattern established by Henry Warner Bowden's *Dictionary of American Religious Biography* (Greenwood Press, 1977) and include the individual's published works (designated by A) and studies of the individual's life and work (designated by B). Most, although not all, of the individuals included in the biographical sketches are mentioned in the historical narrative, and where a name is first mentioned it is followed by an asterisk (*).

This volume also contains a basic chronology of the most important historical events in American Catholicism and a bibliographic essay that accentuates the most useful research tools for the study of American Catholicism and some of the more significant historical studies published since John Tracy Ellis and Robert Trisco's *Guide to American Catholic History* (Second Edition; ABC-Clio, 1982).

I am indebted to my teachers Colman Barry, O.S.B., Gerald Fogarty, S.J., and Robert Handy in particular for introducing me to the study of the religious and specifically Catholic dimension of American life. Many other teachers and historians also have a share in this work, some of whom are acknowledged in the endnotes, but many others remain unacknowledged simply because I have over the years appropriated so many of their interpretations that I no longer remember where I first got them and have unconsciously made their insights my own. I hope, however, that I have given proper citation to sources where I have been explicitly aware of my debt.

I would also like to thank Robert Trisco and Philip Gleason for giving me numerous valuable suggestions to improve the narrative section of this text.

I am grateful for grants from Marquette University's Religious Commitment Fund, the Graduate School, and the sabbatical leave program that enabled me to begin and finish this project. I am also thankful to my chairman, Philip Rossi, S.J., for periodically providing me with a reduced teaching load to complete this text.

Henry Warner Bowden has been a source of encouragement and skillful guide throughout the years this project has been in gestation.

While this project was underway, I had the pleasure of being aided by a number of graduate research assistants who did bibliographic research, prepared some preliminary biographical sketches, critiqued first drafts, and entered numerous corrections into the computer. For their assistance I would like to thank David Schimpf, Dominic Scibilia, Michael Naughton, Rebecca Kasper, Jonathan Zemler, and especially Pam Young, C.S.J., who prepared the final manuscript.

Work on this text has been the preoccupation of my mind for over six years, and no one knows that better than my wife, Phyllis, and our two sons, Brian and Michael. This book is dedicated to Brian and Michael. When they are older, may they appreciate, as I have, the religious tradition out of which we come and learn by experience and study the griefs and anxieties, the sorrows and pains, the joys and hopes, the comforts and challenges that living in such a faith tradition brings.

Part One
ROMAN CATHOLICISM: A HISTORY

1
MISSION CATHOLICISM: 1492–1840

From the sixteenth to the early nineteenth century, Spanish, French, and English missionaries, merchants, explorers, soldiers, governors, and their servants and slaves brought a Catholic presence to the New World. As part of the colonial expansion of their respective empires, the missionaries came to sustain the religious life of their compatriots and to evangelize the newly discovered peoples who inhabited the lands the colonials explored. They established parishes and missions to the Indians on the southern borderlands of the present United States from Florida to the Southwest, along the California coastland, on the northern borderlands from the St. Lawrence Seaway to the western Great Lakes, down the Mississippi River to New Orleans, and on the Mid-Atlantic coastlands of Maryland and Pennsylvania. The term "Mission Catholicism" designates an intermittent Catholic presence along the present borderlands of the United States.

Mission Catholicism existed in numerous isolated and loosely organized religious communities shepherded primarily by missionaries who were, until 1790, without the benefit of the episcopacy and other major ecclesiastical institutions that could ensure a stable and continuous Catholic life. The missionary enterprize was motivated by the long Christian tradition of spreading the faith, but it was also tied to the exploratory, colonizing, commercial, and military aims of the empires it represented. The execution of these motives provided for both the glory and the sadness of Mission Catholicism from the establishment of the first stable Spanish parish and mission in St. Augustine, Florida, in 1565 to the eventual secularization of the Spanish Indian missions in California in the 1830s. Because the missionary efforts were so closely aligned with the strengths and weaknesses of the states they represented, moreover, they generally experienced the fate of the political bodies with which they were legally, or at least culturally, identified. Spanish and French Catholicism within the present borders of the United States waned as soon as did Spanish and French political power; English Catholicism persisted and developed because it was hitched to Anglo-American fortunes.

SPANISH MISSIONS

On 12 October 1492, under the patronage of the Spanish crown, the Italian navigator Christopher Columbus and his sailor companions landed on one of the Bahamian Islands and named it San Salvador. That discovery opened up for the Spanish empire a new era of discovery, expansionism, colonization, cupidity, rapacity, and evangelization—a continuation of late fourteenth- and early fifteenth-century Spanish reconquest and religious revival. By the mid-sixteenth century, Spanish commerical and military powers as well as a full complement of ecclesiastical institutions (including dioceses, bishoprics, schools, plus numerous missions) were well established throughout the Antilles, Mexico, and Central and South America. By that time, too, the Spanish had explored the regions north of their central power bases—from Florida across the southern part of the United States into Texas and Mexico; from Mexico into the northern interiors of New Mexico, Arizona, and Kansas (discovering in the process the Colorado River, Rio Grande, and Grand Canyon); and from Mexico along the California coast to San Francisco.

The Spanish decided to establish military and ecclesiastical institutions on the northern reaches of their southern empire not because they discovered gold or commercial advantage in these lands, but primarily because they feared foreign—French, English, Russian, or American Indian—encroachments upon their southern American empire. In 1565, for example, Spain established a military outpost and a mission at St. Augustine in Florida once it learned that French Huguenots had planted a colony north of St. Augustine. Later, because of the threat of English colonies to the north, Spain sustained St. Augustine as a strategic outpost in the defense of the empire. New Spain established permanent settlements and supported missionary efforts in Texas only at the beginning of the eighteenth century because of French presence at New Orleans and along the Mississippi River. The early establishments in Arizona at the end of the seventeenth and beginning of the eighteenth centuries were in response to the threat of American Indian invasions of Spanish territories further south. The late eighteenth- and early nineteenth-century Spanish movements into upper California were reactions to the Russian settlements in Alaska. The one exception to this defensive posture appears to be the motivation for building Santa Fe and other New Mexican military and missionary outposts in the early seventeenth century.

The missions to the Indians as well as the presidios were, in Herbert E. Bolton's phrase, "outposts of empire." The intersecting of religious and military objectives was clear in the establishment of these two characteristic institutions of the Spanish empire on the northern frontier.[1] The presidio protected the Spanish empire further south, provided military assistance to the Indian missions, and helped enforce Christian discipline within them. The missions themselves provided the benefits of religion to the military, served as buffer zones between the Spanish military outposts and unfriendly Indians, became listening posts that provided the military with intelligence about warring Indian tribes and the movements of the French and English, and supplied the military with Christianized Indians to wage war against unfriendly Indians and invading foreigners.

For three centuries, Spanish missionaries developed five major mission territories on the North American frontiers and worked to convert the Indians to Christianity. Although the duration of these Indian missions varied from territory to territory, they all passed through three similar phases of historical development: establishment and organization, a golden age of success and prosperity, and, because of various internal and external problems, a period of decline and ruin from which they never rebounded even though some Spanish Catholic influence lingered on in these territories. The Florida missions lasted 198 years (1565–1763), those in New Mexico 230 years (1598–1680; 1692–1840), those in Texas 134 years (1659–1793),[2] those in Arizona 142 years (1700–1842), and those in California 65 years (1769–1834).

The Spanish established the missions to evangelize the Indians and thereby save their souls. To accomplish these goals they frequently sought to separate the Indians from their former way of life and to introduce and incorporate them into Spanish culture. The two complementary methods, separation and incorporation, were so integrally related that it was difficult for the Spanish or the Indians to distinguish between them. The missionaries believed that all people, Indians and Spaniards alike, were subjects of sin and redemption. The missionaries' task was to preach the good news of Christian redemption and free the Indians from their condition of sinful bondage. Many missionaries, however, identified the universal condition of sin with the Indian culture, which they saw as pagan and corrupt. Redemption and conversion meant more to these missionaries than freedom from the universality of sin; it meant that Indian civilization itself had to be wiped out and replaced by a Christianized Spanish culture. The Indians had to make a clean break with their past when they converted to Christianity.[3] Such a conception of the missionary task remained the dominant tradition among the Spanish from the sixteenth to the nineteenth century.

The Spanish missionaries emphasized not so much individual conversions as the communal means necessary for living a sanctified Christian life. Prior to baptism the missionaries gave their prospective converts a basic introduction to the Credo, believing that such a rudimentary knowledge of Christianity was all that European Catholic peasants possessed. But even this elementary introduction to Christianity could take years because the missionaries had to learn the Indian languages, discover concepts that could communicate the message of Christian redemption, and convince their prospective converts of the benefits of Christianity.

The missionaries also provided new forms of communal and cultural supports for the Christian neophytes. Once baptized the Indians were generally separated from their tribes to form new Christian communities. Under the guidance of the missionaries, the new Christians lived a routine quasi-monastic life of worship and work. In the ideal setting they were to experience regular hours of prayer, a cycle of annual liturgical celebrations, a cult of Mary and the saints, seasons of fasting, and daily catechetical instruction. Within such a communal life, the children of the new converts would receive baptism and likewise be nurtured in the Christian life.

Life in an Indian mission also demanded Christian discipline. Those who offended the moral and civil standards of mission life were duly punished, and those who ran away were brought back to the missions by the force of the state's military arm. Once baptized and initiated into the Christian community, the converts were expected to live in conformity with Christian standards and the moral expectations of Spanish social life.

The Spanish conceived of the Indian missions as transitory institutions that would provide the means of redemption, a basic evangelical introduction to and experience of Christian living, communal support, discipline, and a system for weaning the Christian neophytes away from their former pagan life-style so that they could eventually be fully incorporated into Spanish Christian congregations and culture. Regular hours for work in fields, tending cattle, preparing food, and building homes, churches, and other institutions for the mission became a significant part of mission life for the Indians and their clergy. Such a sedentary life-style fitted the Spanish pattern of civilization and religion, but it was frequently contrary to the nomadic style of life led by many Indians. The missionaries prepared their new converts to live this kind of disciplined life by giving manual as well as religious instructions. Although they learned how the Indians lived off the land, the missionaries taught them how to use the implements and arts of Spanish culture to provide for themselves in a Spanish Christian society.

Although separation and incorporation were the primary methods of evangelization within the Spanish tradition, there also developed a tradition of adaptation to Indian culture that some missionaries adopted as the chief means of evangelization. This second method, although frequently a part of the practice of separation and incorporation, demonstrated respect for Indian culture and used Indian languages and customs as a means of communicating the Christian gospel. From Bartolomé de Las Casas in the sixteenth century to Eusebio Kino,* S.J., in the eighteenth, moreover, missionaries here and there—horrified by the soldiers' rapacity, the merchants' and traders' cupidity, and the state's destruction of the Indians and their way of life—saw themselves as defenders of the Indians' natural rights and as barriers against the harsh and unjust governmental treatment and official massacres of the Indians. Although some missionaries were rigorous disciplinarians within the Indian missions, they rarely exercised the kind of violence that issued from other quarters of Spanish society. The line between the missionaries' complicity and their actual participation in the demolition of Indian culture was generally very thin, however.

Although the missions had some successes, they did not flourish for long nor did they serve a significant percentage of the Indian population. Eventually they all came to an end. In 1859, John Gilmary Shea, a historian of American Catholicism, wrote that the cause of their annihilation was not some inherent weakness in the mission system. For him, "the interference of government alone crushed them; . . . their ruin is chargeable to the English and Mexican governments, and to the inborn hostility of the Anglo-Saxon race to the Indians."[4] Internal difficulties, however, as well as external forces created, even in times of success, setbacks and eventually a period of decline and ruin.

Most of the missions shared similar internal reasons for their ultimate decline and failure. The mission system itself was supposed to be a transitory institution leading to the full incorporation of Indians into a parish church. For almost three hundred years, Catholicism on the northern frontiers of the Spanish empire was much like a preparatory school that had no available higher education. The Spanish Indian missions, although here and there temporarily successful, never developed Indian churches with native dioceses, bishops, parish priests, and all the sacramental and educational means necessary for nurturing and sustaining a mature Christian community. The Spanish commitment to the missionary efforts on the northern borderlands was never more than tenuous and marginal. Spain did not have the resources or the power to build the institutions necessary to sustain the Catholic church in North America. The establishment of the Spanish church would have brought with it the full complement of Spanish political, financial, and military power—as it had in Mexico and other Spanish dominions—but this never happened in the North American Spanish colonies. In the larger conception of Spanish policy in the Americas, as Bolton pointed out, the borderland missions were from their origins to their end mere defensive "outposts of empire."

Missionary success, even with the full complement of Spanish resources, would have been limited because of the clash of cultures. The Spanish Christian and the Indian cultures never accommodated themselves very easily to one another. The missionaries, soldiers, and governors, moreover, generally agreed that the best way to Christianize the Indians was to destroy their culture or at least keep the baptized Indians separated from their pagan backgrounds. Frequently the converted Indians living in the sedentary missions felt the pull of their former nomadic way of life and ran away, only to be brought back forceably by the arm of the law. Some missionaries, though, believed that it was unrealistic to expect the Indians to separate themselves completely from their former cultures. In 1714, Antonio de Miranda, O.F.M., recommended that the missionary have patience in weaning the Indians from their former life-styles. "Little by little he (the missionary) removes the weeds, and through patience he comes to see the garden free of darnel. But to will that the new plant bear leaves, flowers, and fruit all at once is to will not to harvest anything."[5]

Not all missionaries were as patient or hopeful about Christianizing the Indians or retaining the new converts. Father Joseph Perez, O.F.M., complained in 1817 that, after 130 years of missionary preaching at San Ignacio Mission in Arizona, only those Christian Indians who had died were safe (i.e., saved). "The grownups are full of superstitions, and no matter how the ministers work they do not believe them because they have more faith in their old medicine men."[6] After generations of missionary preaching and teaching, the missionaries could not eradicate the pull of the Indian way of life, and the Indians continued to practice their old religions.

Other internal forces eventually brought the missions to an end. Many missionaries failed to learn the Indian languages and cultures and failed to translate Christianity into Indian ways of thinking and conceiving of things. The Indians themselves, because of their harsh treatment and resistance to Spanish military intrusions and missionary tactics, periodically rebelled and revolted. The cycle of revolt and Spanish retaliations increased the instability of mission life and in many cases brought about the ruin of the missions. Church-state conflicts, usually between the missionaries and the military governors over jurisdiction and control of the Indians and their temporalities, also contributed to the decline. The inability of the Spanish to provide a constant supply of food and other material benefits, which were used to induce the Indians to remain in the missions, caused Indians to abandon their Christian missions. Deadly diseases, some of them brought by the Europeans, were also frequent visitors at the missions, and many Indians feared that the missionaries and the missions themselves were causes of death.

Even if the missions could have held up under the burdens of their own internal difficulties, they could not withstand the external forces that eventually destroyed them. The Anglo-American military force against the missions in Florida, the constant raids of unfriendly Indian tribes in Texas and the Southwest, the loss of Spanish political power and stability in the eighteenth and early nineteenth century, the Spanish removal of the Jesuit missionaries in the late eighteenth century, the Mexican War of Independence (1810–20), the struggle for Texas independence (1820–36), and the Mexican secularization of the California missions in the 1830s–all these things diverted political and economic attention away from the missions and in effect left them without those supports that were necessary for their survival within the Spanish context of the union of church and state.

In terms of Christian intention the missions were successful even though they had only a few lasting monuments to their credit. The gospel was preached, the kingdom of Christ was being spread to the "ends of the earth," genuine converts were undoubtedly made, salvation was made possible for numbers of natives, and missionaries fulfilled their own Christian responsibilities with zeal. These kinds of successes are not easily measured by the historian.

Although Spanish Catholicism was unsuccessful in making many Christian converts of the Indians, it did leave a remnant of Catholic presence in the territories the Spanish missionaries originally discovered and evangelized. That remnant became the foundation of an episcopally organized church. Cuba established a diocese in New Orleans in 1793 and sent a bishop, Luis Ignacio Marie de Penalver y Cardenas-Porro, there until 1801; Mexico appointed Francisco Garcia-Diego y Moreno to the two Californias in 1840. For the most part, though, the Americans would be responsible for establishing the institutional church in those areas. They erected dioceses and sent bishops to Galveston in 1842, Santa Fe and Monterey in 1850, St. Augustine in 1857, and Tucson in 1868. That is a story, however, for nineteenth-century American Catholicism.

FRENCH MISSIONS

The acquisition of fish and fur and a desire to spread the faith brought French Catholics to North America in the seventeenth century. From Acadia to the St. Lawrence Seaway to the Great Lakes and down the Mississippi to the Gulf of Mexico, the French established a colonial empire that encircled the English colonies to the south and east and provided a buffer for the Spanish to the west. Although the French built a few missionary outposts within the present boundaries of the United States, they had little success in sustaining them except in New Orleans, where the French presence continued to have a significant impact throughout the eighteenth and nineteenth centuries. Detroit, Vincennes, and St. Louis, too, maintained some French Catholic connections into the early nineteenth century, but for all practical purposes those towns were soon overtaken by the Americans shortly after the American Revolution. French missionary efforts to evangelize the Indians, although zealous and heroic, also had minimal lasting effects.

After a period of discovery and exploration in the early sixteenth century under Jacques Cartier and a few missionary efforts among the Indians in Acadia in the early seventeenth century, Samuel de Champlain founded Quebec (1608), which became the center of French commercial, political, and ecclesiastical work in the New World. Like Spain, France was a Catholic confessional state. The Gallican church and state enjoyed an alliance in the sixteenth, seventeenth, and eighteenth centuries that made it very difficult at times to distinguish political, commercial, and missionary goals; the three were so intertwined that the successes and failures of one depended upon those of the other two. Financial support for the missionaries, for example, periodically depended upon their benefit to the state's military and commercial objectives, which periodically warred with religious concerns. Church and state used each other to advance their own causes, even when those causes were not entirely compatible or reconcilable. In such circumstances of alliance, tensions between the church and the state were almost inevitable.

By the end of the seventeenth century, New France had developed both a colonial and a missionary church.[7] The colonial church, an extension of the Gallican church, had its headquarters in Quebec, where the first bishop, François de Montmorency de Laval, was consecrated in 1674 and where the French constructed a number of parishes, hospitals, seminaries, schools, and convents to serve the French and the Indians. Quebec was the structural backbone of the colonial church. Within the present borders of the United States the colonial church was for the most part far removed from the center of ecclesiastical power and supervision. Parishes for the French were established, for example, in Cahokia (1698), Biloxi (1699), Detroit (1704), Mobile (1710), New Orleans (1718), Vincennes (1734), Duquesne (1754), and a few other places in the Midwest during the mid-eighteenth century. Although the stories of these churches are significant, the most dramatic of the French efforts to plant the church in New France are found in the missionary efforts toward the Indians.

The French developed a missionary church to the Indians alongside and at times as part of the colonial church. French missionaries (Capuchins, Recollects, and especially Jesuits) evangelized, baptized, and established mission stations among the Abenakis in Nova Scotia and Maine periodically from 1610 to 1763, when France ceded Canada to England; among the Indians along the St. Lawrence Seaway (at Tadoussac, Quebec, Sillery, Three Rivers, and Montreal); among the Hurons below the Georgian Bay from 1634 until the Iroquois massacres of 1649; among the upstate New York Iroquois from the early 1650s to the 1680s; among the Hurons and other tribes in the far west at Sault Ste. Marie (Michigan) and Keweenaw Bay on Lake Superior in the 1660s; and, after Louis Jolliet and Jacques Marquette* explored the Mississippi River in 1673, a few missionaries were sent to the Illinois and other tribes in Michigan, Illinois, and Indiana.

Although the French Indian missions had the same ultimate purposes as the Spanish, they did not always engage in the same missionary strategies. At the beginning of the seventeenth century, many of the Jesuit missionaries tried to adapt themselves to the nomadic Indian life, but soon abandoned this procedure because it proved ineffective in establishing a stable Christian life among the tribes. Later they tried to convert the Indians to a sedentary life that would enable the missionaries to evangelize the Indians more effectively, instruct them in the Christian rituals, wean them from customs and practices that were inconsistent with Christian morality, and preserve them in a disciplined Christian way of life. Like the Spanish to the south and like their Jesuit brethren in Paraguay, the French Jesuits built missions they referred to as "reductions" to separate the Christian Indians from the villages of unconverted Indians.[8] The Jesuit missions to the Georgian Bay Hurons, although brief, were the most effective of the French "reductions." There the Jesuits built prayer huts (or churches) within the Indian tribal territories and, like the Spanish, tried to develop a regular cycle of Christian life and discipline within a Christian communal context.

Although the French Jesuits in particular accepted and lived with many of the existing Indian customs and sought to show the Christian dimension of indigeneous beliefs and morals, they resisted those things in the Indian way of life that they considered contrary to Christianity. Polygamy especially had the force of tradition within the Indian communities and frequently pulled the new converts away from the disciplined Christian life. One Jesuit reported that "of all the Christian laws which we propound to them, there is not one that seems as hard to them as that which forbids polygamy, and does not allow them to break the bonds of lawful marriage."[9] The Indians hated these restrictions upon their liberties, and the Jesuits discovered that the Christian Indians often found a monogamous marriage too difficult and frequently entered into scandalous relationships after conversion. The Indians resisted not only assimilation into a French life-style but also into a Christian moral life that conflicted with their own former religious traditions and customs, which had the sanction of their own communities. The Indian missionaries, like their third-century Christian predecessors, tried to separate the newly baptized and the catechumens permanently from former practices and customs that were opposed to Christian tradition, but they were successful only where they were able to sustain a mission for a period of generations.

Even within the sedentary missions, however, the missionaries soon discovered that the strategy of separation would not be effective unless it were accompanied by a genuine attempt to accommodate themselves to those things in the Indian life-style that were not inherently repugnant to Christianity. As one Jesuit put it in 1667–68:

We must then follow them [because we cannot expect to instruct them when they only occasionally come to us] to their homes and adapt [s'accommoder] ourselves to their ways, however ridiculous they may appear, in order to draw them to ours. And, as God made himself man in order to make men Gods, a Missionary does not fear to make himself a Savage, so to speak, with them, in order to make them Christians. Omnibus omnia factus sum.[10]

Whatever their methods the French missionaries believed that God alone was the founder of the Indian as well as the primitive church. The Jesuits in particular believed that martyrdom was the premier providential sign that God was directing the establishment of the churches in the wilderness. In 1639 the Jesuit Jerome Lalemant feared that the missions might be in bad shape because no priest had yet been martyred for the cause.[11] His fear was unwarranted. In subsequent years the Jesuit Relations (reports the Jesuit missionaries sent back to France) were filled with accounts of the martyrdoms of the Jesuits Isaac Jogues,* Jean de Brébeuf,* and numerous other Jesuits and Indian converts.[12] The story of Indian brutality against Jogues reads like stylized early Christian martyrologies:

He was greeted with a hundred beatings at the entrance to the Village where he was first conducted; there was no good mother's son who did not fling his paw or claw on this poor victim,—some struck him with heavy blows of cords, others with blows of sticks; some pulled and carried away the hair of his head; others, in derision, tore out the hair of his beard. A woman, or rather a Megera, takes his arm and cuts off, or rather saws off, with knife the thumb of his left hand; she cuts a gash, and goes in quest of the joint, with less skill, but with more cruelty than a butcher exercises upon a dead beast; in short, she lacerates and removes the whole mass of the thumb. Another bites one of the fingers of his right hand, injures the bone, and renders that poor finger crippled and useless; others tear out his nails, then put fire on the end of those poor fingers,—laid bare, in order to render the martyrdom more keenly felt. For all these pains, the poor Father had no other Physician or other Surgeon than patience; no other salve than pain, no other cover than the air which surrounded his wounds.[13]

Jogues found the "Royal Road of the Holy Cross" in the *Imitation of Christ* to be a fundamental source of "great peace, and repose in occasions of suffering."[14] Denying self, taking up the cross daily, and shedding one's blood as a witness to the Christian faith were the means of establishing God's glory in the missions. Repeatedly the missionaries recalled for their French reading audience the maxim of early Christianity that the "blood of the martyrs is the seed of the church."

Measured by the rod of human efficiency, historical efficacy, and ecclesiological stability and permanence, the French Indian missions within the present borders of the United States were generally failures. They produced few lasting results and collapsed for many of the same reasons that the Spanish missions miscarried. The French efforts were also doomed by the cession of Canada to England in 1763, the decline of Jesuit presence after the papal suppression of 1773, and a more general lack of sufficient personnel to serve the huge geographical expansion from the Niagara to New Orleans. By the end of the eighteenth century, for all practical purposes, the French Indian missions ceased to have any major impact, although a few Indians in the interiors of Indiana and Illinois throughout the latter half of the eighteenth and early part of the nineteenth century would continue to be served by French priests and would for years carry memories of the French blackrobes within their communities. Measured by the missionaries' standards of Christian witness or by the criterion of human courage and dedication, the Indian missions were a major achievement.

ENGLISH MISSIONS

From 1634 to 1776, English Catholics planted and sustained their religion in the colonies of Maryland and Pennsylvania, and, unlike their Spanish and French neighbors, they did so without the benefit of governmental financial or legal support and without the burden of serving in vast geographical territories. Unlike the Spanish and French, too, English Catholics were geographically surrounded by and lived in the midst of Protestants, who had previously built colonies in Virginia and Massachusetts and who were, from the beginning, a majority even within Maryland. Unlike their coreligionists to the north and south, moreover, the English Jesuits very quickly (i.e., by the 1640s) abandoned any efforts to evangelize and serve the Indians in Maryland (even though they originally intended to do so) and concentrated their religious efforts upon the Catholic colonists. Catholic presence in the English colonies, furthermore, unlike that of the Spanish and French missions, provided a firm foundation for a lasting influence of Catholicism in the United States.

In 1633 the English Catholic Cecil Calvert,* who had inherited his father George's* possessions and intention to establish a colony in the New World, obtained from King Charles I a charter that acknowledged Cecil's "laudable, and pious Zeal for extending the Christian Religion, and also the Territories of our Empire,"[15] and which made him the sole proprietor. The charter indicated that Maryland—like other English, Spanish, and French colonies—was established with mixed political, commercial, and religious motivations. Calvert appealed to Protestant and Catholic investors to initiate the Maryland project, but he received his greatest financial support from seventeen young Catholic gentry. In fact Catholics had, at least during the seventeenth century, a predominance of financial and political clout in the colony. The charter also gave Calvert the same patronage rights over the colony that the bishop of Durham had over that English province—that is, the power to erect and found all churches and chapels and the exemption from all laws of mortmain. To provide for the religious needs, Calvert invited the Jesuits to join the colony and, appealing to their missionary zeal, indicated that he wanted them to evangelize the Indians.

With these purposes in mind, Calvert's two ships, the Ark and the Dove, set sail and landed in Maryland in 1634. The 150 or so persons on board, mostly Protestant, included Calvert's brother Leonard, who was appointed governor of the new colony, three Jesuits (Fathers Andrew White* and John Altham and Brother Thomas Gervase), and a number of young Catholic investors. Although the colony was erected under the authority of a Protestant king, no Protestant ministers came with the first expedition, and in fact ministers of the Church of England would not appear in the colony until twenty years later.

Throughout the colonial period, the Jesuits provided the only Catholic religious leadership in Maryland and Pennsylvania and, as R. Emmett Curran, S. J., has noted, "constituted, almost exclusively, the institutional church in British America."[16] During the first 150 years, 113 Jesuit priests and thirty brothers served within the Maryland Province—although no more than five priests and four brothers served at any one time during the seventeenth century. The numbers of priests increased slightly in the eighteenth century, but by 1772 there were only twenty-three priests in the colony.[17] In terms of numbers, the English Catholic colony was far less impressive than the Catholic colonies to the south and north.

The Jesuits built plantation manors much like those of other Maryland gentlemen upon lands they received or purchased from the proprietor. Like other gentlemen planters, moreover, they eventually bought and sold black slaves to farm their plantations. By 1785, black Catholics, primarily slaves, made up more than 20 percent of Maryland's total Catholic population.[18] These plantations became the primary temporal support for the Jesuits' religious activities. Although the plantations forced the Jesuits to become involved in managing temporalities, which took time away from their religious mission, they freed the Jesuits from the temporal authority and control of the landed gentry (who had controlled the Jesuits in England) and enabled them to enjoy a certain amount of de facto separation from the proprietor and local Maryland government. This separation also, as Gerald Fogarty, S. J., has noted, "planted the seeds from which would grow the American Catholic tradition of religious liberty."[19]

The Jesuits were primarily responsible for sustaining and developing Catholic spiritual life not only in Maryland throughout the seventeenth and eighteenth centuries but also in Pennsylvania, where Irish and German immigrants and Maryland migrants had established Catholic communities at Conewago, Goshenhoppen, and Philadelphia during the eighteenth century. Like itinerant preachers in the nineteenth century, the Jesuits carried the chalice and Bible into the outlying regions of Maryland and Pennsylvania. On Sundays, either at the plantations, which became the liturgical centers of Catholic life during the entire colonial period, or at the mission stations outside the plantations, they observed a regular routine of hearing confessions, celebrating Mass, preaching, and giving catechetical instruction to adults and children.

The Jesuits fostered an Ignatian spirituality by leading prominent laity through the *Spiritual Exercises* and by encouraging study, reading, prayer, and meditation. They also tried periodically to establish some schools in Maryland for the education of Catholics, but because of a lack of resources and the penal laws, these schools never lasted beyond a few years. What little religious education there was took place within the manors, at the liturgical centers, and through the lending libraries some Jesuits set up at their plantations. Jesuits circulated Bibles, theology texts, apologetic works, and particularly devotional and spiritual manuals to the laity.[20] They also established religious confraternities to encourage personal meditation, adoration of the Blessed Sacrament, and devotion to the Sacred Heart—traditions that Jesuits had fostered in their European colleges and universities. It appears from some of the sources that these Jesuits were trying to erect in the Maryland wilderness quasi-collegial Catholic communities. Small prayer groups and reading circles served as cells of Christian growth and development within the larger communities—much like the schools of Lutheran pietism or the class meetings of John Wesley. Building up a devotional elite within the community was consistent with the sixteenth-century Jesuit tradition.

Eighteenth-century Maryland Catholic spirituality, like that in England, was also influenced to a considerable extent by the writings of Richard Challoner, vicar apostolic of London. His *Catholic Christian Instructed* (1737) and *Garden of the Soul* (1740) typified the kind of spirituality that was proposed for eighteenth-century English-speaking Catholics. *The Garden of the Soul* was a spiritual manual intended, as its subtitle indicated, for the English Catholic laity who, "Living in the World, Aspire to Devotion."[21] It prescribed spiritual practices that individuals could perform at home and in the ordinary conditions of their life in English society, and fostered a type of piety that was simple, sober, and unostentatious, befitting cultural circumstances of English and colonial Catholicism. Colonial Catholics did not always have the benefit of clerical and sacramental services. Those who were far removed from the liturgical centers probably conducted their own religious practices and observances within their homes or failed to live an overt religious life. Colonial religious life was a low-profile experience; Catholics carried on their religious traditions as quietly and privately as possible so as not to offend their neighbors and create a cause for open oppression. As the number of clergy and churches increased in Maryland during the latter half of the eighteenth century, the center of religious life, as Jay Dolan has pointed out, shifted from the home to the parish churches,[22] making the public expression of Catholicism more visible than had been the case earlier.

From the very beginning of the Maryland enterprise, Catholics and other Christians enjoyed an unprecedented degree of religious toleration. In 1632, Cecil Calvert gave his brother Leonard some instructions about conduct on board ship that indicate the low religious profile that would characterize the colony in the future: "be careful to preserve unity and peace amongst all the passengers on Shipp-board." They were to give no offence to Protestants, perform their religious services "as privately as may be," and should not even engage Protestants in discussions of religious matters. Calvert's highest priority as proprietor of the new colony was to maintain the colony's political and social harmony. Religion, he warned, should not be a source of civil disturbance.[23]

Until 1649, religious toleration derived from the proprietor's fiat, and thereafter it became the result of a legal enactment that Cecil Calvert had encouraged the Maryland Assembly to make. In 1649, Calvert argued that peace was the goal of all good politics, as it was of all genuine Christianity. God desired unity and peace, he told his colony, and "commands us to love one another; Christian Religion teaches us soe to doe for the accomplishment of Eternal happiness and human polity also adviseth it (for) our temporal felicity in this World."[24] Religious toleration was a necessary means to civil peace and was the surest way to secure God's blessings upon Maryland. The Maryland Assembly wrote an Act Concerning Religion (1649) that privileged Christianity, provided for toleration of all Christians, and imposed civil penalties and fines for blasphemy, derogatory talk against Mary, the apostles, and the evangelists, and for profanation of the sabbath.[25] The colonials had learned from experience, as the act indicated, that the legal establishment of religion had frequently "fallen out to be of dangerous Consequence in those commonwealthes where it hath been practiced."[26]

In 1654, a Puritan-controlled assembly revised the Act of 1649, excluding Catholics from general toleration. The revision, however, did not take permanent effect, and the colony continued to enjoy a general toleration for all Christians until the Glorious Revolution in 1689, when the king replaced the lord proprietor and gradually thereafter Catholics were excluded from the colony's political life. The Church of England became established by law in 1702, and Catholics were finally disfranchised in 1718. The Jesuit Peter Attwood complained that the earlier Maryland tradition, unlike that of other colonies, had extended traditional English freedoms to Catholics. The great reversal of that tradition in the aftermath of the Glorious Revolution was a violation of the common law.[27] The complaint was of no avail. Catholics would thereafter become second-class citizens and feel the sting, if not the rigors, of the establishment and penal law system.

From the beginnings of Maryland until the Glorious Revolution, prominent land-owning Catholic families, many of whom were related to the proprietor by marriage, had enjoyed social and economic prestige in the colony and an almost privileged status in its political life. These court Catholics helped to preserve Catholic freedoms but also caused a great deal of jealousy within the Protestant majority. Such political circumstances help to explain some of the dynamics behind the great reversal after the Glorious Revolution. Prominent Maryland Catholics continued to maintain some of their social and economic prestige, but because of legal restrictions, they no longer took part in Maryland's political activities. This situation enabled them to develop their plantations and commercial interests. The first Charles Carroll illustrates the point. He came to Maryland in 1688 to be Calvert's attorney general, but because of the revolution he was unable to serve in that capacity. Instead he began to lay the foundations for what would become a significant fortune for the Carroll family. Prominent land-wealthy Catholics like them continued to intermarry and pass on their fortunes to their heirs, giving them economic security in a colony where they did not have much political security or exercise any political functions. It would be from many of these prominent Maryland Catholics that significant support for the American Revolution would come between 1765 and 1776.

In 1765, the year of the Stamp Act, 256 Maryland Catholic gentlemen and in 1773 a few Jesuits, desirous of maintaining their low-profile Catholicism, protested against rumors that the vicar apostolic of London, Richard Challoner, wanted to establish a Catholic bishop in Maryland. They saw such an action as an occasion for increased Protestant opposition to Catholicism.[28] These Catholics, moreover, could not have been unaware of the increasing American resistance to the establishment of an Anglican episcopacy in the colonies. Many Anglo-Americans feared what Sydney Ahlstrom has called the "deeply ingrained 'anti prelatical' bias" that was a part of "the drift of American opinion" during the prerevolutionary years in the American colonies.[29] The establishment of an Anglican episcopacy would mean, they feared, the imposition of greater restrictions upon colonial freedoms. The episcopacy was seen as an instrumental means for reinforcing political oppression, a view that only gradually died out in American consciousness.[30] Maryland Catholics did not have any anti-prelatial biases, but they did fear the Protestant animus against the episcopacy and what that animosity might do to their own already limited liberties within the colony.

By 1773, the year of the Boston Tea Party, Charles Carroll of Carrollton,* the third Charles of that family, emerged as a significant political figure in Maryland. Carroll took up his pen in the *Maryland Gazette* to defend local autonomy and the constitutional rights of the Maryland legislature against what he perceived to be the usurpation of governor Robert Eden's proclamation establishing officers' fees in the colony.[31] Under the pseudonym "First Citizen," Carroll took issue with a Maryland attorney, Daniel Dulany, who had supported the governor, defended the legislature's rights, and objected on constitutional grounds to the governor's abuse of power.

In the course of the newspaper warfare with Carroll, Dulany charged, in ad hominem fashion, that Carroll, a Catholic, was disqualified from the debate. He was legally incapable of belonging to any branch of the legislature, could not even vote for representatives, and in fact was disabled by his own Catholic principles, which were distrusted by the laws, from interfering in the election of members.[32] Carroll shot back that his own "speculative notions of religion" and religious affiliation were private matters that had nothing to do with the interpretation of constitutional principles.[33]

Like other Enlightenment figures, Carroll had clearly separated religion and politics, had done much to raise the issues of natural rights and constitutional procedures, and was hailed as a rising star in the revolutionary generation. The fact that he was a Catholic did not seem to bother those who sided with him. His political prominence in this debate, though, did much to bring about a new era of religious toleration and eventually of religious liberty for Catholics.

Toleration for Catholics, however, was not easily won in America, as evidenced by the American reaction to the British Parliament's Quebec Act of 1774. Among other things, that act officially and legally acknowledged the Catholic church in Canada, providing Catholics with the full enjoyment of their religious rights. The First Continental Congress of 1774, like the "Suffolk County Resolves," protested against this act which was interpreted as "dangerous" not only to the Protestant religion but to the "civil rights and liberties of all Americans."[34] The protests manifested the long-standing colonial Protestant antipathy toward Catholicism as well as a fear of the British Parliament's increasing political tyranny.

The American oratory against the act made it impossible for the colonials to win the Canadians over to the cause of the Revolution. In 1776, however, the Continental Congress appointed a committee of Samuel Chase, Charles Carroll of Carrollton, and Benjamin Franklin to seek an alliance with the Canadians in the revolt against England. They also sent John Carroll,* Charles's cousin and a Jesuit priest before the papal suppression of the order in 1773, to accompany the committee, hoping that his Catholicism would help win over the French-

Canadian Catholics. The trip was doomed to failure from the start, but it did reveal a growing awareness of the political, if not religious, openness to and perhaps usefulness of Catholics in the war effort. Religious affiliation could not be overlooked entirely in the common project of war and independence.

During and after the Declaration of Independence, a number of Catholics from Maryland and Pennsylvania participated in the war effort and joined in the political process of constitution-building at the state and federal levels.[35] Daniel Carroll II,* Charles's cousin and John's brother, was elected a Maryland state senator and, together with fellow Catholic Thomas Fitzsimons of Philadelphia, served in the United States House of Representatives during the formation of the United States Constitution and Bill of Rights. Charles Carroll, however, was by far the most significant Catholic involved in the movement toward American liberty. He had written in favor of a constitutional government, acted as an adviser to the Continental Congress since 1774, made a trip to Canada on behalf of the revolutionary cause, helped form the Maryland State Constitution (1776) which acknowledged religious toleration for all Christians, was for a brief period a member of the United States Senate, and was a signer of the Declaration of Independence. In 1829, Carroll told a friend that when he signed the Declaration, he had in view "not only our independence of England but the toleration of all sects, professing the Christian religion, and communicating to them all great rights."[36] For many nineteenth-century American Catholics, Carroll was the paramount symbol of the compatibility of American and Catholic identities.

With the end of the war and the beginning of the process of political reorganization, a new era was dawning for American Catholics—one that would bring greater toleration and eventually religious liberty in the states as well as in the nation as a whole.

2
A FREE CHURCH IN THE REPUBLIC: 1776–1815

From 1776 until 1815, John Carroll was the central figure in the transformation and institutionalization of American Catholicism. Elected as the first American bishop in 1789, he presided over the initial stages of the development of the Catholic community from a tiny, geographically and politically restricted, colonial priestly mission into a free, geographically expansive, and episcopally organized national church. The Revolutionary War, the subsequent establishment of the United States Constitution and Bill of Rights, the French Revolution and the consequent arrival of French émigrés, and westward expansion were crucial events in these developments. By 1815 Catholicism had already undergone what Carroll had in 1783 called "a revolution, if possible, more extrordinary [sic], than our political one."[1]

The Catholic church took institutional shape in a new nation that was significantly influenced by the values of the Enlightenment and republicanism. Carroll, too, had been influenced by a moderate Catholic Enlightenment and had adopted the "language of a Republican."[2] Like many other Christian leaders in American society, he rejected what he considered the dangerous tendencies of an excessive rationalism, but he also tried to accommodate Catholicism to those values in the Enlightenment and in republicanism that he found genuinely consistent with the Catholic tradition.

Like the new nation itself, the American Catholic church was initially shaped in an atmosphere of unprecedented liberty; it became a free church in a free republic. This revolutionary and constitutional arrangement meant more than the removal of civil and political restraints upon Catholics. It meant that the church was on its own with regard to internal and external operations. The church was free to communicate the gospel, promote its spiritual and liturgical life, teach its distinctive doctrines, organize its institutions, and encourage its membership to support Catholic life and institutions voluntarily. Of its very nature, moreover, voluntaryism in religion demanded a spiritual revival that was built upon personal persuasion. Furthermore, Catholic identity, institutions, and particularly the Catholic understanding of freedom and religious authority would have to be established anew amid the changing political and cultural circumstances.

Catholics like John Carroll enthusiastically accepted civil and religious liberties not only because they were beneficial to Catholicism but also because they were thought to be based upon principles of reason and revelation.[3] Religious liberty and toleration, however, were not something American Catholics could take for granted in the early years of the new republic. A few states (e.g., Massachusetts, Connecticut, New York, the Carolinas), although granting toleration to Catholics, still retained restrictions upon full Catholic participation in the political process. Some individuals, too, periodically advocated more rigorous civil and political strictures upon Catholics in the new nation. Such circumstances made John Carroll apprehensive and anxious about the future of full religious freedom for Catholics. In the *Columbian Magazine* in 1787, the *Gazette of the United States* in 1789, and in a 1789 joint address with Catholic laity to George Washington,[4] Carroll advocated the full extension of religious liberty in all the state constitutions on the grounds that Catholics like other Americans had contributed their blood for the country's independence, and in justice they deserved equal political opportunity under the law.

The American Catholic encounter with modernity in the form of religious liberty, separation of church and state, and voluntaryism was not worked out with systematic reflection. American Catholics simply accepted the new dynamics and principles of the age and began to make the practical adjustments that were necessary to build up Catholic religious life and institutions.

Like that of many religious leaders in the new nation, John Carroll's first and abiding concern was for a revival of religious practices. In 1785, he reported that the religious vitality of Catholicism was at a low ebb. Catholics in Maryland and Pennsylvania were "rather faithful" to their religious obligations. Most of them went to confession and received the Eucharist once a year, fulfilling their Easter duty, but they rarely received the sacraments at other times during the year, and even when they did they had little religious fervor. By comparison, though, the new immigrants in the trading centers were weak Catholics, not even fulfilling their Easter duty. Almost all Catholics in the United States, too, failed to instruct their children and slaves in the basic elements of the faith. Consequently, many of the young were very lax in their morals.[5]

Carroll's extant sermons,[6] his diocesan synod of 1791, and his letters and instructions to his clergy stress the need for a general renewal of American Catholic piety. That reformation, made possible by the new political circumstances, centered on the two things he perceived to be most wanting—namely, the restoration of traditional Catholic practices, especially the frequent celebration of the Eucharist and Penance, and a conversion of the heart that was essential for a fruitful reception of the sacraments.

The diocesan synod of 1791 gave its highest priority to the revitalization of sacramental practices.[7] Canonical prescriptions, like those of the diocesan synod, indicate the ideals, not the historical reality. Catholics who lived at great distances from the major liturgical centers rarely had the opportunity, because of the scarcity of clergy, of attending Mass and the sacraments. Many scattered throughout Maryland and Pennsylvania attended Mass only once every other month. Those few families on the frontier settlements in Kentucky, Tennessee, Ohio, Indiana, and Illinois saw a priest perhaps once or twice a year. In those places, the Catholic faith was kept alive, if at all, through family religious services and prayers. Scarcity of clergy, some wandering and inept priests, weakness of Catholic "fervor," and ignorance of the fundamentals of the Catholic religion were continuing obstacles to the realization of the canonical vision. By 1791, however, the simple goals of a religious revival were set. The real work was to instruct the faithful and motivate them to a true conversion of heart.

Catholics needed a host of ecclesiastical and educational institutions as well as competent personnel to help bring about the converted heart. The creation of new structures and an increase in competent personnel were not in themselves the solution to the problem of religious vitality, but they could at least provide instrumental means to aid the revival. American Catholics, like Americans in general, were caught up in the postrevolutionary process of institutionalization—establishing new political institutions to correspond to republican ideology, reforming older models of ecclesiastical policy to adapt to the new political circumstances, and developing new legal institutions and business enterprises for law, order, and prosperity.

Carroll and the former Jesuit priests took some major steps to form a national church in spiritual communion with Rome—analogous to those in France or Spain—but one that would be adapted to the exigencies of the rising new nation. In the early 1780s they already considered themselves a national clergy. They asked Pope Pius VI in 1783, therefore, for an American superior over the missions because they did not want to give any offense to the new civil government by having their own spiritual jurisdiction depend upon some foreign ecclesiastical superior.[8] In 1784, Rome appointed John Carroll as the new American superior.

The appointment of a religious superior of the American missions, however, was not sufficient. The presence of some unruly priests, conflicts in some congregations, and distance from Roman jurisdiction made it increasingly evident by 1788, even to those clergy who had originally resisted it, that the church's future depended upon the establishment of an American bishop to enforce ecclesiastical discipline and create a truly national church. The clergy, accordingly, petitioned Pope Pius VI to allow them to elect their own bishop in order to "arouse the least suspicion and opposition among those with whom we live."[9]

As was generally the case in the late eighteenth century, Rome permitted the clergy to elect their own bishops, and John Carroll became the first to be elected in the United States. With the episcopacy thus established in 1789, American Catholics had the full institutional presence of Catholicism for the first time in 156 years. This presence stabilized American Catholicism and enabled the systematic development of other institutions which provided for the religious and cultural needs of the new nation. Now American Catholicism was no longer a Jesuit or ex-Jesuit mission (even though Rome would consider the United States missionary territory until 1908—a fact that periodically irritated some in the American church).

Shortly after his 1790 consecration in England, Carroll convoked a diocesan synod, in accordance with the decrees of the Council of Trent, to unite his clergy around him and consult with them on a number of issues: for example, the mode for the continuation of the episcopacy, the ordering and uniform administration of the sacraments and ecclesiastical discipline, the exterior government of the clergy, and the means for a decent support of the clergy.[10] Carroll, like other Gallican-trained clergy, repeatedly spoke of a national church, enthusiastically supported American customs and political ideals, and wanted his people to become American Catholics, but this did not mean a severance of communion with Rome. His own experience with the dissolution of the Jesuits made him aware of the dangers of an excessive nationalism and how that could and did injure the church. A synod was one way of bringing about uniform Catholic discipline that would provide a foundation for preserving communion with Rome. The synod met in Baltimore from November 7 to 10, 1791, and enacted a number of decrees that would govern the American church for the next thirty-seven years.

After the synod, Carroll wrote American Catholics a pastoral letter, a practice that would continue throughout the nineteenth and twentieth centuries after national episcopal synods and meetings, outlining the deliberations and stressing in particular the fundamental importance of the Christian education of youth. He encouraged parents themselves to train their children in the virtues of morality and religion and urged those with means to send their sons to Georgetown Academy, which had recently opened. Thorough learning would produce increased piety, and from that piety would flow a constant supply of priestly vocations.[11]

Voluntaryism was also a recurring theme in the pastoral. The need for education, schools, seminaries, and clergy demanded increased voluntary financial support from the laity. Carroll noted that voluntary contributions to the clergy and church were a relatively new practice for most American Catholics. In the immediate past, the Jesuits' plantations had supplied resources for the support of the clergy, but this was no longer sufficient to respond to current exigencies. Carroll appealed to Biblical injunctions and the practice of primitive Christianity. He reminded his people, in particular, that the ecclesiastical canons of the Catholic tradition had divided voluntary offerings into three parts: the first for the minister, the second for the poor, and the third for the building and repair of churches.[12]

The synod also discussed means for the continuation of the American epis-copacy, but apparently nothing was decided. Two options were available: One was to select a coadjutor, the other was to divide the diocese. Carroll preferred division, but Rome decided in favor of a coadjutor, chosen with the consulta-tive voice of the clergy. In 1792, Carroll continued to advocate the election of bishops. Though he was opposed to an "ecclesiastical democracy" of the kind Bishop John Milner of England had likewise opposed in 1792, he sincerely wished "that Bishops may be elected, at this distance from Rome, by a select body of Clergy, constituting, as it were, a Cathedral chapter. Otherwise, we never shall be viewed kindly by our government here, and discontents, even amongst our own Clergy, will break out."[13] For a variety of reasons, not the least of which was Carroll's increasing reluctance to consult a clergy who had periodically opposed him and had been the source of discontent in a few con-gregations, the clergy did not formally participate in the election of new bish-ops.

The first major sign of institutional expansion occurred in 1808, when Rome made Baltimore an archdiocesan see, with suffragan dioceses in Boston, New York, Philadelphia, and Bardstown, Kentucky, and appointed new bishops (i.e., John Cheverus, Luke Concanen, O.P., Michael Egan, O.F.M., and Benedict Joseph Flaget, S.S.*). Distance of the congregations from Baltimore and Car-roll's age (he was seventy-three in 1808) made it impractical for him to con-tinue to administer the loosely organized body. Although the new bishops func-tioned more like mendicant priests than European princes of the church, they provided the kind of institutional leadership and jurisdiction that promised a permanent Catholic presence in these rapidly developing areas.

Like many leaders of this age of new institutions, Carroll saw the future of the country and the church in terms of education and piety. He became an original member of the boards of trustees for St. John's College in Annapolis, Maryland, and the University of Pennsylvania, both nondenominational schools. He also envisioned and helped to establish Georgetown College. In 1783, he told an English correspondent, "The object nearest my heart is to establish a college on this continent for the education of youth, which might at the same time be a Seminary for future Clergymen."[14] The future of the church, the continuation of the ministry, and the adaptation of Catholicism to American ideals and circumstances depended upon the schools.[15]

Lack of money and adequate teachers, the perennial problem of Catholic schools in the United States, plagued the new educational adventures from the beginnings. Catholic education in a republican environment was the basis of "all our hopes," as Carroll put it. By the end of his episcopacy in 1815, he had witnessed the establishment of three seminaries for the education of priests, three colleges for men, and several academies for young women.

Schools demanded faculty, and Carroll had a difficult time supplying an ad-equate one. In 1791, fleeing the terror of the French Revolution, the Paris Sulpicians, an order dedicated to the education of Catholic clergy, came to

Baltimore to establish the first seminary in the United States exclusively devoted to the theological education of the clergy. The Sulpicians' formation of the American clergy, their membership in the episcopacy, their involvement in missionary activities in the West, and their advice to the archbishops of Baltimore had a significant Gallican influence upon the development of antebellum Catholicism.[16] During the Reign of Terror in France, numerous other French clergymen came to the United States for refuge and began to serve the needs of the rising American church, deepening the Gallican dimension of antebellum American Catholicism. The French émigrés were well educated in languages and theology, and with their contacts in France, the new French bishops in particular were able to enlist significant numbers of French clergy to serve in American dioceses.

From 1776 to 1815, the number of clergy was greatly increased not only because of the French Revolution and its aftermath, but also because of the newly established seminary and the immigration of other clergy from Europe. In 1785, for example, John Carroll counted 24 priests, most of them ex-Jesuits; by 1808, there were 68; and by 1830, there were 232.[17] The rapid growth of clergy in the Maryland diocese, the most populous center of Catholicism, illustrates this point. In 1785, there were 19 priests in Maryland; by 1818, there were 52—14 of whom were French, 12 Americans, 11 Irish, and the remainder from other European countries.[18] During the Carroll years, moreover, a number of other religious orders of men established themselves in the United States, increasing the number of clergy. The Augustinians came to Philadelphia in 1796, the Dominicans established St. Rose's Priory in Kentucky in 1806, and the ex-Jesuits became affiliated with the unsuppressed Russian branch of their order in 1804 and were fully restored by papal decree in 1815.

Women religious also contributed to the foundation of the American Catholic educational and social mission during the first period of the church's institutional development.[19] The French Ursulines of New Orleans had established a day school and a boarding school for young women as early as 1727, and during Carroll's days, they continued these services once Louisiana became a part of the United States. The Carmelites (1790), a contemplative order of women, the Poor Clares (1790s), the Visitations (1808), and the Oblates of Providence, founded by Mary Elizabeth Lange* (1828), were all established in Baltimore. Mother Elizabeth Seton* founded the Sisters of Charity of St. Joseph in 1808 at Emmitsburg, Maryland, near Mount St. Mary's, a Sulpician college for young men. They grew rapidly and eventually erected houses, orphanages, schools, and hospitals in New York, Philadelphia, and Baltimore. The Sisters of Loretto (1812), the Sisters of Charity (Nazareth, 1812), and the Dominicans (1822) were established in Bardstown, Kentucky, as were the Sisters of Our Lady of Mercy in Charleston (1829). Mother Rose Philippine Duchesne* and her Religious of the Sacred Heart, a French order of nuns, came to St. Louis in 1818 and by 1829 had founded a number of schools and hospitals from there to New Orleans. The number of women religious increased from none in the 1780s to 1,344 in 1850.[20] Even by 1818, the number of "young American ladies" who aspired to religious life had risen so dramatically that Baltimore's Archbishop Ambrose Maréchal* rejoiced while complaining to Rome that he needed to exercise vigilance "lest more than can be cared for be admitted to the monasteries which exist in my diocese."[21]

The numerical growth and geographic expansion of convents demonstrated the widespread religious revival that was taking place in early nineteenth-century Catholicism, and manifested the essential role women religious played in the expansion, institutionalization, and Christian nurture of American Catholicism.

Social, ethnic, racial, and political diversity characterized the lay Catholic community from the beginning of Carroll's episcopacy, and that diversity increased drastically after his death. The most visible and public-minded Catholics were the old-guard Maryland and Pennsylvania families (e.g., the Neales, Brents, Carrolls, Taneys, Fitzsimons, and Barrys), who had land and wealth, commercial enterprises, foreign educations, social prestige, family ties, and close association with the Federalist Party in politics. They were Catholics by birth, family persuasion, and conviction. Their experiences in colonial times had taught them to separate religion and politics, the spiritual from the temporal realm. Like their Protestant neighbors, they rarely doubted their birthright as Americans and, because of their social positions, were engaged in building the new nation.

Some Catholics outside of Maryland were also "Catholic Citizens," as John Tracy Ellis* called them, who participated actively in American public life.[22] Francis Cooper and Andrew Morris of New York, Father Gabriel Richard* of Detroit, and William Gaston* of North Carolina, for example, were elected either to the United States Congress or to local state legislatures. Roger Brooke Taney* of Baltimore was appointed to the United States Supreme Court. Mathew Carey* of Philadelphia placed his wealth, talent, and pen at the service of numerous common political, economic, and social causes. Robert Walsh,* also from Philadelphia, entered into the spirit of the nation in 1811 when he launched his *Review of History and Politics* to provide a forum for the rise of a national literature that would display the country's genius and promote liberal and useful science. Like others influenced by the spirit of republicanism, he was interested in the common good. Christianity was the fundamental source of this public-spirited mentality, many like Carey thought, and bishops such as John Carroll and Louis William Dubourg* repeatedly spoke of the marriage of religious virtue and public life. Bishop John Cheverus of Boston summed up this attitude when he wrote to Irish Catholic immigrants of Hartford in 1823: "Be sober, honest, and industrious; serve faithfully those who employ you, and show that a good Catholic is a good member of society, that he feels grateful to those who are kind to strangers, and sincerely loves his brethren of all persuasions, though he strictly adheres to the doctrines of his own church."[23]

Other older Catholic families in Maryland and Pennsylvania were farmers, small businessmen, and laborers with varying degrees of wealth and different ethnic and racial origins. Some Native American Catholic families, too, lived in Maine and along the Wabash River in the present state of Indiana. Many Catholic congregations, moreover, had their own local elites—men who were generally elected lay trustees and who financed and governed their congregations' temporalities with a sense of their own responsibility for their local churches. These persons, too, wanted to live in peace with their Protestant neighbors and periodically joined them in common civic enterprises.

The ideal of mingling freely in American society was not just the result of an Anglo-Catholic mentality that had arisen in Maryland and Pennsylvania, as some have argued; it was the necessary result of conditions in the early republic. French, Irish, Italian, German, Spanish, Portuguese, as well as Anglo-Catholics during this period were in tiny Catholic communities that were inevitably a part of the life of their towns and cities. There were not enough Catholics in any single state or city to create a sense of Catholic or ethnic identity separate from their American identity.

Until the 1790s, southern Anglo-Catholics constituted the majority within the Catholic community, even though there were pockets of German, French, and Irish Catholics. Gradually after the 1790s, however, the ethnic character of American Catholicism began to change, and with this change came a host of tensions that would continue to disturb the Catholic community throughout the nineteenth and early twentieth centuries. The French Revolution in 1789 and the San Domingo revolt of 1791 brought a host of black and white French-speaking Catholics to Eastern Seaboard cities. In some, like Baltimore, the Catholic population in 1793 was immediately doubled by boat loads of Catholics from San Domingo. Other seaports experienced similar increases. With the Louisiana Purchase in 1803, the entire lower Mississippi Valley came into the American Catholic communion and significantly increased the number of French and Spanish Catholics in the United States.[24]

Irish immigration also began to change the social character of American Catholicism. Between 1785 and 1805, a steady trickle of Irish Catholic immigrants came to Philadelphia, Boston, New York, Norfolk, and Charleston, bringing enough Catholics to the last four cities to begin new Catholic congregations. The Irish Rebellion of 1798 and continuing economic troubles in Ireland increased Catholic emigration to the United States until it became a veritable flood in the 1830s and 1840s. But, before the Irish immigrants would eventually outnumber the Anglo and French Catholics, they would have little influence upon the selection of the American Catholic hierarchy or the direction of American Catholicism. That is a story that remains to be told.

French and Irish Catholic immigration during the Carroll era, although numerically small by comparison to later years, was significant not only because these immigrants established the first new congregations along the Eastern Seaboard, but also because they were the first Catholics that Americans in those places would come to know. Internal tensions and ethnic hostilities in these first congregations, in John Carroll's estimation, both broke the Catholic bond of peace and community and created a bad reputation for Catholics in American society. He advised the new immigrants to become "not Irish, nor English, or French congregations and churches, but Catholic-American" ones.[25] Creating Catholic-American congregations was no easy task for the new immigrants, but they did set up patterns of assimilation and lay forms of ecclesiastical organization that would influence Catholic presence in these cities for years to come. Necessity, remembered Catholic traditions, the spirit of republicanism in American society, and American laws regarding the incorporation of religious societies were combined in the formation of these new congregations. This combination also produced a crisis within the Catholic community, which will be described later, as the lay Catholic leaders tried to accommodate themselves and their congregations to the ideals and realities of postrevolutionary America.

By the time John Carroll died in 1815, American Catholicism had been significantly transformed. The establishment of the episcopacy, religious orders, schools, and new congregations provided a solid institutional basis for further growth and development. The Catholic population, which John Carroll estimated at twenty-five thousand in 1785, almost quadrupled by 1815 because of natural increase, immigration, and the acquisition of the Louisiana Territory.[26] Catholicism had also expanded geographically. In 1785, Catholics were primarily located in Maryland and Pennsylvania, with a few in New York and throughout Virginia. By 1815, they were spread along the Eastern Seaboard from Maine to Florida, and from Detroit to New Orleans. Anglo and other ethnic Catholics also became a part of the early American movement into the frontiers of upstate New York, western Pennsylvania, Kentucky, and the Ohio River Valley and the Mississippi River Valley where French Catholics had previously established a few pioneer villages. Wherever Catholics went, they intended to preserve the church by establishing as soon as possible the episcopacy as a permanent sign of the church's presence and as a promise of institutional stability, even when numbers did not justify the erection of new dioceses. Frontier Catholicism would develop rapidly in the remaining antebellum period, but during the beginnings of this rapid growth and extension into the West, American Catholics would experience an age of severe crisis that would threaten to shake the foundations that had just been established.

3
CRISES AND IMMIGRANT CATHOLICISM: 1815–1866

From 1815 to the convocation of the first provincial council of Baltimore in 1829, American Catholicism painfully adjusted to a nation that was itself being transformed by the rise of popular republicanism. Because of the internal battles over lay trusteeism, these years in particular were crucial for the gradual institutional transformation of the Catholic church from a loose confederation of local congregations under minimal, and at times ineffective, episcopal supervision to a nationally organized denomination under forceful episcopal leadership.

From the rise of Andrew Jackson to the end of the Civil War, moreover, American society experienced a new age of intellectual ferment, social and religious reform, economic and cultural disruption, conflicts over slavery, and religious and racial antagonisms that challenged the country's republican fiber and tested its own ideals. The first great economic depression, the Mexican-American War of manifest destiny and expansion, the displacement and removals of the Indians, the California gold rush and geographical expansion west of the Mississippi River, the flowering of American Protestant evangelicalism, the rise of Transcendentalism and abolitionism, the tidal waves of Catholic immigration, and the emergence of a virulent anti-Catholic nativism created conditions for the simultaneous growth and social transformation of American Catholicism: numerically from one of the smaller American religious communities to the largest single denomination; culturally from an Anglo-American community to a predominantly immigrant community; and religiously from a simple home-centered spirituality to an emotional, highly organized, and ostentatious devotional spirituality that was parish-centered.

The most significant crisis before the first provincial council, and one that was symptomatic of new anxieties in American culture, was lay trusteeism, a Catholic form of popular republicanism that asserted lay rights and powers at the parish level.[1] Lay trusteeism had its roots in Carroll's episcopacy but became much more volatile and assertive after his death, becoming the first major internal test of American Catholic identity in the new republic. How American or how republican and democratic could the ancient Catholic hierarchical institutions become and still retain their continuity with the Catholic tradition? That was the question of the day. Lay trusteeism arose when Catholic laymen in a few cities and towns formed themselves into voluntary corporations in accordance with the laws of their respective states and/or in conjunction with the ancient Catholic practice of lay patronage in order to purchase property, build churches, and organize their Catholic communities.

Generally, this process put the laymen, who were elected trustees of their churches, in legal control of the properties. The lay trustees also periodically hired and fired their pastors, created major internal congregational conflicts in their fights with pastors and bishops, and used the American courts and legislatures to win a voice and some legal power within their ecclesial communities. The lay trustees considered themselves the governors of the church's temporalities and generally looked upon their clergy as ministers of the church's spiritual affairs—a division of labor that corresponded to the American republican separation of religious and temporal affairs. Many of the articulate trustees argued for the creation of a republican Catholic church, one that would be significantly accommodated to national principles and practices, believing that the church had always adapted itself to the culture of its people in the past.

Baltimore's archbishop, Ambrose Maréchal, and some of the other French-American bishops were not entirely opposed to some form of lay participation within the church, and Bishop John England* even favored some form of diocesan democratic governance that significantly included the lay voice. For the most part, though, bishops and pastors vehemently rejected the trustee form of ecclesiastical republicanism. Most bishops and some pastors entered into a pamphlet war with their lay trustees, periodically took them to the civil courts to settle specific issues, presented petitions before state legislatures, and appealed to the papacy to reinforce the hierarchical nature of the church. When all of these attempts to gain authority over lay trustee–controlled congregations proved ineffective, James Whitfield, Baltimore's archbishop, convoked the first provincial council (1829) where the bishops legislated against the laity holding titles to ecclesiastical properties; reaffirmed the bishop's exclusive right to select, appoint, and remove pastors; and outlawed lay patronage in the United States.

Out of the struggle over lay trusteeism came a strong reassertion of episcopal authority and power within the church; and the means of asserting that power, the provincial council, initiated a distinctive national episcopal conciliar governing tradition that set the tone and direction for nineteenth-century American Catholicism.[2] Although the provincial council did not in fact bring trusteeism to an end (it would reappear again and again, here and there, throughout the remainder of the nineteenth and early twentieth centuries), it mustered a united and nationally organized episcopal force against it that was difficult, if not impossible, for subsequent lay trustees to resist. Henceforth, too, the bishops would have the major voice in articulating Catholic identity, and they identified Catholicism with a strong hierarchical institution where the lines of authority and power were clearly drawn. By 1829 episcopal authority on the national and local levels called for the creation and mustering of new institutional resources to meet the social and religious needs of a vast immigration. Among other things, the development of Catholic episcopalism produced a violent nativism that threatened Catholic internal unity and self-identity.

Between 1830 and 1866 at least two distinctive social traditions of American Catholicism developed. Although united institutionally, doctrinally, and sacramentally, they had different religious and social sensibilities and ways of perceiving and relating to the world around them. In the course of these thirty-six years, the immigrant tradition would become the dominant one. Because of the external conditions of nativism and the internal exigencies of immigrant life, the immigrant form of American Catholicism increasingly developed religious and ethnic solidarity, cultural isolationism, institutional separatism, and an aggressive minority consciousness that was defensive as well as insular. Segregated by internal choice as well as by external alienation though these Catholics were from much of mainstream America, they appropriated many values of the host culture and "Catholicized" them in the process, contributing to the larger religious life of American immigrant peoples and to the general social and educational welfare of the country.

The second social tradition, a numerical minority impulse, was significantly influenced by a romanticism that saw in Catholicism the religious, communal, and sacramental sensibilities which could satisfy the human longing for continuity, community, tradition, and authority in a world perceived to be increasingly torn apart by religious individualism and relativism. This tradition was articulated primarily by the converts Isaac Hecker* and Orestes Brownson* who were at home in the Anglo-American republican tradition and understood Catholicism, when interpreted in the light of their own post-Kantian idealist philosophies, as compatible with American republicanism. Although Hecker and Brownson, like the immigrant Catholics, separated themselves from those elements in American culture that they believed were hostile to the development of a genuine social Christianity, they, unlike the immigrants, encouraged Catholics not simply to preserve Catholicism in its ethnic conclaves but to make America itself Catholic.

The American Catholic population increased by an overwhelming and historically unprecedented 1,300 percent, from about 318,000 in 1830—3 percent of the total American white population—to 4.5 million in 1870, representing about 13 percent of that population.[3] By 1850 Catholicism was the largest single denomination in the country, and although it still represented only a small percentage of the country's total population, it had developed a strong institutional presence from coast to coast. The phenomenal numerical increase and geographical institutional expansion were due to massive immigration, primarily of Irish and German Catholics, the annexation of Texas in 1845, the acquisition of territories in the Southwest and California after the Mexican-American War (1846–48) and the Treaty of Guadalupe Hidalgo (1848), and the acquisition of the Pacific Northwest territories (1846).

Immigration and geographical expansion significantly increased ethnic and regional diversity within American Catholicism. In addition to the Anglo-Americans of Maryland and Kentucky, American Catholicism encompassed the cultural and religious traditions of the French and Spanish as well as the white and African-American Creoles in Louisiana; the free and slave African-Americans throughout the South; the new Irish and German immigrants in the Northeast and Midwest; a few Native Americans in Maine, the Midwest, Southwest, and Pacific Northwest; some French Canadians in the Northeast and Northwest; and Spanish-speaking peoples in Texas, the Southwest, and California.[4] Especially after the potato famine in the 1840s, waves of Irish immigrants were brought to American shores. By 1860, it has been estimated, 63 percent of the Catholic population was of Irish stock.[5] Over six hundred thousand German Catholic immigrants came to the United States by 1870, when they represented about 15 percent of the Catholic population.[6] Already during the late eighteenth and early nineteenth century, a few had established themselves and their separate national parishes in Pennsylvania, Maryland, and New York City. In the post-1830 period, and especially after the revolutions of 1848, they came in large numbers to Cincinnati, St. Louis, and Milwaukee, the so-called German triangle.[7] By the end of the Civil War about 78 percent of the Catholic population was of Irish and German heritage, significantly increasing the foreign character of Catholicism. The center of the Catholic population and presence, moreover, had shifted from Maryland to New York, the Northeast, and Midwest.

The rapid increase of Catholic immigrants, the geographical spread of Catholicism, the manifestations of institutional strength and stability, the emancipation of Catholics in England and Ireland in 1829, and traditional Protestant-Catholic theological antagonisms brought about a virulent hostility toward American Catholics, particularly after 1830. Catholic life in this period cannot be understood outside the context of what Ray Allen Billington called "The Protestant Crusade."[8]

This crusade was verbal, militant, and organized—culminating in the Know Nothing political movement of the 1850s. Catholics were under siege, and their leaders in particular felt the blows of the warfare. In politics, American nativists charged, Catholicism was an enemy of republican institutions and a friend of foreign despotism. Catholic theology, dogmatic and conciliar statements, as well as papal and episcopal church structures were basically opposed to republicanism, democracy, and civil and religious liberties. In religion Catholics were priest-ridden, intolerant, proscriptive, and against free rational inquiry. Catholicism was also against the spirit of the age, the great foe of progress, and clung to outdated religious forms. It was the religion of a dead tradition, having little interior religious life and little respect for the Bible. In social, economic, cultural, and moral life, Catholicism tended to debase its members, hindered their material prosperity, encouraged ignorance and superstition, and failed to insist upon an adequate moral code. In the words of William Ellery Channing, who was himself open to, and supportive of, Catholics in a number of ways, Catholicism belonged to "the dogmatical age of Christianity," an age that was swiftly passing away.[9]

This composite of charges represented a general Protestant assessment of Catholicism that was propagated in secular and religious newspapers, histories, school textbooks, polemical religious debates, and even in some political campaigns. Although most Protestants shared the general assessment of Catholicism, only a few entered into the lurid publishing crusades or into the burning of the Charlestown, Massachusetts, Ursuline convent in 1834, the Philadelphia Bible riots in 1844, and Louisville's "Bloody Monday" battles in 1855.

The Protestant crusade had a considerable effect upon the church's defensive and insular posture in theological reflection, apologetics, institution-building, spiritual programs, missionary endeavors, and especially in the indefinable area of the Catholic imagination. The primary agency for the Catholic defense was the newspaper.[10] The American propensity for reading newspapers and the use of them for anti-Catholic propaganda convinced Bishop John England and others after 1820 to publish their own newspapers as a means of communicating their doctrines and defending themselves before the public. Catholics repeatedly asserted their Americanism and increasingly emphasized those distinctive elements in their tradition (e.g., ecclesiastical unity, hierarchical authority, historical continuity) that distinguished and separated them from their Protestant neighbors. Church leaders, moreover, tried to construct a strong internal religious identity that would enable Catholics to withstand assaults from without. At the same time, they retaliated with their own aggressive counteroffensive.

The American Catholic view of Protestantism was as reductive as the nativist view of Catholicism. Whatever was good in it—that is, the fundamental Christian dogmas—had been retained from the Catholic tradition. Although a number of good people embraced Protestantism, it was a new religious system and a human invention that could not be traced back any further than the sixteenth century. The essence of it was a private interpretation of the Bible which led inevitably to protesting individualism and ultimately to the breakup of all ecclesiastical unity. And being internally divisive, it could not contribute to social and political unity and stability.

Catholic apologists did not see much good in Protestantism, and if they did, they rarely mentioned it. Bishops and missionaries, though, repeatedly and privately reported to Rome and to European missionary agencies that Protestantism was the dominant force in the United States and that it was able to win over a number of Catholics who did not have sufficient clergy or churches. These Catholics implicitly acknowledged the force of Protestantism, and although they publicly assailed Protestantism for its inability to convert the Indians, they privately feared that it was indeed making successful efforts among Indians, African-Americans, and even some immigrants. In fact one of the nineteenth-century motives for missions to the Indians and the westward expansion of Catholicism was the apparent success Protestant missionaries and Bible societies were having in the West.

By the 1850s Catholics were mounting their own crusade to make America Catholic. Few were as bold or, given the nativist mentality of the times, as arrogant and aggressive as New York's Bishop John Hughes* in articulating the Catholic design. Hughes preached:

Everybody should know that we have for our mission to convert the world, including the inhabitants of the United States, the people of the cities, and the people of the country, the officers of the navy and the marines, commanders of the army, the Legislatures, the Senate, the Cabinet, the President, and all! . . . There is no secrecy in all this. It is the commission of God to His Church, and not a human project.[11]

Catholics in the United States hardly had the means to serve their own immigrants much less convert others to their cause. Nonetheless, assertions like Hughes's helped to ignite the powder keg of nativism.

Antebellum Catholic insularity and defensiveness were as much a result of internal demands as a response to external attacks. The almost uncontrollable immigrant invasion and geographical expansion put immediate and massive pressures upon the tiny American Catholic communities to absorb the new immigrants, create internal cohesion and religious solidarity among them, develop institutions to meet their spiritual and social needs, and help them preserve their own personal and communal identity while they accommodated themselves to an American way of life that was itself in the midst of movement and change. Preoccupation with the internal life of the Catholic immigrant community, however, was not solipsistic; it was publicly useful to the nation as well as internally necessary. The Catholic church—especially in its spiritual, educational, and social mission—provided a home and services for the new Americans.

Whether in the East or on the western frontiers, antebellum Catholicism built similar institutions to meet the new immigrants' and pioneers' needs, but the experience of Catholicism in these places was not the same. In the East Catholics had come into areas where Protestants already had well-established patterns of authority and economics. Most Catholic immigrants were foreign to these established patterns and would fit in only as they gained strength in numbers or were able to develop their own religious, economic, and political support systems. On the western frontiers the situation was somewhat different. Here, for the most part, Catholics and Protestants settled the new areas together and had equal opportunity for growth and economic development. Even though the old antagonisms between Protestants and Catholics continued to influence life on the frontier, those antagonisms were mitigated by the necessities of building a common life together.

It is sometimes asserted, and with good reason, that the spread of Christianity to the American frontier was primarily the work of Methodists and Baptists. Lay elders and frontier itinerant preachers moved west as the country did and gradually laid the foundations of Christianity there. Catholicism was primarily an eastern and Great Lakes phenomenon that did not have the mobility of ministry that some Protestant churches possessed. Yet Catholics did move into the frontier with amazing speed and established their fledgling institutions sometimes before, but most of the time alongside, those of American Protestantism.[12]

The national expansion and development of Catholicism were directed and controlled primarily by five institutions that molded and shaped American Catholic consciousness and its orientation to American society for years to come: the national episcopal councils, the local episcopacy, the clergy, communities of women religious, and the schools.

Baltimore's seven provincial and three plenary episcopal councils served a number of functions in the American church.[13] They created a uniform national system of ecclesiastical government, became the primary agency for the expansion of bishoprics in the West, defined the nature of episcopal authority in the church, helped to construct a national Catholic identity, provided a code of uniform ecclesiastical discipline, and encouraged the development of Catholic devotionalism and a disciplined moral life.

The territorial or diocesan bishop, the second institution of antebellum Catholicism, was the primary sign and instrument of the presence and development of Catholicism on the midwestern and western frontiers as well as in the East. The multicultural American church was led by immigrant bishops. Until 1866, 75 percent of all newly appointed bishops were foreign-born. Of the eighty bishops named between 1830 and 1866, 31 percent were Irish, 25 percent American, 20 percent French, 6 percent German, and the rest from other countries (Spain, Italy, Belgium, Canada, and Mexico).[14] Although the Irish constituted the majority of the Catholic population, they did not dominate the hierarchy in proportion to their numbers, but Irish-born bishops did possess some of the largest eastern and midwestern sees during this period. The disproportionate representation of French and French Canadian–born bishops in the American hierarchy reflected both the church's continuing inability to provide enough qualified native clergy for the episcopate and the generally higher standards of education and leadership that characterized the French missionary clergy. These French bishops were the pioneers of Catholicism in many small new dioceses in the South, Midwest, Southwest, and Pacific Northwest.

Almost all the antebellum bishops appointed for the vast territory from the Midwest to the Pacific Ocean followed a similar pattern in establishing the foundations for Catholicism. Because of their foreign educations, connections in Europe, the scarcity of priests, and the general poverty of the Catholics in these areas, the bishops—many times even before they settled in their dioceses—made a trip to Europe to beg for money and to enlist clergy, seminarians, and religious orders of men and women. Like the seventeenth-century French Jesuits, they tried to stir up the missionary zeal of European Catholics to serve the needs of these new dioceses. In this effort they were largely successful, bringing to the United States hundreds of missionaries and thousands of dollars. Clergy serving in the missions or in the new dioceses also went to Europe on recruiting tours. The Jesuit Pierre De Smet,* Indian missionary of the Missouri, went to Europe at least seven times from 1830 to 1870 and brought back over one hundred missionaries for Jesuit enterprises in Missouri and the Northwest.

In spite of their cultural and personal differences, immigrant and American bishops shared a common Tridentine vision about the church. Although they tried to meet the ethnic-based needs of their diverse peoples, they were more concerned about unity and even uniformity of religious life and practice than they were about legitimate cultural diversity.[15] Many bishops also saw themselves as Tridentine reforming bishops. In their reactions to lay trustees, clergy, religious orders, or popular folk religious practices, they intended to establish their own authority and the post-Tridentine parish-centered sacramental tradition of Catholicism.[16]

At the local and congregational levels, the clergy, whether diocesan or members of religious orders, were the third institution to provide for the spiritual and social developments of antebellum Catholicism. The immigrant episcopacy had a predominantly immigrant clergy to assist them in their pastoral initiatives. In 1830, 232 of these priests served about 230 churches; by 1866, 2,770 priests were ministering to 5,067 churches and missions.[17] The greatest number of clergy were from Ireland, and they had, even more so than their bishops, an almost total authority over their Irish people; but that control was dictated not so much by ecclesiastical doctrine or discipline as it was by the Irish veneration of, and attachment to, their priests. Archbishop Gaetano Bedini reported in 1853 that the Irish people "see in their priests not a simple minister of Religion; but their father, their magistrate, their judge, their king, their 'Papa,' their idol. This is not an exaggeration.''[18]

During the antebellum period, women religious became the backbone of the church's educational and social mission. By 1830 there were approximately five hundred in twelve communities,[19] and between 1830 and 1870 forty-seven new communities of women religious emigrated to the United States.[20] By 1870 well over two thousand women—immigrants and native born—were living a religious way of life in communities across the country, building convents, schools, and hospitals; serving the sick in cities and villages that were periodically plagued with epidemics; becoming the heart of the church's care of orphans; and working to improve the lot of immigrant and pioneer alike. African-American women religious—the Oblate Sisters of Providence (Baltimore, 1829) and the Association of the Holy Family (New Orleans, 1842),

German Benedictines (St. Mary, Pennsylvania, 1852), American Dominicans (Kentucky and Ohio, 1820), French Canadian Sisters of Providence (Vancouver, Washington, 1856), and a host of other religious communities provided young women with an opportunity to live an evangelical life and serve real needs in immigrant and pioneer communities. They were an essential part of the church's missionary efforts and an integral part of the institutional means of care and hope. Their social and educational activism was frequently combined with a contemplative quasi-monastic life-style (i.e., seclusion in communal convent living, celibacy, retreat from the materialism and acquisitiveness of American life) that made them signs of contradiction in society. They were generally under episcopal and/or clerical supervision and control, yet they were independent, self-confident builders of the institutions that served the church and the society.

Catholic schools became the fifth institution in which the bishops and their cooperators placed their hopes for the evangelization and education of the people and the continuation of the Catholic tradition. The Catholic school became a primary institutional symbol of the immigrant church, reflecting a symbiotic relationship between Catholicism and American values, simultaneously incorporating purposes of both. It was the church's response to the fundamental need for education in the nation, a defense against the pan-Protestantism of the public schools,[21] an attempt to unite the communication of knowledge with the cultivation of enlightened Catholic piety,[22] and the means of preserving cultural and religious solidarity. The school, moreover, was another Catholic form of voluntaryism that provided educational alternatives in a religiously pluralistic society. It also furthered the general antebellum American desire to create good and virtuous citizens by means of knowledge and religion.

Although the Catholic schools integrated religion and education, they also separated Catholics, particularly on the East Coast, from the Protestantized Americanism current in common schools, further alienating nativists and American Protestants who considered them un-American and sectarian. In some places, especially in the Midwest and West, however, Catholic schools were perceived as a major contribution to American public life, because they were the first, and for a while the only, schools available for all children.

The issue of Catholic schools became the focus of Catholic and national attention after a series of antebellum battles between bishops and common school societies. The most publicized of these was the confrontation between Bishop Hughes and the New York Public School Society in the early 1840s. Hughes's controversy set the tone for subsequent school wars in other parts of the country, and began a century of Catholic slurs against public education, a withdrawal of official Catholic support for the improvement of common schools, and a major step toward their secularization.

The New York school controversy was ostensibly a battle over the use of public funds for Catholic schools, but it provided an occasion for Catholics to establish the rationale, as outlined above, for the very existence of Catholic schools in American society. During the battles Catholics appealed, as they would continue to do for over a century, to the free exercise clause of the First Amendment, and their opponents to the nonestablishment clause. Both the common school proponents and Hughes argued for a link between religion and education, but only the former believed that a true neutrality in regard to religion was possible. For Hughes neutrality in practice turned out to be religious universalism of the pan-Protestant kind. Although the issues were real for both parties, the controversy itself turned nasty, with a host of hermeneutical suspicions on both sides. The intensity of the verbal battle revealed how significant the school issue was. For both sides the schools helped to define the meaning of America and the specific role of religion in society. Were the schools to be the primary agents of a pan-Protestant Americanism or of a specifically Catholic Americanism? [23]

The desire for Catholic schools was shared by all bishops, but not all could put that desire into practice. Throughout the nineteenth century Catholic schools never served more than a very small portion of the Catholic population. It is difficult to say, given the present state of scholarship, just how many were actually established and kept running from 1830 to 1866. [24] Depending upon prevailing economic conditions, parishes opened and closed numerous schools during the period. Most orders of women religious who came to this country opened schools for girls, some of which were free and others of which required tuition. The schools provided education and culture for girls and much needed revenue for the women religious. One report indicates that there were only 20 schools for girls in 1830, but by 1856 the number had increased to 130. [25] This was primarily the result of the arrival of new teaching orders of women religious.

Dominicans, Franciscans, Jesuits, nine teaching orders of brothers, and a number of bishops also established ninety-three new colleges for men in the antebellum period, some of them surviving only a year or two; only twenty-nine are still in existence. Catholic colleges, like many others in the nation, had a very low survival rate throughout the nineteenth century. [26] Generally they had a threefold religious purpose: to provide a preparatory education for boys aspiring to the priesthood, to create a center for missionary activities, and to cultivate moral virtues. The antebellum Catholic colleges many times trained boys from the age of six to twenty, providing elementary as well as higher education.

As the schools emphasized Catholic distinctiveness in American society, so did Catholic piety. Increasingly after 1830 the bishops, clergy, and religious orders, in conjunction with the European Catholic romantic religious revival, fostered a multiplicity of traditional Catholic devotional practices and forms of piety that encouraged the new immigrants to identify their ethnic cultures as well as their religion as Catholic.

Episcopal conciliar legislation and the subsequent pastorals from 1830 to 1866 reflect a gradual transformation in American Catholic piety. Until the

1840s the bishops admonished Catholics to develop a spiritual life oriented to the sacraments but fundamentally centered in family prayer life. Christian catechesis and spiritual reading in the home were fundamental.[27] These recommendations reflected the realities of the agrarian and diaspora conditions under which many Catholics lived, scattered as they were throughout the country, many times without the benefit of clergy and the regular celebration of the sacraments.

After the 1840s the dominant vision of Catholic spirituality shifted, reflecting new sociological circumstances. The great increase in population, the migration from peasant agricultural backgrounds to large cities, the loss of control over the means of production and the product produced, the democratic and republican political atmosphere in which they were living, and the hostility of a Protestant American environment made Catholics receptive to a spirituality that corresponded to their new urban situation.

The primary end of Catholic spirituality was the salvation of souls, and the church was the divinely established means of that salvation. Joseph Chinnici has rightly argued that the church was the center of this vision of the spiritual life. It was perceived as the "society whose divinity overshadowed the humanity of its institutions, its teaching, and practice."[28] The church was also the spiritual homeland and refuge for uprooted immigrants. John Hughes preached in 1835, like Abraham, that the immigrants were commanded to, "Go forth out of thy country and from thy kindred, and from thy father's house, and come into the land that I will show thee. And I will make of thee a great nation, and I will bless thee and magnify thy name, and thou shalt be blessed" (Gen. 12:1). That "great nation" was the church, and the providential signs of its identification with Christ were found in its poverty, suffering, and persecution.[29]

The emphasis upon the church as the means of salvation and the spiritual homeland or refuge for the immigrants was concretely put into practice in a variety of parish-centered and distinctively Catholic spiritual activities such as parish missions, pious confraternities, and devotions to the saints. Through these specific means church leaders hoped to revive the spiritual life of Catholic immigrants, many of whom (especially the poor Irish peasants) had only a minimal attachment to the church and were not, in the period before the Irish Catholic revival of the 1850s, consistent sacramental Catholics.[30]

The parish mission was one of the European pastoral activities that produced, in Jay Dolan's study of the phenomenon, a Catholic Revivalism.[31] It was primarily a preserve of the religious orders—particularly the Redemptorists, Passionists, Jesuits, and eventually the American Paulists—and was intended to revive the religious life of local congregations through intensive preaching over a concentrated period of a week or two. The mission emphasized the renewal of the Christian life of baptized Catholics, leading them to a more fervent reception of the sacraments of penance and the Eucharist. Although a few parish missions began in the early 1830s, they were flourishing by the hundreds by the 1850s and 1860s. Itinerant preachers from the religious orders had the distinct advantage of coming into a parish, appealing to its congregation to convert, and leaving before their message became routine. Although some sermons were doctrinal expositions, most seem to have been, in Orestes A. Brownson's words, an appeal to the heart as well as head, so that individuals would not only know but feel sin and grace. The missions awakened the Christian life through "sensible devotions."[32]

Missionaries also enrolled parishioners in pious societies where the revival might be sustained with communal support. The parish missions, moreover, provided parishioners with an opportunity to purchase religious artifacts for their homes and spiritual books and pamphlets for their continued edification. The mission, as Dolan has indicated, was like a Protestant revival, except it was oriented to the sacraments and to identification of individuals with the ongoing religious life of their parishes. Over the course of the nineteenth and early twentieth centuries, immigrants became a faithful, churchgoing community. How much the missions contributed to this development is difficult to assess, but they seem to have changed the religious habits of a number of immigrants.

The parish mission helped to foster devotional practices within the Catholic community. Some historians like Dolan and Ann Taves have seen devotional Catholicism as the key to the revival of Catholic life during this period. By the mid-nineteenth century devotions to Jesus, the Sacred Heart, the Blessed Sacrament, Mary, and the saints began to flourish in American Catholic piety, replacing to some extent the simple piety of the colonial and early republican age. Devotionalism would continue to characterize Catholic parish piety until the Second Vatican Council in the 1960s, when other forms would replace it. Like other Catholic movements at this time, the devotional development emphasized the unity of the Catholic community in the face of hostility from outside. Indeed, as Taves has argued, devotional Catholicism was another way of separating Catholics from Protestants.[33] Undoubtedly the devotional revolution fostered closer attachments to ecclesiastical authority, but it was much more than an ideological hammer in the hands of the clergy to promote institutional ends. It was an attempt to revive personal and family piety and reaffirm the traditional Catholic doctrine of the communion of saints, while providing a means of preserving religious and ethnic solidarity.

The revival of devotionalism reinforced the Protestant image of Catholicism as a religion of outward forms, rather than interior disposition. Protestants, though, were not entirely alone in their criticisms of Catholic devotional practices. Although some American Catholics, especially the new American converts Hecker and Brownson, accepted in principle the devotions associated with the Catholic doctrine of the communion of saints, they found many practices associated with those devotions to be excessively mechanical and/or so closely tied to ethnic sensitivities that they produced an unnecessary barrier to the development of an American Catholic spirituality. Brownson thought that some devotions to Mary, particularly those recommended by Alphonsus Liguori's *Glories of Mary,* were too effeminate and bathetic for his masculine, Anglo-American heart.[34] At times, too, he charged that some practices associated with the veneration and petitioning of the saints detracted from the central mysteries of Christianity that they were originally intended to illustrate. Some Catholics had an almost superstitious reliance on favorite saints, relics, and sacramentals that made Catholicism particularly unattractive to Protestants, and in fact did a great injustice to the Catholic tradition itself. Catholic spirituality had many times borrowed from the European traditions sentiments that were needlessly alien to American sensitivities, which emphasized the development of personal virtue, liberty, initiative, and responsibility for public life.[35]

In the 1860s Brownson called for a revision of Catholic spirituality that would put it more in accord with the dynamics of American life. The old Catholic spirituality that placed exclusive emphasis on obedience had to be changed in a republican age that demanded an integral relationship between obedience and liberty.[36] Contemporaries, he wrote,

demand personal conviction,—to appropriate, to assimilate to themselves the truth which authority teaches, so that they may have in themselves as Catholics unity of thought and life, and speak from their own thoughts, convictions, and experience as living men, and not merely repeat a lesson learned by rote, and to which they attach no more meaning than the parrot does to her scream of "pretty pol."[37]

Brownson was here signaling a new development in American Catholicism that had existed alongside and within the immigrant tradition since the 1840s, one that was analogous to the devotionalism that dominated the immigrant church.

This new sensibility, which I have elsewhere called "American Catholic Romanticism,"[38] was part of a much wider European and American spiritual and intellectual impulse. In the United States the new sensibility exhibited itself in what Sydney Ahlstrom has called "Romantic Religion in New England" and "Catholic Movements in American Protestantism."[39] Out of these American movements, especially Transcendentalism and Tractarianism, came a number of converts to Catholicism who had a significant impact upon American Catholic life and thought and whose perspectives and sensibilities were shaped more by the issues coming out of the post-Kantian era than they were by those experiences that conditioned the immigrant Catholics.

The new sensibilities of the romantic era—for example, the emphasis upon religious feelings, the recovery of an incarnational view of the church, an organic approach to history and community, the integration of Christianity and social values, and even the emphasis upon authority as necessary for community—appealed to those who converted to Catholicism. To some extent these elements were also being rediscovered in the popular and institutional religious revival and devotional revolutions that were taking place in European and American Catholicism. But the new converts to Catholicism, especially Hecker and Brownson, revealed a romantic Catholicism that differed in some major respects from the popular and institutional Catholicism of the immigrant era.

Unlike Hughes, Bishop Martin John Spalding,* Francis Patrick Kenrick,* and other apologists for the immigrant American Catholic vision, Brownson and Hecker possessed a romantic religious epistemology that emphasized the role of intuition in understanding God and the Catholic tradition. They had been drawn into the modern, post-Kantian religious and philosophical quest to harmonize the subjective and objective dimensions of human and Christian existence. The philosophical and religious questions that were current in New England Unitarianism and Transcendentalism, out of which they emerged, were not even raised in the immigrant community, except to refute them as the wild imaginings of atheistic philosophical geniuses. Brownson and Hecker, on the other hand, took seriously the new religious epistemologies and tried to reconcile intuitive and rational approaches to truth and meaning. What this meant in effect was that both gave far greater significance to the subject than did their American Catholic coreligionists.

Brownson and Hecker certainly spoke out, like their coreligionists, in favor of ecclesiastical authority, the visible church, the sacramental means of grace, and the communion of saints, but they did so from an intellectual position that differed considerably from the dominant immigrant position. For both men there was a dynamic and harmonious dialectic between subject and object, freedom and authority, nature and grace, church and world that did not enter into the world view of Hughes, Spalding, and company. For Brownson and Hecker, union with God was individual, activist, and intuitive as well as communal, sacramental, and rational. What made Catholicism so attractive to them was the dialectical harmony of those elements in the Catholic experience of Christianity. This fundamental perspective was at the heart of their understanding of the necessity and role of the church in preserving fundamental American constitutional values and in maintaining freedom, order, and justice in American society. To make America Catholic was a matter, according to Hecker, of demonstrating that those human and universally valid aspirations of American society were grounded in the authentic Catholic tradition.

Although American bishops repeatedly encouraged lay Catholics to good citizenship,[40] they themselves refused to become involved in partisan politics. Bishops and clergy were extremely sensitive to the Protestant and nativist criticisms of the church's historical involvement in European politics and to the general republican disdain for clerical interference. In their 1837 pastoral the bishops made it clear that, unlike some of the evangelicals who had been organizing for a Christian Party in politics, they refused to identify Catholicism with any political movement.[41] The bishops could count. They knew they could not influence political developments even if they wanted to, and they did not. Catholicism's primary responsibility in the political order was to develop sound moral consciences, not to devise strategies or particular means to achieve penultimate temporal ends.

Slavery was the single economic, political, as well as moral reform issue that divided the nation's conscience perhaps more than any other after 1830. Catholics, like many other Americans, had accepted the institution in practice and in theory. Slavery came with the Spanish Catholics to Florida in the sixteenth century, with the English Catholics to Maryland in the seventeenth, and with the French Catholics to Louisiana in the eighteenth. Catholics throughout the South owned slaves and used them to build their plantations and churches, make their profits, and financially sustain their missionary and evangelical efforts. Large Louisiana and Maryland landowners like Charles Carroll of Carrollton owned hundreds of slaves, while small farmers in Kentucky and Missouri owned one or two. Lawyers and judges like William Gaston of North Carolina, bishops, priests, and religious orders of men and women bought, sold, traded, and punished their own slaves. Catholics were implicated in the slave business throughout the antebellum period.[42]

Many Catholics not only accepted the American institution of slavery, they also found support for it in Catholic teaching, justifying it on biblical, historical, and theological grounds. In the 1840s, in the midst of a presidential campaign that had raised the issue of abolition, Bishop England gave what amounted to a practical Catholic defense of American slavery.[43] Catholics throughout the South and many in the North periodically repeated England's arguments and shared his view that the legislature had the responsibility for any change in practice. The overwhelming majority of Catholic newspapers, both in the North and South, supported slavery and generally accepted England's argument.

The abolitionist movement, which had in the 1830s and 1840s divided three major Protestant churches, did not affect American Catholic unity. American bishops individually and as a national body remained aloof from the moral battles over slavery, except to articulate what they considered the traditional Catholic teaching. In fact, their national pastorals never touch on slavery because the bishops considered it a politically divisive issue. The 1852 national pastoral clearly hints that troubles were brewing in the country, but the bishops merely recommended conscientious religious respect for all public authorities.[44] For most articulate American Catholics, slavery was a civil institution, and if there was to be a change in the institution, it would have to come from civil or legislative means.

Traditional Catholic moral theology viewed slavery as a consequence of original sin,[45] but the institution of slavery was not itself considered essentially sinful. Nonetheless there was a moral dimension to slavery, and Catholics, like other American Christians, developed a moral code of the relative rights and duties of masters and slaves.[46] Francis Patrick Kenrick, the most authoritative moral theologian in the antebellum American hierarchy, reinforced the American Catholic position and enshrined it in his *Theologia Moralis*, a textbook used in some seminaries. Like other Catholic moral theologians, Kenrick argued that slavery did not abolish the natural equality of human beings nor did slaveholders have the right to treat slaves as property or animals. Slavery gave the master a right to the use of the slave's services and nothing more. In exchange the master was to provide due care for his slave and treat him or her humanely.[47] Slaves had a right to a knowledge and practice of religion, lawful and valid marriages, the integrity of family life, and adequate food, clothing, and shelter.[48] No doubt this moral code and the concern for the religious care of slaves was observed in some places, as Stafford Poole and Douglas Slawson have pointed out, but it was by no means uniformly followed.[49]

American Catholics accepted slavery not because they lacked nerve or because of cultural pressure to conform to a dominant tradition; they accepted it willingly and consciously and had a theology and tradition to support it. They were involved in it, moreover, economically, politically, and culturally. Although the institution was not considered sinful in principle, it was so in concrete practice, and some American Catholics experienced ambivalence and internal conflicts in their acceptance of it because of the moral consequences it produced among the slaves and slaveholders. Catholic ambiguity regarding slavery revolved around the distance between the moral code they themselves accepted and the actual practices that they and their culture observed.

Although the dominant American Catholic tradition accepted slavery and called for the observance of a moral code, a minority of American Catholics rejected American slavery and a few called for its abolition. Mathew Carey of Philadelphia was clearly disturbed by slavery, but his only solution was to support the American Colonization Society for the removal of African-Americans to Africa. Judge William Gaston of North Carolina, on the other hand, took a prophetic stand on slavery in 1832, calling for the "ultimate extirpation of the worst evil that afflicts the Southern part of our confederacy."[50] During the North Carolina Constitutional Convention in 1835, he also opposed depriving black freeholders of voting for members of the state senate and house of commons. Two of his judicial decisions moreover affirmed that even slaves had rights to protect themselves against harsh and murderous assaults.[51] Cincinnati's *Catholic Telegraph* and two of New York's pastors, Jeremiah Cummings and Thomas Farrell, also periodically lectured against slavery and called for its abolition.

Even those Catholics who opposed slavery did not join the abolition movement, for most in both the North and South identified abolitionists with religious bigotry and nativism. Indeed, a number of abolitionists were anti-Catholic, and some of them made the traditional identification of Catholicism and slavery, seeing them as "natural allies in every warfare against liberty and enlightenment."[52] In the Catholic mind, abolitionists were associated with all the social and political upheavals in Europe. Catholics periodically called abolitionists Red Republicans, socialists, atheists, and revolutionary advocates of a private interpretation of the higher law. A number of abolitionists, however, tried to gain Catholic support and were not the bigoted nativists many Catholics thought.

The battles over slavery and abolitionism that had split some denominations also split Northern and Southern sympathies more generally and led to the tragedy of the Civil War. On 4 February 1861, shortly after Abraham Lincoln's election, the South organized the Confederate States of America, and two months later with the firing on Fort Sumter in Charleston harbor, the war began. Catholics in large numbers came out of their immigrant communities and entered national public life in new and dramatic ways during the war.[53] Southern Catholic leaders almost immediately sided with the Confederacy. In fact, even before the organization of the Confederate States, Bishop Jean-Pierre Augustin Verot* of St. Augustine, Florida, had preached a sermon on "Slavery and Abolitionism" that was subsequently printed and distributed throughout the South as a Confederate tract,[54] earning for him the title "rebel bishop." Perceiving a crisis in the public state of affairs and the inevitability of a civil war, he decried the slavery issue as the cause of the present troubles—because one half of the nation refused to acknowledge the legitimacy of an institution that God, the church, society at all times, and all governments had acknowledged. Most Southerners justified the separation on the basis of a states' rights theory of government and the right to separate from the federal government's aggression upon the South.

In the North the process of regional attachment was more gradual. There was a considerable amount of sympathy for the South among many Northern Catholics, even among those who were against secession as a solution to the problem. In October 1861 Brownson asserted that he, like most bishops and religious leaders, had for the past fifteen years counseled Catholics to respect and obey the federal government. That government, in Brownson's opinion, was still the legitimate government and "it has never lost its legitimacy by any act of tyranny or oppression. . . . Rebellion against it, therefore, is not only a crime, but a sin." Brownson, however, was disappointed that in the midst of the secession crisis the Catholic population and its leaders had not stood up for the federal government. Of the twelve Catholic newspapers, he could count only two as decidedly loyal, two as occasionally loyal, one that strived to be on both sides, and all the rest as really "secession sheets."[55] Brownson's Yankee American loyalties came to the fore in this assessment, but he also saw a contradiction in those Catholics who were simultaneously siding with Southern revolutionaries while emphasizing in traditional Catholic fashion the authority and unity of the state as well as the church. This did not fit the Catholic pattern.

Some bishops in the North, however, gradually came to share Brownson's view that the Southerners were rebelling against the Constitution and public order. Although Archbishop Kenrick of Baltimore generally stayed out of the battles, Archbishop John Purcell* of Cincinnati supported the Union's cause, as did Bishop John Timon of Buffalo and other Northern sympathizers. Hughes won the wrath of the Southern episcopacy by flying the American flag over his cathedral at the commencement of the war.

For Hughes, as perhaps for other Irish supporters of the Northern cause, the war was justified on constitutional grounds; but it was not for him or for many of his Irish people a war to end slavery. Hughes wanted to keep slavery out of the war issue because he believed that Irish Catholics would not support a war to abolish slavery but only to support the Constitution.[56] Hughes, therefore, was particularly disturbed by the Emancipation Proclamation and told William Seward, Lincoln's secretary of state, so, but he did not express his concerns in public. Such was not the case with James McMaster,* editor of the *New York Freeman's Journal,* and with the editor of the *Metropolitan Record,* both of whom expressed racist sentiments and pitted the African-Americans against the white laboring classes of New York. When the Emancipation Proclamation was followed in 1863 by the enactment of enforced military draft for all those who could not buy their way out with three hundred dollars, the two journals seethed with indignation at the outrage and injustice of the whole thing. These journals either stirred up or expressed a growing class and race hatred that broke out in four days of rioting in New York in 1863.[57]

Catholic sectional patriotism came to the fore during the course of the war, with bishops identifying themselves as citizens of both sections of the country. Patrick Lynch* of Charleston and Hughes of New York were both sent on diplomatic missions by their respective governments. In 1861 Lynch went to Rome, hoping to obtain recognition of the Confederacy, and in 1864 he returned there on a similar mission, only this time as the Confederacy's official representative. Bishop Hughes acted in a similar fashion for the North. For him the war was an opportunity for patriotism, and he lost no time in supporting the government's right to conduct war against the rebellion. In 1861 Lincoln and Seward asked Hughes to make a diplomatic mission to Europe with Thurlow Weed to promote "healthful opinions" in France and England in favor of the North. Hughes enthusiastically accepted, traveling to England, France, and Italy as an emissiary of goodwill. His mission had very little political influence, but it was a move into the public realm that he interpreted as a sign of the fundamental compatibility of Catholicism and Americanism.[58]

Seventy clergy served in the military chaplaincy on both sides of the war,[59] and numerous others took care of bereaved families at home. Nursing sisters, too, provided medical aid, constant care, and spiritual comfort to the ill and dying soldiers on the battlefields or confined to military hospitals. A recent scholar estimated that 640 (or 20 percent) of the 3,200 Civil War nurses were nuns.[60]

When the war came to an end, Catholics, like others, tried to interpret its ultimate historical significance. Martin John Spalding saw the "wicked war" as a divine chastisement "for our Sins."[61] Verot saw it and the Southern defeat as divine vengeance upon a people who had abused their slaves or who had refused or neglected to provide them with a Christian education.[62] The previous antebellum Catholic ambivalence about slavery was almost totally destroyed as Southern Catholics tried to make some divine sense out of the terrible tragedy. Those like Verot who spoke out after the war did so almost exclusively to remind their people that sin was the cause of it all—not the sin of slavery itself, but of the moral abuses that accompanied it.

Brownson interpreted the war as a major turning point in American political theory and an opportunity for Catholics to take a leading role in reestablishing national unity and governmental stability. He believed that a postwar-united Catholicism would be the foremost influence in "forming the character and shaping the future destiny of the American republic." For him, the end of the war demanded that Catholics themselves discover their own universally valid principles and share them with the rest of the country. He believed that Americans, who were not sectarian in their hearts, would respond to a thoroughly catholic (i.e., universal) vision if such a vision could be presented intelligently and responsibly. He wrote *The American Republic* (1866) to argue his case before the American people. The book was also an intellectual peace offering particularly for Southern Catholics who, like himself before the war, had accepted a states' rights view of government. Brownson now rejected that view and called upon Southern Catholics and others to reestablish the metaphysical and theological grounds for national unity and the transcendental source of governmental stability.

The war, Brownson argued, had also brought about a new era of good feeling in American society, perhaps comparable to that following the Revolutionary War. In the midst of the war, he opined that the struggle was making Americans "one people" again.[63] It had made the American people more accepting of Catholics as their fellow citizens, and it had transformed Catholics. He predicted, too, that immigrant Catholics would become Americanized through their participation in the war. Prior to the war those Catholics who were Americanized had been so on the Southern model—a civilization based on slavery, with its center in Baltimore and Virginia. He hoped that the war would Americanize Catholics upon the Northern model—a civilization based on constitutional liberty, with Massachusetts as the center.[64]

The need for Catholic unity in the wake of the war was felt in other quarters. In 1865 Archbishop Spalding of Baltimore called a Second Plenary Council in order, among other things, to demonstrate Catholic unity, provide a uniform disciplinary code, and construct some means to evangelize and assist the freed African-Americans.[65] The call for a council generally resonated well with both Northern and Southern bishops, who were in search of some signs of spiritual and temporal harmony. The Archbishop of New Orleans, John Mary Odin, encouraged Spalding's initiative in this regard, remarking: "The holding of a plenary council will be gratifying to all the bishops of the South. Everything seems to be so gloomy in the future, that it will be beneficial for all."[66]

The plenary council focused upon internal ecclesiastical and disciplinary matters, leaving little time or energy to discuss the church's responsibility to the freed African-Americans, about 150,000 of whom were Catholic. American bishops, however, were not willing or prepared to give them material assistance. The Southern dioceses in particular had been ravaged by the Civil War and were economically and culturally unprepared to care for them. Although one of the council's decrees suggested the establishment of African-American churches, schools, and orphanages, and encouraged bishops and priests to respond to the African-Americans' needs, no specific actions were recommended.[67] The matter was ultimately left up to the individual bishops' consciences. Without any practical organized national effort on behalf of African-Americans, the Catholic response would continue to be meager and ineffective.

The Civil War and the plenary council represented a major turning point in American Catholicism. The immigrant church would continue on into the twentieth century, but it was significantly transformed by the war. Catholic participation in the war efforts was symbolic of the end of an era of isolation from American public life—at least for some leading Catholics. The participation of large numbers of Northern and Southern Catholic soldiers in the war, the two episcopal diplomatic missions, the contributions of priests and nuns, and the sacrifices on all sides brought Catholics more thoroughly into the nation's life than had been the case throughout the previous thirty years. Catholic immigrants had paid their dues to American society with their services and their blood. They would feel a closer attachment to their country than before the war. Young priests (e.g., James Gibbons,* John Ireland,* Edward McGlynn*), sisters, and immigrant families had all participated in the terrible tragedy, and in the process they became more Americanized in their feelings. Nativism, too, had lessened considerably during the war and would not be revived for some years to come—and when it returned it did not have the same virulence as in the antebellum period. If it was an exaggeration to claim, as did James Parton in an 1868 issue of the *Atlantic Monthly,* that the "despised minority" of Catholics was "well on its way to complete acceptance in Protestant American Society," there was at least some truth in the exaggeration.[68]

4
TOWARD AMERICANISM: 1866–1899

From the Second Plenary Council (1866) until the papal condemnation of Americanism (1899), American Catholicism, like the nation itself, was in a period of transition from the devastation brought about by the Civil War to the beginnings, in the North at least, of an unprecedented population explosion, economic expansion, and social mutation caused by accelerated immigration, rapid industrialization, and largely uncontrolled urbanization. These transformations created new political, economic, cultural, and religious problems that called for solutions that were not readily available. The societal problems associated with the material developments were accompanied by a progressive cultural optimism and an American chauvinism that fit into the evolutionary theories of the post–Civil War years. The rise of the natural sciences, scientific history, sociology, psychology, and biblical criticism extended the scientific and technological mind and raised new issues about the role of religion in human life and culture.

In the midst of these social and cultural changes, American Catholicism continued to be preoccupied with its own house, trying to meet its own institutional, social, spiritual, and intellectual problems—some created by the war and others the result of its own internal growth and accommodations to changing conditions in society. During these years the Vatican and a number of American Catholics, moreover, focused upon the fundamental threat of naturalism and the need to reassert a Catholic supernaturalism. These were also years of a slow Catholic transition from antebellum localism and isolationism to late-nineteenth-century nationalism. Although American Catholicism remained institutionally united between the Second and Third (1884) Plenary Councils, between 1884 and 1900 it experienced a crisis that publicly divided bishops and others into warring factions over how the church should respond to new problems and how it should relate to the modern and changing world. These Catholic battles have been tagged "Americanism"[1] because of Pope Leo

XIII's encyclical *Testem Benevolentiae* (1899), which condemned an excessive accommodationist stance toward American and modern culture.

The greatest postwar expansion and development of Catholicism took place in the Northeast and Great Lakes regions. Between 1870 and 1900 the Catholic population increased by 92 percent, from 6.2 million to 12 million (18 percent of the total American population). Some of the increase came from Irish and German immigration, but most of the immigrant increase came and would continue to come in the early twentieth century from southern and eastern European countries. Many of those immigrants settled in northern and Great Lakes cities, where they continued to build the institutions of the immigrant church. There were also, however, a number of second- and third-generation immigrant Catholics in these areas who had fought in the war and were moving into the economic middle class, becoming increasingly involved in the new labor movements, establishing on a national level their own immigrant aid societies and/ or fraternal organizations for mutual support and influence, and emerging into big-city politics. These social and cultural transformations among the immigrant and the emerging middle class would eventually produce some major tensions within the American church as the bishops and clergy identified with one or the other of these groups.

Catholicism in the United States, as elsewhere, was experiencing new intellectual as well as social transformations in the immediate postwar period. Many of the intellectual issues of the day were being defined in Rome under Pius IX. The Vatican's condemnations of Catholic traditionalism and ontologism in the early 1860s, the encyclical *Quanta Cura* (1864) and *Syllabus Errorum* (1864) on the inherent naturalism in modern thought and political practices, and the First Vatican Council (1870) on rationalism, fideism, and papal infallibility set the tone of the papacy against the modern world and provided a host of embarrassing issues for American Catholics who, although sharing some of the pope's perspectives on modern thought, were strong advocates of American republicanism and the freedoms associated with modern constitutional government.

Vatican I reinforced a Catholic supernaturalism to counter a modern world that it perceived as increasingly rationalistic, naturalistic, and/or materialistic. Many American Catholic thinkers shared that view of the world. Even before the council, Brownson and a number of other American Catholics had gradually concluded that a new problem had developed in the postwar world. The antebellum polemical battles with Protestantism were, for the most part, over, and the problem of the church's necessity, important as it still was, was no longer the most significant issue in the modern world. A new age of unbelief had arrived, and it was increasingly evident not only in the naturalism of the theologians, philosophers, scientists, and politicians, but also in the mass culture, in progressive commercialism and materialism and in secularized education. This assessment of the age was not just a narrow-minded Catholic ghetto interpretation of events in the United States and Europe, but a reflection of post–Civil War realities.[2] This interpretation of modern developments, more-

over, was not a wholesale condemnation of modern culture. The Catholic critics did not deny the benefits of scientific achievements, technological progress,
or improvements in communications and transportation, but they were extremely apprehensive about the mentality, ideology, and cultural sensitivities
that were the source and effect of these modern developments. Nonetheless,
for Brownson and some others, the modern world was in decay, and the church
could not accommodate itself to that world without compromising its integrity.

Brownson's interpretation of the modern world and the church's relationship
to it was not, however, the only Catholic interpretation. Isaac Hecker illustrated
a different spirit within post–Civil War American Catholicism, one that was as
anti-naturalistic as Brownson's, but one that was sympathetic to the millennial
and pneumatological optimism of the period. Hecker and his followers were
preoccupied with relations between the church and the age. For them, though,
the age was not exclusively naturalistic; it was full of promise. For Hecker, in
particular, the principal issue of the 1880s was, "How can religion be made
compatible with a high degree of liberty and intelligence?"[3] More optimistic
than Brownson in his understanding of human nature and modern culture, he
saw that the development of free civil institutions and the spread of enlightenment had created an atmosphere in the modern world that contributed to "the
progress of true supernatural life among men." He wrote *The Church and
the Age* (1887) to show that modern liberty, so far as true, and the increase
of intelligence, so far as "guileless," were invaluable helps to the "spread of
Catholicity and the deepening of that interior spirit which is the best result of
true religion."[4] Although both Brownson and Hecker saw the necessity of
Catholicism's becoming incarnate in American culture, their practical judgments differed considerably upon the methods to be used in accomplishing this
goal and upon precisely what in American culture could legitimately be incorporated into American Catholicism. Their own differences represented the kind
of split that would become much more widespread and public in American
Catholicism after the Third Plenary Council.

Throughout the postwar years, Rome received a series of complaints and
appeals from American Catholics about clerical rights, the treatment of immigrants, missions to Indians and African-Americans, schools, and the necessity
of another plenary council to respond to changing conditions. In 1884 Rome
convoked the Third Plenary Council at Baltimore, the first time it had initiated
an American council.[5] The council issued a series of legislative decrees[6] that
provided, among other things, for some clerical consultation in diocesan administration and in the election of bishops, prohibited clerical involvement in
politics (a provision that would have repercussions in subsequent years), and
established measures for a uniform national catechism (the *Baltimore Catechism*), for a national collection to assist the missionary efforts toward African-
Americans and Indians, and for the condemnation of secret societies. The most
significant and most numerous decrees, however, were on Catholic education,
mandating, rather than simply exhorting (as did former conciliar decrees),

Catholics to establish parochial schools within two years of the council.[7] The council also exhorted Catholics to support academies and colleges, restructured seminary education, requiring seminarians to take two years of philosophy and four of theology, and initiated plans for the eventual establishment of a national Catholic university.

The Third Plenary Council was the last national legislative council in American Catholic history, the end of episcopal conciliarism, and the last demonstration of national episcopal unity in the nineteenth century. The council's unfinished business planted seeds for subsequent disunity among the bishops. They failed, for example, to address the immigrant issue adequately[8] and to come to an agreement about the establishment of a Catholic university and about the principles and measures to be used in determining which secret societies should be condemned. But the divisive consequences of this unfinished agenda would not become clear until the pressures of subsequent events made them so.

Gradually between 1884 and 1899 a split evolved in the American Catholic mind. On the one hand, the division was social, reflecting the developing postwar social differentiation within the American Catholic community between the newly arrived immigrants and the increasingly Americanized middle-class immigrants; on the other hand, it was intellectual, embodying two very different evaluations of the modern world. American Catholic leaders in particular broke into at least two major opposing parties in their evaluation of the times and assessments of the proper relationship of the church to the age. The general rupture developed in response to very specific issues: proper pastoral approaches to the immigrants, labor unions, and social justice; the establishment of a Catholic university; the relationship between parochial and public schools; the presence of a Roman apostolic delegate; cooperation with and participation in interdenominational activities; religious liberty and church-state relations; and the relationship between religion and the new sciences.

On the one side were those who wanted to give a Catholic direction to contemporary currents of life and thought by accommodating Catholicism to what was best in the new age while preserving the essentials of faith and ecclesiastical government. This group—variously designated as liberal, Americanist, accommodationist, or transformationist—was led by the archbishop of St. Paul, John Ireland. Associated with him were Bishop John Keane,* Denis J. O'Connell,* Cardinal James Gibbons, the Paulists, the Sulpicians, a few lay and clerical editors and writers, and some professors at the new Catholic University. At times, too, depending upon specific issues, Bishop John Lancaster Spalding* of Peoria, Archbishop John Joseph Williams of Boston, and Archbishop Patrick Riordan of San Francisco aligned themselves with this group.

On the other side were those who also accepted the material achievements of the modern age and appreciated the accomplishments of modern science and technology, but they were extremely critical of what they perceived to be a spirit behind these developments that was essentially hostile to faith and all religious authority. For them the church could not, without losing its integrity and identity with the apostolic tradition, accommodate itself to the outward forms of modern culture and modern patterns of thought. This group—variously called conservative, anti-Americanist, traditionalist, preservationist, intransigent, *refractaire*—was led by the archbishop of New York, Michael Corrigan.* He was joined and periodically egged on by Bishop Bernard McQuaid* of Rochester and Thomas S. Preston, Corrigan's vicar general. The German clergy and bishops, too, led by Archbishop Frederick Katzer of Milwaukee, resisted the accommodationists and upheld a view of Catholicism as a cultural and religious force against the winds of modernity and secularity. The majority of American and European Jesuits also belonged to this group, as did the theologians Joseph Schroeder and Georges Peries at the Catholic University in Washington, D.C., and St. Louis laymen Arthur Preuss, editor of the *Fortnightly Review*, and Condé B. Pallen, editor of *Church Progress*, who represented the thought of German Catholic lay leadership in the country. This group was periodically joined, depending on specific issues, by Archbishop Patrick Ryan of Philadelphia, Archbishop William Henry Elder of Cincinnati, and numerous writers for the *American Ecclesiastical Review* and *American Catholic Quarterly Review*.

The years 1886 and 1887 were crucial, as Thomas Wangler and others have argued, in the emergence of the Americanist party and in a clear identification of the opposing positions.[9] During a commission to Rome for the American hierarchy in those years, Keane, Ireland, O'Connell, and at times Gibbons developed a self-conscious accommodationist perspective toward the modern world and American culture, a sense of "cause," a realization of a "mission," and the beginnings of a "movement." Keane, O'Connell, and Ireland, in particular, became extremely conscious of their opponents and repeatedly tagged them their "enemies," "*refractaires*," and/or "conservatives." They began to see themselves as the "advanced" party, the one truly in touch with the modern world. Their enemies were lost in the hopeless battle of preserving a foreign culture.

During the Roman sojourn three specific issues (the German immigrant problem; the condemnations of the Knights of Labor, Henry George and Edward McGlynn; and the establishment of a Catholic university) split the American hierarchy, and the divisions that originated then would continue and become more public and volatile in subsequent years over other issues. The first problem was the absorption and care of the new immigrants and their adjustment to American conditions. Although much of the national ecclesiastical attention after 1884 was focused upon what was called the "German problem," the immigration issue was much larger, as would become increasingly evident. Of the 6.5 million Catholic immigrants who entered the United States from 1880 until 1920, more than 64 percent came from Italy, Poland, and Austria-Hungary and over 365,000 from Mexico. The largest percentage came after 1890, when German and Irish immigration fell off considerably.[10] By 1920 there were almost 20 million American Catholics, representing about 20 percent of the total population and an increase of about 11 million since 1880.

During this period the Germans were the first to articulate what the immigrant adjustment meant, and what they said in the late 1880s and 1890s would be echoed again and again, with different modulations, by immigrants from French Canada, Mexico, and southern and eastern Europe.[11] German Catholic priests and laity had complained to Rome for some time about their second-class identity in American Catholicism, where they were treated as foreigners, not well represented in the hierarchy, and pressured to Americanize. These complaints came to a head in 1886 when Father Peter Abbelen,* vicar general of Milwaukee, presented a memorial to Rome requesting that all German national parishes be acknowledged as legally equal to English-speaking parishes, that all immigrants and all children born to them in the United States be assigned to national parishes, and that immigrants have pastors who understood their language and fostered their customs. He complained about the Irish-American Catholic insistence on rapid assimilation, which was dangerous to the faith because particular languages and customs, although not essential to the faith, "foster piety and are so dear and sacred to the faithful that not without great dangers could they be taken away from them." Abbelen believed in the inevitability and desirability of gradual Americanization, but he also feared that those who favored a more rapid assimilation would cause the new immigrants to loose their faith.[12] Ever since the late eighteenth century, German Catholics had here and there built national parishes and organizations separating themselves from English-speaking Catholics and from their German- and English-speaking Protestant neighbors, believing that "language saves faith."[13]

Keane and Ireland countered the Abbelen memorial and his arguments for cultural diversity by preparing an "answer" that revealed very different pastoral priorities concerning the immigrants' and American church's future.[14] The real question in the American church, Keane and Ireland argued, was not between the Irish and the Germans, as Abbelen saw it, but between the use of English, the language of all public life in the United States, and the use of foreign languages which prevented the new immigrants from entering into and enjoying the benefits of American life. Although Keane and Ireland saw the necessity of immigrant institutions for "the practice of religion in the language most familiar to them," they saw these facilities as transitional elements in the American church. The bishops protested, however, against the overidentification of the German language and culture with faith, because such an identification would force the Americanized immigrants to reject their religion when, as would inevitably happen, they lost their parents' language and culture. For these bishops history had demonstrated this irreversible process. They saw the transitional necessity of preserving national cultures as a means of preserving faith, but cultural preservation was not the highest pastoral priority because it was all too contingent and not farsighted enough to continue the faith in an American culture. Very much like the Germans, they believed that language and culture were significant bearers of Catholic faith, but the cultural forms that expressed Catholicism most adequately for them were American. Differences over pastoral approaches to language and culture were soon complicated by issues involving social justice.

One of the first of these issues was the church's view of and relations toward labor unions. While in Rome in 1886 and 1887, Keane, Ireland, and Gibbons were forced to articulate their pastoral approaches to labor unions because in 1885 the Knights of Labor had been condemned as a secret society in Canada, and some in the American hierarchy wanted the prohibition extended to Knights in the United States, whose constituency was largely Catholic and whose president since 1879 was the Catholic Terence Powderly.* [15]

The church, Gibbons argued, should permit labor unions like the Knights because they were an efficacious, natural, and just means of seeking redress for grievances. The church, too, should be aligned with the laboring classes because Christ himself sent the church to evangelize the poor. Like England's Cardinal Henry Manning, Gibbons argued that the church was in a new democratic age, one in which the power and influence of the people were providentially rising to new importance. If the church wanted to serve the future, therefore, it had to stand by the people. In fact, for him, "to lose the heart of the people would be a misfortune for which the friendship of the few rich and powerful would be no compensation." A condemnation, he concluded, would be unjust, unnecessary, imprudent, ineffectual, inexpedient, dangerous to the church's reputation, and have financial consequences that would be ruinous for American Catholicism as well as Peter's pence.

While in Rome the Americanist prelates also became involved in the internal ecclesiastical affairs of the Archdiocese of New York, where Archbishop Corrigan had condemned Henry George as a socialist and Father Edward McGlynn for disobedience because he publicly supported and stumped for George during the mayoral campaign of 1886. Gibbons petitioned the Roman Propaganda to withhold a condemnation, which was sought by Corrigan and some other American prelates, of George's works.[16] The Americanist prelates, who generally believed that the church should be on the side of the people, also saw in McGlynn a "friend of the people,"[17] even though they believed Corrigan had a just cause for suspending him in 1887. But the Americanist support for George and McGlynn only aggravated the tensions with Corrigan and those who shared his view of the church and society in the United States.

The third divisive issue that came to the fore during Keane and Ireland's 1886–87 sojourn in Rome was the establishment of a Catholic university, the original intent of their trip. The university eventually won papal approval, opening in Washington, D.C., in 1889 in spite of the opposition of Archbishop Corrigan, Bishop McQuaid, the American Jesuits, many German Catholics, and some opponents within the Propaganda itself. The victory, however, did not settle

American discontent. Loss of support from Corrigan and some German bishops in particular had a significant financial effect because New York was the wealthiest diocese and the Germans were among the wealthiest immigrant groups in the country. Lack of financial aid continued to plague the development of the university throughout the late nineteenth century and into the twentieth.

Soon after the successful Roman mission, the whole issue of Catholic education, not just a Catholic university, became a central bone of contention among American Catholics.[18] The issue of parochial schools came to the fore in 1890 when Archbishop Ireland's address to the National Education Association, "The State School and the Parish School—Is Union between Them Impossible?," warmly acknowledged the need for and benefits of public education, admitting that the state had a right and a duty to provide schooling for all the people. He also made the case for Catholic schools but stated: "I sincerely wish that the need for it [the parish school] did not exist. I would have all schools for the children of the people be state schools."[19]

The German bishops, Corrigan, and even Bishop John Lancaster Spalding— all of whom had done much to support and build up parochial schools—fought fiercely against the Ireland proposal. When Ireland tried to implement a cooperative plan with public schools in Fairbault and Stillwater, Minnesota, the German bishops had had enough and delated the whole experiment to Rome for condemnation. Rome eventually decided the plan could be tolerated, and that decision ended the debate for the time being, but the school question only increased suspicions about a general compromising mentality that existed behind very specific, concrete, Americanist pastoral approaches.

An issue historically and causally connected to the conflict over education was the sending of a Roman apostolic delegate to the United States. In 1893 Pope Leo XIII sent Archbishop Francesco Satolli to Chicago to represent him at the World's Columbian Exposition. Satolli's mission, however, was more permanent: He was also sent to help settle the controversy among the bishops over the education issue and to establish an enduring apostolic delegation. For some time numerous priests in conflict with their bishops had favored an apostolic delegate as a check upon the absolutism of the American episcopacy. Ireland and O'Connell also favored the appointment because they believed that a Roman delegate would further their accommodationist stance. The sending of an apostolic delegate was therefore the result of developing American-Roman connections, one that both Americanists and their opponents had contributed to by their appeals to Rome to resolve local disputes—but also one that Rome desired. It was a part of Roman centralization that had been taking place increasingly during the nineteenth century, one that developed rapidly after the definition of papal infallibility in 1870.

A great number of archbishops and bishops opposed the appointment of an apostolic delegate.[20] Their opposition was based upon a long-standing fear that he would only provide ammunition for a nativist charge that Catholicism represented foreign interventionism. Some argued, too, that it was imposed upon the American bishops without consultation and in opposition to their wishes. This argument was made explicit by McQuaid and especially by Spalding who, in 1894, after the delegation was an accomplished fact, wrote an article for the *North American Review* which charged that in matters of practical ecclesiastical policy, local bishops should make their own decisions.[21]

Another divisive issue was clerical and lay Catholic cooperation with non-Catholics and participation in religious events that were sponsored by either nondenominational groups or by specific Protestant denominations. Participation, cooperation, or even public discussions with Protestants and other non-Catholic religious traditions had, particularly since the days of Pius IX, been discouraged because they were perceived to be actual or potential forms of indifferentism or violations of *communicatio in sacris,* a Catholic prohibition against participating in non-Catholic services. The greatest cause of alarm was Catholic participation in the World's Parliament of Religions, a congress held in conjunction with Chicago's 1893 World's Columbian Exposition. For Archbishop Ireland and a few others Catholic involvement was an occasion to present in a non-polemical way the Catholic viewpoint on a variety of issues. At the end of the parliament, Keane addressed the convention, acknowledging that the parliament itself was a living illustration of the "old saying that there is truth in all religions."[22] This statement was in no way indicative of a spirit of indifferentism, because Keane, like most of the other Catholic participants, made clear what the Catholic claims were in regard to Christianity and the Catholic church, but his statement manifested an attitude that was quickly condemned by his Catholic opponents.

For the conservatives Catholic participation at the parliament and other overtures of cooperation with non-Catholics were manifestations of indifferentism, dogmatic minimalism, neo-Pelagianism, and ecclesiastical egalitarianism. *Church Progress* and the *Western Watchman,* both of St. Louis, and a host of other newspapers bristled with indignation over this kind of leveling tendency, which they saw now as part of the entire liberal program. By 1895 Bishop McQuaid could not contain his anger over what had been taking place in the American church. In a letter to Cardinal Miecislaus Ledochowski, prefect of Propaganda, he characterized the whole movement in the American church as "liberalism," a term that would have its intended effect in Rome.[23]

The apostolic delegate, Archbishop Satolli, also disapproved of the Catholic participation and requested a ruling from the pope. On 15 September 1895, Leo XIII sent him a decision that Satolli himself had anticipated. "Now, although those general meetings have been tolerated by a prudent silence to this day, it would seem, nevertheless, more advisable for Catholics to hold their own assemblies apart."[24] In their own assemblies they were free to invite other religions to participate. The letter indicated that Satolli and the tide of Roman approval were moving away from the liberal camp. Henceforth, Catholic participation in nondenominationally organized religious discussions would be prohibited.

Church-state issues also divided Americanists and their opponents. On this issue Rome was, from the start, clearly on the side of the conservatives. In 1887 Archbishop Gibbons preached a sermon in Rome that underlined the benefits of the American separation of church and state—at a time when the papacy and some European Catholics were having great difficulties with the anticlerical governments of Germany, Italy, and France. He acknowledged that in the United States the government protected the church's freedom without interfering in her spiritual mission.[25] For most of those in the Americanist school of thought, separation of church and state was not only beneficial for American Catholics, but it was, according to Spalding, an irreversible modern tendency and an arrangement that all nations would sooner or later assume, just as they would be forced to accept popular rule, the underlying principle of which, equality, "is a truth taught by Christ, is a truth proclaimed by the Church."[26]

American Catholic enthusiasm for separation of church and state was considerably chastened, however, by Pope Leo XIII's encyclical *Longinqua Oceani* (1895), which extolled the virtues of American Catholicism and the practical benefits of separation of church and state, but which warned American Catholics that it was "erroneous to draw the conclusion that in America is to be sought the type of the most desirable status of the Church, or that it would be universally lawful or expedient for State and Church to be, as in America, dissevered and divorced." The pope recommended, moreover, that in addition to liberty, the Catholic church even in the United States would be better off if "she enjoyed the favor of the laws and the patronage of the public authority."[27]

Ireland and other Americanists were stunned by the encyclical, but some conservatives like the Catholic University's theologian Joseph Schroeder shared its vision of the relationship between church and state and, more significantly, saw that vision as a corrective to the modern tendency to divorce religion from social and political life. Conservatives' views of separation as well as their enthusiasm for the restoration of the pope's temporal powers (lost after Vatican I) were all of a single piece in their understanding of a harmonious relationship between religion and society. Distinguishing between the "thesis" (i.e., the normal state of the union of church and state) and the "hypothesis" (i.e., the historical necessity and benefit of separation), Schroeder indicated that American separation, though beneficial for Catholics, was not the ideal state of affairs and that even the historical development of church-state relations in the United States could have been better.[28] Many like Schroeder saw separation in principle as a manifestation of social rationalism. When pushed to extremes, separation could ultimately turn into a kind of political atheism in which revelation had absolutely nothing to do with political decisions.

The issue of religion's relationship to critical history and the new sciences also divided some within American Catholicism. From 1895 until the encyclical against theological modernism in 1907, a few scholars at the Catholic University and elsewhere, who were sympathetic to and generally supported by the

Americanists, advocated some kind of dialogue with and appropriation of the new scientific methods and the dynamic world view of the period. John Zahm* wrote an extensive study, *Evolution and Dogma* (1895), to demonstrate that an evolutionary and developmental perspective could reinforce the Christian view that the world and humankind had an ultimate dignity, purpose, and unity, and that God was immanent in the processes of history as well as transcendent to the entire development. John Hogan and Francis E. Gigot, Sulpician priests, wrote in favor of restructuring seminary education to introduce modern science and to use the methods of historical criticism in biblical studies.[29]

From the conservative perspective, the dialogue was another form of capitulation to the modern world. The desire to use modern sciences and scientific methodologies tended to obscure the dangers inherent in such an approach because it minimized the church's infallible authority and the authority of tradition itself. In 1891 Joseph Schroeder pointed out this tendency with reference to Canon Bartolo's *I Criteri Theologici*. For him theologians like Bartolo "started out with the very best intentions to reconcile the Church and the world according to their own peculiar ideas, but at last became themselves unable to keep aloof from the dangerous errors which this spirit hides under the most specious forms." Rationalism was the spirit behind these tendencies.[30]

Behind all of the specific issues that divided the Americanists and their opponents were two general conflicting views of the modern age and of how the church should relate to it. Although the Americanists saw the dangers in modern society, they emphasized what was good in it. They were sympathetic to the progressive, optimistic, developmental spirit of the age and saw the Catholic church as a fundamental historical force for religious and cultural improvement. Repeatedly they characterized American culture as democratic, activist, opportunistic, energetic, and aggressive—values they cherished. They also fostered and supported individual initiative, a sense of public responsibility, liberty in politics and religion, and the American constitutional separation of church and state. Because of American political freedom and increasing economic growth, moreover, they saw the United States as the future leader of the world and frequently contrasted the benefits of the New World with the disabilities of the Old. America had its faults, but they were, as Archbishop Ireland frequently said, the mere accidents of the age; what was essential in American culture and therefore consistent with Catholic traditions belonged to a democratic and progressive future.

The anti-Americanists' assessment of the modern world, and to a large extent of American culture, was governed primarily by the views expressed in Pope Pius IX's *Syllabus of Errors*. In this perspective the modern world was characterized by "liberalism," that is, a spirit of individualism, rationalism, socialism, and materialism—and with these aspects of modern culture there could be no compromise. In politics liberalism meant the absolute separation of church and state (a condition in which religion no longer had any influence upon the political order—political atheism, as Orestes Brownson had called it), which meant a historical hostility between church and state. In economics liberalism meant laissez-faire capitalism or socialism—that is, the attempt to absolutize either the individual or the state. In religious and intellectual life liberalism meant rationalism, or the divorce of reason from faith, nature from grace. In ecclesiastical life liberalism meant the attempts not only to restrict the nature and extent of the church's infallibility and authority, but also to accommodate the church to modern culture, ideas, and politics. This group repeatedly criticized modern life, but its members also asserted that they were trying to preserve the primacy of the spiritual order and the absolute necessity of revelation, supernatural grace, and ecclesiastical authority for a proper understanding of the human condition and destiny. They felt these values were severely threatened by developments in modern culture and by those in the church who were sympathetic with them.

Many in the second group saw American culture as part and parcel of liberal modern culture. American culture was primarily Protestant, and Protestantism in their conception was the first historical step toward the rationalism of the Enlightenment and the revolutionary tendencies of modern societies. Americanism was periodically identified with subjectivism, individualism, mammonism, nationalism, and anti-Catholicism. Although they accepted the American constitutional provisions for religious liberty and separation of church and state as beneficial, practical contingencies, members of this group could not see these constitutional arrangements as ideal. Although they acknowledged the practical benefits of modern scientific, economic, and technological advances, they could not accept a progressive or developmental view of history that saw the United States as the harbinger of the future. Although they acknowledged a material development, they could not perceive a spiritual evolution of humanity and rejected a progressive interpretation of history that denied, as they thought, the fundamental realities of human sinfulness or the unchanging structures of the human condition. Although they were patriotic Americans, they criticized what they considered an excessive American nationalism and chauvinism that almost made an idol of the nation and national virtues and tended to forget that Catholicism transcended nationalism and was separate from many values in American society. Yet some in this group had their own kinds of cultural nationalism.

From the late 1880s on the battles between the two world views were played out on the European stage as well. The Americanist program became entangled in civil and ecclesiastical politics, especially in Leo XIII's *ralliement* policy with the Third French Republic. In France the Americanists Ireland, Keane, and Gibbons were well received, especially by those who wanted to establish cordial relations between the government and the Catholic church. The French accommodationists and a few German and Italian sympathizers saw behind the Americanist programs a new religious spirit that they believed was necessary to meet the intellectual and political conditions of modern society. They had some of Ireland's more famous speeches translated into French and Italian and saw the Americanists as members of an international movement to demonstrate the compatibility of Catholicism and modern civilization. The Americanists, too, cooperated and encouraged the cause, speaking in France, attending and participating actively in the International Catholic Scientific Congresses, and working actively in Rome to discredit their opponents' positions and to win Vatican support for their movement. By the mid 1890s Americanism was becoming an international affair and was being used for various purposes in Europe.

The European battle over Americanism became sharply focused after the 1897 French translation of Walter Elliott's * *Life of Father Hecker*.[31] The edition was edited for a French audience and contained a preface by Abbé Félix Klein, a professor of literature at the Institut Catholique in Paris, who introduced Hecker as the pioneer of a spirituality that was needed in a modern scientific age, one that emphasized the interior life of the Holy Spirit and had the potential to transform and invigorate the traditional structures of Catholicism. The French translation with Klein's preface was a manifesto for the renewal of Catholicism in France; for the European conservatives it was a revelation that exposed all that was heterodox in the Americanist movement. Throughout 1897 and into 1898 the conservatives mounted a paper warfare against the book. Charles Maignen, a French priest, led the assault with a series of articles in the Parisian daily *La vérité*. For him Heckerism and Americanism represented, among other things, a neo-Pelagian mentality that stressed the superiority of the natural to supernatural virtues.

The French translation created such a theological and ecclesiastical controversy that Pope Leo XIII took the entire issue of Americanism under his own control. The theological charges against Heckerism and Americanism became the catalyst for the final Roman opposition, but the tide had been building for some years in Rome. The Apostolic Delegate, Francesco Satolli, had, since the World's Parliament of Religion, turned against the Americanists, and once he returned to Rome in 1895, he joined the Jesuits (e.g., Salvatori Brandi, Cardinal Camillo Mazzella) who had opposed the Americanists from the beginning. The encyclical *Longinqua Oceani*, the removals of Denis O'Connell as rector of the North American College in Rome (1895) and of John Keane as rector of the Catholic University (1896), and the silencing of John Zahm and forced withdrawal (1898) of his book *Evolution and Dogma* were clear signs of the growing Roman opposition to the Americanists.

The Spanish-American War (April to August, 1898) also intensified the divisions between the Americanists and their European opponents.[32] Some Americanists, even those like Ireland who tried to negotiate peace, saw the war as a manifestation of American superiority over Spain and, by extension, over the entire Old World. Spain just could not compete with American military might and money. The war revealed for the first time that the future belonged to the United States as a world power. Perhaps no one expressed this American chauvinism less guardedly than Denis O'Connell. In a private letter to Ireland, he asserted that for him the real issue in the war was one of the struggle of "two civilizations": one, the European, which was "all that is old and vile and mean and rotten and cruel and false," and the other, the American, which was all that was "free and noble and open and true and humane."[33] Josiah Strong could not have been more passionately millennialistic or chauvinistic.

The European anti-Americanists interpreted the war as another manifestation of aggressive American jingoism and mammonism that were imperialistic and out of control. It was not just a war between two nations, moreover, but between Catholic Spain and Protestant America. The Spanish-American War further fed an appetite for ecclesiastical war that had been going on for some time in Europe and severely discredited the Americanist cause—ecclesiastical as well as political.

The final blow against Americanism came on 22 January 1899, when Leo XIII published his encyclical *Testem Benevolentiae*.[34] Addressed to Cardinal Gibbons, the encyclical praised American Catholics for their works in promoting Catholicism and distinguished between a theological Americanism, which he condemned, and a political Americanism, which he lauded because it reflected the characteristic qualities, laws, and customs of the country. For Leo, theological Americanism was characterized by three heterodox tendencies: excessive accommodationism, a spirit of religious subjectivism, and a new form of ecclesiastical nationalism. Without actually condemning anyone for holding such positions, the pope sent the American bishops a warning that such tendencies raised the suspicion "that there are some among you who conceive of and desire a church in America different from that which is in the rest of the world." The old fear of ecclesiastical Gallicanism—this time an American-style ecclesiastical nationalism—was a significant part of his concern.

The reaction to the encyclical was swift. The liberals denied that the condemned opinions were held; the conservatives thanked the pontiff for pointing out dangers that actually existed. For Ireland the condemned errors were "Maignen's Nightmare."[35] Like Ireland the other Americanist bishops were angered by the encyclical, and although thanking the pope for it, they were quick to point out that he was condemning a phantom, an imaginary set of errors.

Two archbishops, Corrigan and Katzer, wrote to the pope in the names of their suffragans to express their full adhesion to the letter and indicate that they believed it absolutely necessary to dam up the flood of a false Americanism that would have deluged the country without the encyclical. Corrigan, generally willing to extend the boundaries of ecclesiastical authority, even called the encyclical "your infallible teaching." He acknowledged that he, as much as anyone else, was proud to be an American and to glory in American institutions, developments, and achievements, but "in the matter of religion, doctrine, discipline, morals and Christian perfection, we glory in thoroughly following the Holy See."[36] Archbishop Katzer and his Milwaukee suffragans told the pope that they were "indignant over the fact" that "not a few" in American Catholicism had accepted the condemnations "but did not hesitate to proclaim again and again, in Jansenistic fashion, that there was hardly any American who had held them and that the Holy See, deceived by false reports, had beaten the air and chased after a shadow."[37]

The encyclical did not end the differences in the American church, either with regard to basic orientations to the modern world or with regard to judgments of facts. The leading Americanists would continue until their deaths (Spalding in 1916, Keane and Ireland in 1918, Gibbons in 1921, O'Connell in 1927) to believe that their side had been maligned. They would continue to speak out as they had before and insist that their brand of Americanism was not under condemnation. But the Americanists were chastened, and most of them retired from national and international ecclesiastical and political maneuvers. Their legacy, chastised though it was, continued in new forms into the twentieth century, as shall be seen.

The conservatives believed they had won a major victory. They had stuck by the *Syllabus's* understanding of the dangers inherent in the modern world, and *Testem Benevolentiae* reaffirmed that basic orientation. The leading conservatives died long before their Americanist counterparts (e.g., Corrigan in 1902, Katzer in 1903, McQuaid in 1909), but their legacy would also be continued in new ways by a rising generation of active Jesuits and by a new set of Roman-trained bishops who would gain control of some large dioceses.

5
PROGRESSIVE ERA CATHOLICISM: 1900–1920

Testem Benevolentiae had at least one major effect upon American Catholicism: It ended the intramural battles that had raged through the American hierarchy and Catholic newspapers and journals for the past sixteen years. As American Catholics entered the twentieth century, they could put the old ecclesiastical battles behind them, even if they could not extricate themselves from the different spirits that had been responsible for the battles in the first place. Regardless of their former differences, American Catholic leaders still had to face the problem of providing for the religious needs of their people in the midst of changing American cultural and political circumstances and within the context of a new anti-modernist papacy.

Post-Americanist Catholicism developed during the progressive era of American politics—the era of Presidents Theodore Roosevelt, William H. Taft, and Woodrow Wilson. It was a period of moral, political, and social reforms. The progressive movement represented in part a middle-class mentality that feared the concentration of power in Gilded Age trusts on the one hand and radical labor and populist agitations on the other. Progressives also criticized the persistence of corruption in government and aspired to restore the nation's founding democratic ideals in a transformed and industrialized society. They called upon government to intervene as a moral agent to regulate, though not dissolve, the power of the trusts for the sake of distributing the benefits of the democratic promise to all. Although they used the government as an agent for moral and social reform, they appealed primarily to the moral individual and to moral institutions as the primary agents for the advancement of the public good.

During this period some American Catholics appropriated the spirit of the progressive era, which is usually associated with evangelical Protestant moralism; others rejected that spirit and any form of accommodation to it; still others were not at all involved with the programs of the era, being primarily concerned with the religious needs of immigrant parish communities. The progressive era was another period of immigrant growth, continuing Americanization, a series of intellectual and ethnic crises, and a growing realization that American Catholicism had a new social mission in American society and a religious mission in the world at large. By the end of the era, in the face of World War I, the American hierarchy was again united in a common effort to address national interests. Their unity and developed sense of national, over local, interests would have astounded many participants in the late nineteenth-century Americanist conflicts.

Progressive era American Catholicism also developed within the context of a new papacy that was not only anti-modernist in theology but reformist in its approach to a number of internal ecclesiastical issues and religious practices. Pope Leo XIII died in 1903 and was replaced by Pope Pius X. Modernist theologians met forceful resistance in Pius's 1907 decree *Lamentabile* and his encyclical *Pascendi dominici Gregis,* which condemned modernism as the "synthesis of all heresies." Unlike Leo XIII, Pius X saw irreconcilable differences between the church and the age, believed that a synthesis of theology and modern science was impossible, and thought that Leo's political agenda of *ralliement* had utterly failed. He therefore gave up hope of winning political— French or otherwise—support for the restoration of temporal powers. His encyclical *E Supremi* (1903) outlined his own sense of the church's mission in the modern world to be that of "restoring all things in Christ,"[1] a policy that had ecclesiastical, political, as well as religious implications. On the religious side the pope intended to revive the church's inner life as a fundamental means of transforming, not accepting, the world. Among other things, he initiated reforms in church music, restoring the primacy of Gregorian chant, and promoted the more frequent reception of the Eucharist, giving the liturgical revival a major new impetus. On the ecclesiastical and political sides, he began to assault all modern developments considered hostile to the church's authoritative and doctrinal integrity. Pius X's Vatican tried to eradicate the evils of the modern world by issuing condemnations of modern errors, as had his predecessor Pius IX, and by organizing ecclesiastical machinery to investigate and eliminate any doctrinal or disciplinary deviance within the church.

Lamentabile and *Pascendi* detailed the errors of the modern mind under the rubrics of "vital immanence," "dogmatic evolutionism," "agnosticism," "subjectivism," "historical relativism," and a symbolic view of doctrine. Modernism within the church was perceived not as an attempt to give Catholic answers to very serious problems raised by modern developments but as a capitulation to a mentality that was inherently opposed to the supernaturally endowed doctrinal tradition. The modern mentality was not just attempting to reconcile faith and science; it was, in fact, subjugating the one to the other. In 1910 the pope followed up his condemnations with *Sacrorum Antistitum,* prescribing that all seminary, college, and university professors of theology take an oath against modernism, thus further institutionalizing the anti-modernist stance he had taken.[2]

Although there were not many signs of the existence of theological modernism in the United States,[3] there is no doubt that the papal actions had immediate effects upon American Catholicism. They abruptly killed off any historically minded theological and doctrinal research, ended incipient scholarship in biblical studies, caused the cessation of the publication of the *New York Review,* diminished and eventually eliminated the influence of the modernist faculties at Dunwoodie and other seminaries, and created a climate of opinion and oppression that some quasi-modernists, William L. Sullivan* and John Slattery,* for example, found so objectionable that they left the church.

The reformist papacy created a new American episcopacy during the progressive era that was anti-modernist in its intellectual orientation, Americanist in its loyalties, and modernist in its consolidating administrative practices. Big-city bishops in particular reflected this combination of Romanization and Americanization. John Murphy Farley was appointed to New York in 1902, James Edward Quigley to Chicago and John Joseph Glennon* to St. Louis in 1903, William Henry O'Connell* to Boston in 1906, George William Mundelein* to Chicago and Edward Hanna to San Francisco in 1915, and Dennis Joseph Dougherty to Philadelphia in 1918. Although they were not all cut from the same theological or ecclesiastical cloth, they were all, except for Glennon, educated at some point in Rome and manifested a simultaneous intense loyalty to the Vatican and the United States. All of them, moreover, had been born in the United States, except Farley and Glennon, who were born in Ireland, and Quigley, who was born in Ontario, but all three lived most of their adult lives in the United States.

Big-city bishops of the early and mid-twentieth century were what Edward Kantowicz has aptly called "consolidating bishops." Being Roman to the core did not prohibit them from becoming American and modern in the techniques they used to operate a large institution. Like corporate leaders in American big business, labor, and government, they "brought order, centralization, and businesslike administration to their previously chaotic dioceses."[4] Using standards of efficiency, rational control, and pragmatic effect that were characteristic signs of modernity and the rising corporate structures in American society, the bishops began to centralize and control all parish and diocesan matters from their chancery headquarters. These new corporate executive–type bishops were highly visible and triumphalist in their leadership styles, bringing a new respect for and raising the self-image of American Catholicism. They tried to make Catholicism socially self-confident and vigorous both in the United States and at the Vatican. Building big institutions, staging massive public ceremonies, hiring prestigious first-class legal firms, consulting with successful business managers while cultivating their friendship, using the publicity gimmicks of advertising firms to raise much-needed money to finance their building campaigns—all were tactics used by these bishops to create an image of the church that was both Catholic and American. They also worked diligently to Americanize immigrants through schools and other institutions. When they died, they received national media attention that had rarely been accorded their nineteenth-century predecessors. Catholicism was beginning to be acknowledged as a prominent force in American political, cultural, and economic life, and these forceful bishops helped to bring about the change.

The big-city ecclesiastical princes sponsored a practical, not a theoretical, Americanism that steered away from much systematic reflection on the relationship of Catholic doctrine to American individualism, pragmatism, and corporate capitalism. The episcopal attempts to put the Catholic church on the American map, as Mundelein later phrased it, made them unable or unwilling to think about what values they were incorporating into the church's operational structures.

The episcopal vision and practical implementation of diocesan consolidation, centralization, and control was as American as it was Roman in the early days of the twentieth century, but it was sometimes more vision than reality. Urban as well as other American bishops did not always have the effective and pragmatic or charismatic power to fulfill their episcopal designs. The persistence of local autonomy among strong-willed pastors, college presidents, hospital administrators, superiors of women religious, and social agency leaders periodically frustrated the episcopal will and made centralizing tendencies ineffective and practically impotent. The bishops had to face strong American feudalism and local control over large segments of Catholic life. Many had episcopal authority, but they did not always have the power to make that authority effective.[5]

The consolidating bishops did, however, have prominent allies among the early twentieth-century Jesuits in their anti-modernist and thoroughly ultramontane ecclesiasticism. Many nineteenth-century Jesuits came from Europe, but by the 1920s their membership was increasingly drawn from second- and third-generation American immigrants. They would gradually have a powerful influence upon the educated laity in the American church, primarily because by 1920 they had established and were administering from coast to coast twenty-five major colleges and universities, which they were organizing according to the standards of higher education prevalent in American society.

The late nineteenth-century Jesuits had been predominantly anti-Americanists, but their ultramontane Catholicism took a new twist during the early twentieth century when a few of their leading lights tried to focus Catholic attention upon national and international issues—developing in the process a new kind of activist, conservative, and anti-modernist American Catholic tradition. Although they had been in the Anglo-American colonies since 1634 and had started colleges as early as 1789, they had not had much of a national voice in nineteenth-century ecclesiastical or cultural affairs, except for a popular magazine on spirituality, the *Sacred Heart Messenger*. That changed in 1909 when they began to publish *America* as a national weekly journal of Catholic opinion on a variety of national, rather than purely ecclesiastical, issues. The motivating and innovative force behind *America,* as behind a number of other initiatives during the progressive era, was the Jesuit John J. Wynne,* who became the editor. Wynne's original editorial indicated that it was time American Catholics, in the words of Cardinal John Henry Newman, take "an intelligent interest in public affairs, and not live as a class apart."[6] Coming as it did in the wake of Pius X's *Pascendi, America* was thoroughly orthodox and served the traditional apologetical functions of other Catholic newspapers and magazines, but it also had an activist bent that drove the editors to make Catholic principles part of the American and American Catholic intellectual conversation about public issues. The journal would not be a speculative and intellectually innovative enterprise, but a weekly discussion of vital and practical applications of orthodox Catholic views to contemporary social, political, and cultural questions.

Although the editors of *America* were thoroughly anti-modernist in Pius X's mold, they were also becoming more concerned than their counterparts in the nineteenth century about guiding Catholics to a redemption of society, again following the lead of Pius X to "restore all things in Christ." *America* was a first step in this process, but it represented a confidence among the conservatives that they did indeed have something to contribute to America. The Jesuit policy was defensive, apologetic, and fiercely anti-modernist at first, but it also shifted the conservative focus toward contemporary life—a shift that would much later bring forth Jesuits like John Courtney Murray,* who were not only conversant but also sympathetic with some modern perspectives.

Although there were a few signs that Catholicism was beginning to emerge into American public life, the predominant concerns were still those of the immigrant Catholic communities that were at various stages of settlement, conflict, and development in the large urban areas of Boston, New York, Philadelphia, Baltimore, Chicago, St. Louis, and, to a certain extent, Detroit, Milwaukee, New Orleans, and San Francisco. Southwestern dioceses from Galveston to southern California also experienced a great increase in immigrant population, primarily from Mexico. Until the immigrant restriction laws of the early 1920s, the small southwestern as well as large urban dioceses were in a constant state of flux, trying to absorb the immigrants. The new immigrants brought a rich and dizzying diversity of ethnic Catholic cultures and rites. Each group tried to preserve its own identity and integrity, and each experienced a series of intra-ethnic conflicts, internal church battles, and external hostilities from nativists.

At times the conflicts became so intense and hostile that they led to permanent schisms—as was the case in the late 1890s with a few Polish Catholics who separated themselves from Catholicism and formed an independent denomination, the Polish National Catholic Church, and as was the case with a number of Byzantine-rite Rusin Catholics in Minnesota and elsewhere who permanently separated themselves from the American Catholic church in the late nineteenth and early twentieth centuries and joined the Russian Orthodox Church. How many individual immigrants left the Catholic church to become Protestants or enter the long list of the unchurched is uncertain, but surely the tensions and difficulties of adjustment caused some to withdraw from any allegiance.

Although permanent schisms did occur here and there in American Catholicism, they were not the primary focus of Catholic immigrant attention during the first twenty or thirty years of this century. The primary problem for the numerous southern and eastern European Catholic immigrants was that of preserving their religious and social traditions while they adjusted to new conditions and tried to make a living. Variety characterizes the processes of preservation and accommodation among the different ethnic traditions, but a description of that variety goes beyond the scope of this study. The Irish, Germans, Poles, and French Canadians, for example, brought with them numerous clergy and women religious to help build the institutions that fostered their traditions in the United States and thereby provided institutional means for preservation and assimilation. The Italians, on the other hand, did not bring with them numerous clergy or women religious in the first generation, and consequently their adjustments to American Catholicism were less institutionalized. The Italian peasants, moreover, brought with them various forms of folk Catholicism and an anticlericalism that made their clash with the voluntary and institutional patterns of religious life that had been developing in American Catholicism since the early nineteenth century particularly acute. Intra- and interethnic conflict characterized the progressive era, as the new immigrants sought to establish a home within an American Catholicism that was becoming increasingly pluralistic.

Although progressive era Catholics focused on the continuing immigrant conditions of their church, they also began to develop new missionary initiatives. At a time when liberal Protestants were calling the Christian missionary enterprise into question, American Catholics started to feel an indigenous missionary zeal that was another sign of the emergence of Catholicism from the self-centered preoccupations of the nineteenth century. In the early twentieth century American Catholics created some imaginative ventures in home missions to the unchurched Americans and to those in isolated rural areas, and developed entirely new organizations for foreign missions.

New home missionary movements responded to a variety of unmet needs. The heiress of a large Philadelphia banking fortune, Katharine Drexel,* impressed by the Third Plenary Council's call for assistance to African- and Native Americans, established in 1891 the Sisters of the Blessed Sacrament for Indians and Colored People. When she died in 1955, she and her religious order had established fifty-one houses in twenty-one states and the District of Columbia. By then they also staffed sixty-two schools and had built Xavier University of New Orleans (1925), the only African-American Catholic university in the country.

Some sought to win Protestants or unchurched Americans over to Catholicism. In 1896 the Paulists, under the leadership of Walter Elliott and Alexander

P. Doyle, launched a Catholic Missionary Union whose fundamental purpose was to win converts by developing evangelical methods that were genuinely persuasive as well as respectful of American religious liberty.[7] The most spectacular of the home missions were the lay-led pioneer adventures in public speaking and street preaching organized by Boston's Martha Gallison Moore Avery* and David Goldstein,* both of whom were converts from socialism to Catholicism in 1904 and 1905 respectively. From the early twentieth century until World War II a number of other lay evangelists crisscrossed the country as preachers and apologists for Catholicism.[8] Home missions also received new attention in Francis C. Kelley's* Catholic Church Extension Society, organized in Chicago in 1905 to provide funds and other forms of assistance for rural Catholics.

In the midst of its own continuing dependence upon foreign missionaries to serve the pressing problems of urban immigrants and its own inadequate supply of home missionaries for rural peoples, American Catholicism began to send missionaries to foreign lands. By the beginning of the twentieth century American Protestants had thousands of foreign missionaries and had committed millions of dollars to the endeavor. American Catholics had no more than sixteen religious involved in foreign missions, and their participation was not part of an organized enterprise, but more the result of individual zeal. This situation began to change in 1911 when James A. Walsh* of Boston and Thomas F. Price of Raleigh established the Catholic Foreign Mission Society of America (Maryknoll), demonstrating again an incipient awareness of the American church's wider role in world Christianity and a new awakening of the missionary spirit. Maryknoll, the first American Catholic foreign mission society, built a seminary, attracted priests and eventually sisters to the new order, and in 1918 sent its first group of missionaries to China.

A few middle-class lay and clerical Catholics also crossed the boundaries of their immigrant conclaves to become involved in the progressive era's reformist mentality. Some organized national societies and movements[9] that focused on social, educational, and legislative reforms that were clearly influenced by Pope Leo XIII's perspective on social justice and the common good. Labor priests like Peter Dietz,* Catholic socialists like Fathers Thomas McGrady* and Thomas J. Hagerty, anti-socialists and antiprogressives like Peter Yorke,* lay editors and reformers like Milwaukee's Humphrey Desmond, German Christian solidarists like St. Louis's Frederick Kenkel, and sociologists like Father William Kerby* worked in a variety of ways to promote very different Catholic visions of social and legislative reforms.

John A. Ryan* was undoubtedly the foremost Catholic representative of the progressive social and economic reformist mentality in the early twentieth century. He created a systematic study of the social question by combining the natural law tradition of the Leonine perspective with an empirical examination of the actual economic conditions in American society. Out of this study came his first major book which produced arguments and proposals for *A Living*

Wage (1906), which Richard Ely's introduction called "the first attempt in the English language to elaborate what may be called a Roman Catholic system of political economy." What impressed Ely most about the book, however, was that it got beyond "vague and glittering generalities to precise doctrine" and passed from "appeals to sentiment to reasoned arguments." [10]

Ryan saw state and later federal legislation as a key practical means to regulate and distribute more equitably the nation's wealth. Although critical of certain economic structures and the legislation that supported them, he was not as unalterably opposed to capitalism as was the German Catholic Central Verein, and in fact he hoped to work through the capitalist system to transform it in a more democratic direction. His approach to legislation puts him in the camp of some progressive age Protestant reformers, but his modified Leonine vision makes his own progressivism distinctively Catholic.

Catholic public opinion on the major social and political issues of the progressive era, prohibition and women's suffrage, was as divided as were the perspectives on economic justice. Since the 1840s a few Catholic clerical and lay leaders had been engaged in local parish and state temperance movements, and in 1872 the Catholic Total Abstinence Union (CTAU) was formed as a national movement to promote, exclusively through moral suasion, temperance in the Catholic community. For the exclusive persuasionists, the church and Catholics qua Catholics should stay away from all forms of legislative prohibition. The church should emphasize the supernatural assistance of grace through the sacraments in the reformation of human persons and society. Total legislative prohibition, moreover, was unjustified because drink was not an inherent evil. Perhaps the majority of the CTAU membership opposed reformist movements toward prohibitive legislation, perceiving them to be rooted in Manicheanism, statism or socialism, American activism, pharisaism, and cultural chauvinism. [11] Some bishops, like Milwaukee's Sebastian Messmer, forbade any priest visiting his diocese to speak in favor of prohibition.

After the early 1880s some CTAU members began to advocate prohibitive legislative measures to restrict the sale and licensing of saloons, and by the 1890s a few Catholics—for example, Fathers George Zurcher of Buffalo, John J. Curran of Wilkes-Barre, Pennsylvania, and James T. Judge of Scranton— were avid prohibitionists. Father James M. Cleary of St. Paul, at one time president of the CTAU, became the first vice president of the Anti-Saloon League. Bishops, too, like Spalding, Keane, and Ireland, favored increasing legislation to limit the availability of liquor.

For Catholic prohibitionists the evil of intemperance was so pervasive and so destructive of individual, family, and social life that moral persuasion alone would not be effective. The problems were not just individual; they were part of the entire economic and legal structure of society. Legislative as well as moral reforms were needed. Catholic prohibitionists, moreover, not only cooperated with Protestants in suggesting legislation to restrict the use of alcohol but also wanted American Catholicism—which had all too often been identified with "rum and rebellion"—to be identified with the temperance reformist movements.

Catholics, like other Americans, were also divided on the issue of women's suffrage before and after the progressive era's ratification of the nineteenth amendment. Social activists like Ellen Ewing Sherman, Madaline Vinton Dahlgren, and writers and editors like Katherine E. Conway* opposed women's suffrage. Leonora Barry Lake,* though, was an active suffragist, as were the pro-labor leader Mary Kenney O'Sullivan* and a few other prominent middle-class Catholic women who saw suffrage as a political manifestation and extension of natural equality. Bishops and clergy, too, were divided in their sympathies with the pro- and anti-suffragist movements. Ireland, Spalding, and even the conservative McQuaid favored the establishment of higher education for women and women's suffrage, while Bishop Joseph Macheboeuf of Denver, many of the German clergy, and even Gibbons railed against the evil effects of women's involvement in politics and opposed the ballot.[12]

Many rejected women's suffrage as a threat to the Christian home and inconsistent with a woman's dignity and role in society. Thomas Francis Lillis, bishop of Leavenworth, Kansas, did not believe that it was the "woman's place to approach the polls and vote."[13] Although, as Bishop Messmer noted in 1913, there was no official Catholic position on women's suffrage and even though it was still an open question, he believed that most Catholic theologians and philosophers, although accepting the natural equality of the sexes, denied the claim to political equality.[14] Cardinal Gibbons, too, had rejected the arguments in favor of suffrage, but once the nineteenth amendment was ratified on 20 August 1920, he encouraged all women to exercise their suffrage "not only as a right but as a strict social duty."[15]

Middle-class Catholics, like many others in the United States, revealed a propensity during the progressive era to organize national fraternal and professional societies for a variety of social and reform purposes. The American Federation of Catholic Societies (1901), a national union of various ethnic fraternal and social societies, was one example of this tendency. The AFCS focused attention on national social and moral issues and provided mutual benefit and support for its members. The national organization of Catholic societies of educators, physicians, historians, philosophers, sociologists, and a host of other professional groups also developed during the progressive era and throughout the pre–Vatican II period. These societies tried to create an American Catholic sense of solidarity in responding to professional issues. By organizing themselves nationally these societies were also adopting a characteristically modern principle of organization in their attempts to improve Catholic performance in their functional specialties, develop intercommunication, and provide a means for coordinated activities. In this respect these new institutions played a role analogous to that of the consolidating bishops in the large urban dioceses.[16]

This progressive era tendency also contributed toward the development of a national episcopal organization that would be greatly influential in directing

Catholic presence throughout the twentieth century. The organization of the National Catholic War Council (1917), although brought about because of the needs of World War I, united bishops and isolated Catholic societies into a national force that was able to respond in organized fashion to the American war effort. The initiative for a united effort to muster Catholic support for the war and supply Catholic soldiers with chaplains and religious services came not from the bishops themselves, but from the Paulist John Burke,* editor of the *Catholic World* from 1904 to 1922. He advised the bishops that they must "learn to think nationally." [17] At Burke's suggestion the bishops organized the NCWC as a united Catholic voice—similar to the Federal (later National) Council of Churches of Christ (1908)—capable of asserting Catholic interests in public life. Like some other national Catholic institutions of the period, the NCWC reflected the organizational revolution intrinsic to modernization in the twentieth century.

The NCWC helped the bishops transcend for the moment some of their differences and parochial concerns, and it effectively demonstrated Catholic patriotism. Through the NCWC the bishops helped bring about what Elizabeth McKeown has called "the practical identification of Americanism and Christianity" during the war years. [18] The NCWC also organized an aggressive publicity blitz to broadcast Catholic support for and participation in the war effort and helped to develop lobbying techniques that would serve the bishops well in years to come. Although the War Council was organized to meet pressing national needs, Burke had, even originally, intended that the national body be more than an ad hoc response. He saw it, or something like it, as a permanent federated Catholic response to public issues.

After the signing of the armistice in November 1918, American bishops decided to form the National Catholic Welfare Council (1919; title changed to Conference in 1922) as a more permanent national body to assist in the postwar reconstruction of American society and meet ongoing concerns of American Catholics. The bishops in particular had become increasingly aware of the growing federal control of American life and wanted an effective agency in Washington to protect and advance Catholic interests.

In the midst of establishing the NCWC, the council's administrative committee issued what has come to be called the "Bishops' Program of Social Reconstruction" (12 February 1919), a detailed proposal for legislation to ensure economic and social justice. [19] Written primarily by John A. Ryan, the program was, in the judgment of Joseph McShane, a synthesis of the Leonine vision of social justice and the progressive reform proposals of the age. [20] Among other things, it called for minimum wage legislation; social insurance for unemployment, old age, and sickness; a national employment agency; low-cost public housing projects; regulation of public utilities and monopolies; establishment of consumers' and producers' cooperatives; and equal wages for women.

Some were shocked by the proposals, tagging them socialistic. A few bishops, like Cardinal Gibbons, were unprepared for the negative reactions. He insisted that the program was perceived as a novelty because Catholics themselves had not previously communicated their own sense of social justice. "The Church," he told a 1919 national episcopal assembly, "has a great work of social education and social welfare lying before it." [21] Although Gibbons defended the program, other bishops found some of its proposals too daring. But the program itself was a revelation of the new role in moral leadership the bishops were assuming in American society.

American Catholic leaders were optimistic about their role in society. The war had initiated the hierarchy into the national political process and opened the way for their continued leadership in shaping cultural values. Their own federal movement was not only a manifestation of the collegial temper of some nineteenth-century bishops, but an acknowledgment that modern problems demanded a national organization similar to the Federal Council of Churches. Catholic bishops had, perhaps unwittingly, come to terms with some of the dynamics and institutional developments of the progressive era—but the progressive era was coming to an end.

6
ALIENATION AND ACTIVISM: 1920–1945

American Catholics entered the 1920s with a new feeling of their own Americanism and a new confidence in their ability to contribute to the national welfare. The cultural and social changes associated with the roaring twenties, the Depression of the 1930s, and the development of totalitarianism and religious intolerance in Russia, Mexico, Spain, and Germany, however, made Catholics aware of their continued alienation from aspects of American and modern life. In the midst of these significant changes the neo-Thomist philosophical and theological tradition became a serviceable ideology in articulating an American Catholic identity. Catholics were self-consciously searching for a response to the spiritual, cultural, economic, and political problems of modern American life, producing as a consequence a new kind of Catholic activism in American society, a cautious critique of American Catholic weaknesses, and a discreet call for internal ecclesial reforms. Catholic support for and participation in World War II reaffirmed American Catholic patriotism and nationalism, but it also broke the bonds of a prewar isolationism and laid a foundation for a new kind of internationalism within American Catholic leadership.

In twenty-five years, according to the *Official Catholic Directory,* the Catholic population increased slowly (only 35 percent, from 17.7 million in 1920 to 23.9 million in 1945), especially in comparison to the previous hundred years of immigrant growth. A population increase of only 5 percent during the 1930s shows that the birth rate suffered considerably from the Depression. The slow population growth was accompanied, however, by a phenomenal 82 percent increase in the number of clergy (from 21,019 in 1920 to 38,451 in 1945), a 140 percent increase in seminarians, and an 83 percent increase in women religious. Prior to the 1920s the church had been primarily dependent upon Europe for clergy and women and men religious; thereafter it developed its own native clergy and religious. The postwar growth in religious vocations corresponded to the needs of the increasing number of schools, colleges, universities, hospitals, and social service agencies. What accounts for the tremendous growth of religious vocations during the period, or what does it signify? It is much easier to point to the fact of the growth than to discover its causes. Without denying divine causality, it seems that the growth was the result of a combination of human factors: a concerted effort to recruit young men and women for a religious life, an awareness of the needs within the Catholic community, a growing American Catholic self-confidence, the devastating economic effects of the Depression, and the advantages religious life provided young second- and third-generation immigrants who were conscious of social mobility. Whatever the reasons may have been, there is no doubt that this tremendous growth is in need of a historian for a more systematic analysis.

The gradual evolution of a pragmatic and institutional Catholic Americanism, which had its origin during the consolidating days of the progressive era, continued during the 1920s and 1930s, becoming a part of the Catholic defensive reaction to an aggressive postwar Protestant evangelical crusade to promote 100 percent Americanism. The evangelical battle to protect its long-standing moral hegemony over American culture was an anxious response to the belief that secular values were beginning to threaten the stability and moral integrity of American society, and to the rising visible presence of Catholics and other "foreigners" who challenged Protestant dominance. The campaigns for 100 percent Americanism—for example, the struggle over the justification of prohibition, the immigrant restriction quotas of 1921 and 1924, the Scopes trial of 1925, Oregon's legislative attempt to eliminate private schools, and Alfred E. Smith's political defeat in 1928—reinforced a Catholic sense of alienation, but stimulated a Catholic crusade to Christianize culture, a crusade that was analogous to the Protestant campaign Catholics opposed.

Ratification of the Eighteenth Amendment was the culmination of the nineteenth-century Protestant struggle for a Christian culture in America. Neither the campaign for legislative prohibition nor the Volstead Act of 1920, however, had been popular among most articulate American Catholics. Many Catholic leaders continued to believe that moral persuasion, rather than legislation, was a more effective remedy against the evils of intemperance and alcoholism. Some prominent Catholics, like John A. Ryan, had supported the Eighteenth Amendment, but only on the condition that it could be reasonably enforced. By 1927 even supporters like Ryan were beginning to oppose the Volstead Act, because it was becoming increasingly evident that the law was ineffective and unenforceable, thus making a mockery of this law in particular and of all laws in general.[1] Many articulate Catholics also interpreted the Eighteenth Amendment as another manifestation of the increasing and unjustified involvement of "big government" (i.e., socialism) in individuals' lives—a fear that was similarly behind their opposition to federal involvement in education and child labor. The repeal of Prohibition in 1933 brought no resistance from the organs of Catholic opinion in the United States. Although most Catholics probably shared the Protestant concern for a Christian American culture, they did not agree with

Prohibition as a means, because according to Catholic moral theology, there was nothing inherently evil in the consumption of alcoholic beverages.

One hundred percent Americanism also manifested itself in the rigorous immigrant restriction quotas enacted by Congress in 1921 and 1924, which were clearly prejudiced against southern and eastern Europeans, many of whom since the 1880s were Catholic. The Catholic press again opposed these measures, interpreting them as disguised prejudice against Catholics in America. John A. Ryan and others in the labor movement, however, saw the restriction laws as necessary legislative enactments to provide better wages for working-class Americans. Ryan also believed that Catholics generally were too quick to raise the anti-Catholic complaint.

Whatever the intent of the immigrant restriction quotas, they did have an unintended benefit within the Catholic community. By restricting the constant flow of immigrants, Congress had provided Catholics and especially the consolidating bishops with some time and space to make corporate ecclesiastical planning possible, develop Americanization strategies for the immigrants they had already absorbed into the church, and stabilize a Catholic community that had been in almost constant flux since the 1880s. In spite of the alienation that some Catholics felt because of the restrictions, these quotas coupled with the rise of the consolidating bishops and creation of the NCWC made the 1920s the beginning of a period of organizational strength for American Catholicism. And that organizational strength gave Catholics a sense of self-confidence.

The issues that aroused the greatest public interest in religion in the 1920s were those connected with schools, the primary American agency for passing on American civilization and culture. In 1925 the widely publicized "Scopes Monkey Trial" in Tennessee and Oregon's attempt to prohibit private schools revealed anxieties about the definition, survival, and transmission of 100 percent (meaning evangelical Protestant, fundamentalist, and xenophobic) American culture. Catholics were affected indirectly by the former and directly by the latter. In reacting particularly to the Oregon school case, they emerged in a new way on the American political scene and helped to reinforce constitutional provisions for religious liberty.

In 1922 Oregon enacted legislation that made public schooling compulsory for all children between the ages of eight and sixteen. Backers of the legislation, including the Ku Klux Klan and Scottish Rite Masons, periodically articulated anti-Catholic slogans in their campaigns to win voters' approval. The Oregon law raised the fears of Catholics across the country like nothing else in the most recent past because it challenged the integrity and independence of the entire Catholic school system.

Oregon Catholics, Lutherans, and Seventh Day Adventists were joined by the American Civil Liberties Union, the national office of the Knights of Columbus, the NCWC, and a host of Protestant and liberal secular Americans in calling for a repeal of the law. Catholics in particular rejected the law because, as they argued in state courts and the United States Supreme Court, it violated religious liberty and educational diversity, and reflected a "socialist" movement in society of which Catholics had an almost congenital fear.

In *Sisters of the Holy Names v. Pierce et al.* (1925) the United States Supreme Court handed down a landmark decision that supported the state's responsibility and rights over education and at the same time protected the rights of private and parochial education.[2] This was a legal victory and a milestone in the interpretation of the Constitution.

Catholic schools continued to expand, particularly during the 1920s, and to symbolize something of the relationship of Catholicism to American culture. During the 1920s and 1930s they were gradually transformed from agents of separatism to agents of Americanization. Many Catholic educators, like their counterparts in the public school system, began to worship at the shrine of scientific efficiency, believing that standardization, professionalization, state certification of teachers, and bureaucratic centralization were means for improving education. Accepting these means was part of the Americanization process of the 1920s. Academic and educational excellence, whether in Catholic or public schools, came to be identified with accepting standardized measures. Although American Catholics warred against secularization in the society at large during these two decades, they were themselves captured by the very secular means they adopted in consolidating their dioceses and schools to fight against it. Americanization also meant that the schools would be used to bring American Catholic immigrant children into the mainstream of American economic and political life.

The 1928 presidential campaign and defeat of the Catholic Alfred E. Smith—like the Oregon school case, immigrant restriction laws, and bigotry of the Ku Klux Klan and other "preservers" of Americanism—reinforced the feeling of alienation for a number of articulate leaders of Catholic public opinion and represented the culmination of threats to Catholic self-confidence in the 1920s. Whatever role religion may have had in Smith's actual defeat—and there is much scholarly dispute about it—there is little doubt that many leading Catholics saw it as a threat to their postwar aspirations of rising out of their nineteenth-century second-class status in America.

Smith's candidacy for the presidency brought to the fore some of the larger issues relative to the relationship of Catholicism to American public and constitutional life. The whole question of double allegiance reasserted itself in the campaign: "Can a Catholic be loyal to his church and, as president, to his country?" Charles C. Marshall, an Episcopal layman and political moderate, articulated the fears of many in 1927 when he concluded that the dogmatic principles of the Catholic church were antithetical to American constitutional ideals. He asserted that Smith's election, therefore, might "precipitate an inevitable conflict between the Roman Catholic Church and the American State irreconcilable with domestic peace."[3]

Smith responded to Marshall's charges by outlining a religiopolitical creed that asserted his belief in religious liberty and separation of church and state and argued that no power in the Catholic church could overthrow these political realities.[4] But his creed contained a list of Catholic assertions, not rational demonstrations, and they did not persuade the public. Most Catholics in the 1920s, Smith included, resented the fact that they had to demonstrate their allegiance to their country, but most of them also did not perceive how threatening the Roman church's views and alleged political powers were in a liberal society. American fears, moreover, had recently been reinforced by the publication of John A. Ryan and Moorhouse Millar's *The Church and the State* (1922), which asserted that the state had the obligation to make a public profession of religion. It took more than a decade before an American Catholic, John Courtney Murray, S.J., would begin to develop a very different systematic intellectual response to the church-state issues raised by some Catholic teachings and the Smith candidacy.

Many have argued that Smith lost the campaign not only because of his Catholicism, but also because of his urban identification, his stand against Prohibition, Republican prosperity, and Herbert Hoover's popularity, so even well-developed rational arguments would have failed to convince the public in the context of the late 1920s. Catholic leaders of public opinion, though, were stung by the charges raised during the campaign and by the subtle yet obvious forms of religious prejudice displayed during it.

Although they felt the sting of cultural alienation during the 1920s and 1930s, a few leading Catholics initiated a number of interlocking reform movements that had as their ultimate goals the development of a specific Catholic culture, the Christianization of American culture, and the revitalization of the economic order according to Catholic principles of justice and the common good. The revival of the Thomistic system of philosophy and theology in the 1920s advanced the cause of creating a specific Catholic intellectual culture. The liturgical movement during the mid-1920s fostered the internal and communal life of the church by recovering the liturgical sense and the doctrine of the Mystical Body of Christ. The neo-scholastic and liturgical movements, although different in perspective, were interrelated in intent and with various forms of social Catholicism that developed during the period: the African-American Catholic call for racial justice within church and society; the rising lay consciousness of the "Commonweal Catholics" who published and read *Commonweal* (1924–), a lay Catholic journal of public opinion which nurtured the Catholic sense of lay responsibility for the public good; the increased preoccupations with economic justice during the Depression; the origin of the Catholic Worker movement (1933–), which tried to restore a sense of Christian personalism by advocating and demonstrating in practice the Christian's personal duty to care for the poor and needy; and various other attempts that called attention to the need for reform in the church as well as society.[5]

The intellectual retrieval of Thomism was indicative of the Catholic search for unity and order within an immigrant church that was socially and culturally diverse and within an American society that was increasingly disillusioned and fragmented.[6] During the 1920s the Thomist revival, which had been taking place in European Catholicism since the publication of Pope Leo XIII's encyclical *Aeterni Patris* in 1876, became much more self-conscious, systematically organized, and widespread in the United States. That encyclical, the anti-modernism of Pope Pius X, and the promulgation of the Code of Canon Law in 1917 officially institutionalized Thomist philosophy and theology as the church's authoritative teaching. The Code of Canon Law, for example, stipulated that "teachers shall deal with the studies of mental philosophy and theology and the education of their pupils in such sciences according to the method, doctrine and principles of the Angelic Doctor and religiously adhere thereto."[7]

In 1921 some Catholic critics like Virgil Michel, O.S.B.,* charged that there was not a single journal devoted to neo-scholasticism within the entire English-speaking world and that contemporary Catholics were not conversant enough with modern philosophy to engage it in discussion and debate.[8] In 1923 things began to change. Pope Pius XI published *Studiorum Ducem* in June to commemorate the six hundredth anniversary of the canonization of St. Thomas Aquinas, calling him the "Common or Universal Doctor of the Church; for the Church has adopted his philosophy for her own."[9] The *American Ecclesiastical Review* celebrated the event in July by calling for an American movement "back to St. Thomas."[10] Two years later the Jesuits of St. Louis University began publishing the *Modern Schoolman* (1925–), the first *ex-professo* neo-scholastic journal. Others followed: *Thought* (1926–), *The New Scholasticism* (1927–, which became the *American Catholic Philosophical Quarterly* in 1990), the *Thomist* (1939–). The American Catholic Philosophical Society was organized in 1926 to bring together Catholic neo-scholastic philosophers to discuss and debate the implications of St. Thomas's philosophical system. In 1925 Father Fulton Sheen* published his Louvain doctoral dissertation, *God and Intelligence in Modern Philosophy,* reflecting the rising neo-scholastic interests among younger scholars. By the end of the 1920s a self-conscious intellectual revival was well organized and underway.

In the early 1920s the Thomist system of philosophy and theology was perceived as a grand synthetic vision, transcending time in its unchangeable truths yet pliable and accommodating in its accidental expressions to the "march of the physical sciences" and to newer philosophical insights.[11] The Thomist revival was, in Philip Gleason's considered judgment, part of the American Catholic search for unity. It was an attempt to establish a synthetic intellectual vision that would demonstrate the integral relationship between reason and faith, religion and life. In fact, the Thomistic vision was a comprehensive philosophy of life that influenced not only philosophy itself, but also sociology, law, morality, politics, education, art, economic justice, exegesis, asceticism, and religion. In a time of intellectual disillusionment, political upheaval, and economic disaster, the Thomist view presented a world of order, balance, and reason capped off with the certitude of faith in an ultimately meaningful human existence. The Thomists reasserted the values of human reason and freedom, but they placed them within the vital context of revelation and faith. Reason, in fact, was ultimately oriented to and capable of discovering God's existence. The Thomist vision, moreover, provided an ideological justification for ecclesiastical authority and became the intellectual equivalent of the movement toward institutional consolidation. The Thomist revival, though, was preeminently an attempt to make the supernatural credible in a world perceived to be running madly toward materialism and naturalism.

The Thomist vision was also anti-modernist, and for that very reason it was doubly appealing to many second- and third-generation ethnic American Catholic intellectuals. Individualistic, subjectivist, secularist, relativist, and rationalistic, the modern mind was opposed not only to the Catholic ethnic's sense of tradition and community but also to the anti-modernist mentality that had developed in Western Catholicism since the time of Pius IX and was most recently reinforced by Pius X's assault upon modern thinking. But the point here is that the anti-modernist mind-set in American Catholicism during the 1920s was not something imposed from outside; it was congenial to and almost connatural with the American Catholic experience itself.

The liturgical movement was another major Catholic revival of the 1920s. Like the self-conscious renewal of neo-scholasticism, it sought to combat the twin evils of individualism and totalitarian socialism. It, too, was a search for the unity of the Catholic tradition and an attempt to unpack the social and cultural implications of that unity. It found that unity in a concept of the Mystical Body of Christ, the central Catholic doctrine that simultaneously upheld the dignity and worth of the individual and the communal context of all human reality. It was also an attempt to bring about a restoration of a sense of spiritual interiority, organic communion, and the priesthood of the faithful—dimensions that had been diminished, so the liturgical reformers believed, by an individualism that was characteristic of Catholic devotional piety as well as the modern secular mind. A restoration of an active liturgical sense, it was believed, would do much to make American Catholics conscious of their common responsibility for the welfare of American culture and social life.

Virgil Michel was the primary founder and organizer of the movement. Fathers William Busch of St. Paul Seminary in Minnesota, Gerald Ellard, S.J., of St. Louis University, Reynold J. Hillenbrand, rector of Chicago's diocesan seminary, Martin Hellriegel, a St. Louis pastor, and a number of others joined together to promote the liturgical revival. In 1926 Michel, together with Ellard and Hellriegel, established *Orate Fratres* (*Worship* after 1951) as the movement's primary journal. Michel also founded the Liturgical Press at St. John's Abbey in Collegeville, Minnesota, for the dissemination of popular and scholarly works on the liturgical renewal. The publication of *Liturgical Arts* (1931–72) also raised the consciousness of the importance of art and architecture in American Catholicism. In 1933 Ellard published *Christian Life and Worship,* a textbook used in many Catholic colleges throughout the 1930s and 1940s, to acquaint students with the doctrine of the Mystical Body of Christ and awaken them to the sacramental dimensions of Christian life.

By the time of Michel's death in 1938 the movement, although never more than a minority impulse within American Catholicism prior to the Second Vatican Council, was well organized and beginning to have an effect upon some leading thinkers. After Michel's death leadership of the movement eventually passed to his fellow Benedictine Godfrey Diekmann of St. John's University in Collegeville, a major center of the movement throughout the pre–Vatican II period. After 1940 the liturgical movement was promoted on the national level through the organization of annual Liturgical Weeks and Conferences.

In the midst of the Depression, Pope Pius XI published *Quadragesimo Anno* (1931), and Catholic leaders like Michel began to connect the internal ecclesial liturgical movement with the movement for economic justice. This association of social justice and public worship was, in fact, the distinctive American contribution to a movement that had European origins. For Michel, the German Central Verein, and a few others, public worship was the practical and sacramental expression of the Mystical Body of Christ, the primary source of the Christian spirit, and the font of Christian social consciousness; as such, the liturgy could inspire and empower Christians to work for social justice in the world. For Michel social justice was the virtue that regulated all human actions "in proper relation to the common good."

Like the liturgical reformers, other pioneers promoted a social conscience within American Catholicism during these years. African-American Catholics continued to decry racism in church and society and, under the leadership of Howard University biology professor Thomas Wyatt Turner,* organized the Federation of Colored Catholics in the United States (1925–58), as its 1925 constitution indicated, to unite African-American Catholics, promote Catholic education for them, and stimulate them to more active participation in the struggle for equality in church and society.[12] The federation invited white clergy and laity as associated members. The Jesuits John LaFarge* of Maryland and William Markoe* of St. Louis University became active members and eventually made strong appeals to shift priorities from African-American solidarity to interracial justice. The conflict between Turner's original vision and that of Markoe-LaFarge split the movement in 1933 and for all practical purposes ended its effectiveness. In 1933 the Catholic Interracial Council of the Markoe-LaFarge wing became the primary agency for raising the consciousness of racial injustice in the church and society, but the move toward interracial activity also diminished African-American leadership in the movement and almost completely eclipsed the aim of Catholic African-American solidarity.

Through their publications and meetings, locally organized Catholic Interracial Councils were able to keep the issue of racial justice before the Catholic community, but like other movements toward social justice, they were ineffective in making the demands for racial justice a popular movement within American Catholicism. Many, if not all, Catholic colleges, secondary schools, monasteries, convents, and seminaries throughout the 1920s and into the 1930s continued to be segregated.[13] American bishops as a national body, moreover, did not speak out on the constitutional rights of African-Americans until 1943 and did not make racial discrimination the exclusive subject of a national pastoral letter until "Discrimination and Christian Conscience" in 1958.[14] Desegregation of Catholic institutions would be the work primarily of the post–World War II era.

The primary Catholic reform issue of the Depression concerned the economy, and out of this arose a number of other forms of social Catholicism. The 1919 "Bishops' Program of Social Reconstruction" and the NCWC's Social Action Department, under the general guidance of John Burke and the leadership of John A. Ryan and Raymond McGowan, set the tone for a national Catholic social consciousness, but they were not the only forms of social Catholicism during the 1920s and 1930s. The early pastoral and social work of Robert Lucey* in Los Angeles and his later work among Mexican-American farm workers in the Southwest, the social activism and labor advocacy of a number of young "labor priests" like Peter Dietz and Francis Haas,* the personalism of the Catholic Worker Movement under the leadership of Dorothy Day* and Aristide Peter Maurin,* the social solidarism of the liturgical movement, the social critique and populist polemics of Charles Coughlin* of Detroit, the Jesuit schools of social service, and the advocacy of rural values and the challenge to the government's agricultural policies of the National Catholic Rural Life Conference—these were a few of the individuals and movements that produced a body of literature, a critique of the American social agenda, and a multitude of institutions to foster a Catholic sense of social justice.[15] Although they differed among themselves in selectively appropriating principles from the papal encyclicals and adapting them to the American economic order, they shared a common search for a middle ground between the twin evils of laissez-faire capitalism and socialism. The Catholic vision of social justice upheld simultaneously the inherent dignity and rights of the individual and concern for the common good in the industrial order, themes that were consonant with Pope Leo XIII's 1891 encyclical *Rerum Novarum* and Pius XI's 1931 *Quadragesimo Anno*.

The variety and the specific differences among the diverse kinds of Catholic social reform programs are not easy to depict in a paragraph. John Ryan and the Social Action Department of the NCWC promoted a form of "economic democracy." If the problem, as Ryan saw it, was underconsumption, the solution was an equitable distribution regulated by the government. Ryan's view of the state (especially the federal government after 1930) as a positive agent for social justice corresponded significantly with President Franklin Delano Roosevelt's New Deal—so much so that Charles Coughlin sarcastically referred to Ryan as the "Right Reverend New Dealer." Dorothy Day and the Catholic Workers, on the other hand, encouraged Catholics and others to take personal responsibility for the corporal and spiritual works of mercy. From this initial step Day and others established Catholic Worker houses of hospitality and soup kitchens in various urban areas throughout the 1930s and 1940s. Charles Coughlin differed from others in his conviction that the central cause of the Depression was a money famine, a conspiracy concocted by international bankers to control and limit the supply of money for their own greedy purposes. Although his diagnosis of the disease was constant, his medicine did vary from time to time, but generally he prescribed an increase in the supply of money. The Catholic Rural Lifers supported a form of Catholic and Jeffersonian agrarianism, believing that a stable and healthy rural economy was a strong support for the entire nation. Most Catholic agrarians favored a decentralized and independent economic system that considered rural life as a whole and not as part of an economic industrial system. In the judgment of Edward Shapiro, they "favored more radical economic and social reforms and were more opposed to big business than the 'liberals' of the Catholic University of America." [16] Although the Catholic economic reform programs differed, and although the church, American bishops wrote in 1940, did not prescribe "any particular form of technical Teconomic [sic] organization just as she does not prescribe any particular political organization of the state," she taught that every economic system must be in accord with fundamental justice and the common good. [17]

Economic issues and the effects of the Depression upon the whole culture were not the only concerns of the American Catholic community. Catholics also became increasingly occupied with national and international politics, and by the end of the Second World War some of them had moved into positions of significant political influence which they had not possessed before Roosevelt's presidency. George Q. Flynn has convincingly argued that under Roosevelt and the New Deal, American Catholics were "recognized as a major force in society" and raised to a new level of influence which indicated a transformation in the American political attitude toward the church and in the church's disposition toward the government. Roosevelt placed prominent Catholics (e.g., James A. Farley, Thomas Corcoran, Frank Murphy, Joseph Kennedy, Father Francis Haas) in key administrative positions and courted Catholic favor. Prominent Catholic leaders, on the other hand, accepted much of the New Deal legislation and presented it to American Catholics as an "American version of the papal encyclicals. In this sense the New Deal liberalized American Catholics by showing them the relevance of their Church's teachings on social problems." [18] Catholics also voted in large numbers in support of Roosevelt's four terms. Some studies have revealed that even when other motivational variables like occupation, class, economics, and ethnicity are considered, Catholic votes for Roosevelt and other Democrats during these years were from 27 to 31 percent higher than Protestant votes. [19]

In the realm of international politics Catholics became increasingly concerned during the 1920s and 1930s with the rise of Russian communism, the Mexican persecution of the church, Spanish communism and fascism, Italian fascism, and German National Socialism. These events reinforced their fears about the disintegration of Western Christian culture. Political divisions among Catholics, however, prevented them—even if they wanted to, and they did not—from mounting a Catholic campaign to influence American foreign policy.[20] Although they were divided among themselves on whether communism or fascism represented the greater threat, they were united in their view that the political, like the economic, order should steer a middle path between the Scylla of secular individualism and the Charybdis of totalitarianism (whether of the communist or fascist kind).

American Catholics' preoccupations with Russian communism and even more with religious persecution in Mexico, Spain, and Germany were motivated primarily by their solicitude for their coreligionists in these countries. The problem of religious persecution, in particular, also flowed from an American view of religious liberty, which they saw violated in these countries. The Catholic campaign against foreign governmental persecution of Catholics was another sign that a few Catholics were gradually emerging from their nineteenth- and early-twentieth-century conclaves of ethnic Catholicism. The protests laid a broad foundation for a Catholic international perspective that had been developing here and there since the days of Americanism. But the distinctive Catholic concerns for religious liberty at the international level were not widely shared in the American body politic, thus reinforcing the minority status of their own interests.

From 1917 until World War II Catholic leaders here and there kept alive an opposition to Russian communism, which was generally perceived as totalitarian and antireligious. Although they were united in their anticommunist ideology, American Catholics developed at least three different assessments of communism and different methods of opposing it. Some American Catholics, perhaps the majority, saw their anticommunism as an apocalyptic religious crusade against a diabolic force that could be driven out only by prayer, fasting, and divine intervention. Others—for example, the Catholic Workers, the Commonweal Catholics, and social justice advocates like John A. Ryan, Robert E. Lucey, and Francis Haas—saw the communist critique of unrestrained and individualistic capitalism as valid but sought to combat the appeal of that critique by promoting alternative Christian visions and practices of social justice. Still others, like Fulton J. Sheen, combined elements of both traditions, but he emphasized the ideological aspects of the Catholic war with communism. For him communism was an alien philosophy of life that had a messianic religious force in the world because it demanded an absolute submission to the state. The ideological war with communism had to be carried out in publications, sermons, radio lectures, convert lessons, and other forms of communication that could get to the minds and hearts of the people.[21]

From the Mexican Revolution in 1910 to the decline of religious persecutions of Catholics in 1935, leading American Catholics were divided in their assessment of the role they and the American government should play in coming to the aid of their coreligionists. Some, like Cardinal Gibbons in the pre–World War I era and John J. Burke of the NCWC in the 1920s, believed that American Catholics could best help by working quietly and diplomatically through American governmental agencies to put pressure on the Mexican government to modify and eventually eliminate the persecutions. Others, like Francis C. Kelley of the Church Extension Society during the pre–World War I era and Baltimore's Archbishop Michael Joseph Curley during the 1920s and 1930s, believed that the atrocities and fundamental violations of religious liberties ought to be vigorously publicized in the American press, the American government ought to be criticized for ineffective and inadequate response to the problem, and that violated American sensitivities should be stirred up to put public pressure on the American government to help restore the natural rights of Mexican Catholics.[22] Whether they pursued a diplomatic or heated publishing campaign, American Catholics had little or no measurable effect on public opinion or foreign policy in Mexico, but once again they demonstrated their distress over issues beyond their local churches.

By 1935 American Catholic anxieties over Mexico declined as the persecutions did. From 1936 to 1939 attention shifted to the Spanish Civil War and the persecutions of Catholics in Spain. American Catholics opposed the Popular Front's anticlerical and hostile attacks on the Spanish church and its people and saw the Popular Front as a communist- and secularist-inspired totalitarian regime (operating under the guise of republicanism), but they were divided on the means to preserve the church and its institutions.[23] A public opinion poll taken in 1938 indicated that "39% of Catholics favored Franco; 30% were pro-Loyalist; and 31% were neutral."[24] America, the Tablet, Commonweal under Michael Williams (1935–37), the American bishops' 1937 pastoral "To the Spanish Hierarchy," and a host of diocesan newspapers supported Franco's revolt against the Second Spanish Republic because they saw him as the protector of the church's interests and the best available agent for the restoration of the church's freedom in Spanish society.

A minority of American Catholic journalists and opinion makers—particularly Dorothy Day, the Catholic Worker and Commonweal (after 1937)—together with the Italian clerical antifascist Don Luigi Sturzo and the French philosopher Jacques Maritain believed that Franco's resistance and wartime measures were as cruel and ruthless as those of the so-called Loyalists, and that if Franco did win the war his totalitarianism would be as objectionable as that of the Popular Front. Support for Franco could thus be interpreted as support for a status quo that was badly in need of social reforms to which fascists like Franco were particularly blind. Catholic support for religious liberty should be closely tied to equally adamant support for social justice in Spain. For the consistent pacifist Dorothy Day, furthermore, the church should condemn violence on all sides and not identify itself with military means to win peace.

Catholics were also somewhat divided in their support for Benito Mussolini and Italian fascism, although there appears to have been more support for Mussolini than for Franco. Since the mid-1920s *America, Commonweal,* and numerous other journals and diocesan newspapers favored Mussolini and Italian fascists because they saw them as the true patriots in the war against Bolshevism and as the strongest allies of the church and family. A 1937 opinion poll demonstrated that when given the hypothetical option of choosing between fascism and communism, 61 percent of all Americans favored fascism. A similiar poll in 1939, however, indicated that that support had fallen to 54 percent, but 66 percent of the Catholics in the poll still favored fascism over communism.[25]

But there was also a minority voice in the Catholic community that protested against fascism. Francis Duffy, James Cox, John A. Ryan, and especially the Paulist James Gillis, editor of the *Catholic World,* opposed Mussolini because they rejected his assault on political liberties and his violent undemocratic procedures. After Pope Pius XI's encyclical *Non abbiamo bisogno* (1931), an attack on fascist "statolatry" and fascist assaults on Catholic Action in Italy, Gillis charged that too many American Catholic journals had simply "soft pedaled" the encyclical and been blind to fascist injustices and totalitarian designs.[26]

In the late 1930s some American Catholics also turned their attention to the threat from German National Socialism. For a number of reasons, not the least of which was the 1933 Vatican concordat with Germany, Catholics did not consider Adolf Hitler and Nazi Germany much of a threat until 1935, when Pope Pius XI protested against violations of the concordat and government restrictions on the church's activities.[27] *America,* following in the wake of the papal protests, proclaimed a new Kulturkampf in Germany. By 1936 Catholics like Sheen were beginning to equate communist Russia with Nazi Germany, the one being as demonic as the other in the denials of religious liberties and basic human rights. In March of 1937 Pius XI published his *Mit Brennender Sorge,* condemning the persecution of Catholics in the Reich and protesting against the Nazi divinization of race.[28] Chicago's German-American Cardinal Mundelein followed the pope's encyclical in May of 1937 with an attack on the Nazi-style Kulturkampf.[29] In November American bishops wrote a pastoral "To the German Hierarchy," protesting against the persecution of the church.

Exclusive concern about Nazi persecutions of Catholics made some American Catholics indifferent or numb to Nazi atrocities against the Jews. In 1934 the *Tablet* expressed the opinion of some Catholics when it asked, "Why it is so infamous to restrict certain liberties of 600,000 Jews in Germany and not at all obnoxious to hold in slavery millions of other people in Russia, Mexico, and Spain?"[30] Some Catholics found their own inability to win popular American support for the persecution of their fellow Catholics another sign of the lingering prejudice against them. Other Catholics like Coughlin began after 1937 to assault Jewish bankers and by implication and direct assertion to justify Hitler's and Mussolini's programs as the inauguration of a new Christian social order. Coughlin and *Tablet* Catholics saw Nazi Germany as a force against the evils of the Depression and the Russian communist revolution, both of which were attributed to Jewish sources.

Others rejected Coughlin's and the *Tablet's* anti-Semitism. In 1938, for example, Msgr. Fulton Sheen, among others, addressed a large New York "rally for American Liberty," declaring that "only those who condemn persecution irrespective of where they find it, have any right to be heard." On another occasion he asserted, "I joined the Jews in New York in their protest against the abominable outrages of Hitler against them and their religion. I only ask now that all who believe in freedom, democracy and religion join us in protest against the Reds."[31] In 1938 the Knights of Columbus protested to President Roosevelt about Germany's persecution of the Jews, expressing "the deepest sympathy for the distressed Jews of Europe," and urged the American government to use its influence to help secure their refuge and protection in Palestine.[32] In 1940 Bishop Robert Lucey of Amarillo, Texas, wrote, "We as Christians, as citizens, as human beings must cry out against the horror of this [Nazi] debauchery [against Jews]." Speaking before the National Conference of Christians and Jews in Dallas that same year, he attacked Hitler and protested against the isolationist mentality in America, warning "what is happening to the people of Europe is our business."[33] On 14 November 1941, on the verge of American entrance into the war, the national body of bishops published a pastoral, "The Crisis of Christianity," which condemned religious persecution throughout Europe and singled out the persecutions of the Jews. "We cannot too strongly condemn," they wrote, "the inhuman treatment to which the Jewish people have been subjected in many countries."[34]

Although they protested against religious and civil persecutions in foreign countries, American Catholics, like many other Americans in the late 1930s, remained political isolationists—even after Hitler's rising power, ambitious designs, and military aggression toward Poland, Czechoslovakia, Austria, and other countries. Once Pearl Harbor was bombed on 7 December 1941, however, the isolationism quickly dissipated. Except for Dorothy Day and some Catholic Worker pacifists, most Catholics united with President Roosevelt in the war with the Axis. Although their support was restrained by comparison to that given during World War I, the national body of American bishops placed "our institutions and their consecrated personnel" at the president's disposal for service to the country.[35]

Catholic participation in the war was the culmination of the previous decade's Catholic literary and philosophical assault on totalitarianism, whether in fascist or communist forms. The war brought an end to the Depression, but it produced anxiety and fear at home and abroad about the future of a Christian civilization and the weak possibilities of a just and lasting peace. For many it also brought a common experience of the sacrifice of human life and material goods, a binding together in a united effort to serve the common good, and an idealism about the righteousness of the cause that made the sacrifice and united effort seem redemptive. For many Catholics, in particular, it was another manifestation that they were an integral component of the American system. Fundamental American beliefs and ideals were not only consistent with Catholicism but ultimately grounded in a transcendental revelatory authority which the church proclaimed in the modern world.

Between the world wars a number of American Catholics became increasingly interested in issues beyond their parishes and dioceses and emerged into American political life in ways that were unknown before World War I. Although their concerns were still primarily Catholic, their Catholic interests had become more international than previously, and their Catholic political interests were significantly tied to their anxieties about the survival of a Christian culture, not just the Catholic church. By the end of World War II Catholics were increasingly preoccupied with world peace, the threat of communism, care and relief of war-torn Europe, and the effects of postwar economic and ecclesiastical expansionism.

7
COLD WAR CATHOLICISM: 1945–1965

With the end of World War II the United States entered a twenty-year period of unprecedented economic prosperity, worldwide economic and political influence, and a widespread resurgence of religion in the midst of cold war anxieties over communism. Like many other religious denominations, American Catholicism took advantage of the expanding wealth and built numerous new churches, schools, and other large religious institutions, some of which had been delayed during the previous fifteen years by the Depression and the war. Numerous Catholics, especially the national hierarchy, were convinced that their numerical strength and affluence gave them an exceptional opportunity for moral leadership in American society, but others in American society perceived the increasing Catholic moral crusades as fundamental threats to American democratic liberties. Hopeful, institutionally and numerically strong, and active in the promotion of an American Christian culture, Catholics were withdrawing from their ethnic conclaves, battling each other ideologically, and calling for some moderate reforms in Catholic attitudes and practices. The postwar years began with Catholic anxieties about the twin evils of worldwide communism and secularism, and ended with a confidence that Catholicism had finally emerged into American society and the world community with President John F. Kennedy's election and Pope John XXIII's ecumenical council.

Between 1945 and 1965 American Catholicism experienced a phenomenal growth, one significantly unmatched during the previous twenty years and one not repeated in the post-1965 period. The total Catholic population increased by 90 percent, from 23.9 million to 45.6 million. The number of bishops and archbishops increased by 58 percent, clergy by 52 percent, women religious by 30 percent, and seminarians by 127 percent. One hundred and twenty-three new hospitals, 3,005 new Catholic elementary and high schools, and 94 new colleges were built. Enrollments in Catholic elementary and secondary schools increased by 3.1 million—more than 120 percent—and in Catholic colleges and universities, primarily because of the GI Bill, by a whopping 300 percent, from 92,426 to 384,526. Although the schools expanded rapidly to meet the increasing Catholic population, still they enrolled perhaps no more than 50 percent of all Catholics in primary and secondary education and a significantly smaller percentage in higher education. American Catholics also distributed over $1.35 billion through Catholic Relief Services and the Society for the Propagation of the Faith to aid the world's poor and support missionaries throughout the world. These statistics of numerical and institutional developments and the corresponding increase in financial contributions manifested something not only of the nation's prosperity but also of the general postwar American support for religion and voluntaryism.[1]

The ecclesiastical vision, as officially articulated by the national episcopal pastoral letters from 1945 to 1965, continued to focus on what the bishops repeatedly called the restoration and reconstruction of a "Christian culture" in the United States and Western world. To restore, preserve, or build a Christian culture meant to permeate civilization with the Christian spirit and struggle against the prevailing and pervasive influences of secularism and communism both at home and abroad. These twin objectives, which had been the focus of various Catholic movements in the 1930s, had percolated up to episcopal consciousness and became the foundation of the bishops' programs. In the postwar situation, bishops increasingly called upon all Christians, not just Catholics, to transform society, giving their appeals a more universal ring than they had had during the 1930s.

Secularism, the "practical exclusion of God from human thinking and living," was, the bishops wrote in 1947, the historical source of the rise of fascism, Nazism, and communism and the root of all of the world's travails. It was doing more than anything else to "blight our heritage of Christian culture." The bishops, acknowledging the limits of the historical order, proclaimed the ideals of Christian culture.[2]

The threat of secularism and its particular manifestation in worldwide communism were evident, the bishops repeatedly charged, in the family (where divorce, birth control, and economic injustices threatened to destroy its unity and stability), the entertainment industry (where materialistic values and sexual promiscuity were being promoted), education (which was increasingly being divorced from a religious vision), the economic order (where either laissez-faire capitalism or totalitarian socialism were destroying the individual's and the family's rights to decent and frugal living), the American courts (where religion was being radically separated from the institutions of American culture, particularly education), and the political order (where individual rights were being smashed by totalitarian communism or where political and legal enactments were divorced from natural law and Christian virtues). These threats were a "menace to our Christian and American way of living."[3] The connection between Christianity and America was in the realm of fundamental values, not in the realm of historical and current practices, but the connection itself revealed how closely the bishops had identified the two.

Marriage and family were issues of primary concern for many postwar Americans, especially Catholics, who saw marriage as a sacrament and the foundation of society. To counteract the forces of secularism (manifested in divorce, birth control, and abortion) that threatened the unity, stability, and fertility of marriage, Catholics since the 1930s, but particularly during the late 1940s and 1950s, had established a number of agencies to nurture married life. In 1931 the NCWC established the Family Life Bureau (FLB) as part of its Social Action Department. The FLB was a national clearinghouse for information and studies on the family and was assigned "to promote a program of action that would encourage the building of successful Christian marriages and wholesome Catholic homes." *Integrity* magazine (1946–56), founded by Ed Willock and Carol Jackson* and later edited by Dorothy Dohen,* articulated a radical personalist critique of American individualism and capitalism and fostered a sacramental-personalist approach to family living. The Cana Conference (1943–) and marriage counseling movements sponsored family retreats and days of family renewal to strengthen the spiritual roots of relationships. By the end of the 1940s, moreover, the Christian Family Movement (CFM), under the leadership of Patrick* and Patricia Crowley,* was organized to reform those conditions in society which wrecked havoc on the integrity of modern family life.[4]

The campaign to maintain and promote a Christian civilization in American society also involved a moral crusade against indecency and immorality in the entertainment industry and modern literature. To combat the increasing threat of obscenity and a more general moral laxity, the American bishops established the League of Decency in 1934 and the National Office for Decent Literature (NODL) in 1938. Both institutions evaluated and published their rankings of movies and pamphlets, but the ratings, which started out as moral guidelines for Catholics, soon became in the hands of some church leaders morally binding in conscience. The league, which was an American innovation that Pope Pius XI recommended to the universal church in 1936, also formulated a decency pledge that Catholics took annually during a Sunday liturgy—promising to avoid movies declared objectionable.

Individual bishops and pastors periodically condemned specific movies as occasions of sin and forbade their people to attend them. Urban bishops like Cardinals Francis J. Spellman of New York and Dennis Dougherty of Philadelphia exercised considerable power in blackballing certain movies. Cardinal Spellman publicly declared that some movies could not be seen "with a safe conscience," and others, like *Baby Doll,* were forbidden "under pain of sin." In 1948 Cardinal Dougherty threatened two theater owners that he would direct all Catholics to boycott their theaters for an entire year if they did not within forty-eight hours cease showing *The Outlaw* and *Forever Amber.*[5]

The kind of censorship that was exercised over the entertainment industry was also periodically exercised over the publishing industry. These forms of censorship had as their positive aim the promotion of Christian civilization, but the aggressive and authoritarian tactics that were many times used seriously discredited this manifestation of "Catholic action" in the eyes of some non-Catholics and a few articulate Catholic leaders.

The struggle against secularism came out most forcefully in the battles over education. Many Catholic leaders since the 1930s had fought against the increasing secularization of modern American education from the primary to the university levels. Prevailing philosophies of education, debates over federal aid to education, and Supreme Court decisions revealed this trend. Geoffrey O'Connell, author of *Naturalism in American Education* (1936), and other Catholic university professors at a 1939 conference of the National Catholic Alumni Federation argued that for three decades John Dewey's philosophy of pragmatic secularism had influenced generations of America's public school teachers and created a "threat to the Christian cultural education of the youth of our country."[6] A thoroughly Catholic education, integrating the natural and the supernatural, was the only protection against this fundamental threat, and thus Catholics were facing a challenge of unprecedented proportions in the postwar years as they tried to develop their educational philosophy and educational institutions.

The educational issues that created the greatest public debate were those over federal aid to education, particularly to students in Catholic schools—the two issues were very closely tied in many episcopal lobbying efforts. These issues became magnified by various Supreme Court decisions on aid and the role of religion in public education.

Although in the 1920s and 1930s the Catholic hierarchy had opposed federal aid to public education because of its fear that this would only increase the state's power and authority, which by natural law belonged primarily to parents, by 1944 it had perceived the necessity of some federal aid to schools for the sake of children in economically depressed areas. Two national episcopal statements (1944 and 1955) on private and public education, however, sought to tie federal aid for health, safety, and welfare to all needy children without regard to color, origin, or creed, and to be equitable, to children in any school that met the requirements of compulsory education.

These appeals and the Supreme Court decision in *Everson v. Board of Education* (1947), allowing New Jersey to use tax funds to bus children attending Catholic schools, created a great deal of consternation among some Americans. Again the cry went up that aggressive Catholic bishops, representing a numerous and increasingly powerful Catholic block, were seeking to destroy the Constitution by uniting church and state. In response to these developments, Protestants and Other Americans United for the Separation of Church and State (POAU) was established in 1948. The organization was another sign of the tensions that were developing between some Protestants and Catholics during the cold war.

The fear of Catholic cultural and political aggression became most clearly articulated in Paul Blanshard's *American Freedom and Catholic Power* (1949). Blanshard believed that the time was over when Americans could be silent about the threat of powerful Catholic influences in politics, medicine, art, entertainment, literature, scholarship, and education. In all these areas Catholics were using the power of numbers and institutional force to destroy American freedoms. Blanshard pointed out that he was not against Catholicism or the religious principles of the Catholic people, but against the church's social and political interferences. No doubt there was bigotry in Blanshard's bombshell, but there was also a fundamental difference between his liberal views of the relationship between religion and culture and that of official Catholicism. Blanshard had some historical grounds for asserting that Catholics were politically and culturally aggressive, but he interpreted almost all forms of Catholic action (and the ideology behind it) as censoriousness because he believed that religion ought to be a private affair of conscience. Few Catholic leaders accepted this perspective.

The reaction to POAU, the Blanshard book, and other criticisms of Catholic intentions was immediate and polemical, intensifying the split in the American religious community. Opposition to Catholics' pleas for state aid for their children or to Catholic attempts to provide moral guidance in the culture was motivated, many Catholic writers thought, either by bigotry, moral laxity, indifference to public and common welfare, or by a secularist mentality that made separation of church and state absolute and reduced religious influence to the privacy of individual conscience and total irrelevance in public life. The Jesuit theologian John Courtney Murray sardonically referred to POAU as "PU," asserting that the real threat in American society was not Catholicism but a progressive secularization "that bears within itself the seeds of future tyrannies."[7] Unlike the old nativism, which claimed that Catholicism was anti-American because it was not Protestant, Blanshard's "new nativism," according to Murray, saw Catholicism as anti-American because it proclaimed that there was a source of truth beyond democratic majoritarianism and scientific naturalism.[8]

These charges and countercharges stoked the coals of bitterness, but they also provoked questions about the relationship of the Catholic church to the state and American society, questions that demanded more of an intellectual response than had been provided in the American Catholic past. Out of this experience of conflict and aggressive forms of Catholic action would come a new intellectual struggle (considered later) to define more adequately the Catholic understanding of church-state relations and stimulate more Catholic reflection on the mode of the church's influence in the public forum.

As Catholics criticized the secularization of public education and became involved in the debates over federal aid, their own schools of higher education were undergoing phenomenal changes that made bleak the prospects that Catholic higher education would become the bulwark against naturalism. The postwar expansion of Catholic colleges and universities left little time, financial resources, or energy to scrutinize or develop a Christian educational alternative to the naturalism in secular higher education. Although most administrators within these institutions had a common neo-scholastic philosophical orientation that provided them with an ideological unity and purpose, they concentrated upon building up their professional schools to meet increasing demands and simply let the Christian character of the institution take care of itself.

The development of American Catholic intellectual life did not parallel the institutional expansion of education during these years. In 1962 American bishops, meeting in Rome for the Second Vatican Council, complained in their pastoral letter of that year that the American church, despite its tremendous growth and flourishing condition, could not boast of numerous saints, profound scholars, and brilliant writers as could "some of the older centers of Christian culture."[9] Seven years earlier Msgr. John Tracy Ellis had argued that the immigrant condition of American Catholicism, among other things, had been, but could no longer be, responsible for intellectual narrowness and even anti-intellectualism in education. He and a few others called for more concerted efforts to overcome these conditions.[10]

The primary function of Catholic education, according to some neo-scholastic educators, was not intellectual creativity, but the communication of the wisdom of the ages. For the Jesuit George Bull the "humane use of the mind, the function proper to him as man, is contemplation and not research. . . . In sum, then, research cannot be the primary object of a Catholic graduate school, because it is at war with the whole Catholic life of the mind."[11] How representative Bull's view was is open to question, but it certainly fit in with an unsophisticated scholasticism that tended to dominate Catholic higher education. By the middle of the 1950s though, as indicated, this view was being subjected to considerable internal criticism.

Even prior to the mid-1950s, however, there were some signs of a slowly developing intellectual life within American Catholicism. By the late 1940s philosophy departments and even a few graduate schools of philosophy were captured by disciples of either Etienne Gilson or Jacques Maritain, two widely acknowledged creative leaders of Thomist philosophy. The liturgical movement, with its origins in the 1920s, was also coming into blossom during the postwar years, fostering a historical study of patristic and liturgical sources and a more adequate biblical knowledge. Too much emphasis in Catholic education on apologetics, individual morality, and the "anti" mentality (e.g., anti-Protestantism, anticommunism, and antisecularism) led, Godfrey Diekmann, O.S.B., asserted, to a neglect of the church's essential life—a situation that the liturgical movement was trying to reverse.[12] Biblical study, still in its infancy at the beginning of the postwar years, was nourished by the establishment of the

Catholic Biblical Association and *Catholic Biblical Quarterly* (1938) and encouraged by Pope Pius XII's *Divino Afflante Spiritu* (1943). Historical theology, particularly patristics, was advanced significantly by the German refugee Johannes Quasten, who had been teaching at the Catholic University since 1938. Systematic theology received a major new impetus with the publication of *Theological Studies* (1940), the first scientific journal of theology since the *New York Review*, and the organization of the Catholic Theological Society of America (1946).

The stimulation of theological scholarship produced conflicts within the Catholic community, reflecting differences in methodology between the neo-scholastic and the historical-critical theologians and biblical scholars. Joseph Clifford Fenton,* for example, a theologian at the Catholic University, took issue with some of the biblical scholars whose advanced ideas on inspiration and historical-critical methods contrasted sharply with his own ahistorical neo-scholastic views.[13] Dissensions within the Catholic theological community erupted over a variety of other issues: for example, the kind of theology to be taught at the college level,[14] the possibility of intercreedal cooperation, the understanding of and participation in the ecumenical movement, and the nature of religious liberty and separation of church and state. These incipient postwar theological tensions and diversity would be more fully revealed in the Second Vatican Council. The 1950s neo-scholastic accent on a unified Catholic intellectual vision was—in practice, if not yet in theory—gradually being called into question.

Theologians split into two camps over intercreedal cooperation and the ecumenical movement. John Courtney Murray, S.J., and Gustave Weigel, S.J.,* of Woodstock College argued that circumstances in postwar Europe demanded intercreedal cooperation for the sake of the common good. Such cooperation, countered Joseph Clifford Fenton, Francis J. Connell, C.SS.R., and Paul Hanly Furfey* of the Catholic University, would lead to religious indifferentism.[15] These groups split along the same lines over their approaches to the ecumenical movement: Catholic University professors thought the movement fostered indifferentism, while Woodstock professors considered it necessary to fulfill Christ's will for unity. American Catholic participation in the ecumenical movement, which was predominantly Protestant, was almost nonexistent during these years, except for a very few pioneers who raised the issue of Christian unity to a new level of theological reflection.

The hostilities surrounding the development of POAU and the Blanshard bomb, Protestant suspicions created by certain ill-advised forms of Catholic action, Pope Pius XII's encyclical *Humani Generis* (1950, which was seen as another form of papal repression of theological inquiry),[16] and the papal proclamation of the dogma of Mary's Assumption (1950) curtailed any widespread discussion of Christian unity between American Catholics and Protestants. Nevertheless in the 1950s, in the midst of these tensions, a few Catholics like Gustave Weigel, S.J., George Tavard, A.A., Edward F. Hanahoe, S.A., and

John B. Sheerin, C.S.P., began to crack the ice of the cold war between Protestants and Catholics, researching and publishing articles and books on Protestant theology and entering into some pioneering ecumencial activities with the hope of creating convergence among the churches.

In 1960, after Pope John XXIII had convoked the Second Vatican Council, Weigel was appointed consulter to the newly established Roman Secretariat for Promoting Christian Unity, one of four North Americans to receive the appointment.[17] His standing in the American Protestant community was acknowledged in 1962 when Yale University granted him an honorary doctorate, noting, "You have broken through the Reformation wall and pioneered in Catholic-Protestant dialogue."[18] Weigel saw himself as a "middle generation" ecumenist—one who stood between the hostile and closed mentality of the earlier generation and the more advanced ecumenical approaches of those who would be his successors. The fact that Weigel—along with Murray, Diekmann, and the German theologian Hans Küng—was refused permission to speak at the Catholic University in 1963 indicates that even his moderate openness to the ecumenical movement was throughout the pre-conciliar period considered heterodox—in practice, if not in theory.

The most significant and creative theological development of the period, and the one that ran into the most forceful internal opposition, was John Courtney Murray's views on church-state relations, a perennial problem in American Catholicism. The Catholic understanding of this issue had, of course, been a part of the Protestant-Catholic conflict for generations. The problem of developing an adequate understanding of church-state relations, however, was particularly acute in the postwar years because of what Murray and other Catholics saw as an increasingly secularist interpretation of the First Amendment by the Supreme Court and some liberal Americans like Blanshard—an interpretation that created a virtual wall between church and state, thereby discrediting, if not in fact, at least in theory, any religious influence upon society and legislation.

The problem was compounded by the Catholic church's official understanding of church-state relations (i.e., that the two, although distinct and separate in their ends, belonged ideally in some kind of harmonious institutional union), a view that was contrary to Western political consciousness and institutional developments of the past two centuries. Murray's problem, therefore, was twofold. On the one hand he wanted to show that a Catholic understanding of church-state was indeed not un-American and on the other hand that a true American understanding of the First Amendment need not prohibit Catholics and other religious persons from exercising some influence on the nation's public life. His own perception of the problems that faced Catholics led him to an investigation of historical Catholic sources on church-state and of Western and American constitutional philosophy.

Murray developed a historical interpretation of ancient and recent Catholic teachings and a view of the natural law that supported modern religious liberty, and was critical of the thesis-hypothesis position that had developed in Catholic thinking since the middle of the nineteenth century. His support of religious liberty as a political immunity was severely criticized by Fenton and Connell in this country and opposed by Cardinal Alfredo Ottaviani, secretary of the Holy Office in Rome. By the middle of the 1950s Murray's position had become so controversial that he was silenced and refused permission to publish on the issue. During the presidential campaign of 1960, however, he did publish *We Hold These Truths,* an argument that Catholics could, upon moral grounds, uphold the constitutional principles and practices of the First Amendment.

Although Murray was under a cloud of suspicion and not at first invited as a theological *peritus* to the Second Vatican Council, he had the support of Cardinal Spellman, who in 1947 had called for a better Catholic understanding of the relationship between church and state in the United States and who invited Murray as his own theological expert during the council's second session. Murray eventually contributed to the writing of the council's *Declaration on Religious Liberty (Dignitatis Humanae,* 1965), vindicating his pre-conciliar positions.[19]

American Catholics, like many others in the postwar years, experienced a revival of piety and religion. All the measurable indexes of religious participation had increased significantly: for example, church attendance, contributions to religious causes, and publications of religious literature. In 1954 the nation's Catholic bishops noted the increases in church membership, but they were led to question "how significant such mere statistics may be. One looks in vain for any corresponding increase of religion's beneficent influence upon the nation's life."[20] A year later the sociologist Will Herberg described the renewed interest and activity in institutional religion and President Dwight David Eisenhower's "piety on the Potomac" as superficial, "a religiousness without religion, a religiousness with almost any kind of content or none, a way of sociability or 'belonging' rather than a way of reorienting life to God. It is thus frequently a religiousness without serious commitment, without real inner conviction, without genuine existential decision."[21] By the late 1950s sociologist Andrew Greeley saw possibilities of a spiritual poverty within a Catholic community that had achieved a postwar suburban economic prosperity. "In the midst of plenty, does not prayer become extremely difficult, if not impossible? Does mortification have any meaning to people who have never known material want? . . . Can man, when he has so many things in this world, seriously long for the next?"[22]

The criticisms of the depth of the revival, however valid they might have been, have obscured something of the variety and indeed vitality of the spiritual movements that were taking place within American Catholicism. During the cold war years Catholic piety moved simultaneously in a number of different directions. Catholics in significant numbers continued to be involved in the sacramental life of the church, popular devotional Catholicism persisted with a renewed emphasis upon Marian devotions, jocist cells of reflection and social action persevered, and a liturgically centered piety influenced a few. New styles of Catholic spirituality also arose, with new means of propagating them.

Some Catholics adapted their spirituality to the times, others resisted these efforts as capitulations, still others promoted the retrieval of the contemplative tradition, and many were influenced by the rising missionary consciousness of the postwar period. A few purveyors of piety promoted a revival of spirituality that was particularly adapted to American values and the modern techniques of mass media and advertising. Father Patrick Peyton, C.S.C., for example, organized the nonsectarian "Family Theater Program" (1947) for the Mutual Broadcasting Company and used numerous popular radio and Hollywood stars to promote family prayer with the slogan, "The family that prays together stays together." Bishop Fulton J. Sheen reaffirmed the postwar search for peace and security and stressed the positive influence of religion upon the individual and society through his inspirational television program "Life is Worth Living" (1952–57). The Maryknoll priest James Keller also supported American middle-class values of individualism and activism with his slogan, "It is better to light one candle than to curse the darkness."[23] Keller also used the mass-market techniques of Hollywood and Madison Avenue, radio and TV programs, as well as published pamphlets and books to communicate his message.

Some within the Catholic community thought these popular appeals to the middle class particularly shallow and naive, simply reinforcing a bourgeois mentality and forfeiting any sense of the sacramental, truly personal, and communal dimensions of the Christian tradition. The methods used, moreover, were considered detrimental to the integrity and depth of Christ's message. This critique, articulated by Carol Jackson and others of *Integrity,* was generally followed by a call for a new kind of lay spirituality that connected work and participation in a liturgically centered Catholic spirituality.[24]

The postwar years also saw the revival of contemplation in the Catholic tradition. In the 1940s alone a Gethsemani, Kentucky, Cisterian monastery of the Strict Observance (i.e., Trappist) established six new Trappist monasteries throughout the United States. The monasteries sponsored weekend and more extended retreats for lay persons, inviting all to share in the fruits of an examined interior life. The postwar retrieval of contemplation and prayerful retreats was most clearly articulated and thereby encouraged by a young convert to Catholicism and monk of Gethsemani Abbey, Thomas Merton.*

Merton came to public notice in 1948 when he published his spiritual autobiography, *The Seven Storey Mountain,* which soon climbed to the top of the best-seller list, indicating that Merton had discovered a spiritual yearning in the American soul. In it and in numerous other publications over the next twenty years Merton called for a deepening of the contemplative life in all, not just in monks and nuns. *The Seven Storey Mountain* made that universal call clear.[25] Merton's interests in and associations with liturgical reformers, Catholic Workers, Catholic pacifists, advocates of social justice, and later with the contemplatives and mystics in the Eastern religious traditions demonstrated something of his own personality and special gifts, but they were also indicative of the wider search for spiritual depth in an American culture beset with cold war anxieties and organizational and technological manipulations that absorbed the individual in the externals of human and social life. Contemplation, as envisioned by Merton, was no panacea for cultural anxiety nor a withdrawal from real social and individual problems, but a way of life that continually called individuals to the center of their existence in order to make them active in transforming the world.

The rise of the United States as a world superpower and the widely publicized accounts of the church's persecution behind the Iron Curtain helped to produce for the first time on an extensive scale a missionary consciousness among American Catholics. Stories of the trials of church leaders and missionaries under communist governments became regular reading in popular Catholic magazines and newspapers. Parish and school programs to rescue "pagan babies," prayers for missionaries and the conversion of Russia, Pope Pius XII's 1951 encyclical on missions *(Evangelii Praecones),* and fund drives to assist missionaries in their work of social amelioraton and evangelization were all part of a massive postwar campaign to create "mission mindedness" among American Catholics.

The promotion of a universal missionary zeal and social consciousness for the poor of the world was tied into a spirituality of the Mystical Body and was another part of the anticommunist motif of the era. The one person most clearly successful in articulating these themes was Bishop Sheen, who from 1950 to 1966 was the national director of the Society for the Propagation of the Faith (SPF). Under his leadership the SPF became a well-organized national force within American Catholic dioceses. Between 1950 and 1966, Sheen raised more than $100 million to support a network of 300,000 missionaries, 150,000 schools, 26,000 hospitals, 400 leper colonies, and 5,000 orphanages in various parts of the world.[26]

The postwar years also witnessed at least three new major developments in social Catholicism. The fundamental problems in American society continued to be perceived in terms of secularism, communism, and unguarded or unreserved capitalism, but there were also some signs that these problems were not just external threats to a Catholic vision and way of life. Catholics themselves—in their pursuit of suburbia, wealth, respectability, and a place in the American sun—had been influenced to a considerable degree by bourgeois-mindedness and spiritual bankruptcy. A few Catholics raised their voices not only against a superficial consumer culture but also against those Catholics who had capitulated to it by separating their religious principles and values from their everyday life. During the postwar years the older forms of social Catholicism that had arisen in the early twentieth century and in the Depression continued, but new forms of social Catholicism developed. Some social Catholics tried to transform their culture, others withdrew from its unholy influence, still others tried to dialogue with what was good in it. The older as well as newer forms of social Catholicism were all variously influenced by a neo-Thomist natural law tradition, a doctrine of the Mystical Body, anticommunism, and the papal social encyclical tradition in their perception of the problems of modern culture and their acceptance of the need for change. Social Catholics, however, differed among themselves in the degree of their hostility to economic life-styles engendered by American capitalism, in the extent of the reforms needed, and in the appropriate means of reform.

Labor problems and just wage issues continued in the postwar years, but new urban problems also shifted the concern of some social Catholics. In the midst of these multiple new urban problems (e.g., urban renewal, housing, redevelopment, racism, movement to the suburbs), a few leading Catholics sought to transform the urban culture in which they lived by getting the church as well as the state to respond to them. Chicago, the largest archdiocese in the country, became a virtual seminary for a host of social and religious reform movements that eventually had repercussions throughout American Catholicism. Auxiliary Bishop Bernard Shiel continued to work with the Catholic Youth Organization and transformed it into a movement for social justice. He gathered a number of creative thinkers around himself, delivered numerous talks, and wrote articles on youth, labor justice, neighborhood reclamation, and racism. Reynold Hillenbrand, rector of St. Mary's of the Lake Seminary, formed numerous clergy with a sensitivity to liturgical reform and social justice. Daniel Cantwell and John Egan addressed problems of urban renewal, relocation, and housing for the poor, and lobbied in city and state politics to obtain legislation favorable to persons displaced by urban development.

By 1958 Egan became the executive secretary of the Cardinal's (Albert Meyer) Conservation Committee which, under his leadership, took a more adversarial role toward city officials than had previously been the case among Catholic urban reformers. A few Chicago parish clergy also cooperated with Saul D. Alinsky's "Back of the Yards" movement, organizing laborers and city dwellers to obtain political clout for their neighborhoods. Ann Harrigan established Friendship House in Chicago at the invitation of Bishop Shiel to serve the needs of African-Americans. Patrick and Patty Crowley organized the Christian Family Movement as a jocist organ for stable family relationships and social action. Edward Marciniak, Frank Delany, and Hillenbrand created the Catholic Labor Alliance and worked for industrial reconstruction according to Catholic social teachings. John Cogley and others worked in the Chicago Catholic Workers' house and contributed to rising lay consciousness. In the postwar years Chicago Catholicism buzzed with an activism previously unknown in American Catholicism and perhaps not emulated in such a degree anywhere else in the country. This activism represented supreme confidence: These Catholics believed they had something valuable to contribute to the social and political development of the age. They were not "ghetto" Catholics.[27]

A few social Catholics found conditions in America so contrary to the Christian vision that they called for withdrawal from society as a means of transforming themselves prior to transforming the culture. *Integrity* magazine Catholics like Edward Willock and Carol Jackson, and the Grail, a lay apostolate for women, repeatedly railed against the all-pervasiveness of bourgeois, sensate American culture, and charged that American Catholics as well as others had been desensitized by it and were thus unable to embrace poverty voluntarily and identify themselves with the victims of poverty, dislocation, and alienation in industrialized and mechanized American society. These Catholics wanted to re-Christianize America, but they believed that in order to do so, American Catholics like themselves had to withdraw from the corruptions of a consumerist and secularist culture and move into different forms of Christian communalism where they could abandon themselves to the Absolute.[28]

Other social Catholics wanted to dialogue with what they found good in American culture and appropriate elements of the American tradition and experience into their own social vision and practice. In the past American Catholic social thought was so directed toward the economic plight of workers and critiques of rugged capitalism and socialism that social theorists failed to demonstrate the relevance of Catholic social thought for the professional and entrepreneurial experiences of increasing numbers of postwar Catholics in the fields of medicine, law, dentistry, engineering, and business management. In 1959 a small group of Catholic businessmen who shared a common desire to relate their religious convictions to everyday life formed the National Conference of Catholic (in 1965 changed to Christian) Employers and Managers (NCCEM) to address the common moral and social issues they faced in their own work. The group hoped to develop a continuing exchange with moral theologians so that they could together develop moral guidelines for business and management decisions they were daily called upon to make. The group also encouraged business schools in Catholic universities and colleges to apply the social encyclicals to business and management decisions and develop courses in the ethics of business and management. NCCEM ceased to function in 1968, short-circuited by the Second Vatican Council and decreased interest among businessmen and theologians.[29]

A group of lay Catholics who called themselves "liberal Catholics" also tried to articulate an approach to social justice in American society that appropriated liberal democratic procedures into a Catholic social program. Like other Catholics, they accepted fully the Catholic doctrinal tradition, the papal encyclicals on social justice, the dynamics of the liturgical reform movement, and the Mystical Body understanding of the church, but they became increasingly critical of what they perceived to be a "partisan or sectarian [Catholic] spirit."[30] Neither the withdrawal mentality, nor the belief that Catholics had an exclusive corner on social justice, nor an authoritarian crusade to transform culture would in fact change American society. What was needed was a new method of social justice. Catholics had to cooperate democratically with others in American society to bring about justice. Liberal Catholicism was a "spirit and method".

The use of reason in controversy rather than belligerence, the absence of the chip-on-the-shoulder, the unwillingness to use the truth as if it were one's private possession, the rejection of the sectarian spirit and willingness to deal with others not as if the truth they have were of a different kind from ours or their errors were inevitably born of malevolence—this general approach is often described, in a catch-all word, as liberal.[31]

Catholics, wrote John Cogley, should come forward as individuals, not as a group power block, and play a dynamic role in the "pluralistic" structures of American life.[32] Cogley's recommendation, as Philip Gleason has argued, unwittingly placed more emphasis on individual Catholic participation in American procedurial processes than on the substance of one's own Christian commitments.[33] There was no denial of that substance, but there was certainly a shift of emphasis that had implications for weakening individual and communal ties to the content of the tradition.

One of the foremost social justice issues in the postwar era was racial segregation. The large pre- and postwar migrations into urban and industrial areas brought large numbers of urban Catholics into contact with African-Americans for the first time. In 1940, for example, African-Americans represented 4.1 percent of Chicago's total population; by 1960 they represented 23 percent. This growth in Chicago and elsewhere transformed many Catholic institutions as they responded to the changing urban scene. The migration created a host of negative reactions from white Catholics and others: for example, restrictive housing covenants, violent race riots, institutional and religious segregation, and discrimination policies and practices. The periodic hostilities and racist practices among Catholics were variously motivated by a desire to preserve the value of property, competition in the job market, cultural differences, and long-established and traditional racial attitudes and stereotyping.

In a number of cities African-American Catholics were segregated into their own parishes and schools and not allowed into white parishes, parish schools, colleges, hospitals, and other ecclesiastical institutions. As Steven Avella has convincingly demonstrated, postwar episcopal silence on racism provided an atmosphere for systematic discrimination in the Diocese of Chicago, and what took place in Chicago perhaps resembled what was occurring in other large urban dioceses.[34] Cardinal Mundelein had established a policy of ecclesiastical segregation in 1919, and in the postwar years that policy remained publicly unchallenged by Mundelein's successor, Cardinal Samuel Stritch. In the midst of discriminatory Catholic practices, however, Bishop Shiel and a number of individual clergy and laity protested against racism in the church and society. After 1945 Stritch, as perhaps a number of other more cautious bishops, made a number of case-by-case decisions for the integration of Catholic institutions, but these decisions were generally communicated through private correspondence and not made a matter of public record. Not until the accession of Cardinal Albert Meyer in 1958 was there any official voice against Catholic discriminatory practices and a public reversal of diocesan policies in Chicago.

The archives in Chicago, as perhaps in a number of other urban Catholic dioceses, contain letters from African-American Catholics protesting their maltreatment and the discriminatory practices they experienced in Catholic institutions. One African-American Catholic woman from Chicago's St. Ambrose parish, for example, complained in 1950 about Father Francis Quinn's Sunday sermon in which he was reported to have said:

The Niggers have taken over Corpus Christi church, Holy Angels and St. Anne'[s] and now they are trying to take over this church; but if its [sic] left to me, they will not. Every time I park my car I'm afraid a Nigger will stab me in the back. Just last week a Nigger from Shakespeare school snatched a white woman's purse and when he was questioned he had snatched several other purses. What's the matter with you white people? Are you yellow? Now all Nigger lovers go back and tell the Niggers what I said. . . . Our forefathers from Ireland came over here and prepared the way for us in this church and the Niggers are not going to run us out.[35]

Quinn did not deny the report on his sermon when asked to explain himself to the Chicago chancery, but went on to protest: "The next letter of complaint from the negress will be a complaint that I have no negroes in my school. Isn't that just too bad. I cannot begin to care for my white children. When the day comes that you compel me, that will mark the end of St. Ambrose."[36] When Quinn did refuse to allow an African-American boy into the parish school, the Southern-born Stritch responded forcefully, but privately, ordering the priest to accept the student:

The boy is a Catholic boy of your parish. Clearly he is a child of your flock and has a right to enter your school. In admitting Catholic children of your parish into your school there may not be set up a standard of race or color. You are a pastor of all your people. Merely because the child is a negro is no legitimate excuse for refusing him admission.[37]

Quinn complied but again protested that the admission was the beginning of the end of the parish, identifying it so much with the white population as he had. In 1956 Quinn resigned; by that time the parish was almost entirely African-American.

The Quinn case represents the mixture of Catholic responses to the racial urban transformations in the postwar years: overt Catholic racism, African-American Catholic protests, and official but private reprimands and orders to reverse a standing practice. The pattern in Chicago was perhaps duplicated in many other urban situations where concerned and cautious bishops ruled. This conservative and private approach to racism on a case-by-case basis would also gradually change in the mid-1950s, as more and more bishops would come out publicly in support of racial justice and demand integration in Catholic institutions.

St. Louis's Archbishop Joseph Ritter and Washington's Archbishop Patrick O'Boyle in 1947 and 1948 ordered Catholic schools integrated despite loud protests from certain whites in their dioceses. In 1954, prior to the Supreme Court decision of that year, *Brown v. Board of Education* (ending separate but equal schooling), San Antonio's Archbishop Lucey and Raleigh's Bishop Vincent Waters publicly ended segregation in their dioceses, and after the Supreme Court decision a number of other bishops across the country did the same. In 1955 New Orleans's Archbishop Joseph Francis Rummel, with the assistance of his auxiliary John Patrick Cody,* integrated the schools in that diocese and in 1962 excommunicated those Catholics who publicly defied the order.

As a body the American bishops were slow to register their united voices in support of racial justice. In 1943, the year of the Detroit race riots, the bishops issued a pastoral that supported the constitutional rights of African-Americans and called upon Catholics to work together toward racial peace and harmony.[38] It was not, however, until 1958—after *Brown v. Board of Education,* the 1955 Montgomery, Alabama, boycott, the 1957 establishment of the Presidential Commission on Civil Rights (one of whose members was Father Theodore Hesburgh, C.S.C., president of the University of Notre Dame), and hosts of public protests over violations of civil rights for African-Americans—that the American bishops prepared a pastoral exclusively devoted to the issue of religion and race. That pastoral, "Discrimination and Christian Conscience," forcefully asserted that "the heart of the race question is moral and religious."[39] Although the statement received a generally favorable response in the American press, some critics, like the Montgomery *Journal,* were quick to point out that the bishops had become publicly vocal on the issue of "race mixing" only after the Supreme Court decision.[40] The bishops' pastoral, though, reflected a growing consciousness in Catholicism of the moral and spiritual damage of racial prejudice in church and society.

In 1963, prior to Dr. Martin Luther King, Jr.'s march on Washington, Catholic leaders in Chicago, together with a number of Protestant and Jewish leaders, organized the first major Conference on Race and Religion. By 1963 Catholics and others were beginning to see the necessity of ecumenical cooperation in resolving a significant social issue that continued to disturb the American soul. By then, too, numbers of sisters, priests, bishops, and Catholic laity were willing to unite in public protests against national and local racial policies and legal practices. Washington's Archbishop O'Boyle, for example, was one of the religious leaders who delivered the invocation just before Dr. King's "I Have a Dream" speech. In 1965 numerous women religious, priests, and a bishop or two joined King's march in Selma, Alabama, despite the disapproval of the bishop of Mobile-Birmingham, Thomas Joseph Toolen. By 1965 there was little doubt about where the church stood on the issue of race, even if all Catholics did not comply with the church's teachings.

Postwar Catholics, benefitting from political developments during the FDR era, rapidly emerged into local and national politics. In 1946 World War II participants like Joseph McCarthy of Wisconsin and war heroes like John Fitzgerald Kennedy of Massachusetts were elected respectively to the United States

Senate and House. By 1965 twelve Catholic senators and ninety-one representatives served in Congress, a representation in proportion to their numbers in
society.

The political emergence of Catholics was accompanied by a political division in the American Catholic community, one that had been occasionally
evident since the days of John Carroll, but one that became much more prominent and vocal during the 1950s, as political conservatives and liberals waged
their very different wars against communism and for social justice in American society. The two McCarthys—Joseph R. McCarthy, the junior Republican
senator from Wisconsin (1946–1957), and Eugene Joseph McCarthy, the
Democratic congressman (1949–1958) and then senator (1958–1970) from
Minnesota—symbolized the split in the political allegiances of American
Catholics.

The two McCarthys reveal two very different levels of conscious Catholic
influence on their political activities and decisions. For Senator Joseph Mc-
Carthy, as well as for young Congressman Kennedy, religion was a private and
sacramental affair, and politics was largely pragmatic. Both separated their religious from their political life and showed little interest in the intellectual content of their faith or little inclination to probe the political dimensions or implications of their own religious tradition.[41]

Eugene McCarthy, on the other hand, represented a very different kind of
Catholic politician. He was a Catholic intellectual, well versed in the tradition
of the papal social encyclicals, having taught courses in Catholic social and
political thought at St. Thomas College and St. John's University in Minnesota.
Although he distinguished between religion and politics, he did not separate
the two into independent compartments of his life. His Catholicism, too, was
not the Catholicism of novenas, rosaries, and parish bingo, but the Catholicism
of the Mystical Body, liturgical movement, rural life movement, and social
justice tradition of natural law. Religion was not politics, but politics was a
part of one's religious and moral responsibility to provide for individual liberty
and the common good. The two McCarthys represent extremes in relating religion to politics; most Catholic politicians were probably somewhere on the
spectrum between them.

In the early 1950s Joseph McCarthy's crusade against internal communism,
his army hearings, inquisitorial tactics, and appeals to the fears and anxieties
of the age most certainly reflected the postwar religious culture in which he
was raised. Polls for the period demonstrate that "Catholic McCarthyites out-
numbered the anti-McCarthy Catholics, and his popularity with Catholics was
slightly stronger than with the rest of the population."[42] McCarthy's anticommunism, though, was based primarily on appeals to the American political,
rather than to the Catholic, tradition.

Within the context of the McCarthy era a new Catholic intellectual conservative emerged. The new political conservatives (e.g., William F. Buckley, Jr.,
Russell Kirk, Frederick Wilhelmsen, Thomas Molnar, L. Brent Bozell, Arnold

Lunn) were not card-carrying Catholics identified with explicit Catholic journals, organizations, or movements, as were many of the Catholic political liberals.[43] Even when they did not always appreciate McCarthy's tactics or agree with his specific accusations, many conservative Catholic politicians and intellectuals shared not only McCarthy's antipathy toward "liberals," whom they considered naive or soft on communism, but also his fears of the socialist tendencies of the welfare state. Unlike McCarthy, though, the new conservatives brought "the insights of their faith and the natural law tradition" to the service of the American political tradition.[44]

Shortly after the Senate's censure of Joseph McCarthy, conservative Catholic intellectuals joined Protestant and Jewish political conservatives to establish the *National Review* (1955) and *Modern Age* (1956). Although not specifically Catholic journals, they became the organs for the revival and dissemination of conservative thought. For most of the new conservatives McCarthy was right on the one important fact of the peril of totalitarian communism. They attacked the liberals because they lacked fixed and transcendent values by which to judge issues and because they emphasized almost exclusively procedural, as opposed to substantive, issues. By 1964 some of these new conservatives found a political home with Republican presidential candidate Barry Goldwater. L. Brent Bozell, in fact, became the ghostwriter of Goldwater's *Conscience of a Conservative*.[45]

Although there was considerable support for McCarthy and his anticommunist crusade among American Catholics, a number of American Catholic liberal editors, politicians, educators, labor leaders, and churchmen vehemently opposed his repressive tactics. For them, McCarthyism was a mindless, emotional, superpatriotic, and maliciously conspiratorial hysteria that was destructive of justice, social peace, and the liberal procedures of a democratic society.[46] *Commonweal*—under the liberal leadership of Edward Skillen, John Cogley, James O'Gara, and William Clancy—was in the vanguard of opposition to McCarthyism.[47] Robert C. Hartnett, S.J., editor of *America,* Congressman Eugene McCarthy, Senator Dennis Chavez of New Mexico, Msgr. George Higgins of the NCWC's Social Action Department, and Auxiliary Bishop Bernard Shiel of Chicago were also among the vocal opponents of McCarthy's histrionic methods.

Catholic political liberals, like their conservative opponents, were anticommunists for religious as well as political reasons. The anticommunism of the political liberals, however, stemmed more from the papal encyclicals on social justice than from the more explicitly and directly anticommunist papal encyclicals. For the political liberals, the best means for overcoming communism was the promotion of legislative social programs designed to end hunger, disease, deficient housing, and other social and economic ills, all of which were ultimately responsible for the rise of communism and socialism.

Political liberals also saw the rise and spread of totalitarian communism as a fundamental threat to the liberties for which liberalism had traditionally fought—that is, "maximum human freedom under law, social progress and democratic equality."[48] These Catholic liberals, though, were not ideological or philosophical, but procedural liberals. They did not, for example, share the nineteenth-century philosophical liberals' belief in inevitable progress, an overly optimistic view of human nature, or a dogmatic rationalism. They asserted time and again that totalitarian communism and McCarthyism alike had used methods and procedures that threatened the fundamental rights and liberties of the human person under the guise of promoting the public good. In a democratic and pluralistic society, they argued, Catholics should refuse to engage in pressure censorship or to use coercion in religious and cultural matters; instead, they should be tolerant and civil in public debates and support freedom and democratic procedures to secure a political consensus in society. Because they accepted Catholic doctrine and theology, they were suspect among their liberal political friends; because they sided with the liberals in their politics, they were suspect among conservative Catholics.

By the late 1950s the issue of religion and politics came to the fore once again with the presidential candidacy of Senator John F. Kennedy. By 1959 Kennedy had decided to run, and an interview with him in *Look* (3 March 1959) demonstrated that his Catholicism would be an issue. Kennedy unequivocally supported the separation of church and state and opposed public aid for parochial schools and an American ambassador to the Vatican. One sentence in the interview, however, disturbed some moderate Protestants as well as Catholics. Kennedy was reported to have said: "Whatever one's religion in his private life may be, for the officeholder, nothing takes precedence over his oath to uphold the Constitution and all its parts—including the First Amendment and the strict separation of church and state."[49]

America reacted to Kennedy's "nothing takes precedent" statement by asserting that no religious person—whether Jew, Protestant, or Catholic—could or should reduce religion to the level of private conscience.[50] The Lutheran historian Martin Marty thought that Kennedy's statement revealed an all-too-typical mentality that was "spiritually rootless and politically almost disturbingly secular."[51] The Presbyterian Robert McAfee Brown judged that in Kennedy's effort "to assure his possible constituency that he is just a regular American, he has succeeded only in demonstrating that he is a rather irregular Christian."[52]

Other Protestants were more troubled by Kennedy's Catholicism than by his secularism. Some leaders in the National Evangelical Association, Southern Baptist Convention, Texas Baptist Convention, and newly formed Citizens for Religious Freedom, among others, began to organize against Kennedy, articulating the old anti-Catholic bromides. Other prominent Protestants—among them, Methodist Bishop G. Bromley Oxnam, Eugene Carson Blake, Harold E. Fey, Reinhold Niebuhr, and John C. Bennett, all of whom had intellectual difficulties with Catholic doctrinal and religious positions—called the opposition blindly prejudiced, asserting that these conservative Protestants would oppose any liberal candidate regardless of religious identification.

In the midst of the growing concerns, Kennedy addressed the religion issue directly at a meeting of the Ministerial Association of Greater Houston on 12 September 1960. The talk reaffirmed positions he had taken in the *Look* interview.[53] Although Kennedy's speech may not have eliminated the religious element from the final voting, it went a long way to assuage some people about the dangers of Kennedy's candidacy.[54]

Although Kennedy eventually won the election by a very narrow margin, it was a significant symbolic victory for the American Catholic community, erasing as it did the bitter memory of Al Smith's loss. Catholics who were gradually moving into business, professional life, and politics in ever greater numbers during the postwar years had eliminated one final barrier to their full civic participation. But what did Kennedy's win really mean for the Catholic community? Was JFK's election simply a sign that religion, not just Catholicism, was no longer a matter of much consequence in American political life? Did his election mean that Catholics had arrived in the pluralistic politics of the age, or did it symbolize a more widespread Catholic capitulation to a secular dynamic in the political arena in order to make it in American society? However one interprets the election, it is clear that it was the culmination of an era of Catholic confidence and transition.

The Second Vatican Council (1962–65) was another major symbol of the age of Catholic confidence and transition. The council reflected a sense of ecclesiastical stability that allowed the church to produce a new consciousness of itself, bring forth a number of internal ecclesial reforms and changes, call for a new level of ecclesial involvement in society, and articulate a new dialogical attitude toward Protestants and modernity. To some extent the council confidently put to an end the confrontational or defensive attitude of much of the post-Tridentine era and reflected themes that had been here and there articulated in postwar European and American Catholicism.

On 25 January 1959, just ninety days after he had been elected pope, John XXIII made the surprising announcement that he would call an ecumenical council. After more than three years of preparation it opened on 11 October 1962. Neither American bishops nor laity had any clear ideas of what to expect from a council, and perhaps few saw the necessity for one in the first place. Catholicism in America was strong institutionally. Like Cardinal James McIntyre of Los Angeles, many American Catholics saw "no need for changes."[55]

When the new ecumenical council finally met for the first time, Pope John XXIII made it clear that its primary purposes were pastoral. It was called to revitalize Christian living, reform changeable ecclesiastical practices and structures, nurture Christian unity, engage Catholicism in a compassionate dialogue with the modern world, and promote human dignity and unity, social justice, and world peace.[56]

The council meant free discussion and debate and in fact reflected conflicting theological orientations within the church. The conservative-progressive struggles were closely reported in the press, making many American Catholics significantly aware of ecclesiastical divisions that had previously been hidden in professional journals. When the debates were finished and the votes taken, the council had produced sixteen documents that described in various ways a revitalized understanding of the church's nature and mission in the modern world. The documents on the liturgy, church, revelation, the church's relationship with the modern world, ecumenism, and religious liberty were the most significant of the sixteen. They reflected not only the neo-scholastic theological orientations of the immediate past but also the new biblical, historical, and existential theology that had been developing in France and Germany since the First World War. The very combination of the differing theological orientations provided grounds for both liberal and conservative post-conciliar interpretations of the council's intentions.

The documents, however, reflected and produced a definite shift in Catholic consciousness. Vatican II was the culmination of a twentieth-century Catholic preoccupation with ecclesiology—a view of the church that had moved from a primary emphasis on the institutional and juridical, to the sacramental and spiritual aspects of various Mystical Body theologies, to Vatican II's more comprehensive and multidimensional understanding of the mystery and mission of the church in the world. The council stressed the primacy of the church's mission within the entire economy and mystery of salvation, with Christ as the head and center. Within this context the church was presented as the "People of God," demonstrating the council's desire to emphasize the historical, human, and communal dimension of the church. The church, moreover, was distinguished from the Kingdom of God, thereby reviving the eschatological dimension of Christian and ecclesial life. The council also acknowledged for the first time in any official Catholic document the ecclesial reality of Orthodox and Protestant churches.

Behind many documents was a renewed sensitivity to the historical and mutable dimensions of human existence and Christian faith, both of which were interpreted existentially as a vocation and a mission. Revelation and salvation were understood historically as a series of events that had a beginning, development, and fulfillment. This historical view of human and Christian existence helped to produce a new consciousness of the church's presence in the world and a new willingness to dialogue with the modern mentality.

The council fathers furthermore fostered a spirit of renewal, reform, and change—an élan that Pope John XXIII called *aggiornamento,* a bringing of the church up-to-date. This emphasis represented a dynamic shift of consciousness, especially for those American Catholics who were accustomed to speaking of the church's irreformable nature and unchanging practices. For many American Catholics the church had been presented, at least in the most recent past, as the one permanent and stable institution within a world characterized as a chaotic sea of diversity and change.

The council fathers also emphasized the need for accommodation and legitimate diversity within the unity of the faith. Accommodation and variety were clearly possible in liturgical practices, theological conceptualizations, national customs, and forms of spirituality. Although American Catholics had in the past experienced their own kinds of internal Catholic diversity, their most recent ideological emphasis had been on the unity, not the diversity, of the Catholic tradition. The council taught many Catholics about real diversity within the church.

The council acknowledged, too, the legitimate autonomy of earthly affairs, as a requirement not only of the modern world, but of the Creator's will. Created things and societies enjoy their own laws and values, which must be respected. Religious liberty was one of the manifestations of the developing consciousness of human dignity and autonomy in the modern world that the council also affirmed. The council's *Declaration on Religious Liberty* was the one single document in which the American bishops can claim to have provided some leadership. With the help of John Courtney Murray, S.J., they were able to bring the council to see the religious, moral, and political necessity of recognizing religious liberty in the modern world.

The Second Vatican Council initiated as well a series of internal ecclesiastical reforms and changes at a time in the United States when the church was in a period of institutional strength and stability, and when Catholics were becoming upwardly mobile in American business, professional, and political life. The death of President Kennedy (1963), the civil rights movement, and the rising American involvement in Vietnam forecast, however, something of an era of violence in American society that the bishops did not or could not fully discern during the council. The implementation of the conciliar reforms and the communication of a shifting consciousness that accompanied those reforms were to take place in an American cultural, social, and political context that was in the midst of a radical and revolutionary upheaval. The post-conciliar church would be different from the pre-conciliar church.

8
REFORM, PLURALISM, AND CONFLICT: 1965–1990

The Catholic community, perhaps more than any other religious community in the United States, experienced the combined and simultaneously stimulating and disintegrating hurricane winds of social and religious reforms and upheavals that blew across the country in the 1960s and early 1970s. The implementation of the Second Vatican Council's liturgical and structural reforms and the corresponding transformation of American Catholic consciousness that accompanied them took place at a time of revolutionary change in American political and cultural life. Radical protests against American involvement in Vietnam, rising racial tensions and hostilities in large urban areas, student rebellions on college campuses, changing sexual morals and movements toward sexual emancipation, and the campaign for women's liberation magnified the impact of Vatican II's institutional reforms. When combined, the religious and cultural reformations produced a period of unprecedented turmoil and change. By the late 1970s and early 1980s some Catholics, like many others in American society, were calling for stabilization and conservation in the political order and for a spiritual revival in the ecclesial realm.

During the first fifteen years after the council, a diversity of institutional reforms, new ways of thinking, internal rebellions, conflicts, closings of numerous institutions, and a dramatic decline in denominational identification shook and transformed an American Catholic community whose most recent experience and memory was one of relative institutional stability, unity, and phenomenal growth. The story of developments since the Second Vatican Council needs more critical analysis than has been given or can be given here, but even a cursory review of those developments demonstrates something of the ambiguities of the religious reforms: continuities in the midst of change, strength in the midst of decline, gains in the midst of losses, cultural and religious amnesia in the midst of so-called historical mindedness, signs of transcendence in the midst of the love of secularity, and a thirst for justice and peace in the midst of cultural and ecclesiastical injustices and inequities.

The conciliar reforms were implemented in American Catholicism between 1964 and 1970. The first, most visible, and tangible signs of change were in the liturgy. The entire Mass was put into the vernacular, the altar was turned around, the priest faced the people, and the laity were visibly and audibly involved in the liturgical action through lectors, offertory processions, congregational singing, and active responses to the liturgical prayers. The liturgical and eventually architectural changes were perhaps the most significant because they symbolized in very concrete ways the changing consciousness that had taken place at the Second Vatican Council. Whether the changes themselves were implemented in a rapid and uncontrolled pace or haltingly and begrudgingly, they created an atmosphere of reform that was for the most part foreign to the American Catholic experience of the immediate pre-conciliar era. The liturgy itself had come to symbolize the universal and unchanging nature of the Catholic church. Liturgical forms had remained fairly constant for four hundred years—at least they had remained relatively unchanged in the memories of most Catholics. Now the church was demonstrating that things once considered permanent were changeable. Some American Catholics resisted the innovations because, like some conservative bishops at the council, they were unprepared and saw no need for any modifications in Catholic forms of religious life. Other Catholics found them desirable. For still others, the liturgical changes led to an increasing expectation and anticipation of innovations in many other areas of moral and ecclesial life. For almost all Catholics, the changes created a new Catholic consciousness about the historically conditioned nature of many things Catholic.

This fundamental shift of consciousness took place gradually, but it was constantly reinforced by changes in pious practices, governance, and Catholic life-styles. Many signs of a sectarian identity that were so much a part of pre-conciliar Catholic religious life were eventually eradicated. In a number of churches statues of saints were removed in order to emphasize the centrality of the Eucharistic action within the church and to relegate the cult of the saints to the periphery of Catholic attention. Meatless Fridays, another symbol of Catholic identity in the past, were abrogated; practices of lenten fasting and abstinence were modified; and the practice of auricular confession, the result of the former emphasis on sin, soon fell into disuse. These mutations were not matters of small consequence, because they touched the lives of many Catholics who had been accustomed to thinking about their religious life and their own religious identity in terms of these daily, weekly, and yearly practices and customs. Whether they resisted these changes or accepted them wholeheartedly, American Catholics were fundamentally aware that change itself was an issue in the post–Vatican II period.

Gradually national, diocesan, and parish structures began to be revised to reflect the council's call for dialogue and shared responsibility. Bishops, clergy, religious, and laity struggled to find instrumental means to implement the council's spirit. Sharing ecclesiastical administration and decision-making in the American church was not going to be an easy task for those bishops and priests who had been schooled in a church that emphasized monarchical authority.

But a new style of collegial governance began to be implemented in the years immediately following the council, as the bishops themselves in 1966 established the National Conference of Catholic Bishops (NCCB) and United States Catholic Conference (USCC), a civil reorganization of the NCWC. On the diocesan level many bishops convoked parish councils, diocesan priests' senates, and diocesan pastoral councils—new institutions that attempted to take into account the voices of priests, religious, and laity in issues of ecclesiastical policy. The restructuring process created a great deal of diversity and tension within the church, as some complained about lay involvement in ecclesiastical matters and others criticized episcopal resistance or lack of real "democratic" procedures at the local level. Internal reorganization in the American church took place at an uneven, slow, painful, and, in many dioceses, not well-thought-out pace. By 1969 the bishops were well aware of the need to provide some new legal instrument for adjudicating differences and conflicting opinions within parishes and dioceses and to provide due process procedures to conciliate, arbitrate, and decide between opposing parties. In that year, therefore, the national bishops prepared "The Resolution on Due Process" in order to protect, as the bishops put it, "human rights and freedoms which should always be among the goals of the Church."[1]

The bishops continued to be the most organized voice for the church at the national level through the yearly meetings of the NCCB. Others in the church, however, also became more fully organized at the national level and issued their own statements that complemented and at times competed with the bishops' voice: the National Federation of Priests' Councils (1968), the National Black Sisters' Conference (1968), the National Black Catholic Clergy Caucus (1968), Priests Associated for Religious, Educational, and Social Rights (PADRES, 1969), the Leadership Conference of Women Religious (1971, formerly the Conference of Major Superiors of Women, 1956), *Consortium Perfectae Caritatis* (1971), Las Hermanas (1971). These new national institutions were created to give voice to special interests groups in the church and were typically American in their emphases on democratic procedures. These representative organizations reflected the diversity of opinion in the church, and at times their competing voices paralyzed decision-making and made consensus and common actions impossible except in small groups of very like-minded people. The democratic élan, the aspirations, and the techniques used in these bodies moreover tended to disguise the issue of ecclesiastical authority as defined by the council.

The changing life-styles of some clergy and women religious, too, became most evident in the replacement of religious habits and clerical collars with secular dress, in the public involvement of priests and sisters (most of the time dressed in clerical collars and religious habits), in racial justice marches, and in protests against the war in Vietnam. These transformations were not lost on a people very conscious of visible signs. Removing these signs of separation and emphasizing the integration of religion and life influenced the Catholic imagination. The highly visible social and political activism of sisters and priests represented a fundamentally new image of the clergy and religious and symbolized something of the church's involvement in the world's affairs.

Vatican II's openness to other Christians and other religious traditions was soon translated into multiple new symbolic gestures and forms of ecumencial activity that also diminished a separatist mentality and denominational identity. Vatican II's *Declaration on Non-Christian Religions,* for example, stated the new attitude clearly: "The Catholic Church rejects nothing which is true and holy in these religions. She looks with sincere respect upon those ways of conduct and of life, those rules and teachings which, though differing in many particulars from what she holds and sets forth, nevertheless often reflect a ray of that Truth which enlightens all men."[2]

American Protestant theologians who were invited to the council and many others who did not attend welcomed the new Catholic understanding and appreciation of their own ecclesial traditions and the openness to the search for unity. Douglas Horton, one of the Protestant theological observers at the council, expressed the ecumenical warmth of the era when he wrote:

Because you have made us your friends, nothing important to you can be unimportant to us: we shall never again be indifferent (however we may disagree) to anything in your theology, your polity, your liturgy. Let this relationship of simple human friendship be carried from the center you have created here to the boundaries of Christendom and we have at least the beginnings of ecumenism.[3]

The experience at the council was indeed extended by symbolic gestures from the papacy and carried out by ecumenically minded bishops in their own dioceses. In January of 1964, even before the conclusion of the council, Pope Paul VI made a trip to Jerusalem and had an amicable meeting with the Orthodox Ecumenical Patriarch Athenagoras. In November of 1965 they made a momentus joint declaration lifting the mutual excommunications that the Roman and Orthodox churches issued in 1054. In March of 1966 the archbishop of Canterbury, Michael Ramsay, visited the pope, and they agreed to establish a serious theological dialogue that would lead to unity between their two churches. Such gestures and actions demonstrated something of the new atmosphere created by the council itself.

New post-conciliar structures were also established to carry out the ecumenical directives of the council. Even prior to it Pope John XXIII had established the Secretariat for the Promotion of Christian Unity, which became the primary Roman organ for the direction of Catholic participation in the ecumenical movement. After the council the secretariat established a number of international bilateral dialogues with various Christian churches.[4] In the United States, as in many other countries, the episcopacy established the Bishops' Committee for Ecumenical and Interreligious Affairs (BCEIA) in 1964 to encourage and advise dioceses about ecumenical activities and establish and coordinate national theological conversations with other Christian and non-Christian religions. These dialogues have been the most sustained form of Catholic ecumenical activity in this country.[5] After years of study and conversation, various bilateral committees have produced common statements that outline their current theological agreements and disagreements.[6]

After 1966 diocesan bishops here and there also established their own diocesan ecumenical commissions and bilateral conversations. Some parishes, too, continued to observe the Prayer for Unity Octave and engaged other churches in common social service programs. Mutual prayer services in particular flourished in the immediate wake of the council and then gradually died out for lack of interest, energy, and/or direction. Laity from the various traditions also became engaged in what were popularly known as "living room dialogues," where lay and clerical participants prayed together, shared experiences of their religious traditions, sought mutual forgiveness, and discussed ways of encouraging religious amity and unity at the local level.[7] Although these dialogues created goodwill, they ceased to exist by the mid-1970s.

By the 1980s attitudes had changed on many levels, but the movement toward any kind of organic Christian unity had stalled because the common theological statements of the bilateral commissions have not been officially approved by the churches nor received by lay people, nor have they been integrated into the churches' general life, thought, and practice. The ecumenical statements themselves are published but not widely distributed or read and have not even become subjects of much study in religious education programs or in colleges or universities. In the judgment of some ecumenists, "too much has come too soon for too many."[8]

In the midst of simultaneous social and religious tensions and transformations, the Catholic church, like many other American institutions during the 1960s and early 1970s, suffered for the first time in its history a massive loss of membership, decline in the statistics of institutional identification, and a weakening of authority or influence over significant areas of moral life. The decline took place with the simultaneous social mobility of the Catholic people. Throughout the post-conciliar years, Catholics were becoming solidly identified with the American middle class, had in large numbers received higher education, were moving in increasing numbers into the professional and business class, and were prosperous.[9]

Although the *Official Catholic Directory* in 1988 estimated that there were about fifty-three million Catholics (an increase of about eight million since 1965), Gallup and other polls indicated that about sixty-seven million Americans identified themselves as Catholic. This means that about fifteen million Catholics were either lapsed, alienated, or unchurched (i.e., those who are not officially members of the church or who have not attended church in a six-month period).[10] Some surveys revealed moreover that between World War II and 1982 about 17 percent of baptized Catholics had turned to another denomination.[11]

The decline in denominational identification was also measured by other kinds of statistics. Weekly attendance at Mass, the supreme source of Catholic spirituality, was down from 71 percent in 1963 to 52 percent in 1971, and monthly confessions were down from 38 percent in 1963 to 17 percent in 1971.[12] Although the Catholic population increased by 17 percent, the number of clergy actually declined by 8 percent between 1965 and 1988. The decline was due primarily to the 10,000 who left the priesthood and the startling 85 percent decrease in the number of seminarians: from about 49,000 in 1965 to 7,000 in 1988. Disaffection with the church itself, with the exercise of authority, with the clerical or religious life-style, with some of the church's teachings on sexual ethics, a desire to marry, or any number of other reasons significantly reduced the number of priests in the church from 1965 to 1975. Shortage of clergy became one of the reasons for the closings of many churches and other ecclesiastical institutions in the inner cities.[13] In the midst of renewal and conflict women religious experienced a severe 40 percent decline in membership between 1965 and 1988 (from 179,954 in 1965 to 106,912 in 1988). Like the clergy, sisters in over 500 different religious congregations left their communities for a variety of reasons.

Because of the want of clergy and religious, increased costs, lower birth rates, geographical mobility, internal discontent, and a variety of other reasons, the number of Catholic primary and secondary schools also declined. In 1965 there were 13,396 Catholic primary and secondary schools, serving over 5.6 million students. By 1988 the numbers had declined to 9,050 with only 2.6 million students—a decline of 32 percent in the number of schools and 60 percent in the number of students. Similar reductions were registered in various religious education programs outside of the Catholic schools. Between 1976 and 1988, for example, the number of students attending Confraternity of Christian Doctrine (CCD) classes shrank by 1.1 million.

The sociologist Andrew Greeley and his associates argued that the decline in the number of Catholic schools and their enrollment was primarily the responsibility of a Catholic leadership no longer committed to the value of these schools. The fundamental drop in enrollment can be explained, Greeley contended, by a declining birth rate and by a fundamental shift of the Catholic population from the inner cities to the suburbs—and the failure of the church to follow the Catholic population with a school building program. Most of the Catholic laity, he maintained, were as committed as ever to Catholic schooling and were willing to pay for it because they perceived its benefit; but, with a few exceptions, the clergy and bishops lost their nerve in developing the Catholic school system at a time when most of the empirical evidence demonstrated that Catholic school students, whether from middle-class or economically disadvantaged homes, scored higher academically and developed a stronger religious commitment and sense of social justice than their peers in the public school system.[14] CCD programs across the country became the substitute for Catholic schools in religious education, but those programs themselves, according to Greeley, did not prove as effective as the schools in communicating and fostering Catholic attitudes, beliefs, and practices.

As enrollments in Catholic primary and secondary schools declined in the post–Vatican II period, those in Catholic colleges and universities increased by 46 percent—from 384,526 in 1965 to 563,799 in 1988—even though the total number of Catholic colleges actually declined by 23 percent, from 304 in 1965 to 233 in 1988.[15] The continued growth in Catholic colleges and universities reflected the general trend in American higher education in the post–World War II era, when a much higher percentage of high school graduates was going to college as a primary means of advancing professionally and economically in an American society that increasingly demanded skills associated with higher education.

Despite, or perhaps because of, the continuing growth, Catholic colleges and universities experienced a number of crises—raising fundamental questions about academic freedom, participatory democratic governance with involvement of laity in internal administrative decisions, and the relationship of the internal governance of Catholic colleges and universities to the external supervision of the church's magisterium. At the heart of many of these issues was the recurring problem of Catholic identity.

The key issue relative to the Catholic identity of higher education—an issue that was symbolic of the wider search in post-conciliar American Catholicism—was whether the teaching office of the Catholic church was effectively present in Catholic institutions of higher education through an individual's conscience or through more formal juridical ties. On 23 July 1967 twenty-six college educators, representing ten institutions of Catholic higher education, signed the so-called "Land O' Lakes Statement."[16] Catholic presence in a university was effective and operative through individual consciences, campus ministry programs, religious practices, and the communal bonds of students and teachers. According to the Land O' Lakes Statement, "to perform its teaching and research functions effectively the Catholic university must have a true autonomy and academic freedom in the face of authority of whatever kind, lay or clerical, external to the academic community itself."[17] Such a position was repeatedly advanced from 1969 to 1989 at numerous national and international meetings sponsored by the National Catholic Educational Association and/or the International Federation of Catholic Universities.

Others within the American Catholic academic community—notably Msgr. George A. Kelly and Joseph T. Cahill, C.M., both from St. John's University in Jamaica, New York—pushed for a more juridical definition of Catholic identity at colleges and universities. While accepting academic freedom, this group emphasized the need for academic responsibility and an institutional identification with the church's teaching office. Cahill, president of St. John's, told his trustees in October of 1965 that a Catholic university "must adhere not only to the highest standards of excellence, but also to the teaching, legislation, and spirit of the Roman Catholic Church."[18] Catholic identity could not be effectively secured and a Catholic sense of freedom preserved without a clear institutional acknowledgement of the legitimacy of the magisterium's rights in doctrinal and moral matters. This group was concerned that the principle of autonomy, legitimate as it was in reference to higher education, was being interpreted too absolutely, without regard for the church's authority.

Both sides in the debate saw the issue of Catholic identity to be intrinsically tied to the issue of ecclesiastical authority, as if such authority, whether perceived as necessary or not, were merely external to the task of teaching and research. Rarely did Catholic educators raise the more fundamental issue of the intrinsic relationship between faith and understanding.[19]

Although there were numerous attempts to come to terms with democratization, freedom, and secularity within Catholic higher education in the post–Vatican II era, and although there were numerous attempts to define more precisely what Catholic identity means on a campus, there was, as Philip Gleason argued, no working consensus among Catholic academics and administrators "about what it means, in intellectual terms, to be a Catholic and about how Catholic faith should influence the work one does as a scholar and teacher."[20] Roman documents, which were once thought to settle disputed issues, no longer had the clout to forge a consensus. Thus Catholic colleges and universities continued to discuss the issues of academic freedom, governance, and identity.

The Catholic universities' desire for prestige and prominence as research and scholarly institutions, and the recurring criticisms of failures to be such,[21] also were symbolic of wider concerns in a post-conciliar Catholic community that retained the pre-conciliar sense of cultural inferiority. For some, though, the concerns also reflected the continuing Catholic desire to influence culture and demonstrate that critical scholarship and authentic research were the hallmarks of higher learning and should complement the traditional religious mission of Catholic higher education.

Post–Vatican II American Catholicism experienced an unprecedented period of polarization, conflict, and indeed acrimony as different factions in the church fought with one another over a variety of ecclesiastical, moral, political, and cultural questions. Four issues were particularly divisive: the nature and proper exercise of ecclesiastical authority, social justice, sexual morality and abortion, and the role of religion in politics. Division and conflict, of course, were a part of the much longer history of Christianity. What was particularly new for those whose experience of Catholicism was confined to the relatively halcyon days of the immediate past was not only the widespread and public but also the substantive character of the ecclesial conflicts.

The council had opened up the church to criticism and reform, and during the post-conciliar period it seemed that very little in the church's tradition, from the positioning of the altar to moral and doctrinal issues, was free from at least someone's question or criticism. Conflicts within the church were moreover reflective of and exacerbated by the great cultural revolution in the larger American society that protested against all kinds of institutions. Those Catholics who supported long-held values and institutions were in a position of defense; presumption was no longer on the side of tradition and the church's teaching office, as it had been generally in the pre-conciliar period. Some talked of the "old church" or of "ghetto Catholicism," as if there was very little continuity between pre- and post-conciliar Catholic institutions and experiences. The post-conciliar battle was over the definition of precisely what was and what was not continuous and changeable within the Catholic tradition— and it is that character of the battle that helps to explain so much of the acrimony and bitterness that accompanied it.

Conflicts over the nature and extent of ecclesiastical authority recurred periodically throughout the post-conciliar period. The authority of the papacy and the Vatican bureaucracy came under repeated attacks within the church. Unpopular papal statements on a variety of sexual ethics issues, jurisdictional debates between American theologians and bishops and Vatican officials over the teaching authority of national episcopal conferences, and the Vatican's disciplining of some American bishops and archbishops created and reinforced tensions within the church and produced at least a psychological distancing between America and Rome. Dissensions between non-collegial bishops and their post-conciliar clergy here and there, between non-collegial clergy and their active laity, and between authoritarian bishops and the "new sisters" also reinforced the mentality of conflict and to some extent discredited ecclesiastical authority in general among a large segment of the population.

The most sustained internal conflict was over social justice issues (e.g., war and peace, world poverty, American international aid, other foreign policy questions, the economy, race, and women's liberation). The search for social justice was also one of the defining characteristics of post–Vatican II Catholicism. Although the post-conciliar emphasis on social justice had continuities with pre-conciliar movements in American Catholicism, there were a number of differences: the focus upon justice within the church as well as in society; the emphasis upon social liberation and a preferential option for the poor over the stress upon the economic development of peoples; and human rights perceived in explicitly inclusive terms and in terms of sexual, cultural, and personal empowerments rather than simple immunities. In these emphases post-conciliar American Catholic social thought was modified by its encounter with various liberation movements in North and South American societies.

Following the Second Vatican Council the Catholic community throughout the world was called upon to focus on issues of social justice, but the understanding of what constituted the goal of movements for justice shifted. *Gaudium et Spes,* Paul VI's *Populorum Progressio* (1967), and his establishment of the Pontifical Commission on Justice and Peace (1967) focused on the development of peoples. The Medellin and Puebla Episcopal Conferences in 1968

and 1979, the international episcopal synods on justice (1971) and evangelization of culture (1974) went beyond world development to stress the liberation
of peoples as the core of justice. The 1971 International Synod of Bishops in
Rome articulated that conviction when it wrote that "action on behalf of justice
and participation in the transformation of the world fully appear to us as a
constitutive dimension of the preaching of the Gospel." This meant that "the
redemption of the human race and its liberation from every oppressive situation" was acknowledged as an integral part of the church's mission.[22]

The American bishops, their advisors at the USCC, and numerous theologians and social activists became major advocates for social justice within the
world, focusing in particular on world poverty, the equitable distribution of
goods and services, human and civil rights, and a host of other issues involving
periodic examinations of American foreign policies. The most extensive and
significant of the American episcopal pastorals—*The Challenge of Peace* (1983)
and *Economic Justice for All* (1986)—exemplified and epitomized the post-
conciliar concerns of the official church to demonstrate the interrelated practical, political, and social implications of Christian life and thought. Although
these teaching statements were not necessarily indicative or representative of
actual and popular Catholic practices and perceptions, they indicated the ideals
to which the post-conciliar church aspired.

Dramatic and symbolic activities, publications, official ecclesiastical statements, and papal visits focused on Catholic responsibilities to seek peace and
justice in the world. Of the 188 official public statements, resolutions, and
pastoral letters of the American hierarchy between 1966 and 1988, for example, 52 percent were addressed to issues of national and international social
justice. In contrast, only 12 percent focused on sexual morality and abortion.
The remainder concentrated directly on internal ecclesiastical issues (e.g., ecumenism, celibacy, Mary, the church, the charismatic renewal, schools and
religious education, evangelization).[23]

During the 1960s and early 1970s the Catholic peace movement took a dramatic turn to radical protests against the war in Vietnam. From 1963 to the
Harrisburg Trial in 1972, the so-called Catholic Left, a group of more than 232
Catholics, led high-profile, media-event protests against the war.[24] The demonstrators manifested a sense of unique personal responsibility, an impatience
with the established procedures of the peace movement, and a flair for attract-
ing media coverage.

The Catholic Left became effectively organized into local pockets of resistance, particularly after President Lyndon B. Johnson announced the 1965
bombing of Vietnam. The Baltimore four, the Catonsville nine, the Milwaukee
fourteen, the Chicago fifteen, the Minnesota eight, the Harrisburg seven, the
Camden twenty-eight, the Boston eight, the New York eight, and a host of
other groups of local priests, women religious, and laity burned draft cards in
defiance of federal legislation, poured blood on draft records, raided corporate
headquarters of major industries that supplied the tools of war, burned corpo-

rate and federal documents with napalm, and devised other symbolic actions to demonstrate the violence of the war and their abhorence of it. The most tragic of the protests came on 9 November 1965 when Roger LaPorte, a twenty-six-year-old Catholic Worker volunteer, immolated himself in front of the United Nations Building.

In the midst of the protests, a few individuals—the Jesuit Daniel Berrigan, the Josephite Philip Berrigan, Elizabeth McAlister, a Religious of the Sacred Heart, and laymen Michael Cullen and James Forest—became local and national heroes to the movement as they kept up the public pressure against the war, went on trial, and were imprisoned. The 1968 Catonsville trial, brought against nine Catholic protesters who burned draft files, became an international news event, a focal point for rallying the antiwar movement, and the subject of a book, a play, a television documentary, and a movie. This media event became even more dramatic when Daniel Berrigan refused to turn himself in for imprisonment after the trial, went underground as a fugitive from the law, and was not captured by the FBI until 1970. Such actions heightened the movement's visibility and gave it the publicity it sought.

The symbolic and prophetic protests of the Catholic Left represented a new style in the peace movement and a shift in Catholic approaches to social justice—from rational discussion leading to political consensus (à la John Courtney Murray) to passionate witness to gospel values. The Catholic Left was in continuity with the American civil disobedience tradition, but with a Catholic twist that emphasized visible over verbal protests, and in an age of television the Catholic protesters came into their own. The Catholic Left moreover felt no compulsion to demonstrate their Americanism or loyalty, as had many preconciliar Catholic social justice advocates. Their morality of conscience and the higher law was not self-critical or open to the ambiguity of the human situation or drawn from the natural law tradition so much as it was a morality of prophetic witness.

The reaction to the Catholic peace activists varied from outright disdain to conditional support within the American Catholic population. Cardinal Francis Spellman, an ardent supporter of the war in Vietnam, deplored the demonstrators' tactics and had Daniel Berrigan exiled to Latin America for a period.[25] Spellman, however, was not alone in rejecting the protestors' tactics. By 1971, 69 percent of American Catholics, whatever their views on the war (and by 1971 over 50 percent was opposed), believed that Catholics who raided draft boards were not acting as responsible Christians. And despite the widespread publicity given to the Berrigan brothers after 1968, only 38 percent of the Catholic population could identify them.[26] Statistics like these convinced the sociologist Andrew M. Greeley that the Catholic "radicals" made no difference at all in the Catholic community and that "Berrigan-style protests are counterproductive for the causes they support."[27]

A few pacifists like Dorothy Day and Thomas Merton were also critical of the protesters' destruction of property. Although he abhorred the war in Vietnam, Merton believed that the actions of the Baltimore four and the Catonsville nine in seizing and burning draft files in 1968 put the peace movement on "the very edge of violence. . . . On a long-term basis, I think the Peace Movement needs to really study, practice and use nonviolence in its classic form, with all that this implies of religious and ethical grounds."[28]

By the 1972 Harrisburg trial the radical Catholic peace movement was already in the midst of decline because of internal tensions and a repetitiveness of symbolic activities that had lost their power to provoke. By the end of the war in 1975 the peace movement may have been somewhat chastened, but it would continue to have an impact within the American Catholic community. According to a Gallup and Castelli study, the peace movement and the bishops' peace pastoral made Catholics "doves for a generation."[29] The value of such social analysis as an indicator of real convictions is doubtful, however, especially in light of the overwhelming American Catholic support for the Gulf War in 1991.

Statements of the national episcopacy, resolutions of various religious orders of women and men, congressional lobbying efforts of various members of the USCC, participation in sanctuary movements, production of movies (e.g., *The Mission, Romero*), articles in Catholic journals, and books on liberation (especially by Orbis and Paulist Presses) have focused on national and international responsibility for justice in the world. From 1966 to the 1990s the USCC and the NCCB in particular have published numerous pastorals, statements, and resolutions on hunger in Nigeria-Biafra (1968), human rights in Chile and Brazil (1974), apartheid in South Africa (1975, 1985, 1986), religious liberty in Eastern Europe (1977, 1985, 1988), and military violence in El Salvador (1981, 1983), Namibia (1983), and Nicaragua (1986). Many of these statements called the church to a conversion of consciousness and life-style that would bring Americans to the aid to the world's oppressed. These documents moreover had American foreign policy implications or were directed explicitly to current policies considered unwise or unjust—for example, military aid to El Salvador or to the Contras in Nicaragua. In other words many of the statements had explicit political recommendations indicating, as the bishops said in 1981, that because policy questions "affect people," the church, as "the sign and safeguard of the dignity of the person," must provide a pastoral witness to help shape public policies in accordance with justice.[30]

The American bishops' major effort to get the Catholic people involved in issues of justice and peace was the Detroit "Call to Action" Conference (21–23 October 1976). The convention's theme and its name were taken from Pope Paul VI's apostolic letter *A Call to Action* (1971) and the international episcopal synod's *Justice in the World* (1971). Convoked to celebrate the American bicentennial and discover ways by which the Catholic church could renew itself and translate its faith into forms of justice, this national meeting of American Catholics represented 150 of the 170 dioceses and was composed of 1,340 voting delegates, 47 percent of whom were laity and 53 percent were clergy, including 110 of the nation's 300 bishops.

Cardinal John Dearden,* archbishop of Detroit, presided over the conference. The delegates drew up and sent to the United States' bishops a set of 182 recommendations, not only on social problems, but on a host of internal ecclesiastical matters: for example, parish life, ministry, education, and church government. Some of the recommendations (e.g., lay involvement in the selection of bishops and pastors, the possibility of a married clergy, the ordination of women) made the experiment in American Catholic democratic action at the national level problematic for the bishops.

The numerous recommendations and the process itself proved to be too all encompassing, and the conference itself did not have the practical machinery nor indeed a representative American Catholic consensus to make implementation of the recommendations possible. The conference did, however, symbolize a way of life and decision-making that would be followed in much smaller ways in various dioceses and parishes throughout the country in the period afterward, as more and more people became involved in social justice and local ecclesiastical affairs.

The NCCB's "Bicentennial Consultation: A Response to the Call to Action" (1977) reaffirmed the national bishops' commitment to the "principle of shared responsibility" in the contemporary church, acknowledged that "Call to Action's" process of consultation was imperfect, and rejected some of the conference's recommendations as contrary to doctrine and current church discipline.[31]

In 1978 the NCCB committed itself to a five-year plan (1978–83) for implementing in the diocesan and national church a six-point program that illustrated central themes of "Call to Action": education for justice, concentration on family life, deepening communal life in parishes and communities, promotion of human rights, and focus on world hunger.[32] That same year the national bishops also created the Secretariat for the Laity as a major institution to advise bishops on lay concerns in the church. Even though "Call to Action" did not produce the kinds of changes in the church that some Catholics envisioned, it did influence the consciousness of a number of bishops, who in subsequent years created structures of greater shared responsibility in their dioceses, diocesan offices of justice and peace, and offices for African-American and Hispanic concerns.

The long-term effects and implications of "Call to Action" can be seen on the national level in the major pastoral letters that the bishops produced in subsequent years, and more particularly in the processes by which they prepared and wrote those pastorals.[33] The pastorals themselves were significant first of all because they focused national attention on some of the social justice issues identified at Detroit. Second, the process by which the pastorals were written revealed a new approach to Christian teaching in areas of social justice. Prior to writing the pastorals on peace, the economy, and women's concerns, the bishops consulted a variety of persons with experience and expertise in politics, education, theology, law, economics, and women's issues. Various preliminary drafts of the pastorals were discussed among the bishops themselves, and several hearings were held on them throughout the country as the bishops extended their dialogue before they published the final drafts. Third, the pastorals were intended to spark a national discussion on the ethical dimensions of governmental policy in these areas. Fourth, the bishops distinguished those elements in their pastoral teachings that were doctrinal from those applications of Christian principles that were debatable.

The pastorals were widely discussed in the press, professional journals, Catholic schools, and numerous parish and diocesan meetings across the country. Consultation and dialogue were becoming modes of Catholic action, and the issues were substantial—involving the intersection of Christian values and political policies in the country. The pastorals also evoked creative and critical response from other churches and from a number of intellectuals in American society. One group of prominent conservative lay American Catholic entrepreneurs, labor leaders, and intellectuals, for example, issued their own statement on the economy, written primarily by Michael Novak. The lay letter, although in sympathy with many of the bishops' criticisms of the American economy, called for a more affirmative celebration of the benefits of American democratic capitalism than they thought the bishops were willing to acknowledge.[34]

The twenty-year post-conciliar emphasis on social justice and liberation seems to have had some impact on American Catholic attitudes. Opinion polls indicated that a substantial majority of Catholics favored a number of the justice and peace issues. According to one study, 84 percent supported a bilateral nuclear freeze, 77 percent increased government spending on social programs, 69 percent the ERA, and 68 percent a cut in military spending.[35] By significant margins Catholics were also opposed to President Ronald Reagan's policies in Central America, particularly in providing military aid, and favored greater United States pressure on South Africa.[36] On broad economic themes, too, Catholics were in substantial agreement with their bishops, particularly in their perception that the government ought to play a more activist role in the economy, that circumstances many times force people into poverty, and that there was a need for tax reform and an equitable redistribution of wealth and income.[37] These bread-and-butter issues, of course, were a part of the official Catholic view since Leo XIII and the Depression, but the polls demonstrated that even with increased affluence a majority of American Catholics did not give up their social concerns.

"Call to Action" reflected and further encouraged movements among African-American and Hispanic Catholics. Justice for African-Americans in church and society took a new turn in the post-conciliar period with the rise of Black Power movements, assassinations, and major urban race riots throughout the country. Black Power movements toward separatism and African-American nationalism challenged Dr. Martin Luther King, Jr.'s leadership role in the African-American community, as many began to emphasize the self-determination of African-Americans over integration. With the assassinations of Malcolm X in 1965 and especially of King on 4 April 1968 the fury of frustrations in the African-American community erupted in a long series of urban riots that threatened the stability of society and dignity of human persons.

Within this context the American Catholic church, too, experienced a shift in its approach to racial justice. Some white priests, like James Groppi of Milwaukee, won the confidence of the African-American community and led movements for fair housing, jobs, and dignity, but the leadership on racism was gradually passing to articulate African-American clergy and laity as they protested particularly against racism in the church and called for more self-determination within the structures of American Catholicism.[38]

On 18 April 1968, shortly after the assassination of King, more than 50 of the 150 African-American Catholic priests met in Detroit—under the leadership of Herman Porter, George Clements, and Rollins Lambert—to prepare "A Statement of the Black Catholic Clergy Caucus," a stinging criticism of racism in the church. The opening sentence declared, "The Catholic Church in the United States, primarily a white racist institution, has addressed itself primarily to white society and is definitely a part of that society." The statement called for more African-American participation in all levels of decision-making in the church, greater efforts to encourage vocations among African-Americans, more respect for African-American culture and styles of worship, the establishment of an African-American–led department within the USCC, and dioceses to set aside funds for a permanent leadership training program for African-American laypersons. It also called for African-American assertiveness and self-determination within the Catholic church because of the serious defection of African-American Catholics from it and because the "black community no longer looks to the Catholic Church with hope."[39] The establishment of the National Black Catholic Clergy Caucus (NBCCC, 1968) created a solidarity among the African-American clergy and a new form of militancy and self-determination that had previously been lacking.

Sister Martin de Porres Grey, who was present at the NBCCC meeting in Detroit, later in 1968 helped organize a similar institution, the National Black Sisters' Conference. In the same year the National Black Catholic Seminarians' Association was also founded, and a year later lay Catholics formed a similar national association. In 1970, in response to these solidarity movements, the NCCB established within the USCC a National Office for Black Catholics as a clearinghouse for the African-American voice in national Catholic affairs.[40]

The militant 1960s and early 1970s did indeed make the national bishops, if not the church as a whole, responsive to the appeals and needs of African-American Catholics in the United States. In 1965 Harold Perry, S.V.D., was ordained as the first African-American bishop since the mid-nineteenth century. In 1966, 1968, and 1979 the NCCB published explicit pastoral statements on the issues of racism in church and society. In 1984 the ten African-American bishops published "What We Have Seen and Heard," a pastoral on the gifts of African-American Catholicism. The presence of ten African-American bishops in the American episcopate in 1984 (increased to thirteen in 1988) indicated that the national bishops had also been responsive to the appeals for representation. In 1988, furthermore, Bishop Eugene Marino was appointed archbishop of Atlanta, the first African-American Catholic archbishop in the nation's history. In 1987 Pope John Paul II gave a special audience to African-American Catholic leaders during his visit to the United States. That year also African-American Catholics held a National Black Catholic Congress in Washington, DC, to articulate their concerns.

Although Catholic African-Americans gained representation within the church, some of them were alienated from Catholicism, as was evident in the separation of Washington, DC's charismatic Father George Stallings from the Catholic church in 1989, his subsequent ordination as bishop and archbishop of the separatist African-American Catholic church, and his ordination of African-American Rose Vernell, a former sister, as a priest of Imani Temple in Philadelphia.

The Hispanic movement toward civil rights and justice started with migrant farm workers. A steady stream had been coming into California and the Southwest from Mexico since the 1920s, with a veritable flood after World War II. These workers followed the harvest of the crops—particularly grapes, other fruits, and vegetables—receiving in return starvation wages, poor housing, and miserable living conditions, with no promise of financial stability or growth. Most of them were Spanish-speaking Catholics who received little support from their bishops and clergy, with some notable exceptions like Archbishop Robert Lucey of San Antonio. The workers themselves had little power or recourse against the powerful landowners and growers until, under the leadership of the Arizona-born Mexican-American Cesar Chavez, they began to organize themselves in the early 1960s.

Like the peace protests in the East, the farm laborers' protests on the West Coast used united nonviolent symbolic gestures and tactics to accomplish their goals. In 1962 Chavez established the National Farm Workers Association, which in 1965 affiliated with the AFL-CIO Agricultural Workers Organizing Committee. From 1965 to the middle of the 1970s Chavez led the workers in a series of strikes against the growers in California and other places, fasted and held prayer vigils to demonstrate the necessity of nonviolence, organized protest marches to reveal the workers' plight, called for and engineered national boycotts of grapes, lettuce, and some California wines, and engaged in a number of successful collective bargaining sessions with the growers that eventually won favorable labor contracts.

The presence of large numbers of Hispanics in post-conciliar American Catholicism has also challenged the Catholic church to respond to the new immigrants in ways that were analogous to the challenges presented by earlier periods of immigration. Some estimate that the Hispanic Catholic population grew from about 4.9 million in 1960 to about 13.3 million in 1987, representing in the late 1980s about 20 percent of the American Catholic population.[41] The increasing numbers of Hispanic immigrants demonstrated clearly that the American Catholic immigrant tradition did not cease in the 1960s, when other American Catholics became solidly identified with middle-class America. A large percentage of this Spanish-speaking population was made up of new immigrants primarily from Mexico, Cuba, Puerto Rico, Spain, South and Central America, and the Dominican Republic. Most of the Hispanics, moreover, like other earlier immigrant groups, had low incomes (only 20 percent in 1978 had incomes above $15,000 per year), lacked adequate education and skills, and carried with them particular communal and family traditions and values that clashed with a voluntaristic, technological, urban, and competitive American society. Many also had particular religious sensitivities that did not find ready acceptance in an American Catholic tradition significantly influenced by the republican, Protestant, and capitalistic culture in which it has developed.

In the early 1960s there were only a few Hispanics within the priesthood (and none within the episcopacy) to voice the concerns of their peoples. Although the American bishops had formed the Bishops' Committee for the Spanish-Speaking in 1945, that committee was led by Irish-American Catholics. Not until the 1960s did Hispanic leaders within the church begin to protest the lack of representation in the hierarchy, understanding and respect for Hispanic cultures, and real institutional support for the poor and disadvantaged. In 1969 a number of Hispanic priests, both native-born and immigrants, organized in San Antonio (the scene of much support since the days of Archbishop Lucey in the 1940s) PADRES to voice the concerns of their communities. Soon thereafter a number of other local and national Hispanic organizations developed: Las Hermanas (1971), a group of Hispanic sisters; Father Virgil Elizondo's Mexican-American Cultural Center (San Antonio, 1971), which began as a Spanish language institute and developed into a school for Hispanic culture and theology; the Encuentro movement (1972), a campaign to develop a plan for Hispanic ministries; the NCCB's Secretariat for Hispanic Affairs (1974); and Father Allan Deck's Academy of Hispanic Theologians at the Jesuit School of Theology at Berkeley, CA (1988).

These national organizations and numerous Spanish publications and magazines have encouraged American bishops to recognize "the Hispanic Presence."[42] On 5 May 1970 Patricio Flores was ordained a bishop, the first contemporary Hispanic to be raised to the episcopacy, and was later appointed archbishop of San Antonio. By 1988 twenty more Hispanic bishops had been ordained, more than half of whom were immigrants, continuing the immigrant episcopal tradition of American Catholicism. Hispanics had a voice in the church of the 1990s that they never had in the 1960s. They also enriched the American Catholic tradition with their culture, by contributing the Cursillo and Marriage Encounter movements, and by reminding American Catholics of their own immigrant roots and the need for equality and justice within the religious community. Some surveys indicated, however, that large numbers of Hispanic Catholics continued to be alienated from the institutional church.[43]

The struggle for justice for women in society and church was also part of the new consciousness of the period, as women themselves became the primary voices in the movement for emancipation from traditional cultural, legal, political, ecclesiastical, and theological barriers. The drive for women's liberation had its origins and impetus in secular society, but the Second Vatican Council, as Rosemary Radford Ruether has argued, created an "atmosphere where a discussion among Catholics of women's rights in society and in the Church seemed possible."[44] Vatican II's attention to women was minimal, but it did acknowledge their legitimate social progress and fundamental right to participation in cultural life, and explicitly condemned sex discrimination and prejudices against women as contrary to God's intent. Although the council also admitted that women's roles in the church's mission should be expanded in accord with their greater participation in society, it did not translate that general support into practical reforms.

In the period after the council American Catholics would become divided politically over the Equal Rights Amendment (ERA) and ecclesiastically over increased participation of women in the church. An equal rights amendment had been introduced into Congress as early as 1923 but was never clearly acted upon until the National Association for Women (NOW) pushed for it in 1967. Before 1967 most, although not all, Catholics were opposed to the legislation because they believed that such a bill would endanger family stability. From Congressional passage of the ERA (1972) to its final failure to win ratification in the states (1982), prominent Catholics were found on both sides of the issue, even though an eventual majority of Catholics, according to the polls, favored ratification.[45]

Opposition to the ERA came from the National Council of Catholic Women, the Knights of Columbus, Holy Name Societies, Catholic Daughters, and other Catholic groups who helped organize letter-writing campaigns to state legislatures. Phyllis Stewart Schlafly, founder of the Stop ERA crusade and Eagle Forum, also organized national resistance to ratification because she and others like her believed that the implications of such an amendment would eventually weaken the family, lead to abortion rights and lesbianism, and subject women to the draft and combat duty.

Catholic Women for the ERA, the National Coalition of Nuns, the National Assembly of Women Religious, the Leadership Conference of Women Religious, Network, the St. Joan's Alliance, the Canon Law Society of America, the National Conference of Catholic Charities, and other Catholic groups testified for the amendment before Congress or organized support for its ratification. Throughout the ten-year period of struggle the national bishops (NCCB) at first declared themselves neutral, then when it appeared that ratification might imply abortion rights, they opposed it, but by 1984 they returned to a position of neutrality.

A major dimension of the women's liberation movement within the church was manifested in the religious orders of women. Many congregations struggled to gain control and management of their own renewal processes, define new roles for themselves, and establish social justice as one of their primary missions. The Vatican Council called religious orders to recover their original charisms and adjust their way of life to the changed conditions of the modern world. Many reworked and rewrote their constitutions, democratized their structures, changed their dress and life-styles, and provided a host of new services and ministries that departed somewhat from their previous emphasis on educational and medical work. Mary Ewens, O.P., indicated something of the dynamism, optimism, and final results of the renewal process when she wrote that "the energies of whole congregations were engaged for years in the study of historical sources, the careful revision of constitutions, and consultation with experts in many fields. Finally, the struggle of sisters to reconcile religious life with American culture would be over. No longer would American freedom and independence be suspect."[46] The dynamic of adaptation to the values of the modern world was one of the criteria of successful renewal, and for many it was coupled with a critique of an excessive otherworldliness and the unnecessarily restrictive "traditional structures of a patriarchy."[47]

As some religious orders were studying their own histories, revising their constitutions, and defining new roles for themselves, they encountered opposition here and there among some bishops, Vatican officials, and other groups of sisters. Some like Archbishop Karl Alter of Cincinnati and Cardinal James McIntyre of Los Angeles ran into considerable opposition from sisters in their dioceses when they tried to impose their own regulations on them. In 1965 half of the Glenmary Sisters left the order to form a lay group when Alter tried to legislate for them. In 1968, too, 400 of the 450 Sisters of the Immaculate Heart of Mary did the same when McIntyre vetoed their own chapter decisions. Such ecclesiastical conflicts reflected the tensions involved in the adaptations being tried in the post–Vatican II period, and the clash of old-style episcopal management and the sisters' movement toward self-determining control over their own communities. In 1971 some sisters separated themselves from the Leadership Conference of Women Religious (LCWR), a major national clearinghouse of renewal studies and reforms, and formed *Consortium Perfectae Caritatis*, protesting to Rome against what they considered to be a "this-worldly" social bias among the new sisters.

As a result of higher education[48] and the Vatican Council's call to renewal, many women religious took on a host of new roles. The "new" or "changing" sisters, as they were called in the 1960s, were influenced by the rising women's liberation movements as well as by the new ecclesial directions of the council. In 1966 66 percent of women religious were teaching. By the late 1980s women religious were still involved in teaching, but they had also assumed a number of other roles in the church and society, becoming not only lawyers and physicians, but political advocates for the poor and oppressed, parish administrators, directors of religious education, foreign missionaries in Latin America and other Third World countries, and theologians who have applied feminist critiques of sexist exegesis, anthropologies, and theology and have used a feminist hermeneutic to reconstruct church histories, ethics, and ecclesiologies.

Like earlier generations of immigrants, some sisters and lay women advocated greater participation and representation in all of the church's ministries, calling for the abolition of celibacy as a requirement for ordination, a married clergy, and the ordination of women. Beginning in 1965 with the organization of St. Joan's Alliance and continuing through the first Women's Ordination Conference in Detroit in 1975 to the present, the ordination of women has been the key issue for full inclusion of women in the church. According to opinion polls, American Catholics became increasingly favorable to women priests, from 29 percent in 1974 to 47 percent in 1985.[49]

Although the movements for full inclusion of women in the priesthood had some influence on American Catholics, they had no such influence in Rome. In 1976, in response to growing pressures for women's ordination, the Congregation for the Doctrine of the Faith (CDF) issued a "Declaration on the Question of the Admission of Women to the Ministerial Priesthood," excluding women from ordination on the grounds that women were incapable of "imaging Christ" as priests. Some American theologians, too, have sided with the CDF's arguments against ordaining women.[50]

The American bishops (NCCB) held a number of hearings on women's concerns in the church prior to drafting a pastoral letter on the subject. In 1988, 1990, and 1991 the NCCB published three drafts of "Partners in the Mystery of Redemption," which supported justice for women in society, called for their greater participation in the church's life, but reaffirmed the tradition of excluding them from the priesthood. These drafts failed to satisfy many within the church, and in 1992 the majority of bishops voted against publishing a pastoral on women's concerns because, among other things, the issues were not ripe for resolution within a divided church. Milwaukee's Archbishop Rembert Weakland, O.S.B., summarized the thoughts of many when he said after the vote that the debate over women's role in the church was not over; it was just beginning.

From the 1960s onward a veritable revolution took place in American society on a variety of moral and life-style issues that seriously challenged official Catholic church teachings. Artificial contraception, premarital sex, abortion, and homosexuality became increasingly accepted by the population at large but created ardent divisions both within the church and society. The media in particular concentrated on the divisions over these issues and focused on the public dissent of theologians within the church and on opinion polls that showed growing differences between official church teachings and the beliefs and practices of ordinary Catholics. The questions were repeatedly asked: "When the official church teaches on these issues, who listens?" "From what source do American

Catholics draw their moral values, from the church and its tradition or from their personal experiences and the culture in which they live?'' ''Does the public dissent within the church create a moral vacuum or at least a moral uncertainty in which individuals are left to their own devices to settle the moral issues without the benefit of an undivided teaching voice in the church?'' However the questions were phrased, there was no doubt that the official church's opposition to artificial contraception, premarital sex, abortion, and homosexual activity was countercultural, and, in some circles at least, it reinforced an image of Catholicism as opposed to personal freedoms, women's equality and liberation, and concerns about overpopulation. Although the image did not quite square with the reality, the Vatican did not always make its concern about these issues evident in its own teachings.

The papal encyclical *Humanae Vitae* (1968), prohibiting artificial contraception as immoral, became a major post–Vatican II cause célèbre. It had wide-ranging consequences in the American church because it provoked not only a public opposition among numerous theologians, but also a silent resistance among a growing number of American Catholics and an increasing antagonism to ecclesiastical authority and other church teachings. The encyclical was consistent with *Casti Connubi* (1930), the first major modern papal statement against artificial means of birth control, but it came at a time when there was high expectation that the church was about to change its teaching on the issue. That expectation was created by the general post–Vatican II reform atmosphere and by the fact that Pope John XXIII had created a papal commission on birth regulation in 1962 to reexamine the church's teaching, and Pope Paul VI had broadened the commission's membership during the Second Vatican Council. In 1967 the commission reported a divided opinion to the pope (a report published in the *National Catholic Reporter*): a minority favored retaining the opposition to artificial contraception, while a majority favored changing the teaching. *Humanae Vitae* sided with the minority.

Resistance to the encyclical was immediate in the United States. Theologians at the Catholic University, led by Father Charles Curran, obtained the signatures of eighty-seven theologians who dissented from the papal teaching against artificial contraception. Later over six hundred additional theologians and teachers of theology signed the dissenting statement. Forty priests in the Archdiocese of Washington, DC, also protested against the encyclical and were swiftly suspended from their clerical duties by Archbishop Patrick O'Boyle.

The theologians' public dissent revealed that a fundamental shift in moral categories was taking place in the post-conciliar church: from teleological and essentialist (natural law) categories to personalist and existential categories. Many of the encyclical's theological opponents were proportionalists—that is, those who believe that an action became morally wrong when, all things considered, there was not proportionate reason.[51] The Catholic University theologians and others who signed the dissenting statement were not immediately disciplined, but in 1986, nineteen years after the event, the CDF under Cardinal Joseph Ratzinger declared that Charles Curran could no longer teach at the Catholic University because of his opposition to official church teaching.

The theologians' public dissent unwittingly vindicated a silent sexual revolution that had been going on in American Catholicism since the 1950s, reinforced the contraceptive mentality, and provided warrants for further alienation from the teaching church. Already by 1955, some polls showed, "over four-fifths of Catholic wives capable of conception used some means of birth control, with over one-half of the respondents practicing a method considered immoral by churchmen."[52] Opinion polls from the 1970s to the late 1980s revealed that large numbers of lay Catholics simply ignored the papal ban against contraception. By 1977, one poll demonstrated, 73 percent of Catholics believed that they should be allowed to practice artificial means of birth control.[53]

For the first time in American Catholic history American Catholics publicly as well as privately resisted an official church teaching. American Catholics in the past, of course, did not exactly follow the church's teachings in the areas of economic justice, racial discrimination, or even in the areas of sexual morality, but they rarely protested publicly or questioned the church's authority to teach in these areas. Among the host of reasons that motivated elite and then popular resistance or even indifference to church teaching in the area of sexuality morality was a cultural antiestablishmentarianism, an expectation of change created by the council, and a new notion of ecclesiastical authority that had been issued by the council and by post-conciliar Catholic theologians and journalists.

Father Andrew Greeley and others have argued that the encyclical was responsible for creating a crisis of authority in the church, alienating many Catholics from it, and for damaging the church's entire sexual ethic. The decline in Catholic opposition to premarital sex[54] seems to provide some evidence for Greeley's claim that the church's general sexual ethic has been damaged, but whether that damage came from the encyclical or from other sources seems open to question.

Dissent itself became an issue after *Humanae Vitae* and the focus of much discontent among those Catholics who supported the papal teaching and who saw organized public dissent as an imitation of democratic political maneuvering. According to Msgr. George A. Kelly and a number of others, the theologians' dissent was an attempt to establish a second magisterium in the church, but in effect it only created a situation of uncertainty and doubt which gave rise to a moral relativism and subjectivism. A significant increase in the use of contraceptives can be traced, according to Kelly, to the period of the theologians' published dissent.[55]

If contraception created consternation within the church in the mid-1960s, abortion was to absorb the attention of many Americans after the late 1960s. The push for abortion-on-demand won a major victory in Great Britain in 1967, when it was legalized there. The movement to abolish state laws in the United

States picked up momentum after that victory and became a constant source of concern to American bishops from the late 1960s onward. The campaign to legalize abortion was tied to sexual freedom in general, women's liberation and their right to control reproduction, the problem of unplanned and unwanted children, and the issue of overpopulation. The 1973 Supreme Court decision *Roe v. Wade* abolishing state laws against abortion made it, as some social scientists argued, "one of the most controversial social issues in American society."[56]

Abortion had not been much of an issue at the Second Vatican Council; *Gaudium et Spes* (#27) simply reaffirmed the church's traditional prohibition against it. From the late 1960s onward the American bishops repeatedly taught against abortion, repudiated the Supreme Court's decision, and argued that society and the state had the moral responsibility to "safeguard the life of every person from the very beginning of that life." The bishops perceived themselves as having a preferential option for those unborn "who are least able to defend themselves." Without denying the pain and suffering associated with illegitimacy, emotional distress, poverty, and a host of other problems legalized abortion was supposed to cure, the American bishops asserted in 1969 that "we find no evidence that easy abortion laws will solve these problems."[57] Papal visits in 1979 and 1987 reinforced this official Catholic teaching, as have numerous post-conciliar papal statements.

The abortion issue divided the Catholic church perhaps more than any other. Numerous church leaders, prominent theologians, and philosophers—for example, James Tunstead Burtchaell, C.S.C., John R. Connery, S.J., William May, Germain Grisez, John Finnis, and Joseph Boyle—although differing among themselves in many particulars, upheld the church's official position and saw abortion primarily as a life-and-death, not a liberation, issue. Other theologians such as Daniel Maguire, however, directly opposed the church's position. And still other theologians, those called proportionalists by theologian Richard A. McCormick, S.J., have argued that "just as not every killing is murder, not every falsehood a lie, so not every . . . termination of a pregnancy is necessarily an abortion in the moral sense."[58]

Within the larger American Catholic community, too, the official teaching was not received with unanimity. Numerous Catholics have been active in the national and local pro-life movements. Marlene Elwell, for example, was prominent in organizing the National Right to Life Committee. On the other hand, Catholic feminists like Eleanor Smeal, the former president of NOW (1977–82, 1985–87), became a vigorous exponent of a woman's right to an abortion.[59] The divided Catholic opinion over abortion came out most forcefully during the presidential campaign of 1984. On 7 October 1984 a group of Catholic laity and religious published an ad in the *New York Times* in support of free choice and legalized abortions. The religious in the group were subsequently disciplined by ecclesiastical authority, and on 2 March 1986 a Committee of Concerned Catholics published in the *NYT* a declaration of solidarity with those threatened with ecclesiastical discipline for the positions they took, and asked the American bishops "to protect and defend the right of Catholic religious, scholars and activists to speak out on controversial issues of public policy freely, fully and without reprisal." The issue of abortion, like so many issues of the period, again became associated with those of freedom and authority, ecclesiastical discipline, public policy, and the relation of faith to action.

Since 1974 Catholics have registered an increasing support for the 1973 Supreme Court decision, while Evangelical American Protestants in general have showed increasing opposition to it. A 1984 Gallup poll disclosed that a majority of Catholics believed that abortion should be legal in cases of rape and incest, but 65 percent opposed abortion-on-demand, and 60 percent supported a constitutional amendment to restrict abortions. Catholic opinion on abortion was not only an indicator that official church teachings had not been fully received, but also a manifestation of the general confusion on the morality of abortion and on proper extent of its legality in American society.[60]

The issue of homosexuality came to the fore in American society in 1969 after the Stonewall riot in New York, when homosexual men publicly resisted police harassment. Thereafter the issue of homosexual orientation and life-style became matters of some public debate. Catholic teaching, like that in many other religious traditions, had considered homosexual behavior immoral because it was against biblical prescriptions and the natural law. By the early 1970s the American bishops were distinguishing between homosexual orientations (which were not always freely chosen) and homosexual activities (which were prohibited). A few Catholics, however, questioned the absolute prohibition against homosexual activities in the light of scientific evidence.[61]

Pastoral care of homosexuals also became an issue. In 1969 a group of Catholic homosexuals formed Dignity to plead for respect and pastoral care within the church and for the protection of their cultural and civil rights in society. According to some opinion polls Catholics between 1977 and 1985 became increasingly tolerant of legalizing homosexual relations between consenting adults, supported equal job opportunities for homosexuals (67% in favor, 24% opposed), believed that homosexuals could be good Christians or Jews (67% in favor, 23% opposed), but rejected homosexuality as an alternative life-style (46% in favor, 39% opposed).[62]

Many of the moral issues facing American society and the international community in the post-conciliar period had implications for governmental policies. Catholic church leaders and politicians as well as many others in American society became acutely aware of issues of religion and politics. For American Catholics in particular the old debates of the 1940s and 1950s over religious liberty and separation of church and state gave way to two new issues after the Second Vatican Council. One revolved around the general topic of religion's role in the political process and in helping to influence governmental policies.

The other was specifically focused, particularly during the presidential campaign of 1984, on the responsibilities of a Catholic politician in a democratic society.

The American bishops in particular had, since the council, focused on four moral issues that had governmental policy implications: nuclear strategy, the U.S. policy in Central America, equity in the economy, and abortion. Through pastoral letters, published statements and resolutions, testimonies before congressional hearings, and encouragement of parish educational programs, the bishops and their advisers at the USCC tried to focus national attention on the moral dimensions of governmental decisions. Perhaps no other group in the United States had linked together these particular issues as part of a campaign to stir up a national moral debate and influence government. While affirming their adherence to the separation of church and state, the bishops reasserted that "the Church has a proper role and responsibility in public affairs flowing from its gospel mandate and its respect for the dignity of the human person."[63] Although the bishops and their advisers denied any partisan politics, they took sides periodically on a variety of specific policy choices without indicating that their positions should end the debate. They endorsed, for example, a "No First Use" of nuclear weapons, job-training programs, restrictive amendments on abortion, withdrawal of military aid to Central America, and continued negotiations instead of a declaration of war in the Persian Gulf. Such specific positions were taken not in order to dictate policy choices, but for the purpose of engaging in the democratic political process from a moral and religious perspective.

The issue that created the greatest public confusion and encouraged a new level of debate was that of a Catholic politician's specific responsibilities on abortion. That issue came to the fore during the 1984 presidential campaign, when New York's Cardinal John O'Connor charged that the Democratic vice presidential candidate Geraldine Ferraro had given the false impression that the Catholic position on abortion was not monolithic and that "you can be a good Catholic and believe in abortion . . . that there is solid foundations [sic] for a variance in Catholic teaching on abortion."[64] He also criticized her for separating personal conscience from political responsibility. Ferraro held that a Catholic politician, although personally opposed to abortion, could support the political and civil rights of women to make their own decisions and could support legislative programs that funded and supported abortion, because that was part of the American consensus which she and others were called upon to represent. In 1982 Ferraro had written a letter to Catholics in Congress suggesting that "the Catholic position on abortion is not monolithic and that there can be a range of personal and political responses to the issue." That position was one advocated by moral theologian Daniel Maguire and Catholics for a Free Choice at a 1982 Washington, DC, briefing for some members of Congress entitled, "The Abortion Issue in the Political Process."[65]

The O'Connor-Ferraro conflict had political implications, but it also raised serious issues about the role of religion in politics, issues that New York's Democratic Governor Mario M. Cuomo tried to adjudicate in a speech before a large audience at the University of Notre Dame on 13 September 1984, two days after O'Connor's criticisms of Ferraro's position.[66] Cuomo argued that Catholic bishops had the right to define abortion as immoral for individual Catholics, but that church doctrine did not dictate particular political strategies for converting moral teachings into law. Because law was built upon consensus, and none existed on abortion, the church in the United States should not seek legal remedies for moral problems where there was no consensus. Catholic religious values, he told his audience, need not be the law of the land. The bishops themselves, he opined, had tacitly followed this perspective in the issues of contraception and divorce.

Illinois's Republican U.S. Representative Henry Hyde, two weeks after Cuomo's speech, joined in the debate over the role of religion in politics at another Notre Dame convocation. Hyde argued that the abortion issue was distorted if perceived as a personal, religious, or sectarian issue. The issue was one of public morality, and therefore it belonged to those in public service to address it. For him, it was clearly insufficient for a Catholic public official to hold that his or her personal conscientious objection to abortion ended the matter. Law was not simply a matter of public consensus, but had an educative function to lead people to justice and equity in society. Requiring consensus prior to legislation was, moreover, highly selective in some circles. "No consensus was demanded before adopting the Civil Rights Act of 1964 or Fair Housing legislation—they were right and their proponents helped to *create* a consensus by advocacy and example and by understanding that law itself can be an excellent teacher." Therefore, public officials had the responsibility to teach justice, not just to reflect prevailing values. For him, abortion was not a "Catholic issue," but rather a "moral and civil rights issue, a humanitarian issue and a constitutional issue of the first importance." For Hyde, religiously based values must play a role in public life; otherwise the moral foundations of society will continue to erode.[67]

Whether the law should be reflective or creative of a consensus in society, whether politicians should represent the society's prevailing sense of right or teach justice, and whether the abortion issue was one of private and personal morality or a matter of public justice and morality were questions that continued to divide opinion in the church and society.

In the midst of unprecedented decline and conflict within American Catholicism there arose a number of new movements to revive spirituality. A 1976 *Time* cover story, "U. S. Catholicism: A Church Divided," revealed that despite changes and conflicts the American Catholic people were displaying a "remarkable tenacity" and showing a "spiritual second wind that suggests that U.S. Catholicism might even be on the verge of a new period of vigor."[68] In 1989 Gallup and Castelli, after analyzing recent opinion polls, declared that "American Catholics are in the middle of a religious revival."[69] The revival, though, reflected a shift in Catholic spirituality that took some years to accomplish. It was a revival, moreover, that was continuing simultaneously with the concerns for institutional reforms and in the midst of church divisions.

Although devotional Catholicism continued to characterize the spirituality of many older Catholics during the post-conciliar period, it was gradually replaced by a variety of new forms that emphasized the sacramental, communal, and active dimensions thought to be grounded in the public liturgy, the Bible, and personal experiences of modern Catholics. The ecumenical openness of the Second Vatican Council also encouraged some Catholics to look into forms of spirituality outside of the Catholic tradition.

The charismatic movement was one of the most dramatic, ecumenical, long-lasting, and widespread spiritual movements of the post-conciliar period, touching millions of Catholics in the course of the last twenty-five years.[70] The charismatic movement focused attention on the gifts of the Holy Spirit, the necessity of a new experience of spiritual power, and the need to provide individual and communal witnesses to the faith experience. Catholic charismatics differed from classical Pentecostals primarily in their emphasis on the sacramental context of the spiritual gifts, their allegiance to a teaching church, and their willingness to stay within the institutional structures to renew from within. Another revival of spirituality began to occur during the mid-1970s, when numerous parishes across the country adopted one of any number of parish renewal programs, some of which had been sponsored by the USCC and all of which focused on developing the spiritual life of Catholics at the local level. Perhaps the most successful and widespread of these was RENEW, a diocesan-wide, parish-based pastoral program that originated in the Archdiocese of Newark, New Jersey, in 1976. By 1990 ninety-six dioceses and about one-half of all parishes in the United States had some experience with RENEW.[71]

The national movements toward a recovery of spirituality in American Catholicism were accompanied by a great growth in new and diverse forms of spirituality particularly focused on the special needs of adults, youth, women, divorced people, African-Americans, and Hispanics. Father Virgil Elizondo's Mexican-American Cultural Center, for example, attempted to formulate a spirituality suited to Hispanics. In the parishes, too, diversity characterized the approaches to extra-sacramental spirituality with an increase in the number of Bible-reading and study groups, prayer groups, and an increased emphasis since the mid-1970s on evangelizing lapsed and/or alienated Catholics. The establishment of the National Organization of Catholic Evangelical Directors in 1982 was one indicator of the increased emphasis put on evangelization. Older forms of popular Marian piety, too, continued among Hispanics and other groups and were revived in the 1980s with the alleged Marian apparitions at Medjugorje, Yugoslavia.

Although there were a number of complaints about the institutional church's failures to meet the religious needs of many American Catholics, programs like RENEW, a stabilized (53 percent) Mass attendance by the mid-1970s, widespread participation in prayer meetings, more involvement in church life at parish and diocesan levels, a significant increase in Bible reading, and a large increment in the purchasing and reading of books on spirituality are some of the indicators of a religious revival. Internal disagreements and conflicts, some surveys reported, did not change a sense of belonging to the church. In fact a 1987 poll found that Catholics had more "confidence in the church than in any other institution," with 85 percent saying that their lifetime experiences in Catholicism had been "overall positive."[72]

In spite of the "overall positive" views, serious questions were raised about post-conciliar experiences and developments within American Catholicism. Was American Catholicism able to develop a spiritual integrity as it moved from its ethnic, parochial, and spiritual ghettos into the American mainstream of power and success? Or, had it created a whole host of new ghettos: some oriented to radical protests against church and society, some to social justice activism, some to spiritually satisfying communes, and some to old ethnic and cultural identities? Had the unprecedented changes in theological awareness and in ecclesiastical forms brought about a fundamental spiritual regeneration and a new sense of the reality, mystery, and power of God in human lives? Or, had the transformations simply accommodated themselves to secularity, radical pluralism, and a technological imperative that made ends out of means? Was the selective rejection of official church teachings a new manifestation of basic Christian freedom and personal authenticity, or had it been a sign of American individualism and the decline of faith? Had the decline in identification with and participation in the church been the result of misguided ecclesiastical decisions, radical Catholic aberrations, or the product of a long-standing pretense of belief that was finally shattered once the institutions that supported the pretense began to crumble or show signs of weakness?

Responses to these and a host of other questions produced interpretations and evaluations of post-conciliar American Catholicism as varied and as contradictory as the Catholic experiences themselves. In the late 1960s and early 1970s a number of conservative Catholic groups and individuals rose up in protest against what they perceived to be wrong-headed post-conciliar developments. Traditionalist Catholics associated with Father Gommar De Pauw and the French Archbishop Marcel Lefèbvre rejected as invalid the post-conciliar liturgical reforms and emphasized the unalterable nature of Tridentine sacramental practices. Others—those associated with the *Wanderer,* Catholics United for the Faith, and a host of other conservative lay Catholic organizations—accepted the conciliar declarations and Vatican-initiated reforms but repudiated the liberal interpretations and abuses and censured unauthorized liturgical experimentations, a resurgence of modernism in catechetics, a weakening of magisterial authority, and the minimizing of the supernatural. They periodically charged some American Catholics with unfaithfulness and some leading bishops with heresy and the abandonment of their authoritative offices.[73]

In the early 1970s and thereafter a number of conservative intellectuals, groups, and publications began criticizing the disintegration within American Catholicism that had been occuring since the end of the council.[74] Whether they attributed the breakdown and decline in the church to the popular reform mentality that created the "illusion" of a major discontinuity between the pre-conciliar church and the "New Catholicism," or to the liberal theologians who had blessed an unholy theological pluralism and had capitulated to modernity by collapsing the distinction between the natural and the supernatural, or to the liberal and reform-minded bishops and clergy who had abdicated their authority in the church, or, in Garry Wills's view, to the fatal insufficiencies in the church's very fabric that had protected a pretense of belief that periodically in the church's history called for reform, these voices reflected discontent with many post-conciliar developments. These intellectuals sought to reestablish a sense of the supernatural, reassert the church's interior unity and cohesiveness, and reaffirm loyalty to the church's official magisterium on the ultimate questions concerning God, the human person, and the world. Like the "liberal Catholic" voice of the 1950s, the conservative voice of the 1970s was a minority voice within the Catholic intellectual community. That voice, though, would become more widespread and more moderate in the late 1970s and early 1980s, as the country itself began reacting against the cultural revolution of the 1960s and the church, under Pope John Paul II and Cardinal Joseph Ratzinger, reinforced traditional Catholic values.

The predominant view of post–Vatican II developments was much more favorable to the consequences of reform, change, and pluralism. That view was articulated by a large group of intellectuals who became advisers and church leaders in a number of national and local ecclesiastical institutions: the bishops' national advisers in the USCC, ecclesiastical leaders of other major national organizations (LCWR, Network, NFPC, NBCCC, PADRES, etc.), theological leadership (e.g., in the Catholic Theological Society of America, College Theology Society, Catholic Biblical Association, Canon Law Society of America), educational leadership in the Catholic universities and colleges, directors of religious education programs, and some journalists in the major Catholic newspapers and magazines. The reform-minded leaders in the church were at first critical of the slow and uneven pace of the reforms, but they have been generally supportive of what David O'Brien called *The Renewal of American Catholicism* (1972).

The positive evaluations and celebrations of secularity and pluralism (cultural, ecclesiological, and theological) in the early post-conciliar period contrasted sharply with the generally negative pre-conciliar judgments. In 1960, for example, the theologian Joseph Clifford Fenton could say without much challenge that the scholastic method and terminology were constants in the Catholic tradition that admitted no substantial change.[75] By 1975, seven years after Fenton's death, David Tracy was affirming "an ever increasing pluralism" in theology and seeing it as the occasion of great promise because it enabled individual theologians to learn from a variety of views of humanity and Christianity.[76] Avery Dulles, S.J., and a whole host of theologians joined Tracy in accepting and celebrating reform, revision, and pluralism within unity as fundamental Catholic values.

The year 1975, however, also marked a turning point in the reformist theological and intellectual community that was symbolic of a wider critique of liberal and reform movements within the church and society. That year twenty-four Protestant, Catholic, and Jewish scholars gathered together at Hartford, Connecticut, and published "An Appeal for Theological Affirmation," which called for a recovery of "a sense of the transcendent" and charged that some contemporary theological projects were "false and debilitating to the church's life and work."[77]

After 1975 a split developed within the reform-minded theological community that was indicative of divisions within the larger Catholic community between moderate reformists like Dulles and revisionist theologians like Tracy who were attempting a "basic revision of traditional Christianity and traditional modernity." By revising both traditions Tracy intended to demonstrate "that the Christian faith is at heart none other than the most adequate articulation of the basic faith of secularity itself." Thus a revisionist's theology "is best understood as philosophical reflection upon the meanings present in common human experience and the meanings present in the Christian tradition."[78] Some in American Catholicism interpreted such an attempt as capitulation to modernity, others saw it as a dangerous tendency, and still others understood it as the only acceptable way to dialogue with the modern world.

The very diversity of evaluations of post-conciliar directions created, especially among some who had adult experiences in both pre- and post-conciliar American Catholicism, what Philip Gleason called "psychological marginality." That was the situation of those Catholics who, like new immigrants, belonged to two cultural worlds and felt "semi-detached" from and semi-involved in both worlds simultaneously. Or, as Gleason put it, those who were distanced "from each [culture] by his [and her] attachment to the other."[79] Such Catholics knew and felt the limits as well as the benefits of both past and present assimilationists' and cultural pluralists' experiences and policies within the church. Although they identified totally with neither world and stood in both at the same time, they held in uneasy psychological tension the yearning for God, ecclesial unity and cohesion, and continuity, and simultaneously the desire for freedom, diversity, and change. Such was perhaps the experience of a number of American Catholics at the end of the twentieth century.

As American Catholicism moved into the 1990s and toward the third millennium, it carried with it much hope and a number of serious challenges. How would American Catholics foster and preserve a vital religious life and institutional integrity while responding to and being influenced by a changing American and international environment? How would they respond to the apparent end of the cold war between the major superpowers and take more responsibility for the development of international justice and peace? How would they develop deep religious values and a strong communal identity that would enable them to address effectively the issues of poverty, racism, drug traffic, sexual exploitation, and materialistic consumerism that were destroying individual dignity, family life, and local neighborhoods? How would they respond to and be influenced by the growing Hispanic presence? What would they do to provide for the dignity and participation of women within their own church and society? How would they respond to the serious shortage of clergy within their own communities? These and a host of other questions will test the vitality of American Catholic life and thought in the next generation.

NOTES

CHAPTER 1. MISSION CATHOLICISM: 1492–1840

1. John F. Bannon, ed., *Bolton and the Spanish Borderlands* (Norman: University of Oklahoma Press, 1964), 48.

2. Or 78 years if one considers the permanent presence of the Indian missions from the year 1715.

3. Robert Ricard, *The Spiritual Conquest of Mexico: An Essay on the Apostolate and the Evangelizing Methods of the Mendicant Orders in New Spain, 1523–1572,* trans. Lesley Byrd Simpson (Berkeley: University of California Press, 1966), 284.

4. John Gilmary Shea, *History of the Catholic Missions among the Indian Tribes of the United States, 1529–1854* (New York: P. J. Kennedy, 1882), 119.

5. John L. Kessell, *Kiva, Cross, and Crown: The Pecos Indians and New Mexico, 1540–1840* (Washington, DC: National Park Service, U. S. Department of the Interior, 1979), 319.

6. John J. Kessell, *Friars, Soldiers, and Reformers: Hispanic Arizona and the Sonora Mission Frontier, 1767–1856* (Tucson: University of Arizona Press, 1976), 236.

7. On this, see Cornelius J. Jaenen, *The Role of the Church in New France* (Toronto: McGraw-Hill Ryerson, 1976), viii.

8. Reuben Gold Thwaites, ed., *The Jesuit Relations and Allied Documents: Travels and Explorations of the Jesuit Missionaries in New France, 1610–1791* (New York: Pageant Book Co., 1959), 35:273.

9. Ibid., 25:247; see also p. 249ff. for stories of these problems.

10. Ibid., 51:265.

11. Francis Parkman, *The Jesuits in North America* (Boston: Little, Brown, 1897), 216.

12. For example, *Jesuit Relations,* 34:159–95; 34:223–27; 35:201–5.

13. Ibid., 24:299–301; see also p. 281.

14. Ibid., 34:163.

15. John Tracy Ellis, ed., *Documents of American Catholic History,* 3 vols. (Wilmington, DE: M. Glazier, 1987), 1:95.

16. R. Emmett Curran, ed., *American Jesuit Spirituality: The Maryland Tradition, 1634–1900* (New York: Paulist Press, 1988), 3.

17. R. Emmett Curran, J. T. Durkin, and G. P. Fogarty, eds., *The Maryland Jesuits, 1634–1833* (Baltimore: Corporation of the Roman Catholic Clergymen, Maryland Province, Society of Jesus, 1976), 20.

18. See Thomas O'Brien Hanley, ed., *The John Carroll Papers,* 3 vols. (Notre Dame, IN: University of Notre Dame Press, 1976), 1:179 (hereafter cited as *JCP*).

19. Curran, Durkin, and Fogarty, *Maryland Jesuits,* 10.

20. Thomas Hughes, *History of the Society of Jesus in North America: Colonial and Federal,* 4 vols. (New York: Longmans, Green, and Co., 1907–17), text 1:256.

21. [Richard Challoner], *The Garden of the Soul: A Manual of Spiritual Exercises and Instructions for Christians, Who, Living in the World, Aspire to Devotion* (1740, reprint, New York: D. & J. Sadlier & Co., 1869).

22. Jay P. Dolan, *The American Catholic Experience: A History from Colonial Times to the Present* (Garden City, NY: Doubleday, 1985), 94–95.

23. Ellis, *Documents,* 1:98.

24. Michael James Graham, "Lord Baltimore's Pious Enterprise: Toleration and Community in Colonial Maryland, 1634–1724" (Ph.D. diss., University of Michigan, 1983), 51.

25. See Clayton Colman Hall, ed., *Narratives of Early Maryland, 1633–1684* (1946; reprint, New York: Barnes and Noble, 1967), 269–72.

26. Quoted in John D. Krugler, "Puritan and Papist: Politics and Religion in Massachusetts and Maryland before the Restoration of Charles II" (Ph.D. diss., University of Illinois, 1971), 277.

27. See Graham, "Pious Enterprise," 389; see also Gerald P. Fogarty, "Property and Religious Liberty in Colonial Maryland Catholic Thought," *Catholic Historical Review* 72 (October 1986): 573–600, esp., 587–92.

28. Hughes, *History,* text 2:591; John Tracy Ellis, *Catholics in Colonial America* (Baltimore: Helicon, 1965), 384; idem, *Documents,* 1:125–28.

29. Sydney H. Ahlstrom, *A Religious History of the American People* (New Haven, CT: Yale University Press, 1972), 361.

30. On this American problem, see Carl Bridenbaugh, *Mitre and Sceptre: Transatlantic Faiths, Ideas, Personalities, and Politics 1689–1775* (New York: Oxford University Press, 1962).

31. On this, see Peter S. Onuf, ed., *Maryland and the Empire, 1773: The Antilon–First Citizen Letters* (Baltimore: The Johns Hopkins University Press, 1974).

32. See Elihu S. Riley, ed., *Correspondence of "First Citizen"—Charles Carroll of Carrollton and "Antilon"—Daniel Dulany Jr., 1773, with a History of Governor Eden's Administration in Maryland. 1769–1776* (Baltimore: King Bros., 1902), 118.

33. Ibid., 121, 230.

34. Worthington Chauncey Ford, ed., *Journals of the Continental Congress 1774–1789,* 34 vols. (Washington, DC: U.S. Government Printing Office, 1904–37), 1:34–35, quoted in James J. Hennesey, *American Catholics: A History of the Roman Catholic Community in the United States* (New York: Oxford University Press, 1981), 57.

35. Although some Pennsylvania Catholics joined the Tories in resisting the movement toward independence, most Catholics in Maryland and Pennsylvania supported the war effort. See Martin I. J. Griffin, *Catholics and the American Revolution,* 3 vols. (Ridley Park, PA: the author, 1907–11).

36. Carroll to G. W. P. Custis, February 20, 1829, quoted in Ellen Hart Smith, *Charles Carroll of Carrollton* (Cambridge, MA: Harvard University Press, 1942), 274.

CHAPTER 2. A FREE CHURCH IN THE REPUBLIC: 1776–1815

1. John Carroll to Vitaliano Borromeo, 10 November 1783, *JCP*, 1:80.

2. John Carroll to Charles Plowden, 20 February 1782, *JCP*, 1:65; on the moderate Enlightenment, see Henry May, *The Enlightenment in America* (New York: Oxford University Press, 1976), 3–105. May's description of the moderate Enlightenment did not include any Catholics, but it could have.

3. Patrick Carey, "American Catholics and the First Amendment: 1776–1840," *Pennsylvania Magazine of History and Biography* 113 (July 1989): 323–46.

4. *JCP*, 1:259–61, 365–68, 409–11. On Carroll's argumentation, see Joseph McShane, "John Carroll and the Appeal to Evidence: A Pragmatic Defense of Principle," *Church History* 57 (September 1988): 298–309.

5. *JCP*, 1:180.

6. *JCP*, 3:375–466.

7. *JCP*, 1:527.

8. *JCP*, 1:68.

9. John Carroll, Robert Molyneaux, and John Ashton to Pope Pius VI, 12 March 1788, *JCP*, 1:279–80.

10. *JCP*, 1:520–21, 526–41.

11. Hugh J. Nolan, ed., *Pastoral Letters of the United States Catholic Bishops*, 5 vols. (Washington, DC: National Conference of Catholic Bishops/United States Catholic Conference, 1984–1989), 1:16–27 (hereafter cited as *PL*).

12. *JCP*, 1:533.

13. John Carroll to Charles Plowden, [?] December 1792 [?], *JCP*, 1:548.

14. John Carroll to Charles Plowden, 26 September 1783, *JCP*, 1:78.

15. John Carroll to Leonardo Antonelli, 19 April 1788, *JCP*, 1:301.

16. Harvard, Yale, and Princeton had for years trained men for the ministry, but American Protestants did not establish the first independent divinity school until 1808 at Andover, Massachusetts. On this and the Sulpician influence upon American Catholicism, see the excellent studies by Christopher J. Kauffman, *Tradition and Transformation in Catholic Culture: The Priests of Saint Sulpice in the United States from 1791 to the Present* (New York: Macmillan, 1988), 42 and passim, and Joseph M. White, *The Diocesan Seminary in the United States: A History from the 1780s to the Present* (Notre Dame, IN: University of Notre Dame Press, 1989).

17. For these statistics, see *JCP*, 1:181; and James F. Connelly, *The Visit of Archbishop Gaetano Bedini to the United States of America, June 1853–February 1854* (Rome: Libreria Editrice dell'Università Gregoriana, 1960), 264.

18. Ellis, *Documents*, 1:208.

19. For a social history of the new American establishments, see Barbara Misner, *"Highly Respectable and Accomplished Ladies": Catholic Women Religious in America 1790–1850* (New York: Garland Publishing, 1988). For more general histories of women religious, see Mary Ewens, *The Role of the Nun in Nineteenth Century America* (New York: Arno Press, 1978); James Joseph Kenneally, *The History of American Catholic*

Women (New York: Crossroad, 1990); and Karen Kennelly, ed., *American Catholic Women: A Historical Exploration* (New York: Macmillan, 1989).

20. Mary Ewens, "Women in the Convent," in Kennelly, *American Catholic Women*, 18.

21. Ellis, *Documents*, 1:218–19.

22. John Tracy Ellis, *American Catholicism*, 2d ed., rev. (Chicago: University of Chicago, 1969), 41–83.

23. Quoted in Annabelle M. Melville, *Jean Lefebvre de Cheverus 1768–1836* (Milwaukee: Bruce Publishing, 1958), 222.

24. On the territorial increases, see Gerald Shaughnessy, *Has the Immigrant Kept the Faith? A Study of Immigration and Catholic Growth in the United States, 1790–1920* (New York: Macmillan, 1925), 68–72. Shaughnessy's estimate that in 1803 Louisiana had fifteen thousand white Catholics, primarily Spanish and French, out of an estimated twenty-four thousand seems to me to be a low estimate based on slim evidence.

25. John Carroll to the Congregation of Boston, 30 April 1790, *JCP*, 1:441.

26. John Carroll, Report for His Eminence Cardinal Antonelli on the Condition of Religion in the sections of the United States of America, 1 March 1785, *JCP* 1:179; see also Shaughnessy, *Has the Immigrant?* 63–73.

CHAPTER 3. CRISES AND IMMIGRANT CATHOLICISM: 1815–1866

1. On trusteeism, see Patrick Carey, "The Laity's Understanding of the Trustee System," *Catholic Historical Review* 64 (July 1978): 357–76; and idem, *People, Priests, and Prelates: Ecclesiastical Democracy and the Tensions of Trusteeism* (Notre Dame, IN: University of Notre Dame Press, 1987).

2. On this, see James Hennesey, "Papacy and Episcopacy in Eighteenth and Nineteenth Century American Catholic Thought," *Records of the American Catholic Historical Society* 77 (September 1966): 175–89.

3. For figures, see Shaughnessy, *Has the Immigrant?*, 125, 153.

4. For an extensive treatment of the individual characteristics of the various ethnic groups that made up nineteenth-century American Catholicism, see Dolan, *American Catholic Experience*, 127–348. Much attention has been given to the ethnic variety in American Catholicism, but little attention has been paid to the ways in which the development of American Catholicism has been affected by geography and regional sensibilities. *Catholics in the Old South: Essays on Church and Culture*, ed. Randall M. Miller and Jon L. Wakelyn (Macon, GA: Mercer University Press, 1983), is an exception here. During this period the fundamental outlines of regional variations in Catholicism began to emerge. East Coast Irish Catholics, for example, do not have the same sensibilities and cultural and historical experiences as do those in the South, Southwest, Midwest, or Northwest. It is beyond the scope of the present essay, however, to develop these variations.

5. Jo Ann Manfra, "The Catholic Episcopacy in America, 1789–1852" (Ph.D. diss., University of Iowa, 1975), 14.

6. On this estimate, see Dolan, *American Catholic Experience*, 130.

7. Colman J. Barry, *The Catholic Church and German Americans* (Milwaukee: Bruce Publishing Co., 1953), 44–86.

8. Ray Allen Billington, *The Protestant Crusade: 1800–1860* (1938; reprint, Chicago: Quadrangle Books, 1964).

9. William Ellery Channing, *The Works of William E. Channing, D.D.*, 3d ed., 5 vols. (Glasgow: James Hedderwick and Son, 1840), 2:271.

10. On Catholic newspapers, see Paul J. Foik, *Pioneer Catholic Journalism* (New York: United States Catholic Historical Society, 1930).

11. John Hughes, "The Decline of Protestantism, and Its Causes," in *Complete Works of the Most Rev. John Hughes, D.D., Archbishop of New York: Comprising His Sermons, Letters, Lectures, Speeches, etc.*, ed. Lawrence Kehoe, 2nd ed., rev. and corr., 2 vols. (New York: American News Co., 1865), 2:101.

12. On developments in the Midwest, see Robert Frederick Trisco, *The Holy See and the Nascent Church in the Middle Western United States, 1826–1850* (Rome: Gregorian University Press, 1962); Timothy Walch, "Catholic Social Institutions and Urban Development: The View from Nineteenth-Century Chicago and Milwaukee," *Catholic Historical Review* 64 (January 1978): 16–32; and Thomas W. Spalding, "Frontier Catholicism," *Catholic Historical Review* 77 (July 1991): 470–84.

13. The provincial councils that met in 1829, 1833, 1837, 1840, 1843, 1846, and 1849 were in reality legally binding national synods as much as were the plenary councils that met in 1852, 1866, and 1884. After each of these meetings the bishops prepared pastoral letters for American Catholics, a practice that has continued to the present day after national episcopal meetings.

14. These figures are based upon an analysis of Joseph Bernard Code, *Dictionary of the American Hierarchy* (New York: Longmans, Green and Co., 1940).

15. See, for example, Bishop John Hughes to a correspondent in Rome, 30 March 1858, quoted in John R. G. Hassard, *Life of the Most Reverend John Hughes, D.D., First Archbishop of New York* (New York: D. Appleton and Co., 1866), 389.

16. On this, see, for example, John Hughes, *Pastoral Letter of the Right Rev. Dr. Hughes to the Clergy and Laity of the Diocese of New York* (New York: George Mitchell, 1842), 5; Dale Light, "The Reformation of Philadelphia Catholicism, 1830–1860," *Pennsylvania Magazine of History and Biography* 112 (July 1988): 375–406; and Paul Horgan, *Lamy of Santa Fe: His Life and Times* (New York: Farrar, Straus and Giroux, 1975), 169–251.

17. On these statistics, see Peter Guilday, *A History of the Councils of Baltimore, 1791–1884* (New York: Macmillan, 1932), 193–94.

18. Quoted in Connelly, *Visit of Archbishop Bedini*, 240.

19. This statistic is an estimate based upon accounts in Thomas W. Spalding, *The Premier See: A History of the Archdiocese of Baltimore, 1789–1989* (Baltimore: Johns Hopkins University Press, 1989), 107–9; Clyde F. Crews, *An American Holy Land: A History of the Archdiocese of Louisville* (Wilmington, DE: Michael Glazier, 1987), 88, 106; Misner, "Highly Respectable and Accomplished Ladies," 143, 166; and Ewens, *Role of the Nun*, 32. The phenomenal growth in the number of women religious is illustrated in the diocese of Bardstown, Kentucky, where the number of sisters increased from none in 1815 to 260 in 1836.

20. For statistics, see Ewens, *Role of the Nun*, 86, 201.

21. On the "sectarian" pan-Protestantism of the common schools and the anti-Catholicism of textbooks and readers, see Richard Shaw, *Dagger John: The Unquiet Life and Times of Archbishop John Hughes of New York* (New York: Paulist Press, 1977),

139–45; and *PL,* 1:141–42. Even primary spellers acquainted students with words (e.g., nunnery, abbot, monastic, papist) that would help students understand nativist literature; on this, see Ruth Elson, *Guardians of Tradition: American Schoolbooks of the Nineteenth Century* (Lincoln: University of Nebraska Press, 1964), 53, quoted in Ewens, *Role of the Nun,* 162. Timothy L. Smith, "Protestant Schooling and American Nationality," *Journal of American History* 53 (March 1967): 679–95, is the classic treatment of Protestant religious influence on public schools.

22. *PL,* 1:111.

23. For a history of the controversy, see William Oland Bourne, *History of the Public School Society of New York* (New York: George Putnam's Sons, 1873); Shaw, *Dagger John,* 139–75; Vincent P. Lannie, *Public Money and Parochial Education: Bishop Hughes, Governor Seward, and the New York School Controversy* (Cleveland: Press of Case Western Reserve University, 1968); and Hughes, *Works* 1:41–298.

24. See Dolan, *American Catholic Experience,* 262–93, for an account of the varieties of diocesan responses to the development of a Catholic school system.

25. Connelly, *Visit of Archbishop Bedini,* 264–65.

26. Edward J. Power, *A History of Catholic Higher Education in the United States* (Milwaukee: Bruce Publishing Co., 1958), 34, 255. See also Connelly, *Visit of Archbishop Bedini,* 264–65; and Harold A. Buetow, *Of Singular Benefit: The Story of Catholic Education in the United States* (New York: Macmillan, 1970), 117.

27. *PL,* 1:42, 72, 76.

28. Joseph P. Chinnici, *Living Stones: The History and Structure of Catholic Spiritual Life in the United States* (New York: Macmillan, 1989), 50. See also pp. 35–85 for a description of immigrant bishops' views of the spiritual life.

29. Hughes, *Works,* 2:158–69.

30. Emmet Larkin, "The Devotional Revolution in Ireland," *American Historical Review,* 77 (1972): 625–52.

31. Jay P. Dolan, *Catholic Revivalism: The American Experience, 1830–1900* (Notre Dame, IN: University of Notre Dame Press, 1978).

32. [Orestes A. Brownson], "Revivals and Retreats," *Brownson's Quarterly Review* 15 (July 1858): 289–322.

33. Ann Taves, *The Household of Faith: Roman Catholic Devotions in Mid-Nineteenth-Century America* (Notre Dame, IN: University of Notre Dame Press, 1986).

34. Orestes Augustus Brownson, *The Works of Orestes A. Brownson,* coll. and arr. Henry F. Brownson, 20 vols. (Detroit: T. Nourse, 1882–87), 8:316; see also Patrick W. Carey, ed., *Orestes A. Brownson: Selected Writings* (New York: Paulist Press, 1991), 45.

35. O. A. Brownson, "Rights of the Temporal," *Brownson's Quarterly Review* 18 (October 1860): 464–67.

36. Brownson, *Works,* 20:256, 270–71, 274.

37. Ibid., 256.

38. Patrick W. Carey, "American Catholic Romanticism, 1830–1888," *Catholic Historical Review* 64 (October 1988): 590–606.

39. Ahlstrom, *Religious History of the American People,* 597–632.

40. Only a few prominent lay Catholics during the antebellum period (e.g., Mathew Carey, William Gaston, Roger Brooke Taney) became actively involved in American public and political life.

41. *PL,* 1:85.

42. For more information on American Catholics and slavery, see Benjamin J. Blied, *Catholics and the Civil War* (Milwaukee: the author, 1945); Madeline Hooke Rice, *American Catholic Opinion in the Slavery Controversy* (New York: Columbia University Press, 1944); and Joseph D. Brokhage, *Francis Patrick Kenrick's Opinion on Slavery* (Washington, DC: Catholic University of America Press, 1955).

43. John England, *The Works of the Right Reverend John England, First Bishop of Charleston,* coll. and arr. Ignatius A. Reynolds, 5 vols. (Baltimore: John Murphy and Co., 1849), 3:112, 113–91.

44. *PL,* 1:181.

45. See Rice, *American Catholic Opinion,* 12.

46. See, for example, John England, *A Catechism of the Roman Catholic Faith* (Charleston, SC: Henry J. Egan, 1821), quoted in Peter Clarke, *A Free Church in a Free Society: The Ecclesiology of John England, Bishop of Charleston, 1820–1842, a Nineteenth-Century Missionary Bishop in the Southern United States,* 2nd ed. (Hartsville, SC: Center for John England Studies, 1982), 400.

47. Francis P. Kenrick, *Theologia Moralis,* 3 vols. (Philadelphia: Eugenium Cummiskey, 1841–1843), 1:255–57.

48. For a summary of these rights and their sources in the tradition, see Stafford Poole and Douglas J. Slawson, *Church and Slave in Perry County, Missouri, 1818–1865* (Lewiston, NY: Edwin Mellen Press, 1986), 55–58.

49. John Mary Odin to director of the seminary at Lyons, France, 2 August 1823, quoted in ibid., 59.

50. Gaston's speech at Chapel Hill, North Carolina, "Judge Gaston on Slavery," reprinted in *American Catholic Historical Researches* 8 (April 1891): 71.

51. See Rice, *American Catholic Opinion,* 135–36.

52. Quoted in Billington, *Protestant Crusade,* 425.

53. For an account of Catholic participation in the war, see Blied, *Catholics and the Civil War.*

54. Michael V. Gannon, *Rebel Bishop: The Life and Era of Augustin Verot* (Milwaukee: Bruce Publishing Co., 1964), 31.

55. Brownson, *Works,* 17:156.

56. Hughes to Simon Cameron, 2 October 1861, quoted in Shaw, *Dagger John,* 344.

57. On the draft riots, see ibid., 360–69; and Hennesey, *American Catholics,* 154–55.

58. On Hughes's trip, see Shaw, *Dagger John,* 345–54.

59. Hennesey, *American Catholics,* 155.

60. Ewens, "Women in the Convent," in Kennelly, *American Catholic Women,* 26.

61. Spalding's journal of 5 July 1863, quoted in Thomas W. Spalding, *Martin John Spalding: American Churchman* (Washington, DC: Catholic University of America Press, 1973), 142.

62. Gannon, *Rebel Bishop,* 118.

63. Brownson, *Works,* 17:279.

64. Ibid., 12:509.

65. On the purpose and results of this council, see Thomas Spalding, *Martin John Spalding,* 194–237.

66. Quoted in ibid., 197.

67. Ibid., 215, 222.

68. James Parton, "Our Roman Catholic Brethren," *Atlantic Monthly* 21 (April 1868):

432–51, quoted in Dolores Liptak, *Immigrants and Their Church* (New York: Macmillan, 1989), 48.

CHAPTER 4. TOWARD AMERICANISM: 1866–1899

1. For discussions of Americanism, see Robert D. Cross, *The Emergence of Liberal Catholicism in America* (Cambridge, MA: Harvard University Press, 1958); Robert Emmett Curran, *Michael Augustine Corrigan and the Shaping of Conservative Catholicism in America, 1878–1902* (New York: Arno Press, 1978); Gerald P. Fogarty, *The Vatican and the Americanist Crisis: Denis J. O'Connell, American Agent in Rome, 1885–1903* (Rome: Università Gregoriana Editrice, 1974); Thomas T. McAvoy, *The Americanist Heresy in Roman Catholicism, 1895–1900* (Notre Dame, IN: University of Notre Dame Press, 1963); Margaret M. Reher, "The Church and the Kingdom of God in America: The Ecclesiology of the Americanists" (Ph.D. diss., Fordham University, 1972); idem, "Pope Leo XIII and Americanism," *Theological Studies* 34 (December 1973): 679–89; Thomas E. Wangler, "The Ecclesiology of Archbishop John Ireland: Its Nature, Development and Influence" (Ph.D. diss., Marquette University, 1968); and idem, "The Birth of Americanism: 'Westward the Apocalyptic Candlestick,' " *Harvard Theological Review* 65 (July 1972): 415–36.

2. For this interpretation, see the recent studies by James Turner, *Without God, Without Creed: The Origins of Unbelief in America* (Baltimore: Johns Hopkins University Press, 1985); and Philip Gleason "Baltimore III and Education," *U.S. Catholic Historian* 4 (1985): 273–306.

3. Isaac T. Hecker, *The Church and the Age: An Exposition of the Catholic Church in View of the Needs and Aspirations of the Present Age* (New York: Office of the Catholic World, 1887), 2.

4. Ibid., 1–2.

5. For a general background on the council and a discussion of the issues, see Guilday, *History of the Councils of Baltimore*, 221–49; John Tracy Ellis, *The Life of James Cardinal Gibbons, Archbishop of Baltimore, 1834–1921*, 2 vols. (Milwaukee: Bruce Publishing Co., 1952), 1:203–51; and idem, "Episcopal Vision in 1884 and Thereafter," *U.S. Catholic Historian* 4 (1985): 197–222.

6. Found in *Acta et Decreta Concilii Plenarii Baltimorensis Tertii* (Baltimore: Joannis Murphy, 1886).

7. Gleason, "Baltimore III and Education," 273.

8. See Barry, *Catholic Church and German Americans*, 57–58.

9. See Wangler, "Ecclesiology of Archbishop Ireland"; idem, "Birth of Americanism"; and Reher, "Church and the Kingdom of God."

10. On these statistics, see Shaughnessy, *Has the Immigrant?*, 165, 169, 175, 180.

11. For sources on the new immigrants, see Carey, *People, Priests, and Prelates*, 337 n. 12, 15; 338 n. 18, 19.

12. Barry, *Catholic Church and German Americans*, 289–96.

13. Ibid., 11.

14. Reprinted in ibid., 296–312.

15. Henry Joseph Browne, *The Catholic Church and the Knights of Labor* (Washington, DC: Catholic University of America Press, 1949).

16. For the petition, see Ellis, *Documents*, 2:457–60.

17. Ibid., 1:455.

18. On the school question, see Daniel F. Reilly, *The School Controversy (1891–1893)* (Washington, DC: Catholic University of America Press, 1943).

19. In John Ireland, *Church and Modern Society* (New York: D. H. McBride and Co., 1903), 215–32; quote is from p. 217.

20. On the whole question in some detail, see Ellis, *Life of Gibbons,* 1:595–652.

21. J. L. Spalding, "Catholicism and Apaism," *North American Review* 159 (September 1894): 282–83.

22. John J. Keane, "The Ultimate Religion," in John Henry Barrows, ed., *The World's Parliament of Religions,* 2 vols. (Chicago: Parliament Publishing Co., 1893), 2:1331. See also James F. Cleary, "Catholic Participation in the World's Parliament of Religions, Chicago, 1893," *Catholic Historical Review* 55 (January 1970): 585–609.

23. Letter quoted in Frederick J. Zwierlein, *The Life and Letters of Bishop McQuaid: Prefaced with the History of Catholic Rochester before His Episcopate,* 3 vols. (Rochester, NY: Art Print Shop, 1927), 3:224.

24. Letter quoted in Cleary, "Catholic Participation," 605.

25. Sermon in Ellis, *Documents,* 2:461–63.

26. John L. Spalding, *Education and the Higher Life* (Chicago: A. C. McClurg and Co, 1890), 179.

27. For the encyclical, see Ellis, *Documents,* 2:499–511; quote from p. 502.

28. Joseph Schroeder, "Leo XIII and the Encyclical 'Longinqua,' " *American Catholic Quarterly Review* 20 (April 1895): 381–82.

29. On these early attempts at modernism, see R. Scott Appleby, *"Church and Age Unite!" The Modernist Impulse in American Catholicism* (Notre Dame, IN: University of Notre Dame Press, 1992).

30. Joseph Schroeder, "Theological Minimizers and Their Latest Defenders," *American Ecclesiastical Review* 4 (February 1891): 118.

31. *Le Père Hecker Fondateur des "Paulistes" Américains, 1819–1888* (Paris, 1897).

32. On Catholic negotiations prior to the war, see Marvin R. O'Connell, *John Ireland and the American Catholic Church* (St. Paul: Minnesota Historical Society Press, 1988), 441–55.

33. O'Connell to Ireland, Rome, 24 May 1898, quoted in ibid., 455.

34. Republished in Ellis, *Documents,* 2:537–47.

35. Ireland to George Deshon, 24 February 1899, in the Paulist Fathers Archives, quoted in O'Connell, *John Ireland,* 462, and McAvoy, *Americanist Heresy,* 237.

36. Corrigan to Leo XIII, 10 March 1899, quoted in McAvoy, *Americanist Heresy,* 248–49.

37. Katzer to Leo XIII, Pentecost Sunday, 1899, quoted in ibid., 252–53.

CHAPTER 5. PROGRESSIVE ERA CATHOLICISM: 1900–1920

1. Claudia Carlen, *The Papal Encyclicals,* 5 vols. (New York: McGrath, 1981), 3:5–10.

2. See ibid., 3:71–98.

3. On what little modernism there was, see Appleby, *"Church and Age Unite!"*

4. Edward R. Kantowicz, *Corporation Sole: Cardinal Mundelein and Chicago Catholicism* (Notre Dame, IN: University of Notre Dame Press, 1983), 2. See also idem,

"Cardinal Mundelein of Chicago and the Shaping of Twentieth-Century American Catholicism," *Journal of American History* 68 (June 1981): 52–68; James M. O'Toole, *Militant and Triumphant: William Henry O'Connell and the Catholic Church in Boston, 1859–1944* (Notre Dame, IN: University of Notre Dame Press, 1992); and idem, "The Name That Stood for Rome: William O'Connell and the Modern Episcopal Style," in Gerald P. Fogarty, ed., *Patterns of Episcopal Leadership* (New York: Macmillan, 1989), 171–84.

5. On this, see James M. O'Toole, "The Role of Bishops in American Catholic History: Myth and Reality in the Case of Cardinal William O'Connell," *Catholic Historical Review* 77 (October 1991): 595–615.

6. John J. Wynne, *America* 1 (17 April 1909), 5–6.

7. On the missionary union movement, see Thomas J. Jonas, *The Divided Mind: American Catholic Evangelists of the 1890s* (New York: Garland, 1988).

8. Debra Campbell has done the most to uncover something of this early-twentieth-century lay movement in her "David Goldstein and the Lay Catholic Street Apostolate 1917–41," (Ph.D. diss., Boston University, 1982), but she has concentrated on Goldstein and his Boston-based operation; see also idem, "A Catholic Salvation Army: David Goldstein, Pioneer Lay Evangelist," *Church History* 52 (September 1983): 322–32; and idem, "The Rise of the Lay Catholic Evangelist in England and America," *Harvard Theological Review* 79 (October 1986): 413–37. Other local movements still need a historian.

9. For example, the American Federation of Catholic Societies, 1901; the Catholic Educational Association, 1904; the National Conference of Catholic Charities, 1910; the Catholic Press Association, 1911; the Catholic Hospital Association, 1915; and local Catholic social settlement houses. On the latter, see Margaret M. McGuinness, "Response to Reform: The History of the Catholic Social Settlement Movement, 1897–1915," (Ph.D. dissertation, Union Theological Seminary, 1985); and idem, "A Puzzle with Missing Pieces: Catholic Women and the Social Settlement Movement, 1897–1915," Working Paper Series, Charles and Margaret Hall Cushwa Center for the Study of American Catholicism, University of Notre Dame, ser. 22, no. 2 (Spring 1990).

10. Richard T. Ely, "Introduction," in John A. Ryan, *A Living Wage* (New York: Macmillan, 1906), xii–xiii.

11. On the Catholic movement, see Joan Bland, *Hibernian Crusade: The Story of the Catholic Total Abstinence Union of America* (Washington, DC: Catholic University of America Press, 1951).

12. On the suffragist issue, see James J. Kenneally, "A Question of Equality," in Kennelly, *American Catholic Women*, 125–51.

13. A 1906 address to the American Federation of Catholic Societies, quoted in Alfred J. Ede, *The Lay Crusade for a Christian America: A Study of the American Federation of Catholic Societies, 1900–1919* (New York: Garland, 1988), 237.

14. Quoted in ibid., 238.

15. Ellis, *Documents,* 2:540–42.

16. I am indebted to Philip Gleason for this interpretation.

17. Elizabeth McKeown, *War and Welfare: American Catholics and World War I* (New York: Garland, 1988), 74.

18. Ibid., 50.

19. On the program, see *PL,* 1:255–71.

20. Joseph M. McShane, *"Sufficiently Radical": Catholicism, Progressivism, and*

the Bishops' Program of 1919 (Washington, DC: Catholic University of America Press, 1986).

21. Quoted in ibid., 247.

CHAPTER 6. ALIENATION AND ACTIVISM: 1920–1945

1. John A. Ryan, *Declining Liberty and Other Papers* (New York: Macmillan, 1927), 57–58.

2. *Society of Sisters of the Holy Names, Plaintiff, v. Pierce et al., Defendants, Nos. E 8662 and 8660.* For studies and sources on the Oregon law, see David P. Tyack, "The Perils of Pluralism: The Background of the Pierce Case," *American Historical Review* 74 (October 1968): 74–98; Lloyd P. Jorgenson, "The Oregon School Law of 1922: Passage and Sequel," *Catholic Historical Review* 54 (October 1968): 455–66; Christopher Kauffman, *Faith and Fraternalism: The History of the Knights of Columbus, 1882–1982* (San Francisco: Harper and Row, 1982), 281–85; *Oregon School Cases: A Complete Record* (Baltimore: Westminster Press, 1925); and Thomas J. Shelley, "The Oregon School Case and the National Catholic Welfare Conference," *Catholic Historical Review* 75 (July 1989): 439–57.

3. Charles C. Marshall, "Open Letter to the Honorable Alfred E. Smith," *Atlantic Monthly* 139 (April 1927): 540–49.

4. Alfred E. Smith, "Catholic and Patriot: Governor Smith Replies," *Atlantic Monthly* 139 (May 1927): 721–28; quoted in Hennesey, *American Catholics,* 252.

5. On these reforms, see Arnold Sparr, *To Promote, Defend, and Redeem: The Catholic Literary Revival and the Cultural Transformation of American Catholicism 1920–1960* (New York: Greenwood Press, 1990).

6. Philip Gleason, "In Search of Unity: American Catholic Thought 1920–1960," *Catholic Historical Review* 65 (April 1979): 185–205; William M. Halsey, *The Survival of American Innocence: Catholicism in an Era of Disillusionment, 1920–1940* (Notre Dame, IN: University of Notre Dame Press, 1980); Gerald A. McCool, "The Tradition of St. Thomas in North America: At 50 Years," *The Modern Schoolman* 65 (March 1988): 185–206.

7. Quoted in Pope Piux IX's *Studiorum Ducem* (29 June 1923), in Carlen, *The Papal Encyclicals 1903–1939,* 256.

8. Virgil Michel, "The Mission of Catholic Thought," *American Catholic Quarterly Review* 46 (October 1921): 664.

9. Carlen, *Papal Encyclicals,* 3:252.

10. J. Edward Coffey, "Classroom Disease and the Scholastic Prescription," *American Ecclesiastical Review* 69 (July 1923): 34.

11. Ibid.

12. See Marilyn Wenzke Nickels, *Black Catholic Protest and the Federated Colored Catholics, 1917–1933* (New York: Garland, 1988), 303.

13. On the exclusion of African-Americans from the priesthood, see Stephen Ochs, *Desegregating the Altar: The Josephites and the Struggle for Black Priests, 1871–1960* (Baton Rouge: Louisiana State University Press, 1990).

14. For the 1943 and 1958 statements, see *PL,* 2:48, 201–6.

15. On these movements, see David J. O'Brien, *American Catholics and Social Reform: The New Deal Years* (New York: Oxford University Press, 1968).

16. Edward S. Shapiro, "Catholic Agrarian Thought and the New Deal," *Catholic Historical Review* 65 (October 1979): 598.

17. *PL,* 1:436, 438.

18. George Q. Flynn, *American Catholics and the Roosevelt Presidency 1932–1936* (Lexington: University of Kentucky Press, 1968), xi. See also idem, *Roosevelt and Romanism: Catholics and American Diplomacy, 1937–1945* (Westport, CT: Greenwood Press, 1976).

19. Gerhard Lenski, *The Religious Factor: A Sociological Study of Religion's Impact on Politics, Economics, and Family Life* (Garden City, NY: Doubleday, 1963), 173; and Seymour M. Lipset, "Religion and Politics in the American Past," in Robert Lee and Martin E. Marty, eds., *Religion and Social Conflict* (New York: Oxford University Press, 1964), 92–94.

20. On this, see Wilson D. Miscamble, "Catholics and American Foreign Policy from McKinley to McCarthy: A Historiographical Survey," *Diplomatic History* 4 (1980): 223–40.

21. On the different traditions in American Catholicism, see Donald F. Crosby, *God, Church, and Flag: Senator Joseph R. McCarthy and the Catholic Church, 1950–1957* (Chapel Hill: University of North Carolina Press, 1978), 3–25; and Kathleen Riley Fields, "Bishop Fulton J. Sheen: An American Catholic Response to the Twentieth Century" (Ph.D. diss., University of Notre Dame, 1988), 217–310.

22. For an account of American Catholic responses to the crises in Mexico, see James P. Gaffey, *Francis Clement Kelley and the American Catholic Dream,* 2 vols. (Bensenville, IL: Heritage Foundation, 1980), 2:3–73; Robert E. Quirk, *The Mexican Revolution and the Catholic Church, 1910–1929* (Bloomington: Indiana University Press, 1973); Robert H. Vinca, "The American Catholic Reaction to the Persecution of the Church in Mexico, from 1926–1936," *Records of the American Catholic Historical Society* 79 (March 1968): 3–38; and Ellis, *Life of Gibbons,* 2:208–21. On Curley's role, see Spalding, *Premier See,* 349–52; on the bishops' views, see *PL,* 1:337–65, 408–11; on Burke's role, see John B. Sheerin, *Never Look Back: The Career and Concerns of John J. Burke* (New York: Paulist Press, 1975), 108–54.

23. On American Catholic reactions, see J. David Valaik, "American Catholic Dissenters and the Spanish Civil War," *Catholic Historical Review* 53 (January 1968): 537–55; and idem, "Catholics, Neutrality, and the Spanish Embargo, 1937–1939," *Journal of American History* 54 (June 1967): 73–85.

24. Statistics quoted in J. David Valaik, "American Catholics and the Spanish Civil War, 1931–1939" (Ph.D. diss., University of Rochester, 1964), 396–97.

25. On this, see John P. Diggins, *Mussolini and Fascism: The View from America* (Princeton, NJ: Princeton University Press, 1972), 333, 336–37.

26. Ibid., 330–31.

27. On this, see F. K. Wentz, "American Catholic Periodicals React to Nazism," *Church History* 31 (December 1962): 400–20.

28. Carlen, *Papal Encyclicals,* 3:525–37.

29. On this, see Thomas M. Keefe, "The Mundelein Affair: A Reappraisal," *Records of the American Catholic Historical Society* 89 (1978): 74–84.

30. Alden V. Brown, *The Tablet: The First Seventy-Five Years* ([Brooklyn, NY]: Tablet Publishing Co., 1983), 32.

31. Quoted in Fields, "Bishop Sheen," 181, 212 n. 106.

32. Kauffman, *Faith and Fraternalism,* 335–36.

33. Quoted in Saul E. Bronder, *Social Justice and Church Authority: The Public Life of Archbishop Robert E. Lucey* (Philadelphia: Temple University Press, 1982), 63.

34. *PL,* 2:32.

35. Ibid., 37.

CHAPTER 7. COLD WAR CATHOLICISM: 1945–1965

1. For these statistics, see the *Official Catholic Directory* for 1945 and 1965; *PL,* 2:1; and Fields, "Bishop Sheen," 391.

2. *PL,* 2:74.

3. Ibid., 82.

4. I am indebted for information on these family movements to Jeffrey M. Burns, *American Catholics and the Family Crisis 1930–1962* (New York: Garland, 1988).

5. On the censorship, see Robert I. Gannon, *The Cardinal Spellman Story* (New York: Pocket Books, 1963), 423–30; and Paul Blanshard, *American Freedom and Catholic Power* (Boston: Beacon Press, 1949), 180–210.

6. For the papers of this conference, see *Man and Modern Secularism: Essays on the Conflict of the Two Cultures* (New York: National Catholic Alumni Federation, 1940), 45. On Dewey's pragmatic secularism and the American Protestant Neo-Orthodox reaction against it, see George M. Marsden, *Religion and American Culture* (San Diego: Harcourt Brace Jovanovich, 1990), 200–204.

7. John Courtney Murray, "Religious Liberty: The Concern of All," *America* 77 (7 February 1948): 513–16.

8. John Courtney Murray, "Paul Blanshard and the New Nativism," *Month,* n.s. 5 (April 1951): 214–25.

9. *PL,* 3:13.

10. John Tracy Ellis, "American Catholics and the Intellectual Life," *Thought* 30 (Autumn 1955): 353–86; Walter J. Ong, *Frontiers of American Catholicism: Essays on Ideology and Culture* (New York: Macmillan, 1957); Gustave Weigel, "American Catholic Intellectualist—A Theologian's Reflection," *Review of Politics* 19 (July 1957): 275–307; and Thomas F. O'Dea, *American Catholic Dilemma: An Inquiry into the Intellectual Life* (New York: Sheed and Ward, 1958).

11. George Bull, "The Function of a Catholic Graduate School," *Thought* 13 (September 1938): 368, 378.

12. Godfrey Diekmann, "The Primary Apostolate," in Leo Richard Ward, ed., *The American Apostolate: American Catholics in the Twentieth Century* (Westminster, MD: Newman Press, 1952), 29–46. On Diekmann, see Kathleen Hughes, *The Monk's Tale: A Biography of Godfrey Diekmann, O.S.B.* (Collegeville, MN: Liturgical Press, 1991).

13. On postwar developments and conflicts in biblical studies, see Gerald P. Fogarty, *American Catholic Biblical Scholarship: A History from the Early Republic to Vatican II* (San Francisco: Harper and Row, 1989), 222–350.

14. On this, see Rosemary T. Rodgers, "The Changing Concept of College Theology: A Case Study" (Ph.D. diss., Catholic University of America, 1973).

15. For discussions of Murray's stance in this debate, see Donald E. Pelotte, *John Courtney Murray: Theologian in Conflict* (New York: Paulist Press, 1975), 14–17, 152–54; and J. Leon Hooper, *The Ethics of Discourse: The Social Philosophy of*

John Courtney Murray (Washington, DC: Georgetown University Press, 1986), 11–30.

16. Carlen, *Papal Encyclicals,* 4:175–84.

17. The other three were Gregory Baum, O.S.A., from Toronto; George Tavard, A.A., from Mount Mercy College in Pittsburgh; and Edward Hanahoe, S.A., of the Friars of the Atonement at Graymoor, New York.

18. Cited in Patrick W. Collins, "Gustave Weigel: Ecclesiologist and Ecumenist" (Ph.D. diss., Fordham University, 1972), 283–84.

19. On Spellman's position, see Gannon, *Cardinal Spellman Story,* 397. On Murray's positions, see Pelotte, *John Courtney Murray;* and Hooper, *Ethics of Discourse.*

20. *PL,* 2:173.

21. Will Herberg, *Protestant-Catholic-Jew,* rev. ed. (Garden City, NY: Anchor Books, 1960), 260.

22. Andrew M. Greeley, *The Church and the Suburbs* (New York: Sheed and Ward, 1959), 149.

23. Quoted from a 1948 *Christopher News Notes* in Chinnici, *Living Stones,* 197. Some of Keller's best-selling and widely distributed pamphlets and books include *You Can Change the World: The Christopher Approach* (1948), *Three Minutes a Day: Christopher Thoughts for Daily Living* (1949), *Careers That Change Your World* (1950), and *Government Is Your Business* (1951). On Keller, see Chinnici, *Living Stones,* 194–204.

24. For Jackson's criticisms, see Chinnici, *Living Stones,* 201–02; and Peter Michaels, "It Don't Come Naturally," *Integrity* 2 (January 1949): 42–44. See also Debra Campbell, "The Nunk Controversy: A Symbolic Moment in the Search for a Lay Spirituality," *U.S. Catholic Historian* 8 (Winter/Spring 1989): 81–89.

25. Thomas Merton, *The Seven Storey Mountain* (New York: New American Library, 1948), 408.

26. For these statistics, see Fields, "Bishop Sheen," 391.

27. For a good analysis of postwar Chicago Catholicism, see Steven M. Avella, *This Confident Church: Catholic Leadership and Life in Chicago, 1940–1965* (Notre Dame, IN: University of Notre Dame Press, 1992).

28. For a study of *Integrity* Catholics, see James Terence Fisher, "The Limits of Personalism: *Integrity* and the Marycrest Community, 1946–1956," in *The Catholic Counterculture in America, 1933–1962* (Chapel Hill: University of North Carolina Press, 1989), 101–29. On the Grail, see Alden V. Brown, *The Grail Movement and American Catholicism 1940–1975* (Notre Dame, IN: University of Notre Dame Press, 1989).

29. For background on the NCCEM, see *Social Digest* (May-June 1965): 133. The NCCEM needs a historian.

30. "A Personal Note," *Commonweal* 53 (2 February 1951): 413.

31. "What Is Commonweal?," *Commonweal* 59 (5 February 1954): 445.

32. John Cogley, "Some Things Are Not Caesar's," *Today* (November 1951): 12; and Editorial, "The Catholic and Modern Literature," *Commonweal* 56 (16 May 1952): 131.

33. Philip Gleason, "A Browser's Guide to American Catholicism, 1950–1980," *Theology Today* 38 (October 1981): 375.

34. For most of the information in what follows, I am indebted to Avella's *This Confident Church,* 249–88.

35. Quoted in ibid., 261–62, from Report on 8 A.M. Mass at St. Ambrose, 25 June

1950, in Box 2997, Chancery Files, Stritch Papers, Archives of the Archdiocese of Chicago.

36. Ibid., 262, quoting F. J. Quinn to George Casey, Chancellor, 10 July 1950, Box 2997, Chancery Files, Stritch Papers, Archives of the Archdiocese of Chicago.

37. Ibid., 262–63, quoting Stritch to Quinn, 15 September 1950, Box 2997, Chancery Files, Stritch Papers, Archives of the Archdiocese of Chicago.

38. *PL*, 2:48.

39. Ibid., 202.

40. Ibid., 124.

41. For this assessment, see Crosby, *God, Church, and Flag,* 34–36.

42. Ibid., 243.

43. On this development, see Patrick Allitt, "American Catholics and the New Conservativism of the 1950s," *U.S. Catholic Historian* 7 (Winter 1988): 15–37.

44. Ibid., 15.

45. Ibid., 36.

46. For an example of this view, see "No Islands," *Commonweal* 53 (8 December 1950): 221.

47. On this, see Rodger Van Allen, *The Commonweal and American Catholicism: The Magazine, The Movement, The Meaning* (Philadelphia: Fortress Press, 1974), 107–16.

48. William Clancy, "The Liberal Catholic," *Commonweal* 56 (11 July 1952): 335–37. See also "Catholics and Liberals," *Commonweal* 51 (3 February 1950): 452–53; and "The State of Liberalism," *Commonweal* 52 (23 May 1952): 163–64.

49. Fletcher Knebel, "Democratic Forecast: A Catholic in 1960," *Look,* 3 March 1959, 17.

50. "On Questioning Catholic Candidates," *America* 100 (7 March 1959): 651.

51. Quoted in Patricia Barrett, *Religious Liberty and the American Presidency: A Study in Church-State Relations* (New York: Herder and Herder, 1963), 10.

52. Robert McAfee Brown, "Senator Kennedy's Statement," *Christianity and Crisis* 9 (16 March 1959): 25.

53. John F. Kennedy, "The Refutation of Bigotry," in *"Let the Word Go Forth": The Speeches, Statements, and Writings of John F. Kennedy,* ed. Theodore C. Sorensen (New York: Delacorte Press, 1988), 131.

54. For lay Catholic support for the acceptance of the First Amendment, see Barrett, *Religious Liberty and the American Presidency,* 164–66.

55. For this attitude, see Vincent A. Yzermans, ed., *American Participation in the Second Vatican Council* (New York: Sheed and Ward, 1967), 137, 154.

56. On the council, see, e.g., Walter M. Abbott, ed., *The Documents of Vatican II,* trans. Joseph Gallagher (New York: Crossroad, 1989); Yzermans, *American Participation;* Eugene C. Bianchi, *John XXIII and American Protestants* (Washington, DC: Corpus Books, 1968); Robert E. Tracy, *An American Bishop at the Vatican Council: Recollections and Projections* (New York: McGraw-Hill, 1967); Xavier Rynne, *Letters from Vatican City* (New York: Farrar, Straus, 1963); Douglas Horton, *Vatican Diary 1964: A Protestant Observes the Third Session of Vatican Council II* (Philadelphia: United Church Press, 1965); and Albert C. Outler, *Methodist Observer at Vatican II* (Westminister, MD: Newman Press, 1967).

CHAPTER 8. REFORM, PLURALISM, AND CONFLICT: 1965–1990

1. The resolution is printed in *PL*, 3:486.

2. "Declaration on the Relationship of the Church to Non-Christian Religions," art. 2., in Abbott, *Documents of Vatican II*, 662.

3. Douglas Horton, *Vatican Diary 1965: A Protestant Observes the Fourth Session of Vatican Council II* (Philadelphia: United Church Press, 1966), 193.

4. Dialogues with the Lutheran World Federation (1965), Anglican Communion (1966), World Methodist Council (1966), Old Catholic Churches of the Union of Utrecht (1966), World Alliance of Reformed Churches (1968), Pentecostals (1972), Disciples of Christ (1977), Evangelicals (1977), Orthodox Church (1979), and Baptist World Alliance (1984).

5. Bilateral theological conversations have been established with these churches: Eastern Orthodox (1965), Anglican (1965), Lutheran (1965), Presbyterian and Reformed (1965), United Methodist (1966), American Baptist (1967–72), Disciples of Christ (1967–73), Southern Baptist (1978), Oriental Orthodox (1978), and Polish National Catholic (1985). Periodically theologians and bishops have met with classical Pentecostals (although, as yet, there is no official national dialogue with any of the American Pentecostal churches).

6. For a collection of these statements, see Joseph A. Burgess and Jeffrey Gros, eds., *Building Unity: Ecumenical Dialogues with Roman Catholic Participation in the United States, Ecumenical Documents IV* (New York: Paulist Press, 1989). See also George A. Tavard, "Ecumenical Relations," in Adrian Hastings, ed., *Modern Catholicism: Vatican II and After* (New York: Oxford University Press, 1991), 399–421.

7. For examples of these local efforts, see William B. Greenspun and William A. Norgren, eds., *Living Room Dialogues: A Guide for Lay Discussion Catholic-Orthodox-Protestant* (Glen Rock, NJ: National Council of the Churches of Christ in the U.S.A. and Paulist Press, 1965).

8. Burgess and Gros, *Building Unity*, 6.

9. On social mobility, see Andrew M. Greeley, *The American Catholic: A Social Portrait* (New York: Basic Books, 1977). I do not want to make too much of this social mobility, because the American Catholic population was also significantly increased by new Hispanic immigrants (from Mexico, Cuba, Spain, South and Central America, and the Dominican Republic), most of whom were, like the first waves of Irish, poor, uneducated, and without skills needed in an increasingly technological society. By the late 1980s Hispanics constituted almost 20 percent of the American Catholic population.

10. George Gallup, Jr., and Jim Castelli, *The American Catholic People: Their Beliefs, Practices and Values* (Garden City, NY: Doubleday, 1987), 162–63; see also "Portrait of Religion in U.S. Holds Dozens of Surprises," *New York Times*, 10 April 1991, 1.

11. Robert Wuthnow, *The Restructuring of American Religion: Society and Faith since World War II* (Princeton, NJ: Princeton University Press, 1988), 88–90.

12. For these statistics, see "Has the Church Lost Its Soul?," *Newsweek*, 4 October 1971: 80–89.

13. For sociological studies of the clergy shortage, see Richard A. Schoenherr and Annemette Sorensen, "Decline and Change in the U.S. Catholic Church," Report no. 5, *CROS* (Madison: University of Wisconsin, 1981); idem, "Social Change in Religious

Organizations: Consequences of Clergy Decline in the U.S. Catholic Church,'' *Sociological Analysis* 43 (Spring 1982): 23–52; and Dean Hoge, *The Future of Catholic Leadership: Responses to the Priest Shortage* (Kansas City, MO: Sheed and Ward, 1987).

14. Andrew M. Greeley, *American Catholics since the Council: An Unauthorized Report* (Chicago: Thomas More Press, 1985), 130; Andrew M. Greeley and Peter H. Rossi, *The Education of Catholic Americans,* National Opinion Research Center, Monographs in Social Research, no. 006 (Chicago: Aldine Publishing Co., 1966); and Andrew M. Greeley, William C. McCready, and Kathleen McCort, *Catholic Schools in a Declining Church* (Kansas City, MO: Sheed and Ward, 1976).

15. See *Official Catholic Directory* for these years.

16. See "Land O' Lakes Statement: The Nature of the Contemporary Catholic University," in Neil G. McCluskey, ed., *The Catholic University: A Modern Appraisal* (Notre Dame, IN: University of Notre Dame Press, 1970), 336–41.

17. Ibid., 336.

18. Quoted in George A. Kelly, *The Battle for the American Church* (Garden City, NY: Doubleday and Co., 1979), 56.

19. For an attempt to synthesize the relationship between autonomy and communion in Catholic higher education, see Pope John Paul II's *Ex Corde Ecclesiae,* published in *Origins* 20 (4 October 1990): 268–69.

20. Philip Gleason, "Changing and Remaining the Same: A Look at Higher Education," in Stephen J. Vicchio and Virginia Geiger, eds., *Perspectives on the American Catholic Church, 1789–1989* (Westminster, MD: Christian Classics, 1989), 228.

21. On this judgment, see Conference Board of Associated Research Councils, *An Assessment of Research-Doctorate Programs in the United States,* 5 vols. (Washington, DC: National Academy Press, 1982); Greeley, *American Catholics Since the Council,* 145–47; Ellis, "American Catholics and the Intellectual Life"; Paul Reinert, "In Response to Father Greeley," *Jesuit Educational Quarterly* 29 (October 1966): 124–25; National Catholic Educational Association, "A Working Paper: The Future Development of Catholic Institutions of Higher Education," 15 September 1966; and Greeley, "Why Catholic Higher Learning Is Lower," *National Catholic Reporter,* 23 (September 1983): 5. I am indebted to William P. Leahy, *Adapting to America: Catholics, Jesuits, and Higher Education in the Twentieth Century* (Washington, DC: Georgetown University Press, 1991), 136–47, for these sources and his own interpretations.

22. "Justice in the World," in Austin Flannery, *Vatican Council II: More Postconciliar Documents* (New York: Costello Publishing Co., 1983), 90.

23. On this, see *PL,* vols. 3, 4, and 5.

24. For statistics on the Catholic Left, see Charles A. Meconis, *With Clumsy Grace: The American Catholic Left 1961–1975* (New York: Seabury Press, 1979), 153–66. On the peace movement in general, see Patricia McNeal, *Harder Than War: Catholic Peacemaking in Twentieth-Century America* (New Brunswick, NJ: Rutgers University Press, 1992).

25. Richard Curtis, *The Berrigan Brothers* (New York: Hawthorn Books, 1974), 53–57.

26. For these statistics, see "Has the Church Lost Its Soul?," 89.

27. Andrew M. Greeley, "L'Affaire Berrigan," *New York Times,* 19 February 1971, L:37.

28. Thomas Merton, "A Note for *Ave Maria,*" in *Thomas Merton on Peace,* ed. Gordon Zahm (New York: McCall Publishing Co., 1971), 231–33.

29. *American Catholic People,* 77–90.

30. "Resolution on El Salvador," March 1981, in *PL,* 4:437.

31. *PL,* 4:215–26. For a list of the 182 recommendations and the NCCB's graded response to each one, see Joseph A. Varacalli, *Toward the Establishment of Liberal Catholicism in America* (Washington, DC: University Press of America, 1983), 263–94.

32. "To Do the Work of Justice," in *PL,* 4:243–54.

33. *The Challenge of Peace,* 1983; *Economic Justice for All,* 1986; and the first drafts of *Partners in Redemption,* 1988, 1989.

34. Michael Novak et al., *Toward the Future: Catholic Social Thought and the U.S. Economy, A Lay Letter* (Lay Commission on Catholic Social Teaching and the U.S. Economy, 1984); see also, Michael Novak, " 'Pastoral' of Lay Group Stresses Morality of Economic Systems," *Catholic Herald,* 10 January 1985, 9.

35. Gallup and Castelli, *American Catholic People,* 181.

36. Ibid., 85–87, 89.

37. Ibid., 67.

38. For example, Lawrence Lucas, an African-American priest in New York, published his *Black Priest/White Church: Catholics and Racism* (New York: Random House, 1970), pointing out in some detail the racism that influenced decisions and pastoral programs.

39. Statement in Gayraud Wilmore and James Cone, eds., *Black Theology: A Documentary History, 1966–1979* (Maryknoll, NY: Orbis Books, 1979), 322–24.

40. For personal accounts of the history of the NOBC, see Joseph M. Davis and Cyprian Rowe, "The Development of the National Office for Black Catholics," *U.S. Catholic Historian* 7 (Spring/Summer 1988): 265–89.

41. These figures are based on a Gallup calculation that 70 percent of all Hispanics in the United States are Catholic (Gallup and Castelli, *American Catholic People,* 139–48) and on Hispanic population statistics supplied by Moises Sandoval, *On the Move: A History of the Hispanic Church in the United States* (Maryknoll, NY: Orbis Press, 1990), 88–89.

42. National Conference of Catholic Bishops, *The Hispanic Presence, Challenge, and Commitment: A Pastoral Letter on Hispanic Ministry,* 12 December 1983, in *PL,* 5:42–64.

43. Gallup and Castelli, *American Catholic People,* 139–48, 185.

44. Rosemary Radford Ruether, "The Place of Women in the Church," in Hastings, *Modern Catholicism,* 260.

45. For Catholic reactions to the ERA, see James J. Kenneally, "Women Divided: The Catholic Struggle for an Equal Rights Amendment, 1923–1945," *Catholic Historical Review* 75 (April 1989): 249–63; idem, "A Question of Equality," in Kennelly, *American Catholic Women,* 125–51; and Gallup and Castelli, *American Catholic People,* 103–6.

46. Mary Ewens, "Women in the Convent," in Kennelly, *American Catholic Women,* 41.

47. For an example of such a critique, see Marie Augusta Neal, *From Nuns to Sisters: An Expanding Vocation* (Mystic, CT: Twenty-Third Publications, 1990), 37 and passim.

48. By 1967, 68 percent of women religious had at least a college education. By 1980, 88 percent had college educations and 68 percent of these had postgraduate degrees in almost every discipline. For these statistics, see ibid., 31–32.

49. Gallup and Castelli, *American Catholic People,* 56.

50. "Vatican Declaration: Women in the Ministerial Priesthood," *Origins* 6 (3 February 1977): 517, 519–24. For criticisms of the document, see Leonard and Arlene Swidler, eds., *Women Priests: A Catholic Commentary on the Vatican Declaration* (New York: Paulist Press, 1977). For support, see Donald Keefe, "The Sacrament of the Good Creation: Prolegomena to the Discussion to the Ordination of Women," *Faith and Reason* 9 (Summer 1983): 143–54; and idem, "Gender, History and Liturgy in the Church," *Review for Religious* 46 (November/December 1987): 866–81.

51. On this definition, see Richard A. McCormick, "Moral Theology 1940–1989: An Overview," *Theological Studies* 50 (March 1989): 10.

52. Kenneally, *History of American Catholic Women,* 191, quoting Dorothy Dohen, *Women in Wonderland* (New York, 1960), 92.

53. In 1971 *Newsweek* conducted a survey that indicated that 58 percent of American Catholics believed that they could ignore the pope's condemnation of artificial contraception and remain good Catholics; only 31 percent believed the contrary. See, "Has the Church Lost Its Soul," *Newsweek* 4 October 1971, 81. See also, Gallup and Castelli, *American Catholic People,* 50; and Greeley, *American Catholics since the Council,* 80–100.

54. In 1969, 72 percent of Catholics considered premarital sex wrong; by 1985 only 33 percent considered it wrong. On this, see Gallup and Castelli, *American Catholic People,* 50–51; and Greeley, *American Catholics since the Council,* 85.

55. Kelly, *Battle for the American Church,* 129–98.

56. Gallup and Castelli, *American Catholic People,* 91.

57. *PL,* 3:199. The NCCB has published explicit statements against abortion in 1969, 1970, 1973, 1975, 1985, and a host of other documents where abortion is not the primary focus.

58. McCormick, "Moral Theology 1940–1989," 10.

59. Kenneally, *History of American Catholic Women,* 199.

60. See Gallup and Castelli, *American Catholic People,* 91–102.

61. Anthony Kosnik et al., *Human Sexuality: New Directions in American Catholic Thought* (New York: Paulist Press, 1977), 211–16.

62. Gallup and Castelli, *American Catholic People,* 63–64.

63. "Political Responsibility: Choices for the 1980s," March 1984, in *PL,* 5:95, 108.

64. "Archbishop Calls Ferraro Mistaken on Abortion Issue," *New York Times,* 10 September 1984, A:1.

65. For Ferraro's position, see " '82 Letter Signed by Ferraro," *New York Times,* 11 September 1984, A:26.

66. For the speech, entitled, "Religious Belief and Public Morality: A Catholic Governor's Perspective," see *Notre Dame Magazine* (Autumn 1984): 21–30.

67. For Hyde's speech on 24 September 1984, see "Keeping God in the Closet," in Richard McMunn, *Religion in Politics* (Milwaukee: Catholic League for Religious and Civil Rights, 1985), 39–56.

68. "U.S. Catholicism: A Church Divided," *Time,* 24 May 1976, 59.

69. Gallup and Castelli, *American Catholic People,* 42.

70. For some studies of the charismatic renewal, see Kevin and Dorothy Ranaghan, *Catholic Pentecostals* (New York: Paulist Press, 1969); Edward D. O'Connor, *The Pentecostal Movement in the Catholic Church* (Notre Dame, IN: Ave Maria Press, 1971); Joseph Fichter, *The Catholic Cult of the Paraclete* (New York: Sheed and Ward, 1975); Kilian McDonnell, ed., *Open the Windows: The Popes and the Charismatic Renewal* (South Bend, IN: Greenlawn Press, 1989); and Terrence R. Crowe, "Towards a Common Witness: A Comparative Study of the Assemblies of God and the Catholic Charismatic Renewal" (Ph.D. diss., Marquette University, 1991).

71. For these statistics on RENEW, see Michael P. Hornsby-Smith, "RENEW: Institutional Renewal or Modernist Heresy?," *American Catholic Studies Newsletter* 18 (Spring 1991).

72. Gallup and Castelli, *American Catholic People*, 43.

73. On the conservative reaction, see William Dinges, "Catholic Traditionalism in America: A Study of the Remnant Faithful" (Ph.D. diss., University of Kansas, 1983).

74. For example, James Hitchcock, *The Decline and Fall of Radical Catholicism* (New York: Herder and Herder, 1971), George A. Kelly, "The Uncertain Church: The New Catholic Problem," *Critic* (Fall 1976): 14–26; idem, *The Battle for the American Church* (Garden City, NY: Doubleday, 1979); Thomas Molnar, *The Church: Pilgrim of Centuries* (Grand Rapids, MI: W. B. Eerdmans, 1990); the publication of an *International Catholic Review: Communio* (1974) and *Catholicism in Crisis* (1982–86; later called *Crisis*, 1986–); and the organization of the Fellowship of Catholic Scholars (1978).

75. Joseph Fenton, "Rome and the Status of Catholic Theology," *American Ecclesiastical Review* 143 (December 1960): 409.

76. David Tracy, *Blessed Rage for Order: The New Pluralism in Theology* (New York: Seabury Press, 1975), 3f.

77. The appeal condemned thirteen current themes it so characterized. On the appeal, see Avery Dulles, *The Resilient Church: The Necessity and Limits of Adaptation* (Garden City, NY: Doubleday and Co., 1977), 191–95.

78. Tracy, *Blessed Rage*, 10, 34.

79. Philip Gleason, *Keeping the Faith: American Catholicism Past and Present* (Notre Dame, IN: University of Notre Dame Press, 1987), 5.

Part Two
A BIOGRAPHICAL DICTIONARY OF ROMAN CATHOLIC LEADERS

ABBREVIATIONS FOR STANDARD REFERENCE SOURCES

AER   *American Ecclesiastical Review*, 1889–1975 (also called *Ecclesiastical Review*, 1905–43).

CA1948   *Catholic Authors: Contemporary Biographical Sketches, 1930–47*, ed. Matthew Hoehn (Newark, NJ: St. Mary's Abbey, 1948).

CA1952   *Catholic Authors: Contemporary Biographical Sketches*, ed. Matthew Hoehn (Newark, NJ: St. Mary's Abbey, 1952).

CE   *Catholic Encyclopedia*, 16 vols. (New York: Robert Appleton, 1907–12).

CH   *Church History*, 1932–.

CHR   *Catholic Historical Review*, 1915–.

DAB   *Dictionary of American Biography*, ed. Allen Johnson and Dumas Malone, 20 vols. (New York: C. Scribner's Sons, 1928–58; Seven Supplements, 1973–).

DACB   *Dictionary of American Catholic Biography*, ed. John Delaney (Garden City, NY: Doubleday, 1984).

DAH   *Dictionary of the American Hierarchy, 1789–1964*, by Joseph Bernard Code (New York: Joseph F. Wagner, 1964).

DARB   *Dictionary of American Religious Biography*, by Henry Warner Bowden (Westport, CT: Greenwood Press, 1977).

DCA   *Dictionary of Christianity in America*, ed. Daniel G. Reid et al. (Downers Grove, IL: InterVaristy Press, 1990).

DCB   *Dictionary of Catholic Biography*, by John J. Delany and James Edward Tobin (Garden City, NY: Doubleday, 1961).

NAW   *Notable American Women, 1607–1950: A Biographical Dictionary*, ed. Edward T. James et al., 3 vols. (Cambridge, MA: Belknap Press of Harvard University Press, 1971–80).

NAWM   *Notable American Women, Modern Period: A Biographical Dictionary*, ed. Barbara Sicherman et al. (Cambridge, MA: Belknap Press of Harvard University Press, 1980).

NCAB	*National Cyclopedia of American Biography,* 74 vols. to date (New York and Clifton, NJ: J. T. White, 1893–).
NCE	*New Catholic Encyclopedia,* 15 vols. (New York: McGraw-Hill, 1967–79); vols. 16–18, *Supplements* (Washington, DC: Publishers Guild, 1974–88).
NCR	*National Catholic Reporter,* 1966–.
NYT	*New York Times,* 1851–.
RACHS	*Records of the American Catholic Historical Society of Pennsylvania,* 1884–.
SH	*New Schaff-Herzog Encyclopedia of Religious Knowledge,* ed. Samuel M. Jackson et al., 13 vols. (New York: Funk and Wagnalls, 1908–12; Grand Rapids, MI: Baker, 1963–67).
TS	*Theological Studies,* 1940–.
U.S.CH	*U.S. Catholic Historian,* 1981–.

BIOGRAPHICAL SKETCHES

A

ABBELEN, PETER M. (8 August 1843, Germany—24 August 1917, Milwaukee, WI). *Education:* Gaesdonk, Munich, Germany; St. Francis Sem., Milwaukee. *Career:* ordained, 1868; pastor at Chippewa Falls, La Crosse, and Prairie du Chien, WI, 1868–75; spiritual director, School Sisters of Notre Dame, Milwaukee, 1876–1917; preparatory work for Third Plenary Council of Baltimore, 1884; vicar general, Milwaukee archdiocese, 1906–17; domestic prelate, 1907–17.

Throughout his clerical career, Abbelen was a forceful and articulate advocate for the preservation of German language and culture, which he perceived as the cradle of Catholicism. With the support of Milwaukee's Archbishop Michael Heiss, the German clergy of the archdiocese, and those of the archdiocese of St. Louis, Abbelen went to Rome in 1886 to petition for legislation assigning German immigrants only to national German parishes and their children only to German parochial schools. Abbelen's petition was eventually rejected, but it was significant as the beginning of a major cultural division in American Catholicism that eventually lead to the encyclical *Testem Benevolentiae* (1899).

Bibliography

A. "Memorial on the German Question . . . ," in Coleman J. Barry, *The Catholic Church and German Americans* (Milwaukee, 1953), 289–96; *Venerable Mother Caroline M. Friess: First Commissary General of the School Sisters of Notre Dame in America* (St. Louis, 1893).

B. NCE, 1:6; *Milwaukee Journal,* 24 August 1917, 5.

ALEMANY, JOSEPH SADOC (13 July 1814, Vich, Spain—14 April 1888, Valencia, Spain). *Education:* studied at diocesan seminary, Vich, Spain, 1824–28. *Career:* joined Dominicans, 1830; ordained, 1837; sub-master of Dominican novices at Viterbo, Italy, and assistant rector of Church of Santa Maria Sopra Minerva, Rome, 1837–41; missionary work in OH, KY, and TN, 1841–47; provincial of American Dominicans, 1848–50; bishop of Monterey, CA, 1850–53; archbishop of San Francisco, 1853–84; retired as titular archbishop of Pelusium, Egypt, 1884–88.

After spending nine years of missionary work in Dominican foundations in Ohio, Kentucky, and Tennessee, Alemany was appointed the first bishop of Monterey. His knowledge of Spanish, French, and English as well as his American administrative experience within a religious order made him a likely episcopal candidate to help resolve some of the problems associated with the erection of the first diocesan see in former Mexican territory, where the Franciscan Indian missions had been operating since 1769 and where the gold rush of 1849 had begun to transform the territory. He spent thirty-four years working in what is now Nevada, Utah, California, and Baja California. Lack of priests, opposition from the Mexican government to his appointment, and only a few usable churches made his ministry difficult during the first years of his episcopacy. He did succeed, however, in securing from the Mexican government part of the interest derived from the forced sale of church lands in 1848. After his promotion as the first archbishop of San Francisco, he attended Vatican I (1869–70), where he was a member of one of the commissions exploring papal infallibility, a doctrine that he favored and promoted. In 1884 he chaired an episcopal commission at the Third Plenary Council of Baltimore that examined and promoted a uniform catechism for American Catholics. After the council he resigned from his archdiocesan see and retired to Valencia, Spain, where he tried to rebuild the Dominican order.

Bibliography

B. DACB, 17; DAH, 2–3; DCB, 29; NCE, 1:284–85; Gaynor Maddox, "Joseph Sadoc Alemany, O.P., Archbishop of San Francisco," *Historical Records and Studies* 8 (1915): 223–27; Francis J. Weber, *A Biographical Sketch of Right Reverend Joseph Sadoc Alemany, Bishop of Monterey, 1850–1853* (Van Nuys, CA, 1961); John B. McGloin, *California's First Archbishop: The Life of Joseph Sadoc Alemany, O.P., 1814–1888* (New York, 1966).

AVERY, MARTHA GALLISON MOORE (6 April 1851, Steuben, ME—8 August 1929, Medford, MA). *Career:* charter member, First Nationalist Club of Boston, 1888; joined Socialist Labor Party, 1891; lecturer and member of Massachusetts state committee, Socialist Labor Party, 1892–95; founder, Karl Marx Class, 1896; delegate, national convention of Daniel De Leon's Socialist Trade and Labor Alliance, 1898; Socialist candidate for Massachusetts state treasurer, 1898; lecturer and writer on labor reform and antisocialist issues, 1902–29; cofounder, Catholic Truth Guild, 1917; Catholic lay apostolate, 1917–29.

Reared as a Unitarian, Martha Moore Avery became during the late nineteenth century a socialist propagandist and in the early twentieth century an active Catholic lay apostle. Distress over the effects of industrialization on the American spirit and concern for the plight of workers drove Avery into the incipient American socialist movement in the late nineteenth century. By the late 1890s she met David Goldstein, a fellow socialist, and together they established and managed the Karl Marx Class (in 1901 renamed the Boston School of Political Economy), a forum for socialist lectures and discussions. By 1902, however, both Avery and Goldstein became disillusioned with socialism and began to see it as a fundamental threat to the family and society when the party continued to attack religion and advocate violence and free love.

In 1904, influenced by her daughter's conversion to Catholicism and by Catholic social thinking, she became a Catholic. From 1904 until her death in 1929 she used her propagandist skills, acquired during her socialist period, to attack socialism through her writings, public lecturing, and street preaching. She emphasized social reform via nonsocialist means, promoted Pope Leo XIII's encyclical *Rerum Novarum,* supported labor unions, and refocused her School of Political Economy along these lines. She was also a leader in the Catholic lay group Common Cause Society and was its president from 1922 to 1929. In 1916, with the approval of Boston's Cardinal William O'Connell, she began to preach and teach on street corners and became a founding member of the Catholic Truth Guild. Although she remained a strong advocate for economic and social justice, she disapproved of labor violence, women's suffrage, and birth control.

Bibliography

A. With David Goldstein, *The Nation of Fatherless Children* (Boston, 1903; 2nd ed., 1911); *Bolshevism: Its Cure* (Boston, 1919); *Campaigning for Christ* (Boston, [1924]); "Is Socialism the Remedy?," *Irish World* 24 (January 1903, 4–5; "The Spread of Social Disorder," *America* 14 (6 November 1915); 78–79.

B. NAW, 1:69–71; *American Catholic Who's Who,* 1911; David Goldstein, *Autobiography of a Campaigner for Christ* (Boston, 1936); James J. Kenneally, "Catholicism and Woman Suffrage in Massachusetts," *CHR* 53 (April 1967): 43–57; D. Owen Corrigan, "Martha Moore Avery: Crusader for Social Justice," *CHR* 54 (April 1968): 17–38; idem, "A Forgotten Yankee Marxist," *New England Quarterly* 42 (March 1969): 23–43; Debra Campbell, "David Goldstein and the Lay Catholic Street Apostolate, 1917–41" (Ph.D. diss., Boston University, 1982).

B

BADIN, STEPHEN T. (17 July 1768, Orléans, France—19 April 1853, Cincinnati, OH). *Education:* studied at Sulpician Sem., Orléans, 1789–91; St. Mary's Sem., Baltimore, MD, 1792–93. *Career:* ordained, 1793; pastor, various places in KY, OH, IN, IL, MI, and TN, 1793–1819; pastor, various places in France, 1819–26; itinerant pastor, diocese of Cincinnati, 1826–53.

Badin was one of the first students to graduate from St. Mary's Seminary in Baltimore. An emigré from the French Revolution, he became Bishop John Carroll's first vicar in the Old West. As a pioneer priest, he helped to settle Catholicism in Kentucky and was instrumental in bringing the first bishop, Benedict Flaget, to Bardstown. He was also an apologist for Catholicism on the frontier, publishing two tracts to answer charges about Catholic tenets and their influence on American social and political life. He left Kentucky to return to France in 1819 because of a contentious battle with Bishop Flaget over the ownership of church property. He returned to the United States in 1826 and became a priest in the new diocese of Cincinnati, where he became a missionary priest to the Potawatomi Indians in Indiana and Michigan and where he traveled up and down the Ohio Valley serving newly arrived immigrant Catholics.

Bibliography

A. *The Real Principles of Roman Catholics* (Bardstown, KY, 1805); *Origine et progrès de la mission du Kentucky, Etats Unis d'Amérique, par un témoin oculaire* (Paris, 1821); "The Church in Kentucky: Letters of the Reverend Stephen Theodore Badin to Bishop Carroll," *RACHS* 19 (1908): 258–75, 455–82; 23 (1912): 141–74; *Summary Proofs of the Catholic Doctrine from the Scriptures,* 4th ed. (Detroit, 1829).

B. DAB, 1:488–89; DACB, 27–28; NCE, 2:12; Martin J. Spalding, *Sketches of the Early Catholic Missions of Kentucky, 1787–1827* (Louisville, 1844); J. Herman Schauinger, *Stephen T. Badin: Priest in the Wilderness* (Milwaukee, 1956).

BARRY (LAKE), LEONORA MARIE (13 August 1849, Kearney, County Cork, Ireland—15 July 1930, Minooka, IL). *Career:* teacher, St. Lawrence County, NY, 1865; joined Knights of Labor, 1884; organizer for the Knights of Labor, 1886–89; suffragist and temperance advocate, 1890–1928.

The only child of John and Granger (Brown) Kearney, Leonora emigrated with her parents to the United States in 1852, settling on a farm in Pierrepont, St. Lawrence County, NY. In 1871 she married William E. Barry, an Irish painter and musician. The Barrys gave birth to three children, one of whom died at the age of eight. Upon William's death in 1881, Leonora became the sole support for herself and her two sons. She took a job as an unskilled laborer in a garment factory in Amsterdam, NY, earning wages of sixty-five cents for her first week's work. The low pay and the terrible condition of workers in the mill led her to join the Knights of Labor in 1884. She rose through the local and state ranks of that organization and eventually worked full-time for it from 1886 to 1890. During these years she traveled throughout the country seeking reforms in working conditions and attempting to organize the women members of the Knights of Labor. She found the latter task difficult because of apathy, timidity, and internal struggles within the organization. Barry is credited with helping enact the first Pennsylvania Factory Inspection Act of 1889, even though she refused to lobby among legislators because she considered such behavior unladylike. After her marriage in 1890 to Obadiah Read Lake, a printer, proof-reader, and telegraph editor for the *St. Louis Globe-Democrat,* she resigned from her position with the Knights of Labor because she believed that married women should work outside the home only in cases of economic necessity.

In subsequent years she became active in the women's suffrage movement, successfully campaigning in Colorado in 1893. That same year she addressed the congress of women at the World's Columbian Exposition in Chicago on "The Dignity of Labor." She belonged to the Women's Christian Temperance Union, was an officer of the Catholic Total Abstinence Union of America, and the founder of the Catholic Women's Temperance Union. She exerted much effort for enforcement of the Volstead Act and continued public-speaking engagements until 1928. Afflicted with cancer of the mouth, she died in 1930 at Minooka, IL, which had been her home since 1916.

Bibliography

B. NAW, 1:101–2 (under Barry); *Who's Who in America,* 1914–15 (under Barry); *Women's Who's Who of America,* 1914–15 (under Lake); *Joliet Herald-News,* 16 July 1930; Joan Bland, *Hibernian Crusade: The Story of the Catholic Total Abstinence Union of America* (Washington, DC, 1951).

BAUER, MOTHER BENEDICTA (17 July 1803, Pielenhofen, Germany— 13 October 1865, Racine, WI). *Career:* entered Dominicans, Holy Cross Convent, Ratisbon, Germany, 1820; teacher, Holy Cross Convent school, 1822–45; prioress, Holy Cross Convent, 1845–58; missionary sister, various places in USA, 1858–62; founding mother superior, St. Catherine of Siena Convent, Racine, WI, 1862–65.

From 1845 to 1858 Bavarian-born Mother Benedicta (née Maria Anna Bauer) played a significant role as superior of her order at the Ratisbon Dominican convent. She sent numerous missionary sisters from Germany to the United States to establish parochial schools for German-speaking immigrants. The Ratisbon convent directly established American Dominican foundations in Brooklyn, NY (1853), and from this first convent numerous other convents were directly or indirectly founded: e.g., Jersey City, NJ (1872), Mission San Jose, CA (1876), Grand Rapids, MI (1877), Everett, WA (1890), Adrian, MI (1892), and Great Bend, KS (1902).

In 1858 Mother Benedicta herself came to the United States, where she served in convents in Brooklyn, Ohio, Tennessee, and Green Bay, WI. In 1862 and 1863, in spite of financial hardship during the Civil War, she and two companions built a permanent independent Dominican motherhouse (St. Catherine of Siena) and parochial school at Racine, WI. By the time of her death in 1865, she had four additional educational institutions under her supervision in various parts of Wisconsin and had increased the membership in her Dominican community to eight professed sisters, seven novices, and eleven candidates. She began what would become a large Dominican community in the twentieth century.

Bibliography

B. Mary Hortense Kohler, *Life and Work of Mother Benedicta Bauer* (Milwaukee, 1937).

BISHOP, WILLIAM HOWARD (19 December 1885, Washington, DC—11 June 1953, Norton, VA). *Education:* studied at Harvard Univ., 1906–1908; St. Mary's Sem., MD, 1909–15. *Career:* ordained, 1915; pastor, parishes in diocese of Baltimore, 1915–36; founder and superior, Glenmary Home Missioners, 1937–53; founder, Glenmary Home Mission Sisters, 1939.

Born to a patrician Southern family, William Bishop became involved during the progressive era in the home mission movement. After his ordination in 1915, he served in rural parishes in the diocese of Baltimore, where he became acquainted with the loneliness and difficulties of rural life. In the course of his years as a rural pastor, he became familiar with Francis Clement Kelley and the Catholic Church Extension Society, the Maryknoll founders Thomas F. Price and James A. Walsh, Vincent O'Hara and the Rural Life Movement, and Walter Elliott and Alexander Doyle's Paulist Catholic Missionary Union, a movement in American evangelization and home missions. These movements were concerned with spreading, developing, and maintaining the faith in rural areas and foreign territories. Bishop caught their spirit and, as a rural pastor, began to consider new methods to evangelize, maintain old rural parishes, and establish new ones.

Encouraged by James A. Walsh and supported by Cincinnati's Archbishop John McNicholas, Bishop decided at the age of fifty-two to found a new religious order of priests whose fundamental purpose would be mutual support in serving the rural parishes throughout the United States. He was particularly concerned about what he and subsequent Glenmary Home Missioners called priestless territories and counties in the United States. Under the patronage of Archbishop McNicholas, therefore, he founded at Glendale, OH, an indigenous American order of priests (1937) and one of women religious (1939) to focus upon the religious life of rural Americans. By the time of his death in 1953, he had established a seminary and monastic house for the missionaries and a magazine (the *Challenge,* 1938–) for mutual support and communication, and had seven rural missions throughout the United States, twenty-one Glenmary priests, eleven brothers, fifty-one students for the priesthood, sixteen women religious, and twenty-six novices.

Bibliography

A. "Putting Romance into Farming," *Catholic Rural Life* 6 (November 1927): 1-2; "Considering the Other Sheep," *Landward* 4 (Summer 1936): 2; "Our Frontier Mission," *Landward* 5 (Summer-Autumn 1937): 4; "The Conquest of No Priest Land," *Challenge* 2 (Christmas 1939): 4; "Home Mission Vocation," *Challenge* 2 (Christmas 1939): 6.
B. DACB, 47; NCE, 2:584-85; Robert Hoffman, "Father Bishop, The Story of His Death," *Challenge* 16 (Autumn 1953): 14; Herman W. Santen, *Father Bishop, Founder of the Glenmary Home Missions* (Milwaukee, 1961); Christopher J. Kauffman, *Mission to Rural America: The Story of W. Howard Bishop, Founder of Glenmary* (New York, 1991).

BRÉBEUF, JEAN DE (25 March 1593, Condé, France—16 March 1649, French Canada). *Education:* studied at Univ. of Caen, France, 1609-10; Jesuit Coll., Rouen, France, 1617–22. *Career:* entered Jesuits, Rouen, 1617; ordained, 1622; procurator, Coll. of Rouen, 1623; missionary, French Canada, 1625–29; missionary, France, 1629–33; missionary, French Canada, 1633–49.

Jean de Brébeuf was one of the Jesuit missionaries in French Canada who tried to adapt himself to the Indian way of life in order to win the Indians over to Catholic Christianity. In the late 1630s and early 1640s he became one of the cofounders of the Jesuits' mission to the Hurons below the Georgian Bay— an experiment that tried to provide a regular program of evangelization and Christian communal living in the wilderness, where the Indians were far removed from a French Canadian civilization that was being established in Quebec and Montreal. The experiment drew a number of Hurons into the Jesuit communities, but in 1649 the Hurons, the newly established Christian communities, the Jesuit missionaries, and Brébeuf were massacred by an Iroquois uprising. The missions below the Georgian Bay never survived the Iroquois war.

Bibliography

A. *Travels and Sufferings of Father Jean de Brébeuf among the Hurons of Canada as Described by Himself,* trans. Theodore Besterman (London, 1938).
B. NCE, 10: 506; P. Felix Martin, *Hurons et Iroquois: le Père Jean de Brébeuf* (Paris, 1898); Francis Xavier Talbot, *Saint among the Hurons: The Life of Jean de Brébeuf* (New York, 1949); René Latourelle, *Etude sur les ecrits de Saint Jean de Brébeuf* (Montreal, 1952–53); Joseph P. Donnelly, *Jean de Brébeuf, 1593–1649* (Chicago, 1975).

BRENT, MARGARET (1601 (?), England—1671 (?) Virginia).

Very little is known of Margaret Brent's early life. She emigrated to Maryland in 1638 where, under the orders of Lord Baltimore, she and her siblings were given extensive land holdings. She gradually acquired more, becoming the first woman in Maryland to hold land in her own right. As her wealth increased she lent large amounts of money, and court records indicate that she was a frequent plaintiff seeking redress from her debtors. She led a small body of volunteers in support of the Calvert government during Claiborne's rebellion in 1645. Brent was later executrix for Governor Leonard Calvert, and in this capacity she was involved in much litigation. Her handling of his estate was contested by his heirs, but she was supported by the state assembly. In 1646 she became her brother Giles's attorney. She left for Virginia in 1650 and died there around 1671.

Bibliography

B. DACB, 61–62; W. B. Chilton, "The Brent Family," *Virginia Magazine* 13–21 (1903–13): pass.; Agnes Repplier, "The Elusive Lady of Maryland," *CW* 138 (1933–34): 660–69.

BROWNSON, ORESTES AUGUSTUS (16 September 1803, Stockbridge, VT—17 April 1876, Detroit, MI). *Education:* studied at Balston Acad., Balston Spa, NY, 1818–19. *Career:* schoolteacher, Detroit, 1823–24; Elbridge, NY, 1824–26; ordained Universalist minister, Jaffrey, NH, 1826; Universalist preacher, Hartland, VT, Lichtfield, Ithaca, Geneva, Auburn, NY, 1826–30; corresponding editor, the *Free Enquirer,* 1829–30; editor, *Genesee Republican and Herald of Reform,* 1829–30; political organizer for Workingman's Party, 1829–30; unaffiliated minister in Ithaca, 1831; founding editor, the *Philanthropist,* 1831–32; Unitarian minister, Walpole, NH, 1832–34; Canton, MA, 1834–36; editor, the *Boston Reformer,* 1836–38; organizer and minister, the Society for Christian Union and Progress, Boston, 1836–38; founding editor, *Boston Quarterly Review,* 1838–42; staff, *United States and Democratic Review,* 1842–44; founding editor, *Brownson Quarterly Review,* 1844–64, 1873–75; independent journalist and author, 1844–76.

Orestes Brownson was the foremost American Catholic lay theologian and philosopher of the nineteenth century. At the age of three his father died, and because of his mother's poverty he was, at the age of six, taken from her and raised by relatives. This early experience of separation and poverty had a lasting influence upon his life and thought, making him sensitive to the plight of the poor and the need for communion, central ideas in his later published works. Throughout his life, moreover, Brownson was an active and restless religious pilgrim, manifesting something of the diversity of religious options in early-nineteenth-century America and the fluidity of ecclesiastical affiliation.

His father was a Presbyterian, his mother a Universalist, and after the age of six he was raised in a Calvinist-Congregationalist home. He experienced a religious conversion at age thirteen during a Methodist revival and in 1822 became a Presbyterian. In 1826 he was ordained a Universalist minister, and in 1829 he rejected his Universalism and joined the Workingman's Party, where he devoted himself to causes of social justice. Influenced by William E. Channing, he became a Unitarian minister in 1832 but left the ministry in 1838, moving more and more in the direction of a religious socialism. In 1844 he converted to Catholicism, and he remained in it for the rest of his life, but even within this tradition he vacillated between various Catholic approaches to American culture.

Despite the vicissitudes of his religious and intellectual pilgrimage, Brownson continued to develop in dialectical fashion throughout his life a concept of "life by communion" that he appropriated in 1842 from the French St. Simonian Pierre Leroux. For Brownson God's creative act establishes a dialectical harmonious communion between divine sovereignty and human dependence. That divine creative act is manifested most perfectly and definitively in the Incarnation of the Word. The continuing presence of the Incarnate Word is made manifest in the church. The church thus becomes the medium through which God's creative act and the Incarnation bind a community of believers transcendentally to God, Christ, and history. Thus the church is a historical organism that continually seeks to appropriate and express in outward tradition the inner tradition of God's creative Word.

In a variety of ways and with obvious as well as subtle changes, Brownson applied his doctrine of the dialectical harmony of the divine and the human to his understanding of the individual, the church, society, government, the emerging industrial and economic order, and literature. In the period before the Civil War he focused on the necessity of the church for salvation and for societal peace and harmony. In the period after the war he, like Pope Pius IX, concentrated his intellectual guns on what he perceived to be a rising secularism in science, politics, and religion. Although he criticized the direction of American society after the war, he emphasized the necessity of preserving in dialectical harmony and tension the American spirit of freedom and the Catholic sense of authority and community.

Bibliography

A. *Boston Quarterly Review,* 1838–42; *Brownson's Quarterly Review,* 1844–64, 1873–75; *The Works of Orestes A. Brownson,* ed. Henry F. Brownson, 20 vols. (Detroit, 1882–87); *A Guide to the Microfilm Edition of the Orestes A. Brownson Papers* (Notre Dame, IN, 1966); *The Brownson-Hecker Correspondence,* ed. and intro.

Joseph F. Gower and Richard M. Leliaert (Notre Dame, IN, 1979); *Selected Writings: Orestes A. Brownson,* ed. Patrick W. Carey (New York, 1991).
B. DAB, 3:178–79; DACB, 65–66; DARB, 72–74; NCAB, 7:197; NCE, 2:827–29; NYT, 18 April 1876, 7; SH, 2:281; Henry F. Brownson, *Life of Orestes Brownson,* 3 vols. (Detroit, 1898–1900); Arthur M. Schlesinger, Jr., *Orestes A. Brownson: A Pilgrim's Progress* (Boston, 1939); Theodore Maynard, *Orestes Brownson: Yankee, Radical Catholic* (New York, 1943); Americo D. Lapati, *Orestes A. Brownson* (New York, 1965); Thomas R. Ryan, *Orestes A. Brownson: A Definitive Biography* (Huntington, IN, 1976).

BURKE, JOHN JOSEPH (6 June 1875, New York, NY–30 October 1936, Washington, DC). *Education:* B.A., St. Francis Xavier Coll. (NY), 1896; S.T.B., The Catholic University of America, 1899; S.T.L., 1901. *Career:* joined the Paulists, 1896; ordained, 1899; assistant editor and editor, *Catholic World,* 1903–22; general secretary, National Catholic Welfare Conference, 1919–36.

John Joseph Burke represented the moderately progressive party in American Catholicism during the early twentieth century. As editor of the *Catholic World,* he continued the nineteenth-century focus on Americanization; by 1910 he concentrated on social work, theories of society, and social reforms.

Burke was an Irish-American organizer, and with these skills he made his greatest impact on the history of American Catholics and American society. He helped found the Catholic Press Association in 1911, pioneered in establishing the Paulist Press, organized the Chaplains' Aid Society in 1917, and most significantly, conceived and helped establish the National Catholic War Council in 1917 to unite Catholic efforts to respond to the American war effort.

After the war Burke became the general secretary of the National Catholic Welfare Conference and remained the leading organizer in that organization until his death. Although he feared the centralization and growth of federal government, he used centralized Catholic efforts (the NCWC) to lobby in Washington for Catholic causes across the country. He helped organize protests against the Oregon school case, campaigned behind the scenes against secularization in Mexico, organized apologetical responses to the defeat of Alfred E. Smith, and helped organize efforts in behalf of Catholic education. Burke was also involved in promoting the American Catholic Bishops' Program of Social Reconstruction after the war, trying to focus episcopal attention on the need for progressive economic and social reforms to respond to injustices in American society.

Bibliography
A. Editorials in the *Catholic World,* 1910–22; *St. Theresa: An Autobiography* (New York, 1911); *Christ in Us: Meditations* (Philadelphia, 1934); *Lent and the Mass* (New York, 1936); *Pray for Us: A Collection of Prayers for Various Occasions* (New York, 1936).
B. DAB, 22:72–74; DACB, 70–71; DARB, 78–79; NYT, 31 Oct. 1936, 19; John B. Sheerin, *Never Look Back: Biography of John Burke* (Paramus, NJ, 1975); Elizabeth McKeown, *War and Welfare: American Catholics and World War I* (New York, 1988).

C

CABRINI, FRANCES XAVIER (1 July 1850, Sant'Angelo Lodigiano, Italy—22 December 1918, Chicago, IL). *Education:* studied under Daughters of the Sacred Heart, Arluno, Italy, 1863–68. *Career:* teacher, Vidardo, Italy, 1872–74; Cadogno, 1874–80; founder and mother general of Missionary Sisters of the Sacred Heart, 1880–1917.

In 1880 at the age of thirty, Frances Cabrini established the Missionary Sisters of the Sacred Heart to provide spiritual or corporal help primarily to Italian emigrants. Nine years later, at the invitation of Archbishop Michael Corrigan of New York, she emigrated to the United States, where the Missionary Sisters began working for the immigrants in "Little Italy" in New York City. During the first thirty years of their development, the sisters established schools, hospitals, and orphanages and carried on home and prison visitations, teaching basic Christian doctrines and providing needed social services. Mother Cabrini extended this apostolate to the working class beyond New York into New Jersey, Pennsylvania, Louisiana, Mississippi, Illinois, Colorado, Washington, and California.

At her death sixty-seven missionary communities of over four thousand women religious could be found not only in the United States, but in Nicaragua, Chile, and Argentina. Her industry and steadfastness were manifested by her expertise in providing spiritual and human services, and in her abilities in administration and finance. Mother Cabrini was beatified (1938), canonized a saint (1946), the first American citizen to be so designated, and declared "Patroness of Emigrants" (1950).

Bibliography

B. DAB, 1:146–48; DACB, 78–79; DARB, 81–82; NAW, 1:274–76; NCAB, 27:476–77; NCE, 2:1039; Theodore Maynard, *Too Small a World: The Life of Francesca Cabrini* (Milwaukee, 1945); Pietro Di Donato, *Immigrant Saint: The Life of Mother Cabrini* (New York, 1960); Mary L. Sullivan, *Mother Cabrini, Italian Immigrant of the Century* (New York, 1984); idem, ''Mother Cabrini: Missionary to Italian Immigrants,'' *U.S.CH* 6 (Fall 1987): 25–81.

CALVERT, CECIL (1606, London, England—30 November 1675, London, England). *Education:* studied at Trinity Coll., Oxford, 1621. *Career:* second Lord Baltimore, 1632; proprietor, Colony of Maryland, 1634–75.

Cecil was the eldest son of Anne Myrme and George Calvert, the first Lord Baltimore. In 1632, after his father's death, he inherited the province of Maryland which King Charles I had granted to his father. Cecil, like his father a Catholic, obtained a charter for the colony, gathered Protestant as well as Catholic investors in the new colony, invited the Jesuits Andrew White and John Altham to provide for the colony's religious needs, appointed his brother Leonard to be governor of the colony in 1633, and in 1634 sent colonists to Maryland to further his own and his investors' profits, to fortify the English presence in the New World, and to extend Christianity. Cecil also saw the colony as an experiment in religious toleration. Although he invited Jesuits to the colony, he did so on the grounds that they would be financially self-supporting and subject to civilian control. In 1649, after the death of Charles I and seven years of civil and religious war in England, Cecil had prepared for Maryland ''The Act Concerning Religion'' to protect Catholics as well as others in the free exercise of Christian worship. Calvert twice lost control of the governorship and proprietorship of Maryland to Virginia Puritans, and spent much of his time in England trying to protect his rights and regain what he had lost. When he died in London in 1675, Maryland was again under his proprietary control.

Bibliography

A. Donna M. Ellis and Karen A. Stuart, *The Calvert Papers: Calendar and Guide to the Microfilm Edition* (Baltimore, 1989).
B. DACB, 81–82; DARB, 84–85; NCAB, 7:331–32; NCE, 2:1086; William H. Browne, *George Calvert and Cecilius Calvert: Barons of Baltimore* (New York, 1890); Thomas O'Brien Hanley, *Their Rights and Liberties: The Beginnings of Religious and Political Freedom in Maryland* (Westminster, MD, 1959).

CALVERT, GEORGE (1580, Yorkshire, England—15 April 1632, London, England). *Education:* B.A., Trinity Coll., Oxford, 1597; M.A., 1605. *Career:* clerk of the crown of assize and peace in County Clare, Ireland, 1606; secretary to Lord Robert Cecil, 1606–12; clerk of the privy council, 1613; member of Virginia Company, 1609–20; member of Parliament, 1609–24; knighted, 1617; an under secretary of state, 1619; baron of Baltimore, Longford County, Ireland, 1625; granted province of Maryland, 1632.

George Calvert was the son of Alice Grosland and Leonard Calvert, Catholics who became Anglicans in the face of penal laws. After his education at Oxford and some experience as a minor government official, he became a member of Parliament and a staunch defender of King James I's policies. From 1609 to

1625 he served in a number of responsible governmental positions, being appointed, for example, as a special emissary to France in 1610 at the accession of Louis XIII. In 1620, already having been involved in the colonial Virginia Company, he purchased the Colony of Avalon in Newfoundland and tried to establish a colony there in 1623, but it failed. In 1625, the year Charles I became king of Great Britain and Ireland, Calvert returned to the Catholicism of his youth and, because of it, resigned his seat in Parliament and his position as under secretary of state. In the late 1620s he petitioned King Charles I for colonial lands near Virginia and, after much opposition from the Virginia Company, the king granted him the colony of Maryland. Calvert died in 1632, however, before the charter for Maryland was finalized. His son Cecil inherited the charter and developed the colony.

Bibliography

B. DAB, 3:428–29; DACB, 82–83; DCB, 200–01; NCE, 2:1086; Clayton Colman Hall, *The Lords Baltimore and the Maryland Palatinate* (Baltimore, 1902); Bernard C. Steiner, "The First Lord Baltimore and His Colonial Projects," *Annual Report of the American Historical Association* 1 (1905): 109–22; John Bailey Calvert Nicklin, "The Calvert Family," *Maryland Historical Magazine* 16 (1921): pass.

CAREY, MATHEW (28 January 1760, Dublin, Ireland—16 September 1839, Philadelphia, PA). *Career:* printer's apprentice, *Hibernia Journal,* Dublin, 1775–79; editor, *Freeman's Journal,* Dublin, 1780–83; founder, *Volunteer's Journal,* Dublin, 1783; founder, *Philadelphia Evening Herald,* 1785; cofounder, *Columbian Magazine,* 1786; founder, the *American Museum,* 1787–92; established the Carey publishing firm, 1792–93; director, Bank of Pennsylvania, 1802–1805; founder, Philadelphia Society for the Promotion of National Industry, 1820.

Born the son of relatively prosperous middle-class, Irish Catholic parents, Christopher and Mary Sheridan Carey, Mathew had the advantage of a good education, and by the age of fifteen he was already publishing articles in journals, a practice that he continued for the remainder of his life. At nineteen Carey published his first pamphlet, *The Urgent Necessity of an Immediate Repeal of the Whole Penal Code* (1779), and because it disturbed both conservatives and Irish Catholics, he was forced to flee to France, where he met the marquis de Lafayette and Benjamin Franklin, for whom he worked as a printer's apprentice. He returned to Ireland in 1780, became editor of the *Freeman's Journal,* and established the *Volunteer's Journal,* both of which were pro-American and anti-English. In 1784 the young Carey was imprisoned for publishing an article and cartoon that were considered libelous. After being released from prison he emigrated to Philadelphia.

In Philadelphia Carey continued his publishing interests. In 1786 he cofounded the *Columbian Magazine,* and in 1787 he independently established the *American Museum,* the first nationally distributed literary journal—one that gained for him a national reputation. By 1792 Carey established a bookstore and shortly thereafter a publishing firm that became the nation's largest in the early nineteenth century. Carey also became prominent in American political discussions, siding with the Madisonian and Jeffersonian pro-French Republicans against the pro-British Federalists after 1792. When Jefferson became president, Carey's fortunes began to rise with his appointment to the board of the Bank of Pennsylvania in 1801. In 1814 he published *The Olive Branch* to reconcile opposing parties during the War of 1812. The book quickly became the most widely read political book since *Common Sense,* going through ten editions by 1819. On the economic front Carey supported a strong national bank, wrote at least forty separate works on protectionism by 1826, and continued to write on national economic issues for the remainder of his life.

Carey was also a supporter of the common good and an advocate of social justice. He helped establish the Hibernian Society (1792) for the relief of Irish immigrants, a Sunday School Society (1796) to promote the religious education of youth, and the Philadelphia Society for the Promotion of National Industry to promote a protection tariff for American workers and small manufacturers. He also wrote numerous essays and pamphlets to promote the establishment of public charities, to advocate justice for poor working women, and to support prison reforms. He was a strong public advocate for political freedom and emancipation for the Irish, Greeks, and Polish. He also published pamphlets favorable to the African Colonization movement of the 1820s. In ecclesiastical affairs he published the first Catholic (Douay) Bible in the United States and numerous Catholic apologetical, doctrinal, and devotional works, and he became involved in the trustee debates over William Hogan. Because of his personal charities and his general involvement in the public life of Philadelphia, his funeral procession in 1839 was, after Stephen Girard's, the longest the city had ever seen.

Bibliography

A. *The Olive Branch* (Philadelphia, 1814); *Essays in Banking* (Philadelphia, 1816); *Vindiciae Hibernicae* (Philadelphia, 1818); *Letters on Religious Persecution* (Philadelphia, 1827); *Miscellaneous Essays* (Philadelphia, 1830); "Autobiography," *New England Magazine* (November 1833–December 1834; reprint, Brooklyn, NY, 1942); *An Appeal to the Wealthy of the Land* (Philadelphia, 1836).

B. DAB, 3:489-91; DACB, 86–87; NCAB, 6:278; NCE, 3:108; Earl L. Bradsher, *Mathew Carey, Editor, Author and Publisher* (1912; reprint, New York, 1966); Kenneth W. Rowe, *Mathew Carey: A Study in American Economic Development* (Baltimore, 1933); William Clarkin, *Mathew Carey: A Bibliography of His Publications* (New York, 1984); James N. Green, *Mathew Carey: Publisher and Patriot* (Philadelphia, 1985).

CARROLL, AUSTIN (23 February 1835, Clonmel, County Tipperary, Ireland—29 November 1909, Mobile, AL). *Career:* Sister of Mercy, Cork, Ireland, 1853–56; Sister of Mercy, Providence, 1856–69; foundress, Sisters of Mercy, New Orleans, 1869–1909.

From the time she was eighteen, Mother Austin (née Margaret Anne) Carroll was a Sister of Mercy, following the example and spirit of Mother Catherine McAuley, foundress of the Irish Sisters of Mercy. In 1856 Sister Austin came to the United States to teach the poor in Providence. Following the McAuley spirit, which was to help the poor to help themselves, she taught in various convent academies, helped in soup kitchens, worked in homes for women, helped run a day-care center for children of working women, and participated in sodalities for girls and boys. She continued these works throughout the South after 1869, when she was sent to New Orleans and where she established the Sisters of Mercy. In New Orleans the Sisters of Mercy developed a chapel in a prison, regularly visited, nursed, and provided medicine for the sick, opened an employment bureau for women, and set up a free food and clothing pantry for the poor. By the time of her death in 1909, the Sisters of Mercy had opened sixty-five schools in Louisiana, Florida, Alabama, Mississippi and Belize (Central America), fourteen convents, thirty-eight libraries, and nine residences for orphans, the elderly, and working women. While carrying out these spiritual and corporal works of mercy, Sister Austin also wrote a biography of the foundress of her order, published some forty other books, composed numerous articles for American and Irish journals, and translated a number of spiritual works from French and Spanish sources.

Bibliography

A. *Life of Catherine McAuley* (New York, 1865); *Happy Hours of Childhood: A Series of Tales for the Little Ones* (New York, 1867); *Life of St. Alphonsus Ligouri, Bishop and Doctor of the Church* (New York, 1874); *Leaves from the Annals of the Sisters of Mercy,* 4 vols. (New York, 1881–95); *A Catholic History of Alabama and the Floridas* (1908; reprint, New York, 1970).
B. Mary Heremina Muldrey, *Abounding in Mercy: Mother Austin Carroll* (New Orleans, 1988); Mary Ewens, "Women in the Convent," in *American Catholic Women: A Historical Exploration,* ed. Karen Kennelly (New York, 1989), 28–32.

CARROLL, CHARLES (19 September 1737, Annapolis, MD—14 November 1832, Baltimore, MD). *Education:* studied at Jesuit Bohemian Manor Acad. (MD), 1747; St. Omer's Coll., Flanders, Belgium, 1748–54; Jesuit coll., Rheims, France, 1754–55; law school, Bruges, Belgium, 1756; law school at the Temple, London, 1757–58; Coll. Louis le Grand, Paris, 1759. *Career:* elected to Maryland provincial convention, 1774; member of Committee of Correspondence, 1775; Maryland Association of the Freeman, 1775; deputy to Maryland State convention, 1775; Continental Congress's mission to Canada with Benjamin Franklin, Samuel Chase, and John Carroll, 1776; signer, Declaration of Independence, 1776; elected to Continental Congress, 1776; appointed to Board of War, 1776; Maryland state senator, 1778; US Senator, Maryland, 1789–92.

Charles Carroll was the son of Elizabeth Brooke and Charles Carroll II of Annapolis, wealthy plantation owners. After receiving a cosmopolitan education in Europe, he returned in 1765 to Maryland, where his father gave him Carrollton Manor, a ten thousand-acre plantation. From that time forward he signed his name Charles Carroll of Carrollton to distinguish himself from his father. He married his cousin Mary Darnall in 1768; she gave birth to seven children, two of whom outlived him.

Carroll returned to Maryland at a time of high political turmoil and escalating difficulties with England. By 1770 he became a spokesman for the resistance to what was considered unfair and unjustified colonial taxation. Writing under the pen name "First Citizen" in the *Maryland Gazette,* he protested against the jurist Daniel Dulaney's support of new Maryland taxes. Influenced by Enlightenment cries of civil and religious liberties, he supported the people's right to armed resistance and independence from England, becoming a member of the Continental Congress, a signer of the Declaration of Independence, and an instrumental cause in Maryland's decision to support independence. Also in 1776 the Continental Congress sent Carroll, his cousin John, an ex-Jesuit priest, Benjamin Franklin, and Samuel Chase to Canada to solicit support for independence, but the mission failed. Throughout the Revolutionary War he played a major role in the Board of War and in the Maryland State Constitutional Convention as a state senator. After the war he participated in discussions on the United States Constitution and Bill of Rights. Except for his debates with Dulaney, his Catholicism was not a significant issue in his role as political advocate and statesman. As a strong supporter of the Federalist Party, he opposed Thomas Jefferson's election to the presidency in 1800. Although he also opposed the War of 1812, he commented only periodically on political matters after Jefferson's election and withdrew into semiretirement from public life. He died in 1832, the last surviving signer of the Declaration of Independence.

Bibliography

A. *Letters of the First Citizen, Journal of Charles Carroll of Carrollton,* appendices to vol. 1 of Kate Mason Rowland, *Life and Correspondence of Charles Carroll of Carrollton, 1737-1832, with His Correspondence and Public Papers,* 2 vols. (New York, 1898); *Unpublished Letters of Charles Carroll of Carrollton, and of his Father, Charles Carroll of Doughoregan,* ed. Thomas Meagher Field (New York, 1902).
B. DAB, 3:522–23; DACB, 89–90; NCAB, 7:441; NCE, 3:149–150; Joseph Gurn *Charles Carroll of Carrollton, 1737–1832* (New York, 1932); Ellen Hart Smith, *Charles Carroll of Carrollton* (Cambridge, MA, 1942; reprint, New York, 1971); Thomas O'Brien Hanley, *Charles Carroll of Carrollton: The Making of a Revolutionary Gentleman* (Washington, DC, 1970; Chicago, 1982); idem, *Revolutionary Statesman: Charles Carroll and the War* (Chicago, 1983).

CARROLL, DANIEL, II (22 July 1730, Upper Marlborough, MD—7 May 1796, Rock Creek, MD). *Career:* Maryland state senator, 1777–80; member, Continental Congress, 1780–84; member, U.S. House of Representatives, 1780–91; signer, Articles of Confederation, 1781; signer, US Constitution, 1787; member, Constitutional Convention, 1787–88.

Daniel Carroll, elder brother of Bishop John Carroll, was an active Maryland landowning patriot and politician who not only supported the American Revolution but participated in the major events that shaped the writing of the Constitution. He was a Federalist, as were a number of the Maryland Catholic gentry, who encouraged Maryland voters to support and ratify the Constitution as the "best form of government which has ever been offered to the world." He also became one of four Catholic laymen, representing American Catholics, who signed an address of congratulations to George Washington when he was elected president of the new republic. His farm, moreover, was one of four that were transferred to the federal government as the site for the new capital, in Washington, DC.

Bibliography

A. *Maryland Journal* 16 October 1787, 5–6; *Carroll's Letters to Madison,* in *Madison Papers,* Library of Congress, summary in Bernard C. Steiner, "Maryland's Adoption of the Federal Constitution," *American Historical Review* 5 (October and December 1899): 22–44, 207–24.

B. DAB, 3:523–24; DACB, 90; NCAB, 2:389–90; NCE, 3:150–51; Mary Virginia Geiger, *Daniel Carroll: A Framer of the Constitution* (Washington, DC, 1943).

CARROLL, JOHN (19 January 1736, Upper Marlborough, MD—3 December 1815, Baltimore, MD). *Education:* studied at Jesuit Bohemian Manor Acad. (MD), 1747; St. Omer's Coll., Flanders, Belgium, 1748–53; Jesuit education in philosophy and theology at Watten, Liège, and Bruges, Belgium, 1755–62. *Career:* entered Society of Jesus and novitiate, 1753–55; ordained, 1761; philosophy teacher, Liège, 1762–67; teacher, Bruges, 1767–69; Jesuit tertianship at Ghent, Belgium, 1770; tutor to Charles-Philip, son of Lord Stourton, 1771–73; missionary priest in Maryland, 1774–83; superior of American missions, 1784; bishop of Baltimore, 1789–1808; archbishop of Baltimore, 1808–15.

In 1774, after twenty-six years of education and teaching in Europe, thirty-eight-year-old John Carroll, saddened and disturbed by the political and ecclesiastical machinations that brought about the papal suppression of the Jesuits, returned home to Maryland to become an ex-Jesuit missionary. Maryland at the time was in the midst of his cousin Charles Carroll's "First Citizen" debates with Daniel Dulaney over taxation and representation, and the country was experiencing the effects of the organization of the first Continental Congress in Philadelphia. John Carroll stayed clear of the debates and served missions in Maryland and occasionally in Virginia. In 1776, however, in the midst of revolutionary talk, he reluctantly accompanied Charles Carroll, Samuel Chase, and Benjamin Franklin on a mission to Canada to solicit support for the Revolution. By the Treaty of Paris in 1783, Carroll and other ex-Jesuits, reflecting the times in which they lived, were scrambling to establish a quasi-constitutional form of government among themselves to protect their property rights and govern themselves in serving Catholics in a free country where religious tolerance of Catholics had been increasing significantly since the beginning of the Revolution.

As superior of the American missions and first bishop and archbishop of Baltimore, Carroll became the primary organizer of Catholic institutions in the United States and set the tone for the participation of Catholicism in a new and free republican context. He supervised the establishment of Georgetown College (1791), St. Mary's Sulpician Seminary (1791), the first diocesan synod (1791), the diocesan suffragan sees of Boston, New York, Philadelphia, and Bardstown, KY (1808), and Mother Elizabeth Seton's Sisters of Mercy (1809). After the Louisiana Purchase, he also provided ecclesiastical administration for Louisiana and the two Floridas (1805–15) until a new bishop was appointed. He cooperated, too, with Marylanders in founding St. John's College (Annapolis, 1789) and became a member of the board of trustees of Baltimore College (1803).

John Carroll, like many of his fellow Americans, fits into the wide ambit of the Enlightenment. His advocacy of rational religion, the reasonableness of Catholic Christianity, religious liberty, separation of church and state, voluntaryism, ecclesiastical reforms, tolerance of and respect for other religious traditions, and republican political theory reveal some of the dominant concerns of the Age of Reason. Although Carroll wrote no systematic treatises on any of these, many of his personal letters, pastoral programs, and occasional apologetic writings reveal his enthusiastic acceptance of them.

Bibliography

A. *An Address to the Roman Catholics of the United States of America* (Annapolis, MD, 1784); *The John Carroll Papers,* ed. Thomas O'Brien Hanley, 3 vols. (Notre Dame, IN, 1976).
B. DAB, 3:526–28; DACB, 91–92; DAH, 37; DARB, 90; NCAB, 1:480–82; NCE, 3:151–54; D. Brent, *Biographical Sketch of the Most Reverend John Carroll* (Baltimore, 1843); John G. Shea, *The Life and Times of the Most Reverend John Carroll* (New York, 1888); Peter Guilday, *The Life and Times of John Carroll,* 2 vols. (New York, 1922; reprint, Westminster, MD, 1954); Annabelle M. Melville, *John Carroll of Baltimore: Founder of the American Hierarchy* (New York, 1955); James Hennesey, "An Eighteenth-Century Bishop: John Carroll of Baltimore," *Archivum Historiae Pontificiae* 16 (1978): 171–205; Thomas W. Spalding, "John Carroll: Corrigenda ad Addenda," *CHR* 71 (October 1985): 505–18.

CODY, JOHN PATRICK (24 December 1907, St. Louis, MO—25 April 1982, Chicago, IL). *Education:* North American Coll., Rome, 1926–32; S.T.D., J.C.D., Pontifical Institute of the Apollinaris, Rome, 1932. *Career:* ordained, 1931; staff, Vatican Secretariate of State, Rome, 1933–38; secretary, Archbishop John Glennon, St. Louis, 1938–40; pastoral work in St. Louis, 1938–47; auxiliary bishop, St. Louis, 1947; coadjutor bishop and administrator, St. Joseph, MO, 1954–55; coadjutor bishop and administrator, Kansas City, MO, 1956; coadjutor bishop, New Orleans, 1961; apostolic administrator, New Orleans, 1962; archbishop of New Orleans, 1964; archbishop of Chicago, 1965–82; cardinal, 1967–82.

Returning to St. Louis in 1938 after a thorough Roman experience and education, John Patrick Cody eventually became another of the bright, young, ultramontane episcopal leaders of post–World War II American Catholicism. After episcopal duties in St. Louis, St. Joseph, MO, and Kansas City, MO, he went to New Orleans where, under Archbishop Joseph Rummel, he became a strong advocate between 1961 and 1965 for the rights of African-Americans within the church's schools. He was also a member of the Second Vatican Council's preparatory Commission on Seminaries, Universities, and Catholic Schools. During the council he made only one speech before the bishops, calling for acceptance of the council's Declaration on Christian Education and for the establishment of a post-conciliar commission to investigate more thoroughly the problems (peculiar to each nation) of education in the modern world.

From 1965, when he was made archbishop of Chicago, until the end of his life he became the center of controversy in the post-conciliar church of Chicago, where his pre-conciliar exercise of ecclesiastical authority conflicted sharply with new models of episcopal leadership. Although he instituted reforms within diocesan administration (dividing it into twelve vicariates), raised revenues (through "Project Renewal") for the modernization of parishes and schools, and allowed for the establishment of an independent Association of Chicago Priests (1966) and the Presbyterial Senate (1971), his authoritarian style of leadership in dismissing ineffectual pastors and failing to follow the advice of the new clerical associations created an adversarial relationship between him and numbers of his clergy. The Priests' Association in 1971 voted to censure him and his auxiliaries for not representing their views at the National Conference of Catholic Bishops.

In 1968 Cody provoked some conflict in Chicago when he supported a plan that would bus minority children out of overcrowded, inner-city schools to predominantely white schools in suburban neighborhoods. In 1975 his decision to close several inner-city schools with predominantly minority children for budgetary reasons again brought denouncements upon him. His program of associating poor inner-city parishes with wealthier suburban parishes for resource sharing and his overall commitment to the minority community in the inner city brought praise from the archdiocese's African-American clergy, but his style of leadership did not endear him to the white clergy. When he died in 1982, he was under investigation for improper use of church funds, a charge that was refuted when the grand jury refused to hand down an indictment against him. Although he made great strides in justice and racial equality, his episcopal tenure was challenged by a decline in vocations and respect for episcopal authority, departures from the priesthood, and other difficulties associated with the immediate post–Vatican II era.

Bibliography

B. DACB, 104–05; DAH, 44; NCE, 18:101; NCR, 7 May 1982, 4; NYT, 26 April 1982, B:14; Charles W. Dahm, *Power and Authority in the Catholic Church: Car-*

dinal Cody in Chicago (Notre Dame, IN, 1981); Harry C. Koenig, ed., *Caritas Christi Urget Nos: A History of the Archdiocese of Chicago,* 2 vols. (Chicago, 1981).

CONWAY, KATHERINE ELEANOR (6 September 1853, Rochester, NY—2 January 1927, Boston, MA). *Career:* asst. editor, *Catholic Union Times,* Buffalo, NY, 1880–83; assoc. editor, Boston *Pilot,* 1883–1905; managing editor, 1905–1908; managing editor, the *Republic,* Boston, 1908–11; adjunct professor, St. Mary's College, Notre Dame, IN, 1911–15; retired, 1915–27.

Katherine Conway was a novelist, essayist, and managing editor of the Boston *Pilot* who frequently wrote for Catholic periodicals on the moral virtues of marriage. Her activities also included lecturing in Catholic circles on topics that promoted conservative Catholic moral values and opposed women's suffrage. Periodically she charged that the right to vote diverted women from being homemakers, which was their divinely ordained role. After the World's Columbian Congress (Chicago, 1893), she published a paper, "Woman Has No Vocation to Public Life," that outlined her view on women's roles in society. Ironically she was an energetic public servant and political activist, serving as a member of the Massachusetts Prison Commission, the Massachusetts Association Opposed to the Further Extension of Suffrage to Women, president of the New England Women's Press Association, and trustee of the Boston Public Library. She also taught at St. Mary's College (IN) from 1911 to 1915, where she had a formative influence on Sister Madeleva Wolff. She supported education for women, but she thought it should be exercised only in gender-segregated reading circles and literary clubs.

Bibliography

A. *A Lady and Her Letters; Questions of Honor in the Christian Life; Lalor's Maples* (Boston, 1901); *Bettering Ourselves,* 3d ed. (Boston 1904).
B. *American Women Writers: A Critical Reference Guide from Colonial Times to the Present,* 4 vols., ed. Lina Mainiero (New York: Ungar, 1979–82), 1:393:94; DACB, 112; Myra B. Lord, *History of the New England Women's Press Association, 1885–1930* (Newton, MA, 1932); Paula M. Kane, "The Pulpit of the Hearthstone: Katherine Conway and Boston Catholic Women, 1900–1920," *U.S.CH* 5 (Summer/Fall 1986): 355–70; James J. Kenneally, *The History of American Catholic Women* (New York, 1990), 132–33.

CORCORAN, JAMES ANDREW (30 March 1820, Charleston, SC—16 July 1889, Philadelphia, PA). *Education:* S.T.D., Urban Coll., Rome, 1842. *Career:* ordained, 1842; professor of theology, Charleston Sem., 1843–48; editor, *United States Catholic Miscellany,* 1848–61; pastor, Wilmington, NC, 1861–68; theological advisor, Vatican I, 1869–70; professor of theology, St. Charles Borromeo Sem., Philadelphia, 1871–89; founding editor, *American Catholic Quarterly Review,* 1876–89.

Corcoran was a Southern Catholic editor and perhaps the most thoroughly educated theologian of his day in the American church. As editor of the *Miscellany* during the antebellum period, he commented on various events in American Catholic history and criticized what he considered the revolutionary liberties of European and American reform movements. An apologist for the Catholic church, he asserted the importance of authority in the state as well as in the church. He also demonstrated periodically his attachments to Southern culture, his states' rights view of government, his hatred for the abolitionists, and his disdain for President Abraham Lincoln's election, which he saw as the final insult to the South and the culmination of forces creating a split between the two sections of the country.

As a theologian and canonist, Corcoran frequently advised the American bishops at the Baltimore Provincial Councils in the 1840s and 1850s, and he was the theological expert at the national Plenary Councils in 1866 and 1884. In 1868 Baltimore's Archbishop Martin John Spalding chose him as the theological representative of American bishops to assist in the preparations for Vatican I. During the preparatory sessions for the council, Corcoran became disturbed by what he told Archbishop Spalding was proposed legislation on church and state issues that would, if accepted, condemn "the fundamental principles of our [American and common sense] political doctrine." Although the council eventually defined papal infallibility, a position Corcoran defended, it did not address the church-state issue as Corcoran feared.

To foster Catholic intellectual life in the United States after Vatican I, Corcoran established and became a regular contributor to the *American Catholic Quarterly Review,* a journal of Catholic opinion on theological, historical, social, literary, political, and ethical issues. Within the American Catholic community Corcoran was a conservative ultramontane theologian who upheld traditional values of authority, community, and unity. He was also American in his acceptance of democratic government, separation of church and state, and religious liberty. In the postwar period he repudiated the new evolutionary theories, rising biblical criticism, and the Protestant ecclesiastical propensity toward ever-increasing diversity and disintegration. Although he was a theological educator and considered by many to be brilliant, his students considered him dull as a teacher, and he was never a creative publishing scholar. He was an occasional essayist who was more interested in attacking his opponents' positions than in developing creative alternatives.

Bibliography

A. Numerous articles in *American Catholic Quarterly Review* (1876–1889); *Stock Misrepresentations of Catholic Doctrines* (Cleveland, OH, 1902).
B. DAB, 203–04; DACB, 115; NCE, 4:319–20; John J. Keane, "Monsignor Corcoran," *American Catholic Quarterly Review* 14 (1889): 738–47; Mary Marcian Lowman, "James Andrew Corcoran: Editor, Theologian, Scholar (1820–1889)," (Ph.D. diss., St. Louis University, 1958).

CORRIGAN, MICHAEL A. (13 August 1839, Newark, NJ—5 May 1902, New York, NY). *Education:* studied at St. Mary's Coll., Wilmington, DE, 1853–55; Mount St. Mary's Coll., Emmitsburg, MD, 1859; D.D., North American Coll., Rome, 1864. *Career:* ordained, 1863; professor of dogmatic theology and scripture, Seton Hall Coll. and Sem., South Orange, NJ, 1864–73; president Seton Hall Coll., 1868–77; administrator of Diocese of Newark, 1869–70; bishop of Newark, 1873–80; coadjutor archbishop of New York, 1880–85; archbishop of New York, 1886–1902.

As bishop of Newark and archbishop of New York, Michael Corrigan was a vigorous ecclesiastical administrator, a strong disciplinarian, a friend of the immigrants, and a leader of the conservative party in late-nineteenth-century American Catholicism. During his Newark episcopacy he consolidated the administration of church properties, fought losing battles to obtain state funds for Catholic institutions, instituted a solemn Roman-style liturgy, increased the number of Catholic schools and other ecclesiastical institutions, and because of the growing number of Catholics in New Jersey, provided for the establishment of a new diocese in Trenton.

During Corrigan's New York episcopacy the number of Catholics there increased by 600,000, churches by 78, priests by 296, colleges and academies by 22, parish schools by 89, and industrial and reform schools by 18. After the Third Plenary Council of Baltimore in 1884, Corrigan and Bishop Bernard Joseph McQuaid of Rochester, NY, became the national leaders of a conservative party in the Catholic church, rejecting an accommodationist stance toward American values and institutions. Corrigan petitioned Rome to condemn the Knights of Labor as a secret society and suspended Edward McGlynn, the popular pastor of St. Stephen's Church, because he had supported and, against canonical legislation, campaigned for the populist and (in Corrigan's view) "socialist" Henry George when he ran for mayor of New York in 1886. Corrigan also criticized the establishment of the Catholic University of America at Washington, D.C., because he feared its liberal leadership, and was adamantly opposed to Archbishop Ireland's attempts to create a rapproachment between public and Catholic schools. Corrigan believed that those in the Catholic church who supported these programs were undermining the specific identity of Catholicism, weakening its authority, and confusing its religious aims with specific political and cultural programs and agenda. Corrigan held that American Catholicism could preserve its identity only by staying out of political and social issues, concentrating upon its religious mission and institutional developments, and reinforcing ecclesiastical and civil authority as a primary means for maintaining the unity and stability of church and society.

Between 1886 and 1899 Corrigan periodically complained to Rome that the pastoral approaches of the "liberal" Americanizing bishops were threatening the foundations of Catholicism in the United States. In 1899, when Pope Leo XIII issued his encyclical *Testem Benevolentiae* condemning the so-called heresy of Americanism, Corrigan rejoiced that ecclesiastical authority had finally intervened to curtail a false Americanism, which, if left unchecked, would have destroyed the American Catholic church.

Bibliography

A. *The Diocesan Journal of Michael Augustine Corrigan* (Newark, 1987); *The Letters of Archbishop Corrigan to Bishop McQuaid and Allied Documents*, ed. Frederick J. Zwierlein (Rochester, NY, 1946).
B. DAB, 4:450–52; DACB, 116–17; DARB, 112–13; DAH, 51; NCAB, 1:196; NCE, 4:352–54; NYT, 6 May 1902, 1–2; Joseph F. Mooney, *Memorial of the Most Reverend Michael Augustine Corrigan, D.D.: Third Archbishop of New York* (New York, 1902); Robert Emmet Curran, *Michael Augustine Corrigan and the Shaping of Conservative Catholicism in America, 1878–1902* (New York, 1978); Stephen DiGiovanni, *Corrigan, the Vatican, and the Italian Immigrants* (New York, 1990).

COUGHLIN, CHARLES EDWARD (25 October 1891, Hamilton, Ontario— 27 October 1979, Birmingham, MI). *Education:* studied at St. Michael's Coll., Toronto, 1903–07; Univ. of Toronto, 1907–11; St. Basil's Sem., Toronto, 1911–14, 1915–16; St. Basil's Coll., Waco, TX, 1914–15. *Career:* teacher, Basilian Coll., Waco, TX, 1914–15; ordained, 1916; professor of English, Assumption Coll., Sandwich, Ontario, 1916–23; curate, St. Augustine's Church, Kalamazoo, MI, 1923; pastor, St. Leo's Church, Detroit, 1923; pastor, Sts. Peter and Paul, North Branch, MI, 1925; founding pastor, St. Therese of the Little Flower of Jesus, Royal Oak, MI, 1926–66; organizer, National Union for Social Justice, 1934; organizer, Union Party, 1936; founder, *Social Justice*, 1936–42; retirement, 1966–79.

Charles Coughlin rose to national attention as a radio preacher and lecturer who expressed the popular tensions and anxieties of the Depression era. In 1926 he obtained time on Detroit's WJR radio station not only to raise money for his Little Flower parish in a Detroit suburb that was expanding rapidly but also to combat the assaults of the Ku Klux Klan. His broadcasts brought little attention until he began to cover social and political issues at the beginning of the Depression. When he became a forceful supporter and then critic of candidate and President Roosevelt during the 1930s, he increased his radio audience to an estimated forty million listeners, many of whom sent him money to continue his Sunday broadcasts excoriating the evil effects of capitalism, the New Deal, and communism. After 1938 he also became expressedly anti-Semitic in his propaganda, blaming Jewish bankers in particular for the rise of communism and corruptions of capitalism.

Coughlin's popularity as a radio preacher encouraged him in 1934 to form the National Union for Social Justice, which he considered a badly needed lobby of the people in American society. The union was open to all religious traditions and intended to be a populist organization that pushed for the implementation of social justice as defined in the papal social encyclicals and in midwestern agrarian reforms: e.g., a living wage, control of private property for the common good, a fair profit for the farm, the right of labor to organize, absolute government control of all currency, and the priority of human over property rights. By 1935, however, Coughlin's calls for reforms and social justice turned bitterly against President Roosevelt, and in 1936 he instituted *Social Justice,* a journal for expressing his social agenda, and created the Union Party to run against both the Democratic and Republican candidates for the presidency. Running William Lemke for president proved politically disastrous, but it gave Coughlin an opportunity to express his vitriolic attack on the New Deal. By 1938 Coughlin's Christian Front became an anti-Semitic, isolationist, pro-Nazi organization that periodically charged that a Roosevelt-British-Jewish conspiracy would drive the country into ruin.

In 1942 the government barred Coughlin's journal *Social Justice* from the postal system for violating the Espionage Act, and his new archbishop, Edward Mooney, forced him off the air. He lived in relative obscurity as a parish priest thereafter, retiring in 1966 and dying in Birmingham, MI, in 1979. Coughlin saw himself as an advocate for social justice and the people's priest; many of his opponents saw him as a demagogue and/or populist fascist who provided a link between late-nineteenth-century populism and the McCarthyites of the 1950s or the John Birchers of a later period.

Bibliography

A. *Fr. Coughlin's Radio Sermons, October, 1930–April, 1931* (Baltimore, 1931); *Father Coughlin's Radio Discourses, 1931–32* (Royal Oak, MI, 1932); *Eight Lectures on Capital, Labor, and Justice* (Detroit, 1934); *The New Deal in Money* (Royal Oak, MI, 1934); *A Series of Lectures on Social Justice, 1935–36* (Royal Oak, MI, 1936); *Radio Addresses, January 12, 1936–April 21, 1940* (Royal Oak, MI, 1940); *"Am I An Anti-Semite?* (Detroit, 1939); *Why Leave Our Own? 13 Addresses on Christianity and Americanism* (Detroit, 1939).

B. Britannica 3:675; DACB, 120–21; NCE, 18:108–9; NYT, 28 Oct. 1979, 44; Charles J. Tull, *Father Coughlin and the New Deal* (Syracuse, NY, 1965); Sheldon Marcus, *Father Coughlin: The Tumultuous Life of the Priest of the Little Flower* (Boston, 1973); Alan Brinkley, *Voices of Protest: Huey Long, Father Coughlin, and the Great Depression* (New York, 1982); Mary Christine Athans, "A New Perspective on Father Charles E. Coughlin," *CH* 56 (June 1987): 224–35; Daniel P. Noonan, *The Catholic Communicators: Portraits of Father Charles Coughlin, Archbishop Fulton J. Sheen, Pope John Paul II, Mother Angelica, Father Patrick Peyton, Mother Teresa* (Huntington, IN, 1990).

CROWLEY, PATRICIA (24 July 1913, Chicago, IL–) *Education:* studied at Trinity Coll., Washington, DC, 1932-36. *Career:* cofounder with Patrick Crowley, Christian Family Movement (CFM), Chicago, 1943; co–executive secretary, CFM, 1950–70; copresident, International Confederation of Christian Family Movements, 1967–74. **CROWLEY, PATRICK FRANCIS** (23 September 1911, Chicago IL—24 November, 1974, Chicago, IL). *Education:* B.A., Univ. of Notre Dame, 1933; J.D., Loyola Univ., Chicago, 1937. *Career:* cofounder with Patricia Crowley, CFM, Chicago, 1943; co–executive secretary, CFM, 1950–70; copresident, International Confederation of Christian Family Movements, 1967–74.

In 1937, after graduating from Loyola University Law School, Patrick Crowley married Patricia Caron and began to practice business law in the Chicago area. They had four children of their own (a fifth died as an infant), adopted another, and raised over fifty foster children. During World War II Patrick and five other businessmen began to meet with a priest to discuss liturgy, sacraments, and Christian living. This group, which eventually included their wives, adopted Father Joseph Cardijn's method of "Observe-Judge-Act," which had usually been employed in the arena of social justice, and applied it to families to make them aware of the difficulties in the environment that militated against the development of a Christian home. Through mutual discussion, too, couples were encouraged to transform American society, foster social justice, eliminate racial hatred, and thus create an atmosphere conducive to Christian family life. By 1943 this group, under the leadership of the Crowleys, became known as the Christian Family Movement (CFM). For over twenty years the Crowleys led CFM and published "Happy Family" manuals annually on the sacramentality and social responsibility of families.

In 1957 the Crowleys participated in the Second World Congress of the Laity in Rome, where they received the Vatican's *Pro Ecclesia* award. In the early 1960s they were appointed to the papal commission on birth control and joined the majority on the commission in recommending that Catholics be allowed some measures of artificial contraception. During the turmoil of the late 1960s they became involved in Eugene McCarthy's presidential campaign, Patrick helping to manage it in Chicago. By 1970 the Crowleys were disillusioned with political campaigns, police violence, and in particular the corruption of Mayor Richard Daly's Chicago political machine. After Patrick's death in 1974, Patricia, who had started a travel business in 1970, turned her attention away from CFM and toward issues facing the homeless and single women in society.

Bibliography

A. "The Crowley Family," *Agape* 4 (October 1975), 1–2.
B. DACB, 126; NCR, 29 Nov 1974, 1–2; Bernie Bauer, "Pat Crowley: Model Saint for an Affluent Society," *Agape* 4 (1975), 1–2; John N. Kotre, *Simple Gifts: The Lives of Pat and Patty Crowley* (Kansas City, 1979); "Patty Crowley," *Salt of the Earth* (November/December 1991): 4–5.

CUSHING, RICHARD JAMES (24 August 1895, Boston, MA—2 November 1970, Boston, MA). *Education:* studied at Boston Coll., 1913–15; graduated from St. John's Sem. (MA), 1921. *Career:* curate, Roxbury and Somerville, MA, 1921–22; assistant and director, Society for the Propagation of the Faith, Boston, 1922–39; auxiliary bishop of Boston, 1939–44; archbishop of Boston, 1944–70; cardinal, 1958–70.

Richard Cushing's education for the priesthood and his early pastoral and episcopal experience took place under the watchful eye of Cardinal William O'Connell, archbishop of Boston, who had made valiant efforts to centralize all ecclesiastical developments in Boston. Under O'Connell's tight control before World War II, Cushing flourished and developed an uncommon clerical interest in foreign missions. As archbishop of Boston he continued that interest, creating the St. James Society in 1958 to allow diocesan priests an opportunity to serve in those foreign territories where there was a shortage of clergy, especially in Latin America. As a priest and later as bishop, moreover, he was an effective fund-raiser not only for diocesan educational and charitable projects but also for foreign missions.

In the 1950s Cushing was acknowledged as one of the leading and most beloved churchmen in American Catholicism. Because of his association with the Joseph Kennedy family, moreover, he was catapulted into the public limelight with the election of John F. Kennedy, a significant social development especially for Boston Catholics, who since the early twentieth century under William O'Connell had tried to demonstrate their Romanism and Americanism.

Cardinal Cushing was present at the Second Vatican Council, but he spoke only three times and did not have much influence on conciliar procedures or results. He was not a theologian nor was he inclined to theological discussion. In the post-conciliar period, however, he became a sensitive reforming bishop, especially in his support of the use of English in the liturgy, a wider participation of the laity in the church, and the church's participation in the wide arena of social justice.

Bibliography

A. *That They May Know Thee* (Westminster, MD, 1956); *A Call to the Laity* (Westminster, MD, 1957); *Moral Values and American Society: Pastoral Letter* (Boston, 1961); *The Mission of the Teacher* (Boston, 1962); *Blessed Mother Seton* (Boston, 1963); *Call Me John: A Life of Pope John XXIII* (Boston, 1963); *Saint Patrick and the Irish* (Boston, 1963).

B. DACB, 131; DAH, 59; DARB, 117–18; DCA, 333–34; NCE, 16:112–13; NYT, 3 November 1970, 1; John H. Fenton, *Salt of the Earth: An Informal Portrait of Richard Cardinal Cushing* (New York, 1951); Joseph Dever, *Cushing of Boston: A Candid Portrait* (Boston, 1965); John H. Cutler, *Cardinal Cushing of Boston* (New York, 1970).

D

DAVIS, THURSTON NOBLE (12 October 1913, Philadelphia, PA—17 September 1986, New York, NY). *Education:* B.A., Georgetown Univ., 1937; studied at Woodstock Coll., 1937–42; Ph.D., Harvard Univ., 1947. *Career:* entered Jesuits, 1931; ordained, 1942; professor, Fordham Univ., 1947–49; dean, Fordham Coll., 1949–53; editor, *America,* 1953–68; founder, John LaFarge Institute, 1967; consultant, General Secretary of US Catholic Conference, 1970–76; founder and director, John Courtney Murray Forum, 1968–86.

Thurston Davis came to national prominence in American Catholicism when he assumed the editorship of *America* magazine in 1953. At the time some Catholic liberals feared that he had been sent to *America* to moderate or negate the former editor's (Robert C. Hartnett, S.J.) anti-McCarthyism, but such was not the case. During fifteen years of radical change and revolution in American society and within Catholicism, Davis, although conservative by education and inclination, provided some progressive leadership in *America* on many controversies of the day: e.g., racial justice, religious liberty, contraception, divorce and remarriage, poverty, ecumenism, freedom of the press, and the Second Vatican Council. He renovated an old New York hotel in 1964 and established there America House, a major center for national Jesuit enterprises in the 1960s and 1970s. There he also founded the John LaFarge Institute, which brought together leaders from many fields of study and religious traditions to discuss major religious, moral, social, and international issues. The John Courtney Murray Forum, moreover, he established to provide public lectures on issues relating religious thought to common life in the United States. Davis's editorial policy and participation in the renewal of American Catholicism in the post–Vatican II era was governed by an attitude of Christian hope and optimism. One of his editorials indicated his own Jesuit optimism: "While we take full account of the Fall of Man and the weaknesses of human nature, we scorn fatalism, and we rest our resolute rejection of despair on the capacities of human free will elevated by divine grace and aided by the constant protection of divine Providence.''

Bibliography

A. *Between Two Cities: God and Man in America,* ed. with Donald R. Campion and L. C. McHugh (Chicago, 1962).
B. NCE, 18:113; NYT, 19 September 1986, D:22; R. A. Schroth, "Thurston N. Davis, SJ (1913–1986)," *America* (4 October 1986): 157–58; idem, "What's On Your Minds?," *Commonweal* (24 October 1986): 549–50.

DAY, DOROTHY (8 November 1897, Brooklyn, NY—29 November 1980, New York, NY). *Education:* studied at Univ. of Illinois, 1914–16. *Career:* reporter for the *New York Call,* 1917; assistant editor, the *Masses,* 1917; worked on the *Liberator,* 1917–18; reporter, *New Orleans Item,* 1923; cofounder and publisher, *Catholic Worker,* 1933-80; founder, first house of hospitality in New York, 1935; arrested with Cesar Chavez in a farm workers' demonstration, 1973.

After a stormy bohemian and socialist youth that included a sexual liaison that led to an abortion, a marriage that failed, and a common-law relationship that resulted in the birth of a child and subsequent abandonment by the father, Dorothy Day felt the need for religion and was received into Catholicism in 1927. In 1932 she met the French peasant social philosopher Peter Maurin who directed her thinking toward the papal social encyclicals and the personalism of Emmanuel Mounier. In the midst of the Depression Day found her mission in life: personal service to those suffering from unemployment and homelessness. Within this context she and Maurin began to organize what became known as the Catholic Worker Movement.

On 1 May 1933 she published the first issue of the *Catholic Worker,* calling all Christians to give personal service to society's outcasts, thereby providing personal examples of love in action. For the next forty-seven years she drew numerous young Catholics to more than forty Catholic Worker houses of hospitality across the country. In these houses young Catholics were given the opportunity to serve the poor, pray, discuss and clarify Catholic social thought, demonstrate for peace, and live out the spiritual and corporal works of mercy that Day saw as the heart of the gospel. She and many of her followers were ardent pacifists who were periodically arrested for public demonstrations against militarism, war, and constant preparations for war. She stood steadfast against World War II, the Korean War, the entire cold war militaristic mentality, and the Vietnam War. She and her workers became what Mel Piehl has called the source of Catholic radicalism in the United States, a movement that challenged prevailing moral assumptions in the culture.

Day believed that the human person realized the destiny of history only in a life of practical love that served the immediate needs of the neighbor without demanding or expecting an effective result. The Spirit of Christ, present in the Christian, must be realized in history through the actions of persons who see themselves not as isolated individuals, but united together in the creative and redemptive love of God which transcends all processes of history yet is incarnated in the Christian community. This Christian personalism was not individualism; it was communitarian. Persons—not states, legislation, techniques, social programs, slogans, or even monetary contributions—were responsible for other persons in need.

Bibliography

A. *The Eleventh Virgin* (New York, 1924); *The Catholic Worker*, 1933–80; *From Union Square to Rome* (Silver Spring, MD, 1939; reprint, New York, 1978); *House of Hospitality* (New York, 1939); *The Long Loneliness* (New York, 1952); *On Pilgrimage: The Sixties* (New York, 1972); *Therese* (Springfield, IL, 1979).
B. DACB, 136–37; NCE, 9:507–8; NYT, 1 December 1980, D:12; William D. Miller, *A Harsh and Dreadful Love: Dorothy Day and the Catholic Worker Movement* (New York, 1973); idem, *Dorothy Day: A Biography* (San Francisco, 1982); Mel Piehl, *Breaking Bread: The Catholic Worker and the Origins of Catholic Radicalism in America* (Philadelphia, 1982); Nancy L. Roberts, *Dorothy Day and the Catholic Worker* (Albany, NY, 1984); James H. Forest, *Love Is the Measure: A Biography of Dorothy Day* (New York, 1986); Anne Klejment, *Dorothy Day and the Catholic Worker: A Bibliography and Index* (New York, 1986); Robert Coles, *Dorothy Day: A Radical Devotion* (Reading, MA, 1987); Pat Coy, ed., *A Revolution of the Heart* (Philadelphia, 1988).

DEARDEN, JOHN (15 October 1907, Valley Falls, RI—1 August 1988, Southfield, MI). *Education:* studied at St. Mary's Sem., Cleveland, 1924–28; North American Coll., Rome, 1928–32; Pontifical Gregorian Univ., Rome, 1932–34. *Career:* ordained, 1932; pastoral work, diocese of Cleveland, 1934–37; faculty, 1937–44, and rector, 1944–48, St. Mary's Sem., Cleveland; coadjutor bishop of Pittsburgh, 1948–50; bishop of Pittsburgh, 1950–58; archbishop of Detroit, 1958–88; president, National Conference of Catholic Bishops, 1966–71; cardinal 1969–88; retired, 1980–88.

John Dearden came to public prominence and had the greatest influence upon American Catholicism during and immediately after the Second Vatican Council. He was a bishop, however, before as well as after the council. As bishop of Pittsburgh, he was involved, like most American bishops of the 1950s, with numerous building projects to meet the ever-expanding educational, religious, and social needs of the rapidly increasing Catholic population. Shortly after he was transferred to Detroit as archbishop in 1958, he became one of three American bishops to be appointed to the Doctrinal Commission on Faith and Practice (known as the theological commission) that Pope John XXIII had established to prepare for the Second Vatican Council. From 1959 to 1962 Deardon was involved in the preparation of conciliar documents, and during the council he served on a number of conciliar commissions.

After the council Deardon was elected a member of the United States Bishops' Commission on the Liturgical Apostolate and became a national episcopal leader in the implementation of English in the liturgy. Pope Paul VI also appointed him as a member of the Secretariate for Non-Christian Religions, where he demonstrated the ecumencial concerns of the council. In 1966, when the American bishops established the National Conference of Catholic Bishops, Dearden was elected presiding bishop, a tremendously significant position, because during the years of his presidency (1966–71) the American church experienced a host of inner conflicts that challenged its authority and tradition. His amicability, naturally conservative theological orientation, and progressive openness to reforming conciliar directions combined to make him a capable leader in times of turmoil and upheaval.

Dearden was instrumental in his diocese and in the American church at large in extending to the laity and clergy a participation in church life and in decisions that had not been common prior to the council. In 1976, after two years of local and national preparations, he presided over the American Catholic bishops' bicentennial convention "Call to Action," held in Detroit. Shortly after "Call to Action," Dearden called his own diocesan synod to involve laity and clergy in discussions of local ecclesiastical life.

Changes in the church and society, a lack of adequate financing, and a loss of commitment forced Dearden to close 56 of the 269 Catholic schools in his diocese. Although these closings and a host of other painful changes in his diocese pleased some Catholics, they angered others. In the midst of these struggles he was criticized by reformers for not being progressive enough and by conservatives for being a radical innovator. In 1980 because of turmoil and age, he resigned from his see.

Bibliography

B: DAH, 63; NYT, 2 August 1988, 17; Leslie Woodcock Tentler, *Seasons of Grace: A History of the Catholic Archdiocese of Detroit* (Detroit, 1990).

DE SMET, PIERRE JEAN (30 January 1801, Termonde, Belgium—23 May 1873, St. Louis, MO). *Education:* studied at sem. at Malines, Belgium, 1819–20; Jesuit training, Whitemarsh, MD, 1821–23, and Florissant, MO, 1823–27. *Career:* ordained, 1827; treasurer, St. Louis Coll., 1827–33; travel and recuperation, Belgium, 1833–37; superior of western missions, 1838–46; secretary to the Jesuit provincial, St. Louis, 1846–73.

Pierre Jean De Smet was perhaps the best-known mid-nineteenth-century Catholic missionary to the Indian tribes west of the Mississippi River. At the age of twenty he emigrated from Belgium to the United States, joining the Maryland Jesuits. Two years later he moved to St. Louis, where he finished his Jesuit education and became part of the new and developing St. Louis Jesuit province. Because of repeated illnesses after his ordination, he was sent to Belgium in 1833 to regain his health. In 1838 he returned to St. Louis, where he began working among the Potawatomi Indians near Council Bluffs, IA, and from the early 1840s on he made numerous trips from St. Louis to Oregon, establishing Indian missions in Montana, Oregon, and the Dakotas. From 1843 to 1870 he also made nineteen trips to Europe to raise funds and obtain personnel for his missionary work.

De Smet was extraordinarily successful as a missionary. He genuinely respected the Indians' customs and values, endured personal physical hardship without complaint, and would not be affiliated with white-led operations against the Indians. He was trusted by the Indians and was repeatedly a mediator and negotiator not only between whites and Indians, but also between different Indian tribes: e.g., Blackfeet and Flatheads (1846), Fort Laramie (1851), the Mormon War (1858), Oregon/Washington (1858–59), Upper Missouri (1867 and 1870). He advised the federal government on the Indians' behalf, but his advice was rarely taken. De Smet's writings are prolific firsthand accounts of nineteenth-century Native American customs, traditions, and populations without a flagrant bias against them.

Bibliography

A. *Letters and Sketches* (Philadelphia, 1843); *Oregon Missions* (Ghent, Belgium, 1847); *Voyage au Grand Désert en 1851* (Brussels, 1853); *Cinquant Nouvelles Lettres* (Paris, 1858); *Western Missions and Missionaries* (New York, 1863; reprint, Shannon, Ireland, 1972); *New Indian Sketches* (New York, 1865).

B. DAB, 5:255–56; DACB, 140–41; DARB, 126–27; NCAB, 11:453–54; NCE, 4:804; Hiram M. Chittenden and Alfred T. Richardson, *Life, Letters and Travels of Father Pierre Jean De Smet,* 4 vols. (New York, 1905; reprint, New York, 1969); E. Laveille, *The Life of Father De Smet, S.J. (1801–1873),* trans. Marian Lindsay (New York, 1915; reprint, Chicago, 1981); John Upton Terrell, *Black Robe: The Life of Pierre-Jean De Smet, Missionary, Explorer and Pioneer* (New York, 1964).

DIETZ, PETER ERNEST (10 July 1878, New York, NY—11 October 1947, Milwaukee, WI). *Education:* studied at St. Mary's Coll. (PA), 1894–96; Coll. of St. Francis Xavier (NY), 1897–99; St. Bonaventure Coll. (NY), 1897–99; St. Gabriel, Moedling, Germany, 1900–1902; Univ. of Bonn, 1902–1903; St. Mary's Sem. (MD), 1903–1904. *Career:* ordained, 1904; assistant pastor, St. Mary's Church, Elyria, OH, 1905–1906; editor, *Central Blatt and Social Justice,* 1909–10; organizer, first Social Institute at Oberlin Coll., 1909; founder, Militia Christi for Social Service, 1910; secretary, Social Service Commission of American Federation of Catholic Societies, 1911–18; editor, *Newsletter* of Social Service Commission, 1913–18; editor, *Bulletin,* 1914–18; founder, American Academy for Christian Democracy for Women, Hot Springs, NC, 1915; founding pastor, St. Monica's Church, Milwaukee, 1923–47.

Peter Dietz, an American-born son of German immigrants, became one of the first of a long line of twentieth-century American Catholic labor priests. In 1908 as a Cleveland diocesan priest, Dietz joined the German Catholic Central Verein to begin a fourteen-year career as an organizer and advocate of laborers.

He saw the need to educate them into the Catholic social tradition, and that perception became the driving force behind his many activities in labor's behalf. Within the Central Verein he edited the English-language version of the *Central Blatt and Social Justice,* calling attention to the need for Christianizing the labor movement. In 1910 he became a member of the American Federation of Catholic Societies, initiated a Social Service Commission within the federation, and established Militia Christi, a small group of Catholic laborers within the American Federation of Labor that he hoped would become the Christian leaven for the whole labor movement. From 1914 to 1916, moreover, he became a member of the Wisconsin State Conference of Charities and Corrections and was involved with the National Municipal League, National Economic League, and American Institute of Social Service. In all these activities he was more interested in applying Pope Leo XIII's *Rerum Novarum* (1891) to conditions in American society than he was in developing Catholic social thought.

In 1915, to provide for activist Catholic women in the labor movement, he established the American Academy for Christian Democracy for Women in Hot Springs, NC. This school for systematic social thought and service was transferred to Cincinnati in 1917, but in 1922 the archbishop, Henry Moeller, ordered it closed and forced Dietz to leave the city and return to Milwaukee, where he had been incardinated in 1912. After 1923 Dietz became the founding pastor of St. Monica's church in Milwaukee, and although he continued to speak out on labor and attend national conferences on labor and social justice, most of his efforts were focused on building up the parish.

Bibliography

A. *The Christian Manifesto,* Militia of Christ Series, no. 2 (Milwaukee, 1912); *Need of an Organized Christian Force in the American Labor Movement,* Bulletin no. 6 (Milwaukee, n.d.); *What Shall Our Catholic Societies Do?,* Bulletin no. 3 (1912).
B. DACB, 144; NCE, 4:865; NYT, 13 October 1947, 23; *Milwaukee Journal,* 11 October 1947, 3; Mary Harrita Fox, *Peter E. Dietz, Labor Priest* (Notre Dame, IN, 1953).

DOHEN, DOROTHY M. (15 April 1923, New York, NY—3 January 1984, New York, NY). *Education:* B.A., Coll. of Mount St. Vincent 1945; M.A., Fordham Univ., 1959; Ph.D., 1966. *Career:* social worker, New York Foundling Hospital, 1947–48; free-lance writer, 1948–52; editor, *Integrity,* 1952–56; professor, Fordham Univ., 1960–84; editor, *Sociological Analysis,* 1970–72.

During her years in college Dorothy Dohen became interested in the lay apostolate and Catholic Action that had been encouraged by Pope Pius X. She acknowledged in the 1950s that the popes "have called upon lay Catholics to restore all phases of our temporal order to Christ, and the realization that God calls lay people as well as religious to sanctity, have been the molding influ-

ences of my life and writing.'' As a young woman, too, she had a brief period
of training at the Grail and was interested in the Canon Cardijn's Young Christian Worker Movement. Out of this interest and experience she began writing,
under the pen name Elizabeth Williams, on topics of lay spirituality in *Today,
Torch,* and *Cross and Crown* during the late 1940s. Her first book—and the
real passion of her life—was the *Vocation to Love,* a book on lay spirituality
for people who ''realize that they cannot live their interior life in a vacuum but
must bring Christ to all aspects of everyday living.''

As editor of *Integrity* in the early 1950s, she became a prominent critic of
American Catholic life-styles and forms of spirituality that separated Catholics
from the issues of social justice and an authentic communal life. In the 1950s
her own spirituality and lay social activism became increasingly influenced by
the theology of the Mystical Body and by the renaissance of European Catholic
theology. During the 1960s, as a professor of sociology at Fordham University,
she became very critical of an excessive patriotism in American Catholicism,
one she believed she had discovered particularly among the immigrant American Catholic hierarchy. She quietly opposed sexism in the church and explicitly
encouraged the social activist tradition of American Catholicism. To some extent she was one of the forerunners of the Second Vatican Council's call for
the church's involvement in the world.

Bibliography

A. *Vocation to Love* (New York, 1950); ''Editorial,'' *Integrity* 6 (April 1952): 1; *Two
Studies of Puerto Rico* (Cuernavaca, Mexico, 1957); *Women in Wonderland* (New
York, 1960); *Nationalism and American Catholicism* (New York, 1967).

B. CA1952, 136; NYT, 5 January 1984, B-13; Joseph P. Fitzpatrick, ''Dorothy Dohen,''
Commonweal (1 June 1984): 325–27.

DOHERTY, CATHERINE DE HUECK (15 August 1896, Nizhni Novgorod
[now Gorki], Russia—14 December 1985, Combermere, Ontario). *Career:* nurse,
130th Division, Western Front, World War I, 1916–17; founder, Friendship
House, Toronto, 1930; founder, Friendship House, New York, 1938; founder,
Madonna House, Ontario, 1947.

Catherine de Hueck Doherty became in the late 1930s and throughout the
1940s and 1950s a Catholic social activist who was responsible for establishing
numerous houses of hospitality for the poor and homeless in major cities in
Canada and the United States. She was reared in the Russian Orthodox church
and learned from her mother to see the face of Christ in the poor. In 1912, at
the age of sixteen, she married Boris de Hueck. During World War I she and
her husband served on the Western Front, and after fleeing the Russian Revolution to avoid death at the hands of the Bolsheviks, they emigrated to Finland
and eventually England. While in England from 1918 to 1921, Catherine converted to Catholicism.

In 1921 the de Huecks emigrated to Toronto, where Catherine gave birth to their son, George. During the Depression she decided to give her life over to service to the poor. She established Friendship Houses in Toronto and Harlem to put this commitment into practice. These houses and numerous others throughout the United States served meals, provided clothing, and provided Catholic social education to the inner-city poor. They also became centers for Catholic social activists and seekers like Thomas Merton, who came to discuss contemporary religious and social issues. In 1943 (after having obtained an ecclesiastical annulment) Catherine married Eddie Doherty, and they lived and worked in New York (where Catherine had moved in 1938) until 1946, when she left Harlem's Friendship House because of its exclusive interracial agenda, a mission that she believed to be too narrow.

In 1947 the Dohertys moved to Ontario where Catherine founded Madonna House, an evangelical community dedicated to living and teaching the gospel. Madonna Houses were eventually established in the United States, West Indies, England, France, and Africa. By her death in 1985 at the age of eighty-nine, the Second Vatican Council and the revolution of the 1960s had intervened and challenged the approach she considered so necessary to bring the gospel to the modern world.

Bibliography

A. *Friendship House* (New York, 1947); *My Russian Yesterdays* (Milwaukee 1951); *Where Love Is God Is* (Milwaukee, 1953); *The Gospel Without Compromise* (Notre Dame, IN, 1976); *Sobornost* (Notre Dame, IN, 1977); *Fragments of My Life* (Notre Dame, IN, 1979); *Doubts, Loneliness, Rejection* (New York, 1981); *Urodivoi, Fools for God* (New York, 1983).

B. *Contemporary Authors,* new rev. ser. (Detroit, 1984), 12:139–40; NYT, 16 December 1985, B:18; Edward J. Doherty, *Tumbleweed* (Milwaukee, 1948); Robert Wild, ed., *Journey to the Lonely Christ* (New York, 1987); Omer Tanghe, *For the Least of My Brothers* (New York, 1989).

DORSEY, JOHN HENRY (28 January 1874, Baltimore, MD—30 June 1926, Baltimore, MD). *Education:* studied at St. Thomas Coll., St. Paul, 1888–89; Epiphany Apostolic Coll., Walbrook, MD, 1889–93; St. Joseph's Sem., Baltimore, 1893–94, 1897–1902; B.A., M.A., St. Mary's Sem. (MD), 1897–1902. *Career:* taught at the Josephites' mission schools in VA and MD, 1894–97; ordained, 1902; teacher, St. Joseph's Coll. for Negro Catechists, Montgomery, AL, 1903–1904; assistant pastor, St. Peter's Church, Pine Bluff, AR, 1904–1905; pastor, 1905–1907; chief prefect of boys, St. Joseph's Coll. for Negro Catechists, 1907; missionary, Montgomery, 1908–1909; founder and national chaplain, Knights of Peter Claver, 1909–23; missionary in the South, 1913–17; missionary, Nashville and Memphis, 1917; pastor, St. Monica's Church, South Baltimore, 1918–24.

John Henry Dorsey was the first African-American Josephite priest to be ordained in the United States. Under the leadership of John R. Slattery, the Josephites at the end of the nineteenth and beginning of the twentieth centuries became an instrument for the evangelization of African-Americans. Slattery believed that the development of an African-American priesthood would be the most effective means of evangelization, and Dorsey carried the heavy burden of Catholic evangelization among African-American Catholics in the South. He was, however, never fully accepted among the Josephites nor among the Catholics he was sent to serve. His frequent changes of missionary and pastoral assignments indicate the instability of his ministry and the tragedy of racial discrimination in the Catholic community. Moreover, he was frequently ill, falsely accused of sexual misconduct, and in a dispute with a parent over disciplinary actions in 1924, he was bludgeoned with a heavy block of wood, became paralytic because of the blow, and died in 1926. His life of humiliation and suffering reflected the painful emergence of the African-American priesthood within American Catholicism.

Bibliography

B. NYT, 2 July 1926, 19; "Our Father Harry Dorsey," Baltimore *Afro-American*, 10 July 1926 1–2; "Death of Father Dorsey, Colored Priest, After Lingering Illness," *Colored Harvest* 14 (September-October 1926): 10; Albert S. Foley, *God's Men of Color: The Colored Catholic Priests of the United States, 1854–1954* (New York, 1955; reprint, New York, 1969); Stephen J. Ochs, "The Ordeal of the Black Priest," *U.S.CH* 5 (1986): 45–66; idem, *Desegregating the Altar: The Josephites and the Struggle for Black Priests, 1871–1960* (Baton Rouge, LA, 1990).

DREXEL, KATHARINE (27 November 1858, Philadelphia, PA—3 March 1955, Cornwells Heights, PA). *Career:* foundress and mother superior, Sisters of the Blessed Sacrament for Indians and Colored People, 1891–1937; retirement, 1937–55.

Katharine Drexel, the daughter and heiress of a Philadelphia banking family, was raised in luxury, receiving the benefits of private tutoring and the ease that immense wealth could bring in the second half of the nineteenth century. In the late 1880s on a trip to Rome, she met Pope Leo XIII, who challenged her to become a missionary to serve the needs of African and Native Americans. In 1889 she joined the Sisters of Mercy of Pittsburgh but left in 1891 to found the Sisters of the Blessed Sacrament for Indians and Colored People. Over the next forty-six years, as founder and superior of the new religious order, she distributed over twelve million dollars of her inherited wealth building schools, convents, and social agencies among African- and Native Americans throughout the United States. She also provided teaching staff for the schools and nursing sisters for the hospitals. In 1925 she helped establish New Orleans's Xavier University, the first and only Catholic university for African-Americans. Her benevolence also directly benefited the Bureau of Catholic Indian Missions, John Lafarge's Catholic Interracial Council in New York, African-American parishes throughout the country, the NAACP, and the 1930s campaign for anti-lynching legislation in the South.

Her strenuous physical activities were curtailed by a 1935 heart attack, which forced her into retirement in 1937. For the remaining eighteen years of her life as a resident in the motherhouse of her order, she became a contemplative devotee of Eucharistic devotion and an exemplar of diligence in meditation and prayer. When she died in 1955 at the age of ninety-seven, she left a legacy of fifty-one convents in twenty-one states, forty-nine elementary and twelve high schools, and one national university.

Bibliography

B. DACB, 153; DARB, 131–32; NCE, 4:1059–60; NYT, 4 March 1955, 23; Katherine Burton, *The Golden Door: The Life of Katharine Drexel* (New York, 1957); Consuela M. Duffy, *Katharine Drexel* (Philadelphia, 1966).

DUBOURG, LOUIS WILLIAM VALENTINE (10 January [13/14 February?] 1766, Cap Français, Santo Domingo Dominican Republic—12 December 1833, Besançon, France). *Education:* studied at Coll. of Guienne, France (?); Sem. of St. Sulpice, Paris, 1786–88. *Career:* ordained, 1788; Sulpician instructor, Issy, France, 1788–92; president, Georgetown Coll., 1796–98; missionary and educator, Havana and Baltimore, 1798–1803; superior, St. Mary's Coll. (MD), 1803–12; administrator apostolic, Diocese of Louisiana, 1812–15; bishop of Louisiana, 1815–25; bishop of Montauban, France, 1826–33; archbishop of Besançon, France, 1833.

Being born of aristocratic parents in the West Indies enabled Dubourg to receive an excellent preparatory education to the priesthood. After ordination to the priesthood in 1788 and after teaching in Issy, France, he was forced by the French Revolution to flee to Spain. In 1794 he emigrated to Baltimore, where he became involved in founding a college, teaching, and administration. Like many Americans of his age, he was a planner of many projects, a visionary, and a builder whose ecclesiastical and educational schemes worried his superiors, who believed that Dubourg's enthusiasm could not be matched by the practical resources available. Nonetheless in 1812, when Bishop John Carroll needed an administrator to resolve ecclesiastical conflicts in New Orleans, he selected Dubourg, who was a competent Spanish, French, and English linguist as well as an experienced administrator.

After being named the second bishop of Louisiana in 1815, Dubourg set up his diocesan headquarters in St. Louis (1817–20) rather than New Orleans because he was unable to resolve ecclesiastical conflicts there. To the Louisiana Territory he brought the Lazarist priests, the Order of the Sacred Heart (with Mother Rose Philippine Duchesne), and Belgium Jesuits—all of whom helped build up the institutional presence of the Catholic church in the lower Mississippi Valley. In 1825 he resigned from Louisiana because of continuing ecclesiastical conflicts. Returning to France, he became the bishop of Montauban in 1826 and archbishop of Besançon in 1833. Dubourg was one of the talented, though erratic, Sulpicians who provided significant ecclesiastical leadership at the beginning of the nineteenth century.

Bibliography

A. St. Mary's Seminary and Catholics at large vindicated, against the Pastoral letters of the ministers, bishops, etc. of the Presbytery of Baltimore (Baltimore, 1811); Sons of St. Dominick: a Dialogue between a Protestant and a Catholic, on the occasion of the late Defence of the Pastoral Letter of the Presbytery against the Vindication of St. Mary's Seminary, and Catholics at large, etc. (Baltimore, 1812).

B. DAB, 5:473–75; DACB, 155; DAH, 75; DARB, 133–35; NCAB, 4:435–36; NCE, 4:1081; Annabelle Melville, Louis William DuBourg: Bishop of Louisiana and the Floridas, Bishop of Montauban, and Archbishop of Besançon, 1766–1833, 2 vols. (Chicago, 1986).

DUCHESNE, ROSE PHILIPPINE (29 August 1769, Grenoble, France—18 November 1852, St. Charles, MO). *Career:* entered Order of the Visitation of St. Mary, Grenoble, 1788–92; private charitable work, 1792–1804; member, Society of the Sacred Heart, Paris, 1804–52; secretary general of the society, 1815–18; missionary in the United States, 1818–52.

Prior to the French Revolution at the age of nineteen, Rose Philippine Duchesne became a member of the French Visitandines, but the Terror dissolved her order and forced her to a private life of charitable work in Grenoble, France. In 1804, however, she joined the Society of the Sacred Heart, where during a period of revived French interest in foreign missions, she nourished a desire to serve as a missionary to the American Indians. In 1818, at the invitation of the newly consecrated bishop of Louisiana, William Louis Dubourg, she led a contingent of her sisters to Missouri, where they conducted a school for children at St. Charles. In 1819 the sisters moved their motherhouse to Florissant, where they established a novitiate. With the help of the new bishop of St. Louis, Joseph Rosati, the order built additional schools, orphanages, and academies in New Orleans and the entire lower Mississippi Valley throughout the antebellum period.

Mother Duchesne, like many of the first sisters of the Sacred Heart, was unable to speak English, making it difficult for the order to serve the increasingly English-speaking immigrants and Americanized peoples who were entering the lower Mississippi Valley during the early nineteenth century. Continued French religious customs and practices, too, made it difficult for the order to attract American recruits, and when young American women did join the order they experienced a clash of cultures. Despite the difficulties of language and rough frontier life, Mother Duchesne never lost her desire to serve the Native Americans. That opportunity did not open up for her until 1841, when, at the age of seventy-two, she was sent as a missionary to the Potawatomis at Sugar Creek, KS, where she remained for only a year. The Potawatomis named her

"The Woman-Who-Always-Prays." In 1842 she returned to St. Charles to spend the last decade of her life in penance, prayer, and meditation. She was beatified in 1940.

Bibliography

A. Madeleine-Sophie Barat and Philippine Duchesne, *Correspondence: Texte des manuscrits originaux,* Part I, *Periode de Grenoble (1804–1815),* ed. Jeanne de Charry (Rome, 1988); *Philippine Duchesne, R.S.C.J.: A Collection,* eds. Catherine Collins, Melanie A. Guste, and Anna Thompson (Washington, DC, 1988).

B. DAB, 5:477–78; DACB 156; DARB, 135–36; NCE, 4:1088–89; NAW, 1:524–26; Marjory Erskine, *Mother Philippine Duchesne* (New York, 1926); Louise Callan, *Philippine Duchesne: Frontier Missionary of the Sacred Heart* (Westminster, MD, 1957); Catherine M. Mooney, *Philippine Duchesne: A Woman with the Poor* (New York, 1990).

E

ELLIOTT, WALTER (6 January 1842, Detroit, MI—18 April 1928, Washington, DC). *Education:* studied at Coll. of Notre Dame (IN), 1854; studied law in Cincinnati in office of US district attorney Warner M. Bateman. *Career:* admitted to Michigan bar, 1861; joined Paulists, 1868; ordained, 1872; parish and mission work, 1872–88; organizer, Catholic Missionary Union, 1895; founding editor, the *Missionary,* 1896; cofounder, Apostolic Mission House, Washington, DC, 1902; general consultor of Paulist community in New York, 1902–1909, 1912–28.

The son of Irish immigrants, Walter Elliott was a member of the Fifth Ohio Volunteers during the Civil War, and shortly thereafter he became a lawyer in Detroit. In 1868 he joined the Paulists after he heard Isaac Hecker preach an evocative sermon in Detroit. As a Paulist he was a major force in the home mission movement, continuing Hecker's work of bringing Catholicism to the unchurched and to Protestants. Elliott believed that even though the missions that he conducted for non-Catholics were not successful in numerous conversions, they were valuable because they removed prejudices, misconceptions, and bitterness about Catholicism. Throughout the 1890s and into the early twentieth century Elliott conducted numerous missions for non-Catholics throughout the Midwest and on the East Coast. With fellow Paulist Alexander Doyle, he established the Apostolic Mission House at the Catholic University of America to train diocesan priests for home mission work. He also became involved in Catholic temperance work.

Elliott's biography of Isaac Hecker (1891) became a cause célèbre once it was translated into French and modified for a French Catholic readership. In the United States the book, receiving the imprimatur of the conservative archbishop of New York, Michael Corrigan, caused little stir. In French and other European ecclesiastical circles, however, it became the source of a major debate over Americanism and the church's relationship to the age, and it precipitated Pope Leo XIII's encyclical *Testem Benevolentiae* condemning Americanism. Elliott believed that his book had been misunderstood and never perceived the problems of some of his theologically unsophisticated assertions about Hecker's views of the interior life.

Bibliography

A. *The Life of Father Hecker* (New York, 1891; reprint, New York, 1972); *Missions to Non-Catholics* (New York, 1893); *The Life of Christ* (New York, 1902); *Jesus Crucified* (New York, 1906); *The Sermons of John Tauler,* trans. from the German (Washington, DC, 1910); *Parish Sermons* (New York, 1914); *The Spiritual Life* (New York, 1914); *Manual of Missions* (Washington, DC, 1922); *A Retreat for Priests* (Washington, DC, 1924); *A Retreat for Nuns* (Washington, DC, 1925); *Missions Sermons* (Washington, DC, 1926).

B. DAB, 6:99–100; DACB, 169; NCE, 5:285; NYT, 19 April 1928, 25; Joseph McSorley, "Father Elliott, C.S.P.," *The Catholic World* 127 (June 1928): 296–305; idem, *Father Hecker and His Friends* (St. Louis, 1953); Thomas J. Jonas, *The Divided Mind: American Catholic Evangelists in the 1890s* (New York, 1988).

ELLIS, JOHN TRACY (30 July 1905, Seneca, IL—16 October 1992, Washington, DC). *Education:* B.A., St. Viator Coll., Bourbonnais, IL, 1927; M.A., Catholic Univ. of America, 1928; Ph.D., 1930; studied at Sulpician Sem., Washington, DC, 1934–38; Harvard Univ., 1941–42. *Career:* professor, St. Viator Coll. and Coll. of St. Teresa, Winona, MN, 1930–34; ordained, 1938; professor, Catholic Univ., 1938–64, 1977–89; editor, the *Catholic Historical Review,* 1941–64; professor, Univ. of San Francisco, 1964–76; president, American Catholic Historical Society and the American Society of Church History, 1969; retired 1989–92.

John Tracy Ellis started his career as a historian of medieval Catholicism but switched to the history of American Catholicism by the late 1930s, when the Catholic University of America needed a historian to replace Peter Guilday. Influenced by Guilday's documentary and scientific approach, Arthur M. Schlesinger's (Sr.) social history, and the progressive historian's sense of history as an instrument for promoting authentic reform, Ellis became not only the chief historian of American Catholicism during the second half of the twentieth century but an advocate for change within the Catholic church. Through his graduate seminars at the Catholic University he single-handedly built up a generation of historians of American Catholicism and helped raise the level of historical reflection throughout American Catholicism. Concentrating on biographical studies and institutional histories, Ellis directed the new historians into a host of issues that had never before been critically examined. He authored more than twenty studies and historiographic aids and published over four-hundred articles and essays. His own two-volume biography of Cardinal James Gibbons and his general history of American Catholicism demonstrated his fundamental concern with telling the story of American Catholicism honestly, but with a sense of the usefulness of history for the church's present task.

Through his many graduate seminars at the Catholic University, his histories and other writings, his historiographic aids (documents and bibliographic guides), the *Catholic Historical Review,* and the professional history societies to which he belonged, Ellis called upon historians of Catholicism to give up the apologetic task in their research and writing, be intellectually honest in uncovering the dark as well as the bright sides of the church's history, subject the church's history to objective scrutiny, and realize in the entire process that there is no absolute objectivity in interpreting history. Ellis wanted to integrate the history of American Catholicism with American history in general, and by doing so he hoped to transform public opinion about the church. He stressed repeatedly how the church had contributed to American life and tried to demonstrate, along the lines of other consensus historians, how Catholics had supported mainstream American values.

Like John Henry Newman, one of his favorite authors, Ellis believed that the church itself could mature only if it changed and opened itself to a genuine dialogue with the world around it. When it refused to do so it stagnated and generally turned the relative in history into absolutes. Ellis's approach to American Catholicism was critical as well as celebratory. In a number of histories and essays he called upon the church to reform practices he believed were detrimental to its life and development. He was, for example, an advocate of religious liberty and ecumenical sensitivity prior to the Second Vatican Council and wrote essays to demonstrate the strengths and weaknesses of the American tradition in these areas. He also promoted a more active lay role in the church, more widespread participation in the selection of bishops, the vernacular in the liturgy, and the development of intellectual life in Catholic education. His 1955 essay "American Catholics and the Intellectual Life" blasted Catholic failures to produce national leaders and to exercise commanding influence in intellectual circles. That essay stirred up a major national debate in American Catholicism on academic life and promoted a critical examination of the historical and cultural sources of these failures, an examination that has continued into the late twentieth century.

Ellis spent thirty of his eighty-seven years within the context of the Second Vatican Council and post-conciliar church. He identified those times as revolutionary. By the late 1970s he asserted that American society suffered from the triumph of secular humanism, the excesses of individualism, a breakdown in the concept of authority, a widespread collapse of the traditional Protestant ethic, and a resurgence of hedonism. Post-conciliar Catholicism, he believed, had succumbed to these aspects of the national ethos, made a sudden break with its past, had unrealistic expectations for change and reform, lacked inspired leadership, suffered a breakdown of traditional moral standards, and experienced something of the "plague of infidelity." But these negative characterizations had to be balanced with a post-conciliar spirit that he considered beneficial—that is, the strong faith of a majority, the emergence of a spirit of openness, the evolution of new participatory channels of decision making, the attraction of new religious experiences, a widening realization of the value of Catholic schools, and a slowly dawning consciousness that change and innovation were not necessarily the path to improvement. The church was indeed undergoing massive changes, but it had experienced such revolutionary transformations in the past, and therefore there should be no place for Catholic pessimism or despair. Ultimately he believed the church would survive the ecclesiastical and social revolution, not because of its own integrity or skill, but because of a divine promise.

Bibliography

A. *Anti-Papal Legislation in Medieval England, 1066–1377* (Washington, DC, 1930); *The Life of James Cardinal Gibbons,* 2 vols. (Baltimore, 1952); *American Catholicism* (Chicago, 1955; rev. ed., Chicago, 1969); *Documents of American Catholic History* (Milwaukee, 1955, 1961; 3 vols.; Wilmington, DE, 1987); *American Catholics and the Intellectual Life* (Chicago, 1956); with Robert Trisco, *A Guide to American Catholic History* (New York, 1959; rev. ed., Santa Barbara, CA, 1982); *Catholics in Colonial America* (Baltimore, 1965); *Faith and Learning: A Church Historian's Story* (Lanham, MD, 1989).

B. CA1952: 156–57; NYT, 17 October 1992, 10; *Washington Post* 17 October 1992, 8; "Right Reverend Monsignor John Tracy Ellis," in *The Book of Catholic Authors,* ed. Walter Romig, 6 vols. (Grosse Pointe, MI, 1942–60), 5:82; Francis J. Weber, "John Tracy Ellis: Historian of American Catholicism," *American Benedictine Review* 17 (Winter 1966): 467–69; J. Douglas Thomas, "Interpretations of American Catholic Church History: A Comparative Analysis of Representative Catholic Historians, 1875–1975," (Ph.D. diss., Baylor University, 1976), 162–205; *Studies in Catholic History: In Honor of John Tracy Ellis,* ed. Nelson H. Minnich, Robert B. Eno, and Robert T. Trisco (Wilmington, DE, 1985); Henry Bowden, *Church History in an Age of Uncertainty* (Carbondale, IL, 1991), 196–206.

ENGLAND, JOHN (23 September 1786, Cork, Ireland—11 April 1842, Charleston, SC). *Education:* studied at St. Patrick's Coll., Carlow, Ireland, 1802–1808. *Career:* ordained, 1808; pastoral work in Cork, 1808–1812; president, Coll. of St. Mary, Cork, 1812–17; editor, the *Religious Repertory* (1810, 1818) and the *Cork Mercantile Chronicle,* 1814–18; pastor of Bandon, Ireland, 1817–20; bishop of Charleston, SC, 1820–42.

As a young priest in Ireland and as a bishop in the United States, John England represented that side of late-eighteenth- and early-nineteenth-century Catholicism that was open and accommodating to an Enlightenment mentality that prized reason, democracy, religious liberty, voluntaryism in religion, and separation of church and state. In Ireland as in the United States, moreover, he fostered a wide participation of clergy and laity in ecclesiastical decision making. In Ireland he supported clerical nominations of bishops and simultaneously opposed the state's veto powers over them. In his diocese of Charleston, SC, he established a constitutional form of government that incorporated laity and clergy in the management and supervision of parish and diocesan temporalities. Like many Gallican-influenced clergy and bishops of his day, he emphasized the rights, dignity, and integrity of the national church, pressuring the archbishops of Baltimore to convoke national councils of bishops to provide a forum for an efficient and effective episcopal governance of the American church.

From 1820 until his death in 1842 England became something of a national spokesman and apologist for the compatibility of Catholicism and American democratic traditions. He was frequently called upon to preach in Protestant as well as Catholic churches within and outside of his own diocese. In 1822 he established the first explicitly national Catholic newspaper, the *U. S. Catholic Miscellany,* to provide information, defend the church, and give Catholics a voice in national affairs. His national prominence was acknowledged in 1826 when he was invited to address the United States Congress, the first Catholic clergyman to do so. The Vatican, too, recognized his skills when it appointed him apostolic delegate to Haiti (1833–37) to reestablish diplomatic relations between that country and the Vatican.

In his own diocese England erected a seminary for the education of native American clergy (1825), a philosophical and classical school for Charleston students (1832), and a school for African-Americans (1835) that was forced to close because of resistance from prominent Charleston city fathers, and he founded the Sisters of Our Lady of Mercy in Charleston in 1827. He also founded the Brotherhood of San Marino, the first Catholic society for workingmen in the United States, organized an Anti-Duelling Society in Charleston, edited catechisms, and prepared a new edition of the Missal. Although he considered slavery personally repugnant, he defended the institution itself as compatible with Scripture and the Christian tradition. His ideological support of slavery and his view of the compatibility of Catholicism and American democracy won him many friends in Charleston but also demonstrated clearly the difficulties inherent in his accommodationist stance toward the world in which he lived.

Bibliography

A. *The Works of the Right Reverend John England, First Bishop of Charleston,* ed. Ignatius A. Reynolds, 5 vols. (Baltimore, 1849); ed. Sebastian G. Messmer, 7 vols. (Cleveland, 1908).

B. DAB, 6:161–63; DACB, 171–72; DAH, 84; DARB, 152; NCAB, 5:28–29; NCE, 5:352–53; Peter Guilday, *The Life and Times of John England, First Bishop of Charleston (1786–1842),* 2 vols. (New York, 1927; reprint, New York, 1969); Joseph L. O'Brien, *John England, Bishop of Charleston* (New York, 1934); Patrick Carey, *An Immigrant Bishop: John England's Adaptation of Irish Catholicism to American Republicanism* (Yonkers, NY, 1982); Peter Clarke, *A Free Church in a Free Society* (Greenwood, SC, 1982).

F

FENTON, JOSEPH CLIFFORD (16 January 1906, Springfield, MA—7 July 1969, Chicopee, MA). *Education:* B.A., Holy Cross Coll., 1926; S.T.L., J.C.B., Grand Sem./Univ. of Montreal, 1930; S.T.D., Institutum Angelicum, Rome, 1931. *Career:* ordained, 1930; curate, Boston, 1931–34; professor of philosophy, St. Ambrose Coll., Davenport, IA, 1934–35; professor of special dogmatic theology, St. Bernard's Sem., Rochester, NY, 1935–38; professor of fundamental dogmatic theology, Catholic Univ. of America, 1938–64; dean of School of Theology, Catholic Univ. of America, 1941–45; editor, the *American Ecclesiastical Review,* 1944–64; cofounder, Catholic Theological Society of America, 1946; cofounder, Mariological Society, 1949; counselor, Sacred Congregation of Sem. and Univ., 1951–69; member, Preparatory Theological Commission for Vatican II, 1960–62; peritus, Vatican II, 1962–65; consultor for Doctrinal and Mixed Commissions, 1962–65.

Joseph Fenton was a leading mid-twentieth-century American representative of a neo-scholastic theology that prevailed in Roman schools prior to the Second Vatican Council. Like many Roman theologians in the post–Vatican I and postmodernist period, he believed that the scholastic method of theology and even its terminology were constants that could not and would not experience any substantial change without threatening the authenticity of the word of God. Throughout his career as a professor of theology at the Catholic University, as editor of the influencial *American Ecclesiastical Review,* and as peritus at the Second Vatican Council, he appealed to the authority of Vatican I, the papal encyclical tradition, and other ecclesiastical pronouncements as the source of his theological argumentation. For him the appeal to these authorities was the surest way to ward off the dangers of a twentieth-century modernism that was as threatening to divine revelation as were Gnosticism, Montanism, and Arianism in the early church. In the late 1940s and throughout the 1950s he upheld the thesis-hypothesis tradition on separation of church and state and fought against John Courtney Murray's innovative approaches to religious freedom as manifestations of modernism. At the Second Vatican Council he generally supported the theological positions of Cardinal Alfredo Ottaviani and the conservative Roman scholastic theological tradition.

Bibliography

A. *The Theology of Prayer* (Milwaukee, 1939); *The Concept of Sacred Theology* (Milwaukee, 1941); *We Stand with Christ: An Essay in Catholic Apologetics* (Milwaukee, 1942); *The Calling of a Diocesan Priest* (Westminster, MD, 1944); *The Concept of the Diocesan Priesthood* (Milwaukee, 1951); *The Catholic Church and Salvation: In the Light of Recent Pronouncements of the Holy See* (Westminster, MD, 1958).

B. NCR, 16 July 1969, 5; Matthew Hoehn, ed., *Catholic Authors,* vol. 2 (Newark, NJ, 1948): 243–44; Barbara Harte and Caroline Riley, eds., *Contemporary Authors,* 1st rev., vols. 5–8 (Detroit, 1969): 369–70; Donald E. Pelotte, *John Courtney Murray: Theologian in Conflict* (New York, 1976).

FENWICK, EDWARD (19 August 1768, St. Mary's County, MD—26 September 1832, Wooster, OH). *Education:* studied at Holy Cross Coll., Bornhem, the Netherlands, 1788. *Career:* joined Dominicans, 1788; ordained, 1793; instructor, Holy Cross Coll., 1793; teacher, Carshalton Coll., near London, 1794–1800, 1802–1804; superior of United States Dominicans, 1805; founder, Coll. of St. Thomas Aquinas and St. Rose's Church and priory (KY), 1806; missionary in KY and OH, 1806–21; bishop of Cincinnati, 1821–32; founder, the Athenaeum, St. Francis Xavier Coll., Cincinnati, 1829; founder, the *Catholic Telegraph-Register,* 1831.

Edward Fenwick was a member of a distinguished native Maryland Catholic family. He was sent to Europe for an education, and while there he joined the Dominicans. In 1804, after his education, a short teaching career, and brief imprisonment during the French Revolution, he returned to the United States, where he served as a missionary in Maryland and then in 1806 established the first American province of Dominicans near Springfield, KY. From this new establishment he and other Dominicans served the rapidly increasing immigrant Catholic populations in Kentucky and Ohio. He also brought the Dominican sisters to St. Rose's Convent in 1806 and 1807 and built the College of St. Thomas near Springfield. As the first bishop of Cincinnati, he was responsible for Catholicism in a major part of the old Northwest after 1821. In Cincinnati he built numerous churches, a cathedral, and schools, imported Dominican sisters and the Sisters of Charity, established St. Francis Xavier College, and founded a diocesan newspaper. He also expressed great concern for Indian rights and welfare and organized primary and adult education for Indians, but he was unable to provide any institutional barrier against the crush of the white westward movement. His missionary and educational activities in Cincinnati created fears in eastern Protestants like Lyman Beecher, whose *Plea for the*

West (1832) tried to awaken American nativist instincts to win the West from the threat of a Catholic takeover.

Bibliography

B. DAB, 5:328–29; DACB, 182; DAH, 90–91; NCAB, 5:186; NCE, 5:885–86; Victor F. O'Daniel, *The Right Reverend Edward Fenwick, O.P., Founder of the Dominicans in the U.S., Pioneer Missionary in Kentucky, Apostle of Ohio, First Bishop of Cincinnati* (New York, 1920).

FLAGET, BENEDICT JOSEPH (7 November 1763, Contournat, Auvergne, France—11 February 1850, Louisville, KY). *Education:* studied at Univ. of Clermont, France, 1779–81; Sem. of St. Sulpice, Clermont, 1781–83; Sem. of St. Sulpice, Issy, France, 1783–86. *Career:* joined Sulpicians, 1783; ordained, 1788; teacher, moral and dogmatic theology, Grand Sem., Nantes, France, 1788–91; missionary, Indiana, 1792–95; teacher, Georgetown Coll., 1795–98; teacher, Sulpician Coll., Havana, 1798–1801; teacher, St. Mary's Sem. (MD), 1801–1808; teacher, Mount St. Mary's Coll. and Sem. (MD), 1808–10; bishop of Bardstown, KY, 1808–41; bishop of Louisville, 1841–50.

Benedict Joseph Flaget was one of a number of French Sulpicians who fled the Terror in 1791 and emigrated to the United States. After sixteen years of pastoral and educational work in Indiana and Maryland, Flaget was elected the first bishop of Bardstown, KY, which became the premier diocesan see of Catholicism in the Midwest, from Detroit on the north to Tennessee on the south, and from the Alleghenies on the east to the Mississippi River on the west—a territory that contained eight future states. Flaget directed the establishment of Catholicism during the beginnings of the antebellum westward expansion, which saw in the course of a few years a migration that greatly increased both the Catholic and Protestant population.

Flaget traveled throughout this territory on horseback, preaching the gospel, hearing confessions, teaching catechism, celebrating Mass, establishing congregations, and settling local ecclesiastical disputes. He also traveled throughout Europe from 1834 to 1838, awakening among laity and clergy the missionary spirit, raising much-needed funds, and inviting clergy and sisters to serve the fledgling institutions in the vast frontier territory over which he had supervision. During his tenure as bishop of Bardstown (and later Louisville, where the see was moved in 1841), he supervised the establishment of St. Thomas Seminary and St. Joseph's and St. Mary's Colleges; the founding of the Sisters of Charity of Nazareth and the Sisters of Loretto; the settlement of the Trappists at Gethsemane (1848); and the construction of two cathedrals. He attracted to his diocese and to the priesthood, moreover, a number of young men who eventually became leading bishops in the United States: e.g., Francis Patrick Kenrick, Martin John Spalding, John M. Henni, Ignatius Reynolds, Leo de Neckere, John Baptist Mary David, and Guy Ignatius Chabrat.

Flaget's deep French Sulpician spirituality, his prudential administrative skills, his respect for American institutions, and his Gallican sense of the national church endeared him to his priests and people and made it possible for him to elicit their cooperation in establishing the foundations of Catholicism in the midwestern frontier. At his death Catholicism was the largest denomination in the country and in the Midwest eleven new dioceses had been erected in the territory he once traversed as the sole bishop.

Bibliography

A. "1815 Report to Rome," *CHR* 1 (1915): 305–19; "1812 Diary," *RACHS* 29 (1918): 37–59, 153–69, 231–49.

B. DAB, 6:445–47; DACB, 190–91; DAH, 94–95; DARB, 162–63; NCAB, 6:333–34; NCE, 5:956–57; Martin J. Spalding, *Sketches of the Life and Times and Character of the Right Reverend Benedict Joseph Flaget* (Louisville, 1852; reprint, New York, 1969); Abbé Desgeorges, *Vie de Monseigneur Flaget, Evêque de Bardstown et Louisville, par le prêtre qui accompagnerit pendant ses voyages en Europe* (Paris, 1855); J. Herman Schauinger, *Cathedrals in the Wilderness* (Milwaukee, 1952); Clyde F. Crews, *An American Holyland: A History of the Archdiocese of Louisville* (Wilmington, DE, 1987).

FRIESS, MOTHER CAROLINE (21 August 1824, Choisy-le-Roi, France— 22 July 1892, Milwaukee, WI). *Career:* entered School Sisters of Notre Dame, Neuburg vorm Wald, Bavaria, 1840; mother superior, School Sisters of Notre Dame in America, 1850–92.

Born to a Bavarian father and French mother, Mary Catherine Josephine Friess and her family moved from Paris to Bavaria when she was three years old. Educated in Benedictine convent schools, she entered the School Sisters of Notre Dame as Sister Caroline at the age of sixteen, emigrated with three other sisters to establish parochial schools for German immigrants in the United States at the age of twenty-three, and became the mother superior of her order at the age of twenty-six. Between 1847 and 1850 the four original sisters had grown to sixteen and had established three schools in Baltimore and one each in Pittsburgh, Philadelphia, and Buffalo. Sister Caroline returned to Bavaria in 1848, but her order sent her back to the United States in 1850 to establish the convent motherhouse and a school in Milwaukee, where she became mother superior of her order.

In 1851, shortly after reaching Milwaukee, she and two other sisters established St. Mary's as the first parochial school there. By the time of her death in 1892, she had developed a vibrant religious community that had 2,000 sisters; she and her sisters had opened and staffed 265 parochial schools in 16 states and 29 dioceses throughout the United States and Canada, serving 70,000 pupils; she had supervised the establishment of a number of orphanages for 1,500 children; and she had opened 4 institutes of higher education for women. For forty-two years she traveled from Milwaukee to New Orleans, Baltimore, Boston, Buffalo, and hundreds of other cities and towns in the Midwest and

South, establishing new branch convents of the School Sisters and opening schools and orphanages.

Like women religious in other parts of the country during the nineteenth century, she and her sisters faced periodic public assaults on their way of life. In 1873, for example, a Milwaukee journal, the *Christian Statesman,* published a scurrilous attack on the convent school and School Sisters. The independent and resolute Sister Caroline sued the editors of the journal for libel to regain the good reputation the sisters had earned in Milwaukee. The suit dragged on for two years before the editors decided to settle out of court by publishing a retraction of their scandalous and unfounded attacks.

Three years after her death the Maryland Notre Dames opened the first Catholic college for women. In 1913 her sisters also opened Mount Mary College for women in Milwaukee. From her beginnings in Milwaukee Sister Caroline was convinced that a sound religious and secular education was absolutely essential for women in the United States—to provide women for leadership roles in their homes, the church, and society.

Bibliography

A. *The Letters of Mother Caroline Friess,* ed. Barbara Brumleve (St. Louis, 1991).
B. P. M. Abbelen, *Venerable Mother Mary Caroline Friess, First Commissary General of the School Sisters of Notre Dame. A Sketch of Her Life and Character* (St. Louis, 1893); Mary Hester Valentine, *Mother Caroline and Higher Education of Women: School Sisters of Notre Dame—Pioneer Educators in Milwaukee* (Milwaukee, 1992).

FURFEY, PAUL HANLY (30 June 1897, Cambridge, MA—8 June 1992, Washington, DC). *Education:* A.B., Boston Coll., 1917; studied at St. Mary's Sem. (MD), 1918–19; Sulpician Sem., Washington, DC, 1919–22; Ph.D., Catholic Univ. of America, 1926; studied at Univ. of Berlin and Univ. of Frankfurt, 1931–32. *Career:* ordained, 1922; instructor, Catholic Univ. of America, 1925–31; professor and chairman, Sociology Department, Catholic Univ. of America, 1934–66; director, Juvenile Delinquency Evaluation Project, New York, 1956–61; codirector, Bureau of Social Research, 1959–71; retired, 1966–92.

Sociologist Paul Hanly Furfey was for almost sixty years one of the most articulate spokesmen for Christian personalism in the United States. Through seventeen published books and numerous articles from 1936 until 1978 he emphasized the roles of the church as well as the state in supporting the dignity and development of the person, and each person's responsibility for others in need. Furfey promoted what Charles Curran has called a "Catholic radicalism"—i.e., a radical interpretation of traditional Catholic philosophy and theology, a literal and personalist interpretation of the New Testament, and a supernatural sociology. Employing a Mystical Body understanding of the church, he called Catholic Christians in particular to witness gospel values by taking up the spiritual and corporal works of mercy and denying the seduction of materialistic and consumerist values.

Furfey called for social structural reform as well as personal conversion in his attempts to encourage the regeneration of society according to Christian values, but his emphasis was generally on the need for individual and communal commitment to the poor. He supported the Catholic Worker Movement and cofounded the Fides Neighborhood House and El Poverello House in Washington, DC, as support facilities for the poor; he also chose to live among the poor who were subjects of his lifetime study. Furfey was a moderate pacifist (holding that a just-war theory was not categorically wrong) who protested repeatedly against exaggerated nationalism in the United States before, as well as after, World War II and especially during the Vietnam War in the 1960s, when he established Emmaus House in Washington, DC, as a center for anti-war activity.

Bibliography

A. *Fire on the Earth* (New York, 1936); *Three Theories of Society* (New York, 1937); *This Way to Heaven* (Silver Spring, MD, 1939); *A History of Social Thought* (New York, 1942); *The Mystery of Iniquity* (Milwaukee, 1944); *The Respectable Murderers* (New York, 1969); *Love and the Urban Ghetto* (New York, 1978).
B. CA1947: 254–55; *Washington Post* 11 June 1992, C:6; *American Catholic Who's Who* 23:275; Charles Curran, "The Catholic Worker and Paul Hanly Furfey," in *American Catholic Social Ethics* (Notre Dame, IN, 1982), 130–71.

G

GALLITZIN, DEMETRIUS AUGUSTINE (22 December 1770, The Hague, the Netherlands—6 May 1840, Loretto, PA). *Education:* studied at St. Mary's Sem., Baltimore, 1792–95. *Career:* ordained, 1795; pastor of various communities in MD and PA, 1795–99; founding pastor, Loretto, 1799–1840.

Son of Prince Demetrius Alexejewitsch Gallitzin, Russian ambassador to Holland, and the German Countess Amelia von Schmettau Gallitzin, the young Russian Orthodox Prince Demetrius became a Catholic in 1786, a year after his mother had returned to her Catholic faith. In 1792 his parents sent him to tour the United States in order to broaden his education. Shortly after his arrival in the United States, Demetrius became interested in the priesthood and in serving the developing Catholic community. In 1799 he conceived of and established at Loretto, PA, in the Alleghenies, a small Catholic colony, and for the next forty years he became the pioneer missionary to Catholics within a hundred-mile radius of the western Pennsylvania town. Using his considerable fortune, he purchased large tracts of land, invited Catholic immigrants to buy the land from him and settle in the area, and built sawmills, gristmills, tanneries, schools, and other institutions and businesses to provide for life on the frontier.

Gallitzin was a horseback-riding missionary whose princely background and theological education made him a strong authoritarian figure, one who was not always congenial to the free aspirations and democratic inclinations of pioneer Catholics. Periodically before the late 1820s he was in conflict with certain leading lay members of his congregation, but eventually he won over his opponents and ran the Catholic church in the area like a priestly prince.

Demetrius came to some national attention in 1816 when he published *Defense of Catholic Principles* in response to a Protestant minister's attack on "popery." This pamphlet, the first widely distributed American Catholic apol-

ogetical tract, went through many editions and was used by Catholics throughout the country to explain their beliefs, religious practices, and customs, and
to demonstrate the compatibility of Catholic and American principles and practices of religious toleration. His defense of the Catholic faith and his development of Catholicism in western Pennsylvania earned for him a place of high
reputation among the American Catholic bishops who nominated him twice for
the episcopacy (once for Cincinnati and once for Detroit) but he declined to be
considered.

Bibliography

A. *Defense of Catholic Principles* (Pittsburgh, 1816); *An Appeal to the Protestant Pub-
lic* (Ebensburh, PA, 1819); *A Letter to a Protestant Friend on the Holy Scriptures*
(Ebensburg, PA, 1820); Grace Murphy, ed., *Gallitzin's Letters: A Collection of
the Polemical Works of the Very Reverend Prince Demetrius Augustine Gallitzin,
1770–1840* (Loretto, PA, 1940).
B. DAB, 7:113–15; DACB, 203–04; NCAB, 23:297–98; NCE, 6:268–69; Peter Henry
Lemcke, *Life and Work of Prince Demetrius Augustine Gallitzin*, trans. Joseph C.
Plumpe (New York, 1940); Stasys Maziliauskas, *Pioneer Prince in USA: An His-
torical Account of Prince Demetrius Augustine Gallitzin and His Eminent Relatives*
(Troy, MI, 1982).

GASTON, WILLIAM JOSEPH (19 September 1778, New Bern, NC—23
January 1844, Raleigh, NC). *Education:* studied at Georgetown Coll., 1790–
92; graduated, Princeton Coll., 1796; studied law with François X. Martin,
1797–98. *Career:* elected to NC Senate, 1800; Federalist presidential elector,
1808; elected to the US House of Representatives from NC, 1813, 1815; justice, NC Supreme Court, 1833–44.

William J. Gaston was a prominent Catholic layman in North Carolina during more than forty years of active public and political life as a trustee of the
state university, state senator, United States Congressman, and State Supreme
Court justice. For more than twenty of those years he was also Bishop John
England's trusted financial and legal adviser and confidential consultant on various diocesan and national ecclesiastical matters. Gaston was the first Catholic
to serve in North Carolina's legislature and supreme court, even though the
state constitution required that no one could hold public office who denied "the
truth of the Protestant religion." In 1835, after being nominated to the state
supreme court, Gaston was instrumental in mitigating this religious test for
public office. As judge he also upheld some civil rights for slaves and unsuccessfully advocated the enfranchisement of freed African-Americans. Although
a plantation slaveholder, he spoke out periodically against the Southern system
and called for its abolition.

Bibliography

A. *Speech of the Honorable Judge Gaston, delivered in the Recent State Convention of
North Carolina* (Baltimore, 1835); *Speech on Religious Toleration by Judge William Gaston . . .* (Raleigh, NC, 1836).

B. DAB, 7:180–81; NCAB, 3:513–14; NCE, 6:300; J. Fairfax McLaughlin, "William Gaston," *RACHS* 6 (1895): 225–51; W. B. Hannon, "Judge William Gaston: Statesman and Jurist," *Journal of the American Irish Historical Society* 10 (1911): 253–58; Edward F. McSweeny, "Judge William Gaston of North Carolina," *Historical Records and Studies* 17 (1926): 172–88; J. Herman Schauinger, *William Gaston: Carolinian* (Milwaukee, 1949); Walter F. Pratt, Jr., "The Struggle for Judicial Independence in Antebellum North Carolina: The Story of Two Judges," *Law and History Review* 4 (1986): 129–59.

GIBBONS, JAMES (23 July 1834, Baltimore, MD—24 March 1921, Baltimore, MD). *Education:* studied at St. Charles Coll. (MD), 1855; St. Mary's Sem., Baltimore, 1857–61. *Career:* ordained, 1861; pastoral work in MD, 1861–68; vicar apostolic of NC, 1868–72; bishop of Richmond, 1872–77; coadjutor archbishop of Baltimore, 1877; archbishop of Baltimore, 1877–1921; cardinal, 1886–1921.

Born in Baltimore the son of Irish immigrants, James Gibbons moved to Ireland with his family in 1837, and in 1853, after his father's death, his mother and the Gibbons children returned to the United States, where they took up residence in New Orleans. After two years as a grocery clerk James returned to Maryland, where he matriculated at St. Charles College and St. Mary's Seminary. Ordained in 1861 he began serving various parishes in the Baltimore area, volunteered as a chaplain to Union troops at Forts McHenry and Marshall during the Civil War, and in 1865 became Archbishop Martin John Spalding's secretary. As assistant chancellor of Baltimore he helped prepare the agenda for the Second Plenary Council of Baltimore (1866). His affability, practicality, and ecclesiastical experience made him a prime candidate for the episcopal office in the post–Civil War period. At the age of thirty-four he was made the vicar apostolic of North Carolina and became one of the youngest bishops to participate at the First Vatican Council (1869–70).

In 1872 he was made bishop of Richmond, and while there he published *The Faith of Our Fathers* (1876), an introduction to Catholic faith and practice that reflected his missionary experiences among non-Catholics in Virginia and North Carolina. The text was a widely distributed popular and irenic apologetical tract that demonstrated a Catholic acceptance of foundational American institutions and principles. Having lived in a predominantly Protestant Southern culture during the early years of his priestly and episcopal career made him sensitive to Protestant feelings.

In 1877 he was appointed archbishop of Baltimore, an office he served for the next forty-four years. Throughout these years he became the leading Catholic churchman in the country, mediating between the American and Roman church. In 1884 he was appointed the apostolic delegate to the Third Plenary Council of Baltimore, and after that time he was the symbol of Catholicism in the United States, mediating between Catholic and American values. Although he was known for his "masterly inactivity" in administering national ecclesiastical interests, he was considered a moderate Americanist, fighting against a Vatican condemnation of the Knights of Labor, warding off an official public condemnation of Henry George's works, supporting the establishment of the Catholic University of America, and articulating the value of the American form of religious liberty before Roman audiences.

During the 1890s he sided with the Americanist bishops but was a voice of ecclesiastical moderation, trying to preserve unity among the Americanist and anti-Americanist bishops. When Americanism was condemned by Pope Leo XIII in 1899, he argued that no such heresy in fact existed in the United States. In the early twentieth century he was instrumental in establishing the Maryknoll missionaries, preserving the Catholic University from financial failure, and erecting the National Catholic War Council. No other Catholic bishop in the United States during his episcopacy had as much influence on national Catholic life. Throughout his fifty-three-year episcopal career he represented Catholic interests before the American government and was personally acquainted with six American presidents.

Bibliography

A. *The Faith of Our Fathers* (Baltimore, 1876; and many subsequent editions); *Our Christian Heritage* (Baltimore, 1889); *Collections and Recollections in the Life and Times of Cardinal Gibbons,* ed. John T. Reilly, 10 vols. (Martinburg, WV, 1890–1904); *The Ambassador of Christ* (Baltimore, 1896); *Discourses and Sermons* (Baltimore, 1908); *A Retrospect of Fifty Years* (Baltimore, 1916; reprint, New York, 1972).

B. DAB, 7:238–42; DACB, 212–13; DAH, 108–9; DARB, 173–75; NCAB 29:77–79; NCE, 6:466–68; NYT, 25 March 1921, 1, 9; SH, 4:484; Allen Sinclair Will, *Life of Cardinal Gibbons, Archbishop of Baltimore,* 2 vols. (New York, 1922); John Tracy Ellis, *The Life of James Cardinal Gibbons,* 2 vols. (Milwaukee, 1952); Thomas W. Spalding, *The Premier See: A History of the Archdiocese of Baltimore, 1789–1989* (Baltimore, 1989), 123–233.

GLENNON, JOHN JOSEPH (14 June 1862, County Westmeath, Ireland—9 March 1946, Dublin, Ireland). *Education:* studied at All Hallows Coll., Dublin, 1883–84; Univ. of Bonn, 1885. *Career:* ordained, 1884; pastoral work in Kansas City, MO, 1884–96; coadjutor bishop of Kansas City, 1896–1903; archbishop of St. Louis, 1903–46; cardinal, 1945–46.

In 1883 at the age of twenty-one, John Glennon emigrated from Ireland, where he had received his education, to Kansas City, MO, where he was ordained to the priesthood. After twelve years of pastoral work in the diocese he was made coadjutor bishop. In 1903 he began a forty-three-year reign as archbishop of St. Louis, where he became one of the early twentieth-century consolidating urban bishops.

Archbishop Glennon started his career in St. Louis by holding the fifth (1905) and sixth (1908) diocesan synods in order to establish disciplinary and ecclesiastical unity. Throughout his long tenure he also fostered and consolidated

Catholic social work in the diocese, providing, for example, care and education for deaf-mute children of the poor, homes for orphans and homeless men, and Catholic settlement schools and day nurseries. He was responsible, too, for constructing and financing numerous churches, schools, hospitals, and a new seminary to meet the needs of a steadily growing Catholic population. In 1908 he began construction of a major cathedral, Byzantine in style, which became a landmark of ecclesiastical architecture in St. Louis. The large cathedral and even the laying of its cornerstone, which included an ostentatious parade of representatives from all seventy-nine city parishes, were symbolic of big-city ethnic Catholicism in the early part of the twentieth century.

Under Glennon's supervision, St. Louis Catholicism developed the institutions that were symbolic of a community that was ambitious, seeking prestige and influence in the city and manifesting that ambition in numerous social and educational projects. Glennon consolidated these projects by his own episcopal presence, his businesslike administrative efficiency, his eloquence, and the force of his personality and authority. He was able to articulate in word and stone the common purpose and aspirations of the Catholic community in St. Louis. In 1945 Pope Pius XII acknowledged his contributions and services by making him the first cardinal of St. Louis, giving the Catholic community there another symbol of its importance and maturity.

Bibliography

A. "The Dawn of Missouri's History," *St. Louis Catholic Historical Review* 3 (October 1931): 227–31; "The Coming of the Jesuit Fathers to St. Louis," *St. Louis Catholic Historical Review* 5 (April–July 1923): 93–98.

B. DACB, 218; DAH, 112; DCB, 490; NYT, 10 March 1946, 1; John E. Rothensteiner, *History of the Archdiocese of St. Louis,* 2 vols. (St. Louis 1928), 2: 635–764; Thomas B. Morgan, *Speaking of Cardinals* (New York, 1946, 206–44; Nicholas Scheidner, *The Life of John Cardinal Glennon, Archbishop of St. Louis* (Liguori, MO, 1971).

GOLDSTEIN, DAVID (27 July 1870, Spitalfields, Middlesex, England—30 June 1958, Boston, MA). *Education:* studied at New York Public Schools, Hebrew Free School, and Spanish Jewish Synagogue, 1876–81. *Career:* member, Socialist Labor Party, 1888–1903; cofounder with Martha Moore Avery, Catholic Truth Guild, 1917; founder, Catholic Campaigners for Christ, 1936; columnist, *Boston Pilot,* 1945–58.

After emigrating to the United States in 1871, David Goldstein grew up in a Jewish family in New York and attended both public and Jewish schools. At age eleven he became a cigar maker, the trade of his father. In 1888 the Goldstein family moved to Boston, where David joined the cigar makers' International Union and the Socialist Labor Party. In the latter he met Martha Moore Avery, who would be his mentor and colleague for the remainder of her life. Both were active propagandists for the socialist movement, lecturing and debating on street corners and in city parks. In 1896 they established in Boston the Karl Marx Class (which became in 1901 the Boston School of Political Economy), a free, weekly lecture series that was followed by discussions of Marx's writings. The socialist priest Thomas McGrady lectured periodically for the class prior to his departure from the priesthood in 1903, the same year that both Goldstein and Avery resigned from the Socialist Labor Party because they believed that American socialism had become unnecessarily critical of Christian doctrines and had advocated free love and violence.

From 1903 until his death Goldstein became a vigorous critic of socialism because he saw it as a fundamental threat to both religion and traditional family values. Having come to believe that he shared the official Catholic opposition to socialism and Catholic support for a stable family system, he joined the church in 1905. As a Catholic he used the propaganda techniques he had learned in the socialist movement to attack socialism and to preach and teach Catholic positions on justice and family life. In 1917 he and Avery, who had converted to Catholicism in 1904, founded the Catholic Truth Guild in Boston as an agency for lay Catholic propaganda. Supported by Cardinal William O'Connell, Goldstein effectively organized street preaching and lecturing in Boston and criss-crossed the nation from 1917 to 1941 as one of the first lay American Catholic evangelists. By the mid-1930s he changed the name of his one-man movement to Catholic Campaigners for Christ and continued to advocate Catholicism as the source of family and social values. The highly organized and innovative preaching tours waned after World War II because of Goldstein's age, changing directions of the Catholic lay apostolate in the United States, and lack of Catholic support for his aggressive techniques.

Bibliography

A. With Martha Moore Avery, *Socialism: The Nation of Fatherless Children* (Boston, 1903, 1911); with Avery, *Bolshevism: Its Cure* (Boston, 1919); with Avery, *Campaigning for Christ* (Boston, 1924); *Campaigners for Christ Handbook* (Boston, 1931, 1934); *Autobiography of a Campaigner for Christ* (Boston, 1936); *Jewish Panorama* (Boston, 1940); *Letters of a Hebrew-Catholic to Mr. Isaacs* (St. Paul, 1943); *What Say You?* (St. Paul, 1945).

B. NCE, 6:601–2; NYT, 1 July 1958, 31; Debra Campbell, "David Goldstein and the Lay Catholic Street Apostolate: 1917–1941" (Ph.D. diss., Boston University, 1982); idem, "A Catholic Salvation Army: David Goldstein, Pioneer Lay Evangelist," *CH* 52 (September 1983): 322–32; idem, "David Goldstein and the Rise of the Catholic Campaigners for Christ," *CHR* 72 (January 1986): 33–50.

GUÉRIN, MOTHER THEODORE (2 October 1798, Etables, France—17 March 1856, St. Mary-of-the-Woods, IN). *Career:* member, Sisters of Providence, Ruillé-sur-Loire, 1823; superior, Sisters of Providence, Rennes, France, 1824–34; founding superior, Sisters of Providence, St. Mary-of-the-Woods, IN, 1840–56.

In 1840 Mother Theodore (née Anne Thérèse) Guérin came to the United States to establish the Sisters of Providence in response to an invitation from the bishop of Vincennes, IN, Celestine René Lawrence Guynemer de la Hai-landière (1798–1882). With six other French sisters she cleared a plot of land outside of Vincennes and built a suitable convent called St. Mary-of-the-Woods. The sisters established almost immediately St. Mary's Institute as a school for young girls in the area. By the mid-1840s Mother Theodore had had a number of conflicts with her bishop over the community's rule and her fitness as supe-rior. By 1847 Bishop de la Hailandière had become so exasperated with what he considered her obstinacy and disobedience that he excommunicated her. The bishop himself resigned his see in 1847, and his successor almost immediately restored Mother Theodore to her community, where she continued to direct a thriving religious order in Indiana. By the end of the century the Sisters of Providence had grown to over one thousand and had established the College of St. Mary-of-the-Woods, eighty elementary schools and academies in Balti-more, Boston, Chicago, Indianapolis, Fort Wayne, Peoria, Rochford, and other places. In 1920 the Sisters of Providence sent their first American missionaries to China.

Bibliography

A. *Journals and Letters of Mother Theodore Guérin, Foundress of the Sisters of Prov-idence of Saint Mary-of-the-Woods, Indiana,* ed. Mary Theodosia Mug (Saint Mary-of-the-Woods, IN, 1937).
B. DACB, 229; Joseph B. Code, *Great American Foundresses* (New York, 1929).

GUINEY, LOUISE IMOGEN (7 January 1861, Roxbury, MA—2 November 1920, Chipping Campden, Gloucestershire, England).

Daughter of Irish immigrants and a graduate of convent schools, Louise Im-ogen Guiney became a poet, essayist, and literary scholar. In the late nine-teenth century she was a significant part of the Boston and New York literary revival, having among her acquaintances Oliver Wendell Holmes, Thomas Bai-ley Aldrich, and T. W. Higginson. Although influenced significantly by earlier Romantic writers, she tried to develop a link between the Romantic age and the genteel tradition of the 1890s. Throughout her life she was a practicing Catholic and became somewhat of a link between her culture and that of the Boston literary establishment. Although she enjoyed creative writing and loved literature, her published works never sold well, and she was forced by financial circumstances to hire herself out as a piece writer. Like other creative writers in the late nineteenth century she endured poverty, and when forced to work outside her chosen vocation she experienced a drain upon her own genius. In 1901 she moved to England and continued to publish, but she never achieved a significant following there either. She does represent, though, something of the rising middle-class Catholic literary tradition in the late nineteenth century.

Bibliography

A. *A Roadside Harp* (Boston, 1893); *Patrins* (Boston, 1897); *Recusant Poets* (New York, 1939).

B. DACB, 230–31; NAW, 2:101–2; Eva M. Tenison, *Louise Imogen Guiney: Her Life and Works, 1861–1920* (London, 1923); S. M. Parrish, ''Currents of the Nineties in Boston and London: Fred Holland Day, Louise Imogen Guiney, and Their Circle'' (Ph.D. diss., Harvard University, 1954).

H

HAAS, FRANCIS JOSEPH (18 March 1899, Racine, WI—29 August 1953, Grand Rapids, MI). *Education:* studied at St. Francis Sem. (WI), 1904–13; Johns Hopkins Univ., 1920–21; Ph.D., Catholic Univ. of America, 1922. *Career:* ordained, 1913; curate, Holy Rosary parish, Milwaukee, 1913–15; professor of English, St. Francis Sem., 1915–19; professor of sociology, Marquette Univ., 1922–31; editor, *Salesianum,* 1922–31; president, National Catholic Sch. of Social Service, 1931–35; rector, St. Francis Sem., 1935–37; dean, Sch. of Social Science, Catholic Univ. of America, 1937–43; bishop, Grand Rapids, MI, 1943–53.

Like other articulate mid-twentieth-century Catholics, Francis J. Haas hoped to see a Christian culture embodied in social, economic, and political living. Influenced by the papal social encyclicals, his own advanced study of sociology, and the work of pioneer thinkers like John A. Ryan, Haas became a strong advocate of the dignity of labor and the need to establish a more equitable distribution of wealth in American society. Like Ryan he became an activist for a living wage, but unlike Ryan he placed more emphasis upon labor unions (freed from the influence of socialism) than social legislation as a means for obtaining it. The capitalist system, in his estimate, was not in itself vicious, but it was in need of adjustments like collective bargaining to bring about wage justice and mutual benefit for labor and management, thereby providing for the greatest public good.

By the beginning of the 1930s Haas had an established reputation as a fair-minded mediator between labor and management. President Roosevelt acknowledged Haas's skills in 1933 when he appointed him to the National Labor Relations Board. Throughout the New Deal years Haas served as a special strike mediator, a member and negotiator of the United States Department of Labor, and chairman of the Committee on Fair Employment Practices. He also helped organize and lecture at numerous summer schools of social action for Catholic priests from 1937 to the mid-1940s, and was influential in drafting the American Catholic bishops' pastoral "The Church and Social Order" (1940). In the late 1930s and early 1940s he also wrote against and negotiated to end racial discrimination in trade unions and industry. In 1946 President Truman appointed him a member of the Civil Rights Commission in recognition of his efforts for racial justice. The last ten years of his life were spent as the bishop of Grand Rapids, MI, where he manifested the same commitment to fairness and social justice that had characterized his labor-management activities.

Bibliography

A. *Shop Collective Bargaining: A Study of Wage Determination* (Washington, DC, 1922); *Man and Society: An Introduction to Sociology* (New York, 1930).
B. DACB, 233; DAH, 121; DARB, 187–89; NCAB, D:34; NCE, 6:875; NYT, 30 August 1953, 88; Thomas E. Blantz, *A Priest in Public Service: Francis J. Haas and the New Deal* (Notre Dame, IN, 1982).

HALLINAN, PAUL J. (8 April 1911, Painesville, OH—27 March 1968, Atlanta, GA). *Education:* B.A., Univ. of Notre Dame, 1932; studied at Our Lady of the Lake Sem., Cleveland, 1932–37; M.A., John Carroll Univ., 1953; Ph.D., Case Western Reserve Univ., 1963. *Career:* ordained, 1937; assistant pastor, St. Aloysius, Cleveland, 1937–42; army chaplain, 1942–45; assistant pastor, St. John's Cathedral, Cleveland, 1945–58; Newman chaplain, Cleveland Coll., 1945–58; president, National Association of Newman Club Chaplains, 1952–58; bishop, Charleston, SC, 1958–62; archbishop, Atlanta, 1962–68.

Like many of the young men who became priests in the 1930s, Paul Hallinan received a post–Vatican I theological education, one in the United States that promoted a muscular Christianity. His love for church and country was reinforced during World War II when he became a chaplain. In the postwar years, however, as he became involved in the Newman movement, he was gradually exposed on the local and national level to some moderately reforming movements within the church—particularly the social justice and liturgical movements. His interests in reform and change were also fostered by his reading of John Henry Newman and formal study of history at John Carroll and Case Western Reserve universities (1953–56); he did not actually finish writing his doctoral dissertation until he was archbishop of Atlanta in 1963.

As a bishop of Charleston and Atlanta he became known for his moderate reform measures within the church, supporting civil rights, integrating the church's institutions, and engaging in other civil and ecumenical projects. At the Second Vatican Council, where he was a member of the Liturgical Commission, he was an active voice for liturgical renewal, following the lead of scholars like Frederick R. McManus and Godfrey Diekmann, O.S.B. After the council, as a member of the International Committee on English in the Liturgy and the United States Bishops' Commission on the Liturgical Apostolate, he tried to moderate between the radical liturgical innovators who took reforms into their own hands and those priests and bishops who resisted any change. Hallinan loved tradition and appreciated the historical forms of the liturgy, but he understood tradition as a living thing that required, rather than precluded, change.

Bibliography

A. "Richard Gilmour: Second Bishop of Cleveland 1872–1891," (Ph.D. diss., Case Western Reserve University, 1963); *How to Understand Changes in the Liturgy* (Atlanta, 1964); *Days of Hope and Promise: The Writings and Speeches of Paul J. Hallinan, Archbishop of Atlanta,* ed. Vincent A. Yzermans (Collegeville, MN, 1973).
B. DACB, 236; DAH, 124; John T. Ellis, "Archbishop Hallinan: In Memoriam," *Thought* 43 (1968): 539–72; Thomas J. Shelley, *Paul J. Hallinan: First Archbishop of Atlanta* (Wilmington, DE, 1989).

HARRIS, MARY (see JONES, MOTHER MARY HARRIS).

HAWTHORNE, ROSE (see LATHROP, ROSE HAWTHORNE).

HEALY, JAMES AUGUSTINE (6 April 1830, Macon, GA—5 August 1900, Portland, ME). *Education:* B.A., Holy Cross Coll. (MA), 1849; Grand Sem., Montreal, 1849–51; Sem. of St. Sulpice, Paris, 1851–54. *Career:* ordained, 1854; pastoral work in Boston, 1854–75; bishop of Portland, 1875–1900.

James Healy, son of an Irish immigrant father and African-American mother, was one of three talented mulatto brothers, all of whom became priests and obtained prominent positions within the American Catholic community. James was graduated from Holy Cross summa cum laude, and after education for the priesthood he was appointed Archbishop John Joseph Williams's secretary, chancellor of the diocese of Boston, assistant at St. John's Church, rector of the cathedral, and founding pastor of Boston's St. James's Church. Healy was active in charitable works, among them the Home for Destitute Catholic Children, the House of the Good Shepherd, St. Anne's Foundling Home, and the Catholic Laymen's Union.

As bishop of Portland for twenty-five years, the French-speaking Healy took a special interest in the French Canadians and Native Americans of his diocese. Because of his knowledge of Indian life, he was appointed a consultant to the United States Government's Bureau of Indian Affairs. At the time of his death Healy had established more than sixty new parishes, sixty-eight mission stations, and eighteen new schools and convents, and had developed stable welfare institutions in the diocese.

Bibliography

B. DACB, 246–47; DAH, 128; NCE, 6:964; NYT, 6 August 1900, 7; Albert S. Foley, *Bishop Healy: Beloved Outcaste* (New York, 1954). William Lucey, *The Catholic Church in Maine* (Francestown, NH, 1957).

HECKER, ISAAC THOMAS (18 December 1819, New York, NY—22 December 1888, New York, NY). *Education:* studied at Redemptorist novitiate, St. Trond, Belgium, 1845–46; Redemptorist training, Witten, the Netherlands, 1846–47; training at Clapham, London, England, 1848–49. *Career:* ordained, 1849; pastoral work in England, 1849–51; Redemptorist missionary in United States, 1851–57; founder and superior, Congregation of Missionary Priests of St. Paul the Apostle, 1858–88.

In the course of his forty-five years as a Catholic, Isaac Thomas Hecker had a significant impact on American Catholic life and thought. After his death his spiritual legacy continued in the religious order he founded, and his intellectual influence continued in his late-nineteenth-century Americanist heirs. The son of German immigrants, Hecker was baptized a Lutheran, reared within the context of his mother's warm Methodist piety, and educated for a very brief period in the New York Public Schools. In the early 1830s, after his father's foundry business failed, he left school and worked at various jobs to help support the family. During his teenage years and early twenties he joined his brothers' bakery business and became involved with the Loco Focos. In 1842, after meeting Orestes A. Brownson, he went to live with communitarians at Brook Farm and Fruitlands in Massachusetts and for a short time with the Henry Thoreau family, seeking a way of life that suited his quest for meaning and spiritual solace. Influenced by his experiences in Massachusetts, by Brownson, by reading Johann Adam Moehler, and by his own search for spirituality and communion, he converted to Catholicism in 1844 at the age of twenty-five.

In 1845 he became a Redemptorist, and after education for the priesthood in Europe he returned to the United States in 1851 to conduct parish missions for non-Catholics as well as Catholics along the East Coast. These missionary experiences made Hecker and other American Redemptorists believe that the German Redemptorists in the United States should establish a branch of the order that would be sensitive to American culture and attractive to young Americans who could carry on an American-style evangelization program among non-Catholics. In 1857 he took this idea to Rome, where he and his American Redemptorist companions were dismissed from the order. Pope Pius IX did, however, allow Hecker and the other former American Redemptorists to establish in 1858 the Congregation of Missionary Priests of St. Paul the Apostle (i.e., Paulists), whose primary mission was the evangelization and conversion of non-Catholics in the United States. Hecker conducted numerous parish missions throughout the country after 1858, became a theological consultant and advisor to archbishop Martin John Spalding at the Second Plenary Council of Baltimore (1866) and the First Vatican Council (1869–70), published the *Catholic World* (1865–) as a journal of religious thought and opinion, and established the Catholic Publication Society (1866) to distribute to non-Catholics as well as Catholics low-cost Catholic apologetical and spiritual tracts. Throughout the post–Civil War period he focused his attention and much of his writing on the themes of the compatibility of *The Church and the Age* (1887), the title of an anthology of his significant writings.

Influenced by post-Kantian idealism, Hecker became one of the foremost American Catholic representatives of the Romantic mood in American religion. His concentration on the correlation of the subjective search for meaning and the objective response in the church's sacramental and spiritual tradition helped him develop a new apologetic for Catholicism, one sensitive to the benefits of American cultural and political values. After his death in 1888 his views became the subject of an international ecclesiastical controversy which ended when Pope Leo XIII's encyclical *Testem Benevolentiae* (1899) condemned Americanism as a complex of heretical ideas that some conservative European Catholics had exaggeratedly identified with Hecker.

Bibliography

A. *Questions of the Soul* (New York, 1855); *Aspirations of Nature* (New York, 1857); *Catholic World*, 1865–88; *The Church and the Age* (New York, 1887).

B. DAB, 8:495; DACB, 247–48; DARB, 196–97; NCAB, 9:166–67; NCE, 6:982–83; SH, 5:196; Walter Elliot, *The Life of Father Hecker* (New York, 1891); *Le Père Hecker. Fondateur des 'Paulistes' Américains 1819–1888* . . . , intro. by Mgr. Ireland; preface by l'Abbé Félix Klein (Paris, 1898); Charles Maignen, *Etudes sur l'Américanisme: Le Père Hecker, Est'il un Saint?* (Paris, 1898); Vincent F. Holden, *The Early Years of Isaac Thomas Hecker, 1819–1844* (New York, 1939); idem, *The Yankee Paul: Isaac Thomas Hecker* (New York, 1958); John Farina, *An American Experience of God: The Spirituality of Isaac Hecker* (New York, 1981); idem, ed., *Hecker Studies: Essays on the Thought of Isaac Hecker* (New York, 1983); David J. O'Brien, *Isaac Hecker: An American Catholic* (New York, 1992).

HENNEPIN, LOUIS (12 May 1626, Ath, Belgium—after 1701, Rome, Italy). *Career:* missionary, the Recollet Order of Friars Minor, 1673–74; Quebec, 1675–82; France, the Netherlands, and Rome, 1675–17??.

After coming to Canada in 1675, François de Montmorency de Laval, bishop of Quebec, appointed Hennepin the Lenten and Advent preacher and had him study Indian dialects so that he could become a missionary to the Indians. In 1678 he accompanied René Robert, Sieur de la Salle, on his expedition as far west as Lake Peoria, where Hennepin left that expedition and traveled to the Mississippi River and north as far as St. Anthony Falls (which he named) in Minneapolis. Captured by the Sioux, he and some of his companions were rescued by the French explorer Daniel Guysolon Du Lhut and then returned to Montreal. In 1682, shortly after returning from the West, he returned to France and the Netherlands, where he wrote some accounts of his travels and made claims about his own discoveries that historians have seriously questioned.

Bibliography

A. *Description de la Louisiane* (Paris, 1683); *Nouvelle découverte* (Antwerp, 1697); *Nouvelle Voyage* (Utrecht, 1698).

B. DAB, 8:540–41; DACB, 251–52; NCE, 6:1016–17; John Gilmary Shea, *Discovery and Exploration of the Mississippi Valley* (2nd ed., Albany, NY, 1903); J. Delanglez, *Hennepin's Description of Louisiana* (Chicago, 1941); A. Lovant, "Le Père Louis Hennepin: Nouveaux jalons pour sa biographie," *Revue d'histoire ecclésiastique* 45 (1950) 186–211.

HEUSER, HERMAN JOSEPH (28 October 1852, Potsdam, Germany—22 August 1933, Overbrook, PA). *Education:* studied at Berlin and Breslau; St. Charles Borromeo Sem. (PA), 1870–76. *Career:* student teacher, St. Charles Borromeo Sem., 1870–76; ordained, 1876; professor, St. Charles Borromeo Sem., 1876–1927; founding editor, *American Ecclesiastical Review,* 1899–1914, 1919–27; founding editor, the *Dolphin,* 1900–1908; retired, 1927–33.

Herman Heuser was a priest-theologian, seminar professor, editor, author of fifteen books, and promoter of clerical spirituality. Conservative by nature and by education, he taught a post–Vatican I theological tradition that respected the distinction between faith and reason, supported a papal-centered ecclesiology, and warred against rationalism, evolutionism, and materialism. He promoted this message as a seminary professor, cofounder with James Corcoran of the *ACQR,* founding editor of the *AER,* a journal intended primarily for the continued education of the clergy, and founding editor of the *Dolphin,* a general literary magazine and book supplement to the *AER.* In 1896 he was appointed theological advisor to the Pontifical Commission on Anglican Orders. Because of his orthodox reputation, the apostolic delegate in 1907, during the controversy over modernism, appointed him a general censor of all Catholic publications in the United States. Heuser wrote for his own journals and published a number of historical works and books on spirituality. He was also instrumental in writing the constitutions for the Sisters of Mercy of Marion, PA, and for Mother Katherine Drexel's Sisters of the Blessed Sacrament. In 1927 he retired from active teaching and editing and deeded the *AER* to the Catholic University.

Bibliography

A. *Canon Sheile of Doneraile* (New York, 1917); *Autobiography of an Old Breviary* (New York, 1925); *In the Workshop of Saint Joseph* (New York, 1925); *From Tarsus to Rome* (New York, 1927); *House of Martha in Bethany* (New York, 1927).

B. DACB, 256; NCE, 6:1091–92; H. T. Henry, "Some Memories of the Founder of the *Review,*" *AER* 100 (1939): 8–21.

HODUR, FRANCIS (1 April 1866, Zarkack, Poland—16 February 1953, Scranton, PA). *Education:* studied at Univ. of Jagielon, Poland; graduated from St. Ann's Coll., Univ. of Krakow, 1891. *Career:* ordained, 1893; pastor, Catholic churches in Scranton and Nanticoke, PA, 1893–97; independent Polish Catholic priest, Scranton, 1897–1904; bishop, independent Polish Catholic synod, 1904–1907; bishop of Polish National Catholic Church, 1907–53.

Francis Hodur was the founding bishop of the Polish National Catholic Church, a new denomination created as a result of conflicts within the American Catholic church between local Polish Catholic immigrant congregations, who desired autonomous control over their ecclesiastical properties and religious customs, and American Catholic bishops, whose national legislation forbade such autonomy. After studying for the priesthood in Poland, Hodur emigrated to the United States in 1891 and was ordained for the diocese of Scranton, which had a large Polish Catholic immigrant population by the end of the nineteenth century. In 1897 the eighty-one-year-old Irish immigrant bishop of Scranton, William O'Hara, demanded, in accord with Baltimore canonical legislation, that the Polish immigrant parish of the Sacred Heart sign over its property deeds to him. The action precipitated a split in the congregation, and dissaffected members separated themselves from Sacred Heart, established a new independent parish, St. Stanislaus, and obtained Hodur to serve as their priest, independent of any episcopal control.

By 1904 disaffected Polish Catholics throughout the country created a synod independent of the American Catholic communion and elected Hodur as its first bishop. He was ordained bishop by an Old Catholic bishop in order to preserve a legitimate episcopal line within the community. Hodur and the new synod made allowances for Polish language in the liturgy, lay participation in the selection of clergy and bishops, and lay controls over ecclesiastical temporalities. In 1907 the Hodur synod was amalgamated with other disaffected Polish Catholics in Chicago, and together they created the Polish National Catholic Church. From 1907 until his death in 1953 Hodur consecrated nine other bishops for the new denomination, which resembled in most respects Polish Catholic sacramental and spiritual traditions while being innovative in ecclesiastical administration and governance, and he saw the establishment of 165 parishes with over 250,000 members in the United States and a number of missions in Poland. Hodur, like many of the Polish immigrants he represented, experienced the need to preserve his Catholic religious and ethnic heritage, but unlike other American Polish Catholics, he used the methods of democratic participation to accomplish his goal.

Bibliography

A. *Jedenascie Wielkich Zasad [Eleven Great Principles]* (Scranton, PA, 1923); *Prace i Pisma Ksiedza Biskupa F. Hodura [Life and Writings of Bishop F. Hodur]* (Scranton, PA, 1939).
B. DARB, 209–10; NYT, 17 February 1953, 34; Theodore Andrews, *The Polish National Catholic Church in America and Poland* (London, 1953); Joseph W. Wieczerak, "Bishop Francis Hodur and the Socialists: Associations and Disassociations," *Polish American Studies* 40 (Autumn, 1983): 5–35; William J. Galush, "Both Polish and Catholic: Immigrant Clergy in the American Church," CHR 70 (July 1984): 407–27.

HOGAN, WILLIAM (1788, Limerick, Ireland—3 January 1848, Nashua, NH). *Education:* studied at St. Patrick's Sem., Maynooth, Ireland, 1813–14. *Career:* pastoral work, diocese of Limerick, 1814–19; priest in Albany, NY, 1819; assistant pastor, St. Mary's Cathedral, Philadelphia, 1820–23; US consul at

Nuevitas, Cuba, 1843; lecturer, author, and lawyer in NC, GA, MA, and NH, 1824–48.

William Hogan was one of the more notorious vagabond priests of the early nineteenth century. Educated for the priesthood in Ireland, he did pastoral work in the diocese of Limerick until 1819, when, without obtaining his bishop's official permission, he left the diocese and emigrated to Albany, NY, where he served in a parish for a short time, and then in 1820 to St. Mary's Church in Philadelphia. From 1820 to 1823 Hogan was at the center of a bitter and litigious conflict between the newly arrived Irish immigrant bishop Henry Conwell and the lay trustees of St. Mary's, who retained and supported Hogan after Conwell suspended and then had him excommunicated for disobedience and for leading a church into schismatic separation from the bishop of the diocese. In Philadelphia "Hoganism" became the code word for the assertion of lay and clerical rights in the church—lay rights to select pastors and bishops and to hold and control ecclesiastical properties. Hoganism was an attempt to reform the structures of the church according to the democratic élan of the age.

Though Hogan was brash, impetuous, and haughty, he was also a popular preacher and effective organizer. The young cleric's popularity threatened the new bishop's position in the community, but the bishop's quick and ill-tempered suspension of Hogan made the bishop himself not only unpopular but also a threat to good order and compassionate leadership in the church.

Hogan's attacks upon Bishop Conwell and his published charges against his fellow Irish immigrants eventually made him a persona non grata in Philadelphia Catholicism. In 1824 he left the Catholic church, married, was eventually admitted to the bar in New Hampshire, and for the remainder of his life he lectured and published on the un-American and despotic character of Catholicism, feeding the rising nativist hostility of the era.

Bibliography

A. *Nunneries and Auricular Confession* (Hartford, CT, 1855); *Popery As It Was and Is* (Hartford, 1856).
B. DACB, 262; DARB, 210–11; NCE, 7:47; Francis E. Tourscher, *The Hogan Schism and Trustee Troubles in St. Mary's Church, Philadelphia, 1820–29* (Philadelphia, 1930).

DE HUECK DOHERTY, CATHERINE (see DOHERTY, CATHERINE DE HUECK).

HUGHES, JOHN JOSEPH (24 June 1797, Annaloghan, County Tyrone, Ireland—3 January 1864, New York, NY). *Education:* studied at Mount St. Mary's Coll. and Sem. (MD), 1819–26. *Career:* ordained, 1826; pastor, St. Joseph's Church, Philadelphia, 1827–32; pastor, St. John's Church, Philadelphia, 1832–37; coadjutor bishop of New York, 1838–42; bishop of New York, 1842–50; archbishop of New York, 1850–64.

John Hughes, fourth bishop of New York, was from the beginning of his clerical career in Philadelphia a combative apostle for Catholic doctrines, practices, and institutions. In 1817 at the age of twenty, Hughes emigrated from Ireland to the United States and shortly thereafter matriculated at Mount St. Mary's College and Seminary in Emmitsburg, MD, to study for the priesthood. After ordination in 1826 he became engaged in pastoral work in Philadelphia, earning a reputation as a vigorous opponent of trusteeism and an articulate and bellicose defender of the faith in the midst of a rising tide of nativism in the early 1830s.

During the twenty-six years (1838–64) he was bishop of New York, he was perhaps the most visible symbol of Catholicism in the United States. In New York he worked to mold Irish and German immigrants into one Catholic body and defended their rights to exist as Catholics in a rapidly changing American society. His public struggles against the New York lay trustees, the Common School Society of New York, and the "Protestant Crusade" reinforced his authority in the immigrant Catholic community and enabled him to foster an ethnocentric form of Catholicism that was sharply distinguished from the dominant American Protestant community. Rather than Americanize Catholicism, as Carroll and England had tried before him, he wanted to resist Americanizing efforts, stand firm in what he considered the unchanging Catholic tradition, and build up an American society that would be Catholic in its root principles and values. This stance made Hughes severely critical of a number of American values, especially the developing capitalistic system. For him Protestantism was the root of all contemporary ills; the only solution to present problems, therefore, was to return to the unified Christendom of Pre-Reformation days. This romantic idealization of the era of Christendom informed much of his criticism of current troubles and many of his proposals for a just and harmonious society.

Hughes believed in a strong national church with a vigorous episcopal leadership guided by conciliar legislation and not episcopal whim. He participated actively in the Baltimore provincial and plenary councils on the national ecclesiastical level and convoked regular diocesan and archdiocesan synods in New York to govern the local church. After 1840 he became a forceful advocate of Catholic schools, giving diocesan priority to school, over church, construction. He also established Fordham College and St. Joseph's Seminary in 1841 and helped found the North American College in Rome in 1859. In 1856 he started construction on St. Patrick's, which was to be the new Cathedral of New York, a church symbolic of the growing wealth and status of the Catholic community in that city.

He was acknowledged on the national scene as the most powerful and articulate episcopal spokesman of the era. In 1847, in response to the invitation of fifty-four members of the United States Congress, Hughes preached a sermon on "Christianity, the Only Source of Moral, Social, and Political Regeneration" before Congress. In the midst of the Civil War President Lincoln sent him on a goodwill mission to Europe to win favor for the Union.

Hughes had a quasi-despotic control over local ecclesiastical affairs, was a vigorous opponent of lay trusteeism, and was quick-tempered in response to any internal lay or clerical opposition to his rule; but his own forcefulness, ability to excite and control crowds, popularity among the Irish people, and establishment of numerous institutions to serve the immigrants' material, educational, and social needs won him the respect of numerous politicians and the elite in American society, even when they disagreed with his religious perspectives and feared his authoritarian ways.

Bibliography

A. With John Breckenridge, *Controversy Between Rev. Messrs. Hughes and Breckenridge, on the Subject "Is the Protestant Religion the Religion of Christ?"* (Philadelphia, 1833); with Breckenridge, *A Discussion of the Question, Is the Roman Catholic Religion, in any or all its Principles or Doctrines, Inimical to the Civil or Religious Liberty and of the Question, Is the Presbyterian Religion in any or all its Principles or Doctrines Inimical to Civil or Religious Liberty* (Philadelphia, 1836); Lawrence Kehoe, ed., *Complete Works of the Most Rev. John Hughes, D.D., Archbishop of New York, comprising his sermons, letters, lectures, speeches, etc.*, 2 vols. (New York, 1865).

B. DAB, 9:352–55; DACB, 267–69; DAH, 138; DARB, 218–20; NCAB, 1:193–95; NCE, 7:196–98; John R. G. Hassard, *Life of the Most Reverend John Hughes: First Archbishop of New York* (New York, 1866; reprint, New York, 1969); Richard Shaw, *Dagger John: The Unquiet Life and Times of Archbishop John Hughes of New York* (New York, 1977); R. Laurence Moore, *Religious Outsiders and the Making of Americans* (New York, 1986).

I

IRELAND, JOHN (11 September 1838, Burnchurch, County Kilkenny, Ireland—25 September 1918, St. Paul, MN). *Education:* studied at preparatory sem., Merimieux, France, 1853–57; Marist sem., Montbel, France, 1857–61. *Career:* ordained, 1861; pastoral work, St. Paul, 1861–75; coadjutor bishop of St. Paul, 1875; bishop of St. Paul, 1884–88; archbishop of St. Paul, 1888–1918.

John Ireland, first archbishop of St. Paul, became known in the American hierarchy as the "consecrated blizzard of the Northwest." His zealous advocacy of American values and attempts to get the Catholic church to assimilate those values made him the chief American Catholic spokesman for harmony between the church and the optimistic Gilded Age.

Because of the Irish famine in 1850, John Ireland, age twelve, emigrated with his family to the United States, joined the westward migration to Chicago and to St. Paul, and, as his recent biographer indicates, never looked back to Ireland again. In 1861, after a French education for the priesthood, he returned to Minnesota and did pastoral work for a year before volunteering as Civil War chaplain of the Minnesota Infantry Regiment during the first three months of 1863. He continued his pastoral work in the diocese after his chaplaincy duty, becoming a strong local and national advocate for temperance and Catholic colonization in the Midwest. In 1869 and 1870 he represented St. Paul's Bishop Thomas Langdon Grace at the First Vatican Council. For forty-three years, as bishop and first archbishop of St. Paul, Ireland became a dynamo of institutional Catholicism in the middle Northwest. He built or helped build the College of St. Thomas (1885), St. Thomas Seminary (1894), St. Catherine's College (1905), the Cathedral of St. Paul (1915), and the Basilica of St. Mary (1915). These institutions symbolized his drive to see the development of an educated Catholic elite whose presence in the halls of political and economic power would make a Catholic difference in American society.

Ireland became a national figure of Catholic life because he was an eloquent and gifted orator and because he reflected the progressive and optimistic views of his age. His call for Americanization of the immigrants, Catholic cooperation with the public schools, the establishment of a Catholic University, and his public advocacy of these causes in the press, pulpit, and papal courts made his enemies suspect him of trying to create a schismatic church, one democratic in structure and reductionistic in theology. The Catholic national and international debates over Americanism in the 1890s culminated in the papal condemnation of 1899, ending, for all practical purposes, Ireland's effective ministry at the national level. Thereafter he focused his attention on building up the ecclesiastical institutions of his own diocese.

Bibliography

A. *The Apostolic Church* (St. Paul, 1882); *The Church and Modern Society,* 2 vols. (St. Paul, 1896, 1904).
B. DAB, 9:494–97; DACB, 273–75; DAH, 141–42; DARB, 225–27; NCAB, 9:226; NCE, 7:610–13; NYT, 26 September 1918, 13; James H. Moynihan, *The Life of Archbishop John Ireland* (New York, 1953; reprint, New York, 1976); Thomas Wangler, "John Ireland's Emergence as a Liberal," *RACHS* 81 (June 1970): 67–81; Marvin R. O'Connell, *John Ireland and the American Catholic Church* (St. Paul, 1988).

IRELAND, MOTHER SERAPHINE (1 July 1842, Burnchurch, Ireland—20 June 1930, St. Paul, MN). *Career:* novice, Sisters of St. Joseph of Carondelet, St. Paul, 1858–60; teacher, St. Joseph's Academy, St. Paul, 1860–63, 1868–72, St. Joseph's Academy, St. Louis, 1863–68, St. Teresa's Academy, Hastings, MN, 1872–75, St. Anthony's School, Minneapolis, 1875–77; superior, St. Paul Catholic Orphanage, 1877–82; mother superior, Sisters of St. Joseph, province of St. Paul, 1882–1921; retired, 1921–30.

Mother Seraphine (née Helen), the sister of Archbishop John Ireland, helped to develop the Sisters of St. Joseph of Carondelet in Minnesota and the upper Midwest. While she was provincial superior of the order, she opened thirty-seven new institutions: thirty parochial schools, five hospitals, St. Agatha's Conservatory of Music and Art (1884), and the College of St. Catherine (1911), the second Catholic college for women in the United States. When she became superior in 1882, there were 162 sisters; when she retired from office, there were 913. Like her brother, she believed that Catholic men and women ought to become engaged in the country's social and economic life, and to do so Catholics needed a professionally competent education. She also believed that the sister-teacher ought to receive a thorough academic education, and therefore she sent many of her sisters to college summer schools. Many of them received degrees at the University of Chicago, the University of Minnesota, and universities in Germany so they could teach with competence and certification at the parochial and college levels. She also saw to it that teachers and schools received state certification and that her new college was accredited by the North Central Association.

Bibliography

B. DACB, 275; Helen Angela Hurley, *On Good Ground: The Story of the Sisters of St. Joseph in St. Paul* (Minneapolis, 1951).

IVES, LEVI SILLIMAN (16 September 1797, CT—13 October 1867, Manhattanville, NY). *Education:* studied at Hamilton College, 1816; studied theology with John H. Hobart, New York, 1819–22. *Career:* missionary curate and rector, Batavia, NY, Philadelphia and Lancaster, PA, 1823–27; assistant rector of Christ Church and rector of St. Luke's Church, New York, 1827–31; bishop of NC, 1831–52; agent for Catholic charities, New York, 1854–67.

Levi Ives was one of a number of elite converts to Catholicism during the middle of the nineteenth century. Like a few others he came to Catholicism from the Tractarian movement in the American Protestant Episcopal church. He became a Catholic because he longed for community, stability, and continuity with historic Christianity in an age that was alive with the ferment of freedom, revolutions, reforms, and revivalism.

Raised in a Presbyterian family, Ives became an Episcopal priest in his early twenties and was elected second bishop of North Carolina in 1831. As bishop he worked to evangelize the slaves of the North Carolina plantations. In 1845, influenced by the Tractarian movement, he established at Valle Crucis, NC, a religious community called the Brotherhood of the Holy Cross. This semi-monastic community developed a program of devotional practices, venerated saints, and believed in transubstantiation. Ives's community came under some criticism within the Protestant Episcopal church. In 1852, however, he left that church because he had lost confidence in its apostolicity, and on a trip to Europe he became a Catholic. When he returned to the United States, he moved to New York, where he taught rhetoric in St. Joseph's Seminary and where, in 1863, he organized the New York Catholic Protectory to provide material and spiritual benefits for the poor and homeless youth of the city.

Bibliography

A. *The Apostles' Doctrine and Fellowship* (New York, 1844); *The Obedience of Faith* (New York, 1849); *Trials of a Mind in Its Progress to Catholicism* (New York, 1854).

B. DAB, 9:521–22; DACB, 177; DARB, 227–28; NCAB, 5:409; NCE, 7:776–77; NYT, 14 October 1867, 5; SH, 6:71; John O'Grady, *Levi Silliman Ives* (New York, 1933).

J

JACKSON, CAROL (5 May 1911, Oshkosh, WI—). *Education:* B.A., Wellesley Coll., 1937. *Career:* cofounder and coeditor, *Integrity,* 1946–52.

Baptized a Catholic, Carol Jackson claimed that in her college years she was an atheist. In 1941, after meeting Father Francis Wendell, O.P., a leader of the lay apostolate in New York, she became an active Catholic. In Wendell's approach to Catholicism she found a home and a refuge from a world she believed was falling apart in selfish individualism and the bourgeois search for gain. Using the pseudonym Peter Michaels, she wrote periodically for *Torch,* a Dominican publication, berating bourgeois capitalism and the sensate culture it had produced in America in the early 1940s. Through Wendell she met Edward Willock, who had been influenced by Dorothy Day's Catholic Worker personalism and voluntary poverty, and the two of them founded and edited *Integrity* magazine, which aimed to integrate "religion and life for our times." Under her editorship, *Integrity* continued her apocalyptic attacks on American culture, criticized middle-class Catholics for their nerveless pietism, and called upon them to bring the sacramental, truly personal, and communal aspects of their tradition to a world in need of transformation. Through *Integrity* she urged Catholics as workers, consumers, citizens, spouses, parents, individuals, and as families to become involved in social reconstruction by renewing their personal commitment to Christ and the Mystical Body.

Bibliography

A. Peter Michaels, *Designs for Christian Living* (New York, 1947); *This Perverse Generation* (London, 1949); "The Frustration of the Incarnation," *Integrity* 1 (October 1946): 13–23; "It Don't Come Naturally," *Integrity* 2 (January 1949): 42–44.
B. CA1952, 261–62; *The American Catholic Who's Who 1952–53,* 230; Jeffrey M. Burns, *American Catholics and the Family Crisis 1930–1962* (New York, 1988), 170–212; James Terence Fisher, "The Limits of Personalism: *Integrity* and the

Marycrest Community, 1946–1956,'' in *The Catholic Counterculture in America, 1933–1962* (Chapel Hill, NC, 1989), 101–29.

JOGUES, ISAAC (10 January 1607, Orléans, France—18 October 1646, Mohawk territory, now Auriesville, NY). *Education:* Jesuit training at Rouen, 1624–46, La Flèche, 1626–29, and Paris, France, 1633–36. *Career:* grammar instructor at Rouen, 1629–33; ordained, 1636; missionary among Hurons and Iroquois, 1636–46.

At the age of twenty-nine Isaac Jogues, a newly ordained Jesuit priest, emigrated from France to Canada to fulfill his desire to be a missionary among the Native Americans. Like many other young seventeenth-century French Jesuits, he was drawn to the missions by Jesuits who returned from the New World to light the fire of missionary zeal. Very conscious of Tertullian's dictum that ''the blood of martyrs is the seed of Christianity,'' the young Jesuits desired to give witness to the gospel and plant the church among the Native Americans. As many letters reveal, the Jesuits' missionary spirit was tied to their mystical and physical identification with Jesus, even to the point of suffering and death.

For ten years Jogues traveled throughout the Great Lakes region from Quebec to Sault Ste. Marie and lived among the Hurons and Iroquois, evangelizing and baptizing them. During his first five years in Canada (1636–41) he lived in Jesuit missions and worked among the Hurons in the territory between Montreal and Lake Superior. In 1641 he explored as far as Sault Ste. Marie, giving the place its name. During a 1642 trip back to Jesuit headquarters in Quebec, Jogues, a lay assistant, René Goupil, and a few Hurons were captured by the Mohawks, an Iroquois tribe, and taken to central upstate New York, where Goupil and some of the Huron Christians were killed; Jogues was mutilated and made a slave of the tribe. For about nine months he lived among his captors, evangelizing and baptizing over sixty children, many of whom died. In 1643, with assistance from the Dutch at Fort Orange (Albany, NY), Jogues escaped and was taken to New Amsterdam and eventually back to France.

Jogues returned to Canada in 1644 and in 1645 became the first Jesuit to reside among the Mohawks, one of whom tomahawked him to death on 18 October 1646. The story of Jogues martyrdom, retold repeatedly in France, reaffirmed the missionary zeal there and continued to be a significant part of the American Catholic consciousness and imagination, particularly in the first half of the twentieth century. In 1925 Jogues was beatified and in 1930 canonized, giving papal confirmation to a cult that began in the seventeenth century.

Bibliography

A. *Narrative of a Captivity* (New York, 1856; reprint, New York, 1977); *The Jogues Papers,* trans. and arr. John Gilmary Shea (New York, 1857); ''Novum Belgium,'' in *Narratives of New Netherland, 1609–1664*, ed. J. Franklin Jameson (New York, 1909).

B. DAB, 10:74–75; DACB, 280; DARB, 233–35; NCE, 10:506; Felix Martin, *The Life of Father Isaac Jogues*, trans. John Gilmary Shea (New York, 1885); John J. Wynne, *The Jesuit Martyrs of North America* (Auriesville, NY, 1925); Martin J. Scott, *Isaac Jogues, Missioner and Martyr* (New York, 1927); Francis Talbot, *Saint Among the Savages* (New York, 1935); Glenn D. Kittler, *Saint in the Wilderness* (Garden City, NY, 1964).

JONES, MOTHER MARY HARRIS (1 May 1830 [?], Cork, Ireland—30 November 1930, Silver Spring, MD). *Career:* convent teacher, Monroe, MI, 1859; operated dressmaking business, Chicago, 1860; teacher, Memphis, TN, 1861–?; a founder of Social Democratic Party, 1898; organizer, United Mine Workers of America, 1900; a founder of Industrial Workers of the World, 1905.

Mary Harris "Mother" Jones was for more than sixty years an activist labor union organizer, supporter, and political advocate. She was baptized a Catholic in Ireland and remained so for a number of years after emigrating to the United States, but she left the church during her activist socialist period at the end of the nineteenth and beginning of the twentieth centuries. She returned to the church during the final years of her long life.

After a brief teaching career in Monroe, MI, she moved to Memphis, TN, married George Jones, and gave birth to four children; George and the children died of yellow fever in the Memphis epidemic of 1867. After this devastating experience Jones became a labor activist, speaking out and supporting railroad employees and miners in the 1870s, joining the Socialist Labor Party in 1895, supporting Eugene V. Debs for president in 1896, and helping to organize the United Mine Workers of America in 1900. In Pittsburgh, Birmingham, St. Louis, Denver, Philadelphia, Milwaukee, and various other cities and towns, she brought her socialist gospel of labor reform and justice for workers.

She was a "mother" to the predominantly male laboring force, trying to transform them into a universal family, but she was also a prophet of justice who designated the laborers themselves as God's chosen people. As a pioneer labor agitator she was able to merge the authority of a prophetic leader with the empathy of a peer to bring about a practical redefinition of the woman's role in American society. Throughout most of her career her religion seems to have had little influence on her activities; at least she gave very little explicit reference to the relationship between her socialism and her Christianity or her sense of justice and her Catholicism.

Bibliography

A. Mary F. Parton, ed. *The Autobiography of Mother Jones* (1925); Edward M. Steel, ed., *The Correspondence of Mother Jones* (Pittsburgh, 1985).

B. NAW, 2:287–88; *Britannica,* 15th ed., vol. 6 (1990): 609; NYT, 2 May 1930, 24; 1 December 1930, 21; Dale Fetherling, *Mother Jones, the Miner's Angel* (New York, 1974); James J. Kenneally, *Women and American Trade Unions* (Montreal, 1981); Mari Boor Tonn, "The Rhetorical Personae of Mary Harris "Mother" Jones: Industrial Labor's Maternal Prophet" (Ph.D. diss., Univ. of Kansas, 1987).

K

KEANE, JOHN (12 September 1839, Ballyshannon, County Donegal, Ireland—22 June 1918, Dubuque, IA). *Education:* studied at Calvert Hall, Baltimore, 1856; St. Charles Coll. (MD), 1862; St. Mary's Sem., Baltimore, 1862–66. *Career:* ordained, 1866; pastor, St. Patrick's Church, Washington, DC, 1866–78; bishop of Richmond, VA, 1878–88; rector, Catholic Univ. of America, 1889–96; titular archbishop of Damascus and member of Propaganda, Rome, 1897–1900; archbishop of Dubuque, IA, 1900–11; retirement, 1911–18.

John J. Keane and his family emigrated from Ireland to St. John's, New Brunswick, in 1846, when he was seven, and two years later moved to Baltimore. After education for and ordination to the priesthood, John was assigned to St. Patrick's Church in Washington, DC, where he eventually met Isaac Hecker, who became a friend and enduring influence on his life and thought. Keane received from Hecker an appreciation of the importance of the indwelling of God in the soul, the pastoral need to emphasize personal sanctification, and the positive relationship between the church and the world. For Keane, as for Hecker, the Holy Spirit was working simultaneously in the individual, the church, and the age. The pastoral task was to find the right balance and synthesis in the movement toward personal and social salvation in the post–Civil War era.

As a young priest he was especially interested in the temperance movement, education, and the formation of young adults—becoming a leader in the formation of the Catholic Total Abstinence Union (1872) and the Catholic Young Men's National Union (1875). As bishop of Richmond he continued the interests of his early priesthood, organized the Confraternity of the Servants of the Holy Ghost, and wrote *A Sodality Manual for the Use of the Servants of the Holy Ghost* (1880) to foster devotion to the Holy Spirit. In 1884 he attended the Third Plenary Council of Baltimore, wrote the council's pastoral, and was appointed to a committee established to found the Catholic University of America.

In 1886, on behalf of the American bishops, he went to Rome to work out arrangements for the establishment of the Catholic University, and while there he, together with Archbishops John Ireland and James Gibbons, fought against the Abbelen Memorial and the condemnation of the Knights of Labor and Henry George's published works. That trip to Rome helped transform his consciousness about the church in the United States, and thereafter he was more clearly identified as one of the leading Americanists in it. In 1889 he was appointed the first rector of the Catholic University of America, a position that allowed him to appoint the faculty and act as liberal spokesman for the cause of Catholic higher education in the United States.

As a bishop and educator Keane was ecumenically sensitive, attending and speaking at the World's Parliament of Religions and the World's Columbian Congress in Chicago in 1893, and giving the Dudlean lecture at Harvard. Because of his "liberal," or Americanist, activities, however, Pope Leo XIII removed him as rector of the Catholic University in 1896 but gave him a dignified exodus by making him a titular archbishop and assigning him to a consultant position in Rome. After the papal encyclical condemning Americanism in 1899, Keane was appointed archbishop of Dubuque, where he continued to carry out his progressive causes, but failing health caused him to resign his position in 1911.

Bibliography

A. *The Providential Mission of Pius IX* (Baltimore, 1878); *The Providential Mission of Leo XIII* (Baltimore, 1887); *Onward and Upward,* compiled by M. F. Egan (Baltimore, 1902).

B. DAB, 10:267–68; DACB, 285–86; DARB, 241–42; DAH, 147; NCAB, 6:285; NCE, 8:139–40; NYT, 23 June 1918, 18; Patrick H. Ahern, *The Catholic University of America 1887–1896: The Rectorship of John J. Keane* (Washington, DC, 1949); idem, *The Life of John J. Keane, Educator and Archbishop, 1839–1918* (Milwaukee, 1955); Joseph P. Chinnici, ed., *Devotion to the Holy Spirit in American Catholicism* (New York, 1985), 35–47.

KELLEY, FRANCIS CLEMENT (24 November 1870, Vernon River, Prince Edward Island—1 February 1948, Oklahoma City, OK). *Education:* studied at St. Dunstan's Coll., 1885–88; St. Raphael's Sem., Chicoutimi, Canada, 1888–89; Nicolet Sem., Nicolet, Canada, 1890–93. *Career:* assistant secretary to Bishop James Rogers, Chatham, Canada, 1889–90; ordained, 1893; pastoral work in Diocese of Detroit, 1893–1907; founder and president, Catholic Church Extension Society, 1905–24; founder and editor, *Extension Magazine,* 1905–24; bishop of Oklahoma City–Tulsa, 1924–48.

Kelley is known primarily for his establishment of the Catholic Church Extension Society, which helped to provide financial support to rural parishes throughout the United States. Having served as a resident pastor in Lapeer, MI, in the early 1900s, Kelley perceived the need for assistance to rural priests who frequently served extremely large territories with few Catholics and little organized support from the rest of the church. The Extension Society was an attempt to raise missionary consciousness, stir up national attention, and gain financial support for the missions in rural areas where pastorless and churchless people were abandoning or becoming indifferent to religion. Kelley propagated his vision for a new missionary endeavor in rural America by preaching and lecturing throughout the country, and by publishing *Extension Magazine* as the official organ of the movement. By 1919 the Extension Society was collecting and distributing five hundred thousand dollars annually.

During the early twentieth century Kelley was also a vehement public opponent of the persecution of Catholics in Mexico and wrote a number of articles and books to publicize the atrocities. Although he embarrassed some bishops like Cardinal James Gibbons by his outspoken and at times ill-tempered advocacy of the Mexican cause, he did help provide much needed financial and personal assistance to exiled Mexican bishops and clergy. As a busy rural pastor and bishop, he also wrote a number of works to revive the spiritual life among rural peoples.

Bibliography

A. *The First American Catholic Missionary Congress* (Chicago, 1909; reprint, New York, 1978); *The City and the World* (Chicago, 1913; reprint, New York, 1970); *The Book of Red and Yellow* (Chicago, 1915); *Letters to Jack* (Chicago, 1917); *Story of Extension* (Chicago, 1922); *The Epistles of Father Timothy* (Chicago, 1924); *Blood-Drenched Altars* (Milwaukee, 1925); *The Forgotten God* (New York, 1932); *The Bishop Jots It Down* (New York, 1939).
B. CA1948, 376–78; DACB, 288–89; DAH, 149; NCE, 8:144–45; NYT 2 February 1948, 19; James P. Gaffey, *Francis Clement Kelley and the American Catholic Dream,* 2 vols. (Bensenville, IL, 1980).

KENRICK, FRANCIS PATRICK (3 December 1796, Dublin, Ireland—8 July 1863, Baltimore, MD). *Education:* studied at Urban Coll. of the Propaganda, Rome, 1814–21. *Career:* ordained 1821; theology teacher, St. Thomas Sem., Bardstown, KY, 1821–30; coadjutor bishop of Philadelphia, 1830–42; bishop of Philadelphia, 1842–51; archbishop of Baltimore, 1851–63.

After receiving his education for the priesthood in Rome, Francis Patrick Kenrick emigrated to Bardstown, KY, where he taught in the local seminary, served pastoral functions in the diocese, and became a local apologist for Catholicism and Bishop Benedict Flaget's theological advisor at the First Provincial Council of Baltimore in 1829. By that time he already had an established reputation as a good theologian, a scholar, and an apologist for the church. In 1830, after the council, he was appointed coadjutor bishop of the trustee-plagued diocese of Philadelphia, where he immediately reestablished episcopal authority, interdicted a trustee-held church, and enacted diocesan legislation against trusteeism.

As bishop Kenrick brought about a major reformation in Philadelphia Catholicism that included, in addition to his strong sense of episcopal authority, the establishment of the St. Charles Borromeo Seminary (1832) and the *Catholic Herald* (1833) and supported the founding of the Augustinian Villanova College (1842) and the Jesuit St. Joseph's College (1851). He also fought against the so-called Philadelphia Bible Riots of 1844 and sought to establish a strong Catholic school system to counter nativism in the public schools. Although a forceful and authoritarian reforming bishop, after the model of St. Charles Borromeo, Kenrick was retiring and scholarly. In the late 1830s and early 1840s he published seven volumes of his dogmatic and moral theology for use in American seminaries and a number of apologetic tracts (including his major work on the Roman primacy), and began a new English translation of the Bible. He was the most scholarly and productive of the antebellum nineteenth-century bishops.

As archbishop of Baltimore, Kenrick organized and presided over the first Plenary Council of Baltimore (1852), helped promote the establishment of the North American College in Rome (1859), struggled against a virulent nativist Maryland anti-popery campaign in the 1850s, and at the beginning of the Civil War tried to remain politically neutral when the sentiment of a great majority of his flock sided with the South. As the chief moral theologian in the country, Kenrick had held that "under certain protective conditions" the institution of slavery was moral, but he also believed that loyalty to the nation took precedence over loyalty to the state. He died in Baltimore, four days after the Battle of Gettysburg.

Bibliography

A. *Letters of Omega and Omicron on Transubstantiation* (Louisville, 1828); *Theologia Dogmaticae,* 4 vols. (Philadelphia, 1834–40); *The Catholic Doctrine on Justification* (Philadelphia, 1841); *Theologia Moralis,* 3 vols. (Philadelphia, 1841–43; reprint, Baltimore, 1860–61); *The Primacy of the Apostolic See Vindicated* (Philadelphia, 1845; many subsequent rev. eds.); *A Treatise on Baptism: Also A Treatise on Confirmation,* rev. and corr. ed. (Baltimore, 1852).

B. DAB, 10:339–40; DACB, 296–97; DAH, 152–53; NCAB, 1:485; NCE, 8:155–56; NYT, 9 July 1863, 4; Hugh J. Nolan, *The Most Reverend Francis Patrick Kenrick* (Washington, DC, 1948); Joseph D. Brokhage, *Francis Patrick Kenrick's Opinion on Slavery* (Washington, DC, 1955); Thomas W. Spalding, *The Premier See* (Baltimore, 1989), 154–78.

KENRICK, PETER RICHARD (17 August 1806, Dublin, Ireland—4 March 1896, St. Louis, MO). *Education:* studied at St. Patrick's Coll. and Sem., Maynooth, Ireland, 1827–32. *Career:* ordained, 1832; chaplain, Carmelite Convent, Dublin, 1832; pastoral work, diocese of Philadelphia, 1833–41;

coadjutor bishop of St. Louis, 1841–43; bishop of St. Louis, 1843–47; archbishop of St. Louis, 1847–95; retired, 1895–96.

After ordination in 1832, Peter was invited by his brother Francis, then bishop of Philadelphia, to come to the United States and serve in that diocese, where, from 1833 to 1841, he became rector of the cathedral, president of St. Charles Borromeo Seminary, founding editor of the *Catholic Herald* (1833–63), and vicar general.

During his long tenure as bishop of St. Louis, he helped to establish and build up numerous institutions to serve the growing number of German and Irish Catholic immigrants who rushed into the city and diocese. In the early 1840s his diocese embraced the states of Missouri and Arkansas, the western portion of Illinois, the territories now constituting Kansas, Nebraska, and Oklahoma, and a number of Indian missions in the territory east of the Rocky Mountains. The diocese had about 100,000 Catholics, 65 churches, and 74 priests. Although the geographic size of his archdiocese was substantially reduced by the end of his episcopacy, it had experienced dramatic growth: for example, the Catholic population had increased by 100,000, the number of churches by about 235, priests by 200, and parish schools by 130. As metropolitan he was also instrumental in developing Catholic dioceses and institutions throughout the Midwest, from Wisconsin on the north to Alabama on the south and Santa Fe on the west.

Kenrick was influenced in his early Irish education by a Gallican approach to ecclesiology that emphasized the significance and quasi-autonomy of the national church. In the United States he favored those policies that demonstrated the American character of the Catholic church and participated actively in the three national Plenary Episcopal Councils of Baltimore in 1852, 1866, and 1884, which set the canonical standards and governing policies for the church. Despite his allegiance to his adopted country, however, he did not accept American policies that he believed were contrary to his people's interests. During the Civil War he refused to fly the United States flag above the cathedral, and after the war he refused to abide by the Drake Constitution, which would have required clergymen to swear a special oath of loyalty.

In 1869 and 1870 Kenrick took an active role at the First Vatican Council, where he became the leading American opponent of the definition of papal infallibility, arguing in his *Concio in Concilio Vaticano habenda et non habita* (1870) that the teaching of papal infallibility was a theological opinion, not a definable doctrine, because the evidence from scripture and tradition was either silent on the issue or opposed to it. Although he eventually accepted the council's definition of papal infallibility, he never repudiated the arguments of his *Concio,* and he refused to make any public statements on his position after returning.

Although Kenrick was an effective ecclesiastical leader, he irritated the German clergy within his own diocese for the favoritism he showed to the Irish clergy and their parishes. Some of his own fellow bishops, especially Baltimore's Archbishop Martin John Spalding, also found him uncooperative at the national episcopal councils, and some were annoyed with his published objections to papal infallibility.

Bibliography

A. *The New Month of Mary* (Philadelphia, 1840); *The Holy House of Loretto* (Philadelphia, 1841); *The Validity of Anglican Ordination* (Philadelphia, 1841; rev. ed., Philadelphia, 1848).
B. DAB, 10:340–41; DACB, 297; DAH, 153; NCAB, 13:30; NCE, 8:156–57; NYT, 5 March 1896, 1; *Life of the Most Reverend Peter Richard Kenrick, D.D., Archbishop of St. Louis* (St. Louis, 1891); John J. O'Shea, *The Two Kenricks* (Philadelphia, 1904); Samuel J. Miller, "Peter Richard Kenrick: Bishop and Archbishop of St. Louis, 1808–1896," *RACHS* 84 (March, June, September, 1973): 3–163.

KERBY, WILLIAM J. (20 February 1870, Lawler, IA—27 July 1936, Washington, DC). *Education:* studied at St. Francis de Sales Sem., Milwaukee, 1884–92; S.T.L., Catholic Univ. of America, 1894; studied in Berlin, 1895; Ph.D., Univ. of Louvain, Belgium, 1897. *Career:* ordained, 1892; teacher, St. Joseph Coll., Dubuque, IA, 1894; professor of sociology, Catholic Univ. of America, 1897–34; founder and organizer, National Conference of Catholic Charities, 1910; cofounder, National Catholic School of Social Service, 1918; editor, *American Ecclesiastical Review,* 1927–36.

William Kerby belonged to the progressive wing of the faculty at the Catholic University of America. He wanted to integrate as much as possible the sciences—sociology in his case—with theology and a Christian way of life. Like John A. Ryan, he was interested in the problem of social justice and wrote his Louvain dissertation on the socialist movement in the United States. He, like a few others, believed that socialism would lose its appeal in the United States if Catholics and others would work to alleviate the economic injustices and abuses that made socialism possible in the first place. Laissez-faire capitalism, the cause of socialism, demanded radical social reform, and until that was accomplished the threat to individual human dignity and the common good would suffer from the twin evils of capitalism and socialism.

Kerby was particularly sensitive to the influences of social and economic structures, not only upon individuals and communities, but also upon the study of the Bible and theology. He wanted clerical candidates in particular to be aware of the social forces that influenced the Bible, theology, and the people in the parishes. After 1919 he became increasingly aware of the need for a revived spirituality in American Catholicism, wrote prolifically in the *AER,* and gave numerous retreats to both priests and lay people to promote traditional forms of spiritual exercises. He emphasized in particular the importance of personal and social experience within the spiritual life. His own spiritual writings are an attempt to create a dialogue between spirituality and sociology, pointing out the intersection between social and individual religious experience. He was particularly aware of how the changing social circumstances of modernity (e.g., industrialization, bureaucratization) brought forth new questions about God and communal life, and he called for a new approach to the development of a modern spiritual life. His own vision of a revived spirituality was integrally connected to his call for social reform in the economic order.

Bibliography

A. *Le Socialisme aux Etats-Unis* (Brussels, 1897); *The Social Mission of Charity* (New York, 1921); *Prophets of the Better Hope* (New York, 1922); *Introduction to Social Living* (Washington, DC, 1948).
B. DACB, 299; NCE, 8:164–65; NYT, 28 July 1936, 19; John J. Burke, "Monsignor William J. Kerby—An Appreciation," *AER* 95 (September 1936): 225–36; Timothy N. Dolan, "Prophet of a Better Hope: The Life and Work of Monsignor William Joseph Kerby" (M.A. thesis, Catholic University of America, 1981); Bruce H. Lescher, "William J. Kerby: A Lost Voice in American Catholic Spirituality," *RACHS* 102 (Spring 1991): 1–16.

KINO, EUSEBIO FRANCISCO (1 August 1645, Segno, Italy—15 March 1711, Magdalena, Mexico, later AZ). *Education:* entered Jesuit novitiate, Upper German Province, 1665; studied at Freiburg, Ingolstadt, and Munich, Germany, 1665–70; studied theology at Ingolstadt, 1673–77. *Career:* instructor in grammar, Innsbruck, Austria, 1670–73; missionary in Mexico, 1681–83; missionary and cartographer, Atondo expedition, lower CA, 1683–85; missionary, Pimeria Alta, Mexico, 1687–1711.

Eusebio Kino, S.J., was the first permanent evangelist and founder of missions among the Pima Indians of northern Mexico and what is now southern Arizona. After finishing a very promising Jesuit education in which he became competent in mathematics and cartography, Eusebio decided to devote his life to the Jesuit missions. He joined the Spanish Jesuits and was sent to Mexico to work among the Native Americans. From 1683 to 1685 he explored lower California, set up mission stations, and tried to evangelize the Indians there, but a drought forced him and the other Jesuits and Spaniards who had joined the exploration to withdraw to Mexico.

In 1687, two years after he left lower California, he was sent to evangelize the Pima Indians of northern Mexico, establishing the first mission at Nuestra Señora de los Dolores, which became the center of missionary activities that extended as far north as the Gila and Colorado rivers. For the next twenty-four years he explored the area, made maps and sent them to Mexico City and Spain, discovered that California was not an island, and brought some relative material prosperity to the missions by raising cattle, planting wheat, and providing for relative peace among the warring Indian tribes and Spanish soldiers. Like Spanish missionaries throughout the seventeenth century, he tried to convert the Indians to Christianity by bringing them the benefits of a Spanish culture that valued a sedentary life of steady work in agriculture and/or cattle raising. Periodic Indian uprisings against the Spanish invasion of the territory indicate that the Indians themselves were not willing to accept Christian and Spanish styles of life. Throughout his twenty-four years of missionary service, however, Eusebio baptized an estimated 4,500 Pima Indians, and by the time he died he had established seven missions in the area, serving about 2,000 Christianized Indians.

Bibliography

A. *Kino's Historical Memoir of Pimeria Alta,* trans. and ed. Herbert E. Bolton (Berkeley, CA, 1919, 1948); *Kino Writes to . . . the Duchess of Aveiro,* ed. Ernest J. Burrus (St. Louis, 1965).
B. DAB, 10:419–20; DACB, 303; DARB, 245–46; NCE, 8:201–2; Rufus K. Wyllys, *Pioneer Padre: The Life and Times of Eusebio Francisco Kino* (Dallas, 1935); Herbert E. Bolton, *Rim of Christendom: A Biography of Eusebio Francisco Kino, Pacific Coast Pioneer* (New York, 1936); Charles Polzer, *A Life of Eusebio Francisco Kino: Arizona's First Pioneer and a Guide to His Missions and Monuments* (Tucson, 1968); Ernest J. Burrus, *Kino and Manje: Explorers of Sonora and Arizona* (St. Louis, 1971).

KOHLMANN, ANTHONY (13 July 1771, Kaiserberg, Alsace—11 April 1836, Rome, Italy). *Education:* studied at Coll. of Fribourg, Switzerland, 1790s. *Career:* joined Congregation of the Fathers of the Sacred Heart, 1796; military chaplain, Austria and Italy, 1796–98; director, sems. in Bavaria, Berlin, Amsterdam, 1798–1802; joined Russian Jesuits, 1803; novice master, Georgetown Coll., 1804–8; pastor and administrator, Diocese of New York, 1808–15; novice master and president, Georgetown Coll., 1815–24; professor of theology, Gregorian Univ., and consultant to Vatican congregations, Rome, 1824–36.

Kohlmann came to public attention in the United States primarily because of a civil court decision on confessional secrecy and because of his writings on Unitarianism. Having become a member of the Russian branch of the Society of Jesus, the only one not suppressed after the universal papal decree of 1773, he was sent to the United States to help establish Jesuit institutions. In 1808 Bishop John Carroll sent him to New York, where he administered the church until a bishop arrived in 1815. In New York he became involved in what became known as "The Catholic Question," a civil suit against Kohlmann to reveal a confessional confidence that involved stolen property. A Protestant lawyer, Richard Riker, argued Kohlmann's case before the court in 1812 and won a major ruling on religious liberty in favor of confessional secrecy. The case was published the following year, and Kohlmann added an exposition of Catholic teachings to the publication.

In the early 1820s, as president of Georgetown College, Kohlmann, who had since the ordination of the Unitarian Jared Sparks in Baltimore in 1819 been following the major American debates on Unitarianism, published two volumes on Unitarianism because he saw its rise as a threat to Christianity in general and Catholicism in particular. He envisioned his publication as part of a common effort to defend "the public faith of the Christian world" against what he perceived to be the latest manifestation of the revolutionary reforming tendencies in American society that had little respect for the mystery and continuity of tradition. Unitarianism was a threat in America because it had the charm of novelty that could seduce many unsuspecting Christian souls. In the days before the rise of organized nativism, he aligned himself with Protestant anti-Unitarians like Moses Stuart, whom he considered a "respected friend and brother in arms" against a "common foe." Like other anti-Unitarians and Cartesian-influenced Catholics, he defended Christianity against Unitarian rationalism, appealing to the factual evidence of revelation to support his contention that reason could discover the external credibility of the Christian mysteries, but it was incapable of discerning their intrinsic credibility.

Bibliography

A. *The Catholic Question in America* (New York, 1813); *Unitarianism Philosophically and Theologically Examined: In a Series of Periodical Numbers; Comprising a Complete Refutation of the Leading Principles of the Unitarian System*, 2 vols. (Washington D.C., 1821, 1822).
B. DAB, 10:488–89; DACB, 305; NCAB, 24:390–91; NCE, 8:245; J. Wilfred Parsons, "Father Anthony Kohlmann, S.J.," *CHR* 4 (1918): 38–51; Jules Joachim, *Le Père Antoine Kohlmann, S.J., 1771–1836* (Paris, 1937).

L

LaFARGE, JOHN (13 February 1880, Newport, RI—24 November 1963, New York, NY). *Education:* B.A., Harvard Coll., 1901; Univ. of Innsbruck, Austria, 1905; Jesuit novitiate, St. Andrew's on the Hudson, Poughkeepsie, NY, 1905–7; M.A., Woodstock Coll., MD, 1910; ascetical-theological studies at St. Andrew's on the Hudson, 1916–17. *Career:* ordained 1905; instructor, Canisius Coll., 1907; instructor, Loyola Coll. (MD), 1908; pastor, St. Mary's County, MD, 1911–26; editorial staff, *America,* 1926–63.

For almost sixty years (1905 to 1963) the Jesuit John LaFarge played a significant role in the public life of American Catholicism as an organizer and advocate for social justice, a participant in rural life and liturgical movements, and an editor of the influential Jesuit magazine *America.* After completing his education and early Jesuit training and experience as a scholastic-teacher, LaFarge was sent to do pastoral work in rural St. Mary's County, MD, where from 1911 to 1926 he served African-American and white Catholics. This pastoral experience made him aware of the plight of rural peoples and African-Americans in particular. In 1924 he founded the Cardinal Gibbons Institute, an industrial school for African-Americans in Ridge, MD. Although the school closed during the Depression in 1933, after LaFarge had left rural Maryland, it did provide agricultural training for many who had no other means of education. While in Maryland he also became associated with and supported Thomas Wyatt Turner's Federation of Colored Catholics (1921–58).

In 1926 LaFarge left Maryland for New York, where he joined *America*'s editorial staff and founded the Catholic Laymen's Union, an African-American group for mutual spiritual formation and racial studies. By 1934 the Laymen's Union evolved into the first Catholic Interracial Council of New York and became part of a much larger national movement for interracial justice. LaFarge, together with William Markoe, S.J., was responsible for changing Turner's original emphasis on racial and religious solidarity to interracial cooperation for justice. From 1933 to 1963 LaFarge made a major national effort to encourage interracial cooperation in areas of social justice by establishing various college, high school, and parish Interracial Councils, writing articles in *America* and the *Interracial Review,* giving speeches across the country, and publishing books on the race question. He believed that only through an intense educational campaign and organized cooperation could racial justice be accomplished in the United States.

For LaFarge the Catholic communal and social vision was the only hope for justice and equality in American Society, and only through active Catholic cells of laity could this vision be put into practice. He became an officer in the Catholic Association for International Peace (1926), a member of the National Catholic Rural Life Conference (1927), a chaplain of the Liturgical Arts Society (1933), and a member of various other national Catholic movements because he believed that only an integrated Catholic communal and social life could effectively transform a society that was becoming increasingly secular and materialistic in the twentieth century. Although he was an activist, he criticized the hectic pace of American life and periodically called for a return to the spiritual roots that enabled the activist to work for justice and human dignity.

Bibliography

A. *Jesuits in Modern Times* (New York, 1928); *Interracial Justice* (New York, 1937); *The Race Question and the Negro* (New York, 1945); *The Manner Is Ordinary* (New York, 1954); *The Catholic Viewpoint on Race Relations* (Garden City, NY, 1956); *On Turning Seventy* (New York, 1962).
B. DACB, 310–11; DARB, 251–53; NCAB, 49:155–56; NCE, 8:314–15; NYT, 25 November 1963, 19; Edward S. Stanton, "John LaFarge's Understanding of the Unifying Mission of the Church," (Ph.D. diss., St. Paul University, Ottawa, 1972); Marilyn Wenzke Nickels, *Black Catholic Protest and the Federated Colored Catholics, 1917–1933: Three Perspectives on Racial Justice* (New York, 1988).

LAKE, LEONORA BARRY (see BARRY, LEONORA MARIE).

LAMY, JEAN BAPTISTE (11 October 1814, Lempdes, France—13 February 1888, Santa Fe, NM). *Education:* studied at Royal Coll., Petite Sem., and Grand Sem., Clermont-Montferrand, France, ?–1838. *Career:* ordained, 1838; assistant pastor, Chapre, France, 1838–39; missionary priest in OH and KY, 1839–50; vicar apostolic of NM, 1850–53; bishop of Santa Fe, 1853–75; archbishop of Santa Fe, 1875–85; retirement 1885–88.

Jean Baptiste Lamy's life as bishop and archbishop of the missionary frontier diocese of Santa Fe became the subject of Willa Cather's best-selling *Death Comes for the Archbishop* (1927). In 1839 Lamy, a priest who had caught the missionary zeal of early-nineteenth-century France, emigrated to the diocese of

Cincinnati, where he did pastoral work for more than a decade. Although he had desired to convert the Indians, he spent most of his time serving immigrant congregations who needed his ministry.

In 1850, after the 1848 Treaty of Guadalupe Hidalgo, Lamy was made the vicar apostolic of Santa Fe, a vicariate that had previously been under the ecclesiastical jurisdiction of the Mexican diocese of Durango. The Santa Fe vicariate included not only New Mexico, but also large parts of Arizona, Nevada, Utah, California, and Colorado. Over the course of the next thirty-five years, Lamy would help to establish Catholic institutions throughout this large region of the country. His diocese included numerous Native Americans, Hispanics, new immigrants from Ireland and Germany, and a growing number of Protestant American soldiers and politicians who were sent to New Mexico to govern the new American territory and establish the railway and commercial networks that would eventually tie Santa Fe to the East and West coasts. Lamy came into a territory that had about 250 years of Spanish and Mexican Catholic history. His French education and American pastoral experience had not prepared him for the rugged frontier Hispanic culture and folk Catholicism that he met in Santa Fe, nor were the few leading Spanish-speaking priests and people ready to welcome his authority and control after years of ecclesiastical life without episcopal supervision and canonical discipline. His early years in Santa Fe were therefore spent in establishing his authority, canonical discipline, and American-style ecclesiastical institutions for education, social services, and religious ministry. Lamy's importation of French émigré clergy and women religious only helped to increase the clash of cultures on the frontier during his early years.

To help build up the substructure of Catholic life in the diocese, Lamy secured the assistance of the Sisters of Loretto for Catholic schooling (1852), the Sisters of Charity (1865), who built the first hospital and orphanage west of the Pecos River, the Christian Brothers (1859), and the Society of Jesus (1867), all of whom contributed to his educational and missionary efforts. Blessed with the able administrative talents of his lifelong friend and vicar general Joseph P. Macheboeuf, the first bishop of Denver (1868–89), he quintupled the number of clergy, restored twenty old churches, and built forty-five new ones. His public support for spiritual and material developments in the region earned him the respect of Protestants and Jews alike. Their contributions, too, helped to fund the building of the Cathedral in Santa Fe (started in 1869). His rapport with Americans and with the American government, however, remained a continuing irritation and source of contention for those Hispanic Catholics who were pushed aside because of the railway culture that took over the territory after 1850.

Bibliography

B. DAB, 10:566–67; DACB, 315; DAH, 160; DARB, 253–54; NCAB, 12:49–50;
    NCE, 8:355–56; Louis H. Warner, *Archbishop Lamy: An Epoch Maker* (Santa Fe,
    NM, 1936); Paul Horgan, *Lamy of Santa Fe* (New York, 1975).

LANGE, MARY ELIZABETH (? 1784, Santo Domingo, Haiti—3 February
1882, Baltimore, MD). *Career:* founding mother superior, Oblate Sisters of
Providence, Baltimore, 1829–32.

Born in what is now the Dominican Republic, Mary Elizabeth Lange and
her family moved to Cuba sometime during or after the late-eighteenth-century
Haitian revolution, and about 1812 they emigrated to the United States. Shortly
after their arrival Elizabeth and two other Haitian women began teaching Haitian children in the lower chapel of St. Mary's Seminary in Baltimore. In 1829
Father Nicholas Joubert, an émigré priest from Santo Domingo, encouraged
and helped these women to establish in Baltimore the Oblate Sisters of Providence, the first African-American order of women religious in the United States.
The order received papal approval in 1831, and Mother Mary Elizabeth Lange
became the first superior of the small community of three African-Americans.
The primary aim of the new order was to provide Christian education for African-American children. By 1834 the small community had grown to twelve
members, three of whom had been slaves, and by the time of Mother Elizabeth's death, the order had grown to about fifty. Throughout her life the sisters
established numerous missions and schools in Baltimore and other cities. These
schools offered slaves and other African-American girls courses in "refined and
useful education," but many of them lasted for only a few years before they
were closed because of financial hardship. The sisters also served the sick and
dying in the Baltimore community repeatedly during times of cholera epidemics, set up orphanages, and led a communal life of prayer as well as service.
In the early 1990s the Archdiocese of Baltimore initiated procedures for Mother
Elizabeth's beatification.

Bibliography

B. Maria M. Lannon, *Mother Mary Elizabeth Lange* (Washington, DC, 1976); M. Reg-
    inald Gerdes, "To Educate and Evangelize: Black Catholic Schools of the Oblate
    Sisters of Providence," *U.S.CH* 7 (Spring/Summer 1988): 183–200; Lannon, *Re-
    sponse to Love: The Story of Mother Mary Elizabeth Lange, O.S.P.* (Washington,
    DC, 1992).

LATHROP, ROSE HAWTHORNE (MOTHER ALPHONSA) (20 May 1851,
Lenox, MA—9 July 1926, Hawthorne, NY). *Career:* nurses' training, New
York Cancer Hospital, 1896; received as Dominican tertiary, 1899; first vows,
1900; cofounder, Dominican Congregation of St. Rose of Lima (Servants of
Relief for Incurable Cancer), 1900; founder, *Christ's Poor,* 1901.

The third daughter of Nathaniel Hawthorne, Rose was herself an active writer, but she is known in American Catholicism more for her foundation of the Servants of Relief for Incurable Cancer, an order of women religious who established some of the first American hospices and hospitals for those with the incurable disease. As a child Rose lived in England and Italy, where her father was a United States consular officer. In 1871, after returning to Massachusetts, the state of her birth, she married George Parsons Lathrop, and thereafter they moved to New York, where he became an editor of the *Atlantic Monthly.* Throughout her marriage she wrote short stories and verse; her work appeared in several periodicals, and in 1888 she published a book of her poems, *Along the Shore.* The Lathrops were received into the Catholic church in 1891, and they cowrote *A Story of Courage* (1894), a book about the Georgetown Sisters of the Visitation.

In the late 1890s she separated from her husband (who died in 1898) because of his drinking problem and established the Dominican Congregation of St. Rose of Lima (Servants of Relief for Incurable Cancer) to provide for those she saw neglected by church and society. The new community of women religious grew gradually, pioneering in hospice work and establishing St. Rose's Free Home in New York and Rosary Hill in Hawthorne, NY, both hospitals built to serve the terminally ill. They also established a motherhouse and novitiate in Hawthorne. Mother Alphonsa, as she became known, also published *Christ's Poor,* a magazine that helped to gain the necessary financial support for her ministry.

Bibliography

A. *Along the Shore* (Boston, 1888); "Woman and Mammon," in *The World's Columbian Catholic Congress and Educational Exhibit* (Chicago, 1893), 82–83; with George Lathrop, *A Story of Courage: Annals of the Georgetown Convent of the Visitation of the Blessed Mary* (Boston, 1894); *Memories of Hawthorne* (Boston, 1897).

B. DACB, 319; NAW, 2:372–74; NCAB, 9:194; NCE, 8:411–12; NYT, 10 July 1926, 11; Katherine Burton, *Sorrow Built a Bridge: A Daughter of Hawthorne* (New York, 1937); Theodore Maynard, *A Fire Was Lighted: The Life of Rose Hawthorne Lathrop* (Milwaukee, 1948); M. Joseph, *Out of Many Hearts* (Hawthorne, New York, 1961); Patricia Dunlavy Valenti, *To Myself a Stranger: A Biography of Rose Hawthorne Lathrop* (Baton Rouge, LA, 1991).

LIGUTTI, LUIGI G. (21 March 1885, Udine, Italy—28 December 1983, Rome, Italy). *Education:* B.A., St. Ambrose Coll., Davenport, IA, 1914; S.T.B., St. Mary's Sem., Baltimore, MD, 1917; M.A., Catholic Univ. of America, 1918. *Career:* ordained, 1917; professor of classical languages, Dowling Academy (IA), 1918–20; pastor, Woodbine, IA, 1920–26; pastor, Granger, IA, 1926–40; part-time and later full-time executive secretary and director, National Catholic Rural Life Conference, Des Moines, 1938–58; editor, *Land and Home,* 1942–47; editor, *Christian Farmer News Letter,* 1947; editor, *Christian*

Farmer, 1947–51; director of international affairs, NCRLC, 1958–70; canon, Santa Maria Maggiore, Rome, 1970–83; president of Agrimissio, Rome, 1971–83.

Luigi Ligutti emigrated from Italy with his mother in the early twentieth century and moved to Iowa, where he received a college education. After ordination he did pastoral work in Iowa, where he became familiar with the economic, social, and agricultural problems of rural living. In 1940, after years of being associated with the National Catholic Rural Life Conference, he became its executive secretary, and until 1960 the Catholic rural life movement was identified with his name. For twenty years his homey and farm-spun humor, grasp of papal social encyclicals, and experience with farming families combined to make him an effective and stimulating propagandist for the needs and the values of rural life.

After World War II the NCRLC, under his leadership, became a forceful advocate not only for rural peoples in the United States but also for those in developing countries throughout the world. Because of his interest in world hunger programs, the Vatican appointed him as observer to the United Nations' Food and Agriculture Organization (FAO) in 1946. In the postwar years Ligutti believed that the Catholic church in America, like the national government, had to assume leadership in solving world agricultural problems, especially those associated with food production, distribution and marketing, housing, sanitation, health, and diet. In the early 1960s Ligutti had an influence on Pope John XXIII's *Mater et Magistra,* the Second Vatican Council's *Gaudium et Spes,* and Paul VI's *Octogesima Adveniens.* In 1971 he established Agrimissio, an international organization headquartered in Rome and partially funded by the NCRLC to promote agricultural production in developing countries.

Bibliography

A. *Rural Roads to Security* (Milwaukee, 1939); *Catholic Farmer,* 1947–51.
B. NCE, 18:249; NCR, 13 January 1984, 25; Vincent A. Yzermans, *The People I Love: A Biography of Luigi G. Ligutti* (Collegeville, MN, 1976); Raymond W. Miller, *Monsignor Ligutti: The Pope's Country Agent* (Washington, DC, 1981); David S. Bovee, "Luigi G. Ligutti: Catholic Rural Life Leader," *USCH* 8 (Fall 1989): 143–58.

LORD, DANIEL ALOYSIUS (23 April 1888, Chicago, IL—15 January 1955, St. Louis, MO). *Education:* B.A., Loyola Univ. (IL), 1909; studied at St. Stanislaus Sem., Florissant, MO, 1909–14; M.A., St. Louis Univ., 1915. *Career:* entered Jesuits, 1909; professor, St. Louis Univ., 1917–20; ordained, 1923; editor, the *Queen's Work,* 1925–48; director, Sodality of the Blessed Virgin, 1925–48; retired, 1948–55.

The Jesuit Daniel Lord was a prolific writer and apostle to young Catholics throughout the mid-twentieth century. He published thirty books, almost three hundred pamphlets, sixty-six booklets, fifty plays, twelve musicals, and six pageants and prepared hundreds of talks throughout his career as an educator of American Catholic youth. He was particularly preoccupied with raising the level of religious, social, and ethical consciousness among the young and getting them to act in socially responsible ways. During the late 1920s and 1930s he became an adviser to Cecil B. De Mille's *King of Kings,* helped draft the Motion Picture Production Code, and was active in setting up moral standards for the League of Decency. For him literature, motion pictures, and the performing arts were effective communicators of moral values in society, and he worked throughout his life to establish moral codes for producing, reading, and viewing these arts.

Perhaps Lord's most important contribution to twentieth-century Catholicism was his revival among young people of the Sodality of the Blessed Virgin, the largest Catholic youth organization in the country, with over two million members by 1940. The Sodality was a Jesuit society of young men and women who assisted one another in fostering a Christian way of life. When Lord became director in 1925 he gradually transformed it by linking spiritual development with Catholic action. As editor of the *Queen's Work,* the Sodality's organ of communication with a circulation of over 100,000 in the late 1930s, he also tried to develop an intellectual elite among high school and college students. Through lectures, retreats, national Sodality conventions, and the Summer Schools of Catholic Action (1931–48), he fostered reading and writing habits among the young as well as a deep moral and spiritual life. His literary models were G. K. Chesterton and Hilaire Belloc in particular. Throughout his life he was a major participant in the American Catholic literary revival.

Bibliography

A. *Armchair Philosophy* (New York, 1918); *Six One-Act Plays* (New York, 1925); *Religion and Leadership* (Chicago, 1933); *Storm-tossed; If Communists Had the Truth, or Catholics Had the Zeal* (St. Louis, 1936); *Some Notes on the Guidance of Youth* (St. Louis, 1938); *The New Sodality Manual* (St. Louis, 1945); *Our Part in the Mystical Body* (St. Louis, 1955); *Played by Ear* (Chicago, 1956).
B. CA1947: 436–37; DACB, 328–29; NCE, 8:990; NYT, 16 January 1955, 95; J. T. McGloin, *Backstage Missionary* (New York, 1958); W. B. Faherty, "A Half-Century with *Queen's Work,*" *Woodstock Letters* 92 (1963): 99–114; "A Revival Is Organized: Daniel A. Lord and the Sodality Literary Campaign," in Arnold Sparr, *To Promote, Defend, and Redeem* (New York, 1990): 31–50.

LUCE, CLARE BOOTHE (10 April 1903, New York, NY—9 October 1987, Washington, DC). *Career:* associate and managing editor, *Vanity Fair,* 1929–34; Connecticut representative, US Congress, 1942–46; US ambassador to Italy, 1953–57.

Clare Boothe Luce—wife of Henry R. Luce, publisher of *Time, Fortune, Life,* and *Sports Illustrated*—was herself a playwright of some Broadway hits, editor, war correspondent, author, politician, and United States ambassador. She was a leading light in the Republican Party, becoming a keynote speaker at the 1944 Republican National Convention. After taking instructions from Msgr. Fulton J. Sheen, she became a Catholic in 1946 and was perhaps the most prominent Catholic female politician. After her conversion she continued to be active in the Republican Party, labored for the presidential nomination of Dwight David Eisenhower, became a renowned anti-Communist, raised money for her church, unsuccessfully sought Senate seats in 1952 and 1964, and became the first Catholic ambassador to Italy. Even though she believed that a woman's first duties were to her husband and to the education and rearing of children, she was herself an activist.

Bibliography

A. *The Women* (New York, 1937); *Kiss the Boys Goodbye* (New York, 1939); *Europe in the Spring* (New York, 1940); *Margin of Error: A Satirical Melodrama* (New York, 1940); "The Real Reasons," *McCall's* 74 (February to April 1947): passim.
B. NCAB, F:435; NCE, 18:266–67; NYT, 10 October 1987, 1, 41; Alden Hatch, *Ambassador Extraordinary: Clare Boothe Luce* (New York, 1956).

LUCEY, ROBERT EMMET (16 March 1891, Los Angeles, CA—1 August 1977, San Antonio, TX). *Education:* studied at St. Vincent's Coll., Los Angeles, 1905–1907; St. Patrick's Sem., Menlo Park, CA, 1907–12; S.T.D., North American College, Rome, 1916. *Career:* ordained, 1916; pastoral work, Diocese of Los Angeles, 1916–34; bishop, Amarillo, TX, 1934–41; archbishop, San Antonio, 1941–69; retired, 1969–77.

As a young priest in the Diocese of Los Angeles, as bishop of Amarillo, and as archbishop of San Antonio, Robert Lucey was for more than fifty years one of the leading social activists in twentieth-century American Catholicism. Born in poverty and influenced by the papal social encyclicals, Lucey became one of the early radio preachers for social justice as a young priest in Los Angeles, where he also became known for his pastoral work on behalf of the poor and homeless, especially in the 1930s. As bishop of Amarillo he became a forceful advocate of New Deal programs and more effective governmental intervention to bring about an equitable distribution of economic benefits. He was generally pro-labor and became an early supporter of the Congress of Industrial Organizations.

As archbishop of San Antonio during World War II and throughout the Truman and Eisenhower administrations, he supported the Allies, was a charter member of the Committee to Defend America, maintained his New Deal pro-labor views, insisted that the church hire only union workers, and became an early and ardent advocate of federal labor regulation and protection of Mexican-American migrant farm workers (periodically supporting striking farm workers). Prior to *Brown v. Board of Education* (1954) he, moreover, began to integrate the Catholic schools in San Antonio.

Throughout his clerical career he was a promoter of the Confraternity of Christian Doctrine (CCD), believing, as he said at the Second Vatican Council, that many if not most Christians in contemporary society did not know the "eternal truths and the doctrines necessary for salvation." The function of CCD, as organized in the United States, was to use the laity as cells of learning to impart the knowledge and love of Christ. Without a thorough Christian formation program, the work for justice and peace would, he believed, be ineffective and inert.

Although Lucey participated in the Second Vatican Council, he made few oral interventions. After returning from the council in 1965 he became a strong supporter of fellow Texan Lyndon B. Johnson's wars on poverty and Vietnam, becoming a member of the President's National Advisory Council for the war on poverty. After the council, too, Lucey, like many other pre-conciliar bishops, came into bitter conflict with some of his own priests and laity over ecclesiastical authority and the direction of post-conciliar reforms. In 1969, because of pressure from his own younger priests and the apostolic delegate, he resigned his archepiscopal see and retired in San Antonio.

Bibliography

B. DACB, 331; DAH, 170–71; NCE, 18:267–68; NYT, 2 August 1977, 32; Saul E. Bronder, *Social Justice and Church Authority: The Public Life of Archbishop Robert E. Lucey* (Philadelphia, 1982); Stephen A. Privett, *The U.S. Catholic Church and Its Hispanic Members: The Pastoral Vision of Archbishop Robert E. Lucey* (San Antonio, 1988).

LYNCH, PATRICK N. (10 March 1817, County Monaghan, Ireland—26 February 1882, Charleston, SC). *Education:* studied at Urban Coll. of Propaganda, Rome, 1833–40. *Career:* ordained, 1840; pastoral work in Diocese of Charleston, SC, 1840–57; bishop, Charleston, 1857–82.

As a priest and bishop Patrick Lynch was one of the leading Southern Catholics prior to and during the Civil War. Because he was a precocious youth, Bishop John England of Charleston sent him and James Andrew Corcoran to Rome to obtain doctorates in theology. After ordination Lynch became a professor at St. John the Baptist Seminary (1840–45), editor of the *U. S. Catholic Miscellany,* coeditor of Bishop England's collected works, rector of Charleston's cathedral and seminary (1847–51), and administrator of the diocese (1854). His prominence in the administration of the diocese after his return from Rome made him a likely candidate for the episcopacy in 1857 when Bishop Ignatius Reynolds died. As a bishop with Southern sympathies and a states' rights ideology, Lynch sided with the South during the Civil War and saw the institutions that Southern Catholics had built up during the antebellum period destroyed. Twice Lynch went to Europe during the war to plead the Southern cause. He was in Rome when the war ended in 1865 but had to wait for a presidential pardon for his part in the "Southern conspiracy" before he was allowed to return to the United States. He spent his postwar years collecting funds in the North, trying to rebuild diocesan institutions, and healing the wounds of war. During the Vatican Council (1869–70), the Roman-trained Lynch supported the dogma of papal infallibility.

Bibliography

B. DAB, 11:521–22; DACB, 332; DAH, 172; NCE, 8:1111–12; *News and Courier* (Charleston), 27 February 1882, 6; *Irish-American* (New York), 11 March 1882, 3; Richard C. Madden, *Catholic in South Carolina: A Record* (Lanham, MD, 1985).

M

MARÉCHAL, AMBROSE (28 August 1764, Ingres, France—29 January 1828, Baltimore, MD). *Education:* studied at Univ. of Orléans, France, 1787; Suplician sem., Bordeaux, France, 1789–92. *Career:* ordained, 1792; missionary priest, MD, 1792–99; professor, St. Mary's Sem. (MD), 1799–1801; professor, Georgetown Coll., 1801–1802; professor, various sems., France, 1803–11; professor, St. Mary's Sem., 1812–17; archbishop of Baltimore, 1817–28.

Ambrose Maréchal was one of the numerous talented French émigré Sulpicians who served in the United States after the devastation of the French Revolution. As a theologian and later as archbishop of Baltimore, Maréchal tried to blend an American federalism, which he had inherited from Bishop John Carroll and many of the Maryland Catholics, and a theological Gallicanism with an ancien régime culture. The mixture itself provided for an aristocratic ecclesiastical governance of the American church that clashed periodically not only with republican-minded lay trustees in various parishes but also with republican-minded bishops like John England, who wanted American Catholicism to appropriate some American cultural values and practices in the church's modus operandi. Maréchal's controversies with lay trustees, his unilateral exercise of episcopal authority among the bishops, and his preference for a low-profile style of American Catholicism reflected his refined French culture, but this also was a part of American Catholicism that was giving way to the rising Irish-American Catholic subculture: highly visible, combative, republican in political sympathies, and anti-Anglo in culture. As archbishop of Baltimore Maréchal presided over a church that was in a significant period of cultural and social transition, from the predominance of a Southern Maryland culture to that of an Irish immigrant culture.

Bibliography

A. *Pastoral Letter of Archbishop Maréchal to the Congregation of Norfolk, Virginia, 1819* (2nd ed., Baltimore, 1820); "Maréchal Visitation Diary, 1818–1825," *RACHS* 11 (December, 1900): 417–54.

B. DAB, 12:279–80; DACB, 343–44; DAH, 179; DARB, 289; NCAB, 1:482–83; NCE, 9:197–98; Ronin Murtha, "The Life of the Most Reverend Ambrose Maréchal, Third Archbishop of Baltimore, 1768–1828," (Ph.D. diss., Catholic University of America, 1965); Christopher J. Kauffman, *Tradition and Transformation in Catholic Culture: The Priests of Saint Sulpice in the United States from 1791 to the Present* (New York, 1988), 88–111.

MARKOE, WILLIAM MORGEN (11 May 1892, St. Paul, MN—6 December 1969, Milwaukee, WI). *Education:* studied at St. Thomas Coll. (MN), 1906–12; St. Louis Univ., 1912–13; Jesuit sem., Florissant, MO, 1913–18; M.A., philosophy, Mt. St. Michael's Scholasticate, Spokane, WA, 1918–21; studied theology, St. Louis Univ., 1923–27. *Career:* scholastic, St. Francis Sioux Indian Mission (SD), 1921–23; ordained, 1926; assistant pastor and pastor, St. Elizabeth's, St. Louis, 1927–41; editor, *Chronicle/Interracial Review,* 1930–33; asst. pastor, Sts. Peter and Paul's Church, Mankato, MN, 1941–42; pastor, Sacred Heart, Denver, 1942–48; missionary, Missouri Province Jesuit mission band, 1948–51; professor of theology, Marquette Univ., 1951–61; retired, 1966–69.

The Jesuit William Markoe became known primarily for his activities on behalf of interracial justice during the 1920s and 1930s. As a young Jesuit seminarian in St. Louis between 1920 and 1925, Markoe authored over twenty-five articles in *America,* advocating justice for African-Americans, criticizing Catholicism's neglect and apathy in this regard, calling for an increase in African-American clergy, and promoting African-American Catholic lay leadership. As a young Jesuit priest he became an assistant pastor and then pastor of St. Elizabeth's African-American parish, where he began to publish the *Chronicle* (which later became the *Interracial Review*) as a parish organ to raise the consciousness of race problems within the church. He also joined Thomas W. Turner's Federated Colored Catholics but split with the organization in 1933 because he believed it should have focused on interracial justice rather than African-American Catholic solidarity. In 1934 the Catholic Interracial Council was formed as a result of the split, and Markoe made *Interracial Review* its national organ.

Markoe continued his active ministry at St. Elizabeth's after the split with Turner's group and continued to concentrate on race problems in the church throughout the 1930s. For reasons that are not entirely clear, Markoe abandoned his advocacy of interracial justice in the early 1940s and pursued other pastoral and educational interests for the remainder of his life.

Bibliography

A. "Catholics, the Negro, a Native Clergy." *America* 25 (24 September 1921), 535–36; "Catholic Church and Slavery," *America* 28 (12 February 1923), 415–17; "An Interracial Role," Marquette University Archives (Milwaukee, 1963).
B. Marilyn Wenzke Nickles, *Black Catholic Protest and the Federated Colored Catholics, 1917–1933: Three Perspectives on Racial Justice* (New York, 1988).

MARQUETTE, JACQUES (1 June 1637, Laon, France—18 May 1675, near Ludington, MI). *Education:* entered Jesuit novitiate, Nancy, France, 1654; studied philosophy at Pont-à-Monsson, France, 1657–59; studied Algonkian at Trois Rivières, Canada, 1666–68. *Career:* ordained, 1665; taught in Jesuit schools in France at Auxerre, 1656–57, Reims, 1659–61, Charleville, 1661–63, Langres, 1663–64, and Pont-à-Monsson, 1664–65; missionary to various North American Indian tribes, 1669–75.

Jacques Marquette entered the Jesuit novitiate when many French Jesuit houses resounded with stories of the new missions to Native Americans in Canada. After twelve years of formation and teaching in Jesuit schools, the newly ordained Marquette was sent to Trois Rivières in Canada, where he learned the Algonkian language and culture for two years before being sent to Sault Ste. Marie in 1668 to live with and evangelize the Indian tribes there.

After eighteen months at Sault Ste. Marie, he moved to the Jesuit mission, La Pointe du Sainte Esprit, on Lake Superior near present-day Ashland, WI. Because of threats of invasion from the western Dakota Sioux tribes and the belief that his evangelical work was ineffective, Marquette abandoned the mission in 1671 and moved the Huron tribes to the Sault Ste. Marie region, where he established a new mission, St. Ignace, on Mackinac Island. Two years later he joined the Canadian Louis Jolliet and explored the Mississippi River as far as the Arkansas River, determining that the Mississippi flowed into the Gulf of Mexico. The explorers returned to Canada but had opened up the Mississippi Valley for further exploration and evangelization. Marquette evangelized the Illinois Indians in 1674 but became ill and died on a return trip to St. Ignace in 1675 at the age of thirty-eight.

In 1905, after much controversy in Wisconsin, a statue of Marquette, representing the state, was placed in the Washington, DC, Hall of Statues.

Bibliography

B. DAB, 12:294–95; DACB, 345–46; DARB, 289–91; NCAB, 12:220–21; NCE, 9:254; SH, 7:191–92; Reuben G. Thwaites, *Father Marquette* (New York, 1902); A. Hamy, *Au Mississipi: La première exploration* (Paris, 1903); Agnes Repplier, *Père Marquette* (Garden City, NY, 1929); August W. Derleth, *Father Marquette and the Great Rivers* (New York, 1955); Joseph P. Donnelly, *Jacques Marquette* (Chicago, 1968); Raphael N. Hamilton, *Father Marquette* (Grand Rapids, MI, 1970).

MAURIN, ARISTIDE PETER (9 May 1877, Outlet, France—15 May 1949, Newburgh, NY). *Career:* novice in the Christian Brothers, Paris, 1893–1903;

promoter of the Sillonist social reform in France, 1903–1909; homesteader and laborer in Canada and the United States, 1909–33; writer and lecturer for the *Catholic Worker,* 1933–49.

Peter Maurin was a French peasant who became a Christian Brother in France and then a member of Marc Sangnier's Sillon movement before he emigrated to Canada in 1909 at the age of thirty-two. After working on a farm and as a day laborer in Canada for fourteen years, he moved to New York to earn a living. Seven years later he met Dorothy Day, and in 1933 they initiated the Catholic Worker Movement and published the *Catholic Worker,* a periodical dedicated to promoting Catholic social teachings.

Influenced by the personalism of Emmanuel Monier and the papal social encyclicals, Maurin believed that the modern world, in the midst of the great Depression, needed a renewed awareness of the spiritual dignity and worth of the human person to avoid the traps of modern individualism and collectivism. Real reform of social conditions and in personal living would not be brought about, he believed, by large unions, governmental initiatives and regulations, or large business enterprises. Modern humanity was in need of communal reflection, responsible and caring personal work and action, and communal worship and prayer to bring about the necessary social and personal regeneration.

Maurin propagated these ideas through his *Catholic Worker* column "Easy Essays" and through the example of his simple and unostentatious life of charitable service. Although he was not an organizer, he provided the ideas and inspiration for the establishment of houses of hospitality, farming communes, spiritual retreats, protest movements, and round-table discussions that gave many people hope and a chance. His decentralized "Christian communism" influenced Dorothy Day and a host of other young Catholics, who spearheaded a number of radical peace and justice movements in the 1930s and 1940s. When he died in 1949 he owned nothing and was buried in the secondhand clothing that demonstrated his view that a simple life was a Christian life.

Bibliography

A. *Easy Essays* (New York, 1936); *Catholic Radicalism: Phrased Essays for the Green Revolution* (New York, 1949).

B. DAB, 24:561–63; DACB, 350–51; DARB, 299–300; NCE, 9:507–8; NYT, 17 May 1949, 25; Arthur Sheehan, *Peter Maurin: Gay Believer* (Garden City, NY, 1959); Marc H. Ellis, *Peter Maurin: Prophet in the Twentieth Century* (New York, 1981).

McCLOSKEY, JOHN (10 March 1810, Brooklyn, NY—10 October 1885, New York, NY). *Education:* studied at Mount St. Mary's Coll. and Sem., Emmitsburg, MD, 1822–34; Urban Coll. of Propaganda, Rome, 1835–37. *Career:* ordained, 1834; pastoral work in Diocese of New York, 1834, 1837–41; president, St. John's Coll. (Fordham), 1841–42; rector, St. Joseph's Sem., 1842–43; coadjutor bishop of New York, 1844–47; bishop of Albany, NY, 1847–64; archbishop of New York, 1864–85; cardinal, 1875–85.

John McCloskey was the first American Catholic to be created a cardinal, a dignity that symbolized Rome's acknowledgment of the growing importance and maturity of the American Catholic church in general and of the Diocese of New York in particular. After twelve years of education at Mount St. Mary's, McCloskey was ordained and immediately appointed a professor of philosophy in the new seminary at Nyack-on-the-Hudson. The same year the seminary was destroyed by fire, and the studious young priest went to Rome for additional higher education. In 1837 he returned and was simultaneously made pastor of St. Joseph's Church, where he fought with lay trustees until they were able to accept him as their pastor, president of the newly founded St. John's College, and rector of St. Joseph's Seminary. By 1843 Bishop John Hughes needed a coadjutor bishop to assist him with the growing Catholic population, and he chose McCloskey, who already had extensive acquaintance with diocesan administration. When the Diocese of New York was divided in 1847, McCloskey was made the first bishop of Albany. In the course of the seventeen years of his Albany episcopate, McCloskey saw the diocese more than double in population and institutions.

In 1864 he became the archbishop of New York, and in 1869 and 1870 he attended the First Vatican Council, where he initially opposed the definition of papal infallibility as inexpedient. McCloskey's seventy-five years in New York witnessed a tremendous transformation of Catholicism from a tiny minority of despised immigrants to a relatively prosperous body. The completion of St. Patrick's Cathedral on Fifth Avenue in 1879 (a project that started under Bishop Hughes in 1858) was only one symbol of immigrant growth, generosity, ingenuity, and religious dedication. Catholicism in New York, moreover, passed from the aggressive and energetic internal and external antebellum battles of Bishop Hughes to the calm leadership of Archbishop McCloskey, who governed the diocese with a paternalism that provided for liberty and diversity as well as authority and unity. McCloskey's leadership provided a transition between the antebellum and late-nineteenth-century ecclesiastical and civil controversies.

Bibliography

B. DAB, 11:591–92; DACB, 357–58; DAH, 185–86; DCB, 783; NCE, 9:6–8; NYT, 10 October 1885, 1; John Farley, *The Life of John Cardinal McCloskey, First Prince of the Church of America, 1810–1885* (New York, 1918); James J. Walsh, *Our American Cardinals* (New York, 1926), 122–69.

McGLYNN, EDWARD (27 September 1837, New York, NY—7 January 1900, Newburgh, NY). *Education:* S.T.D., Urban Coll. of Propaganda, Rome, 1860. *Career:* assistant pastor, St. Joseph's parish, New York, 1860–66; pastor, St. Stephen's parish, New York, 1866–86; president, Anti-Poverty Society, New York, 1887–92; pastor, St. Mary's parish, Newburgh, NY, 1894–1900.

After receiving his education for the priesthood in Rome, Edward McGlynn became the first vice president of the newly established North American College (1859) in Rome, and a year later he received a doctorate in theology. He returned to New York in 1860 and became involved almost immediately in pastoral work, especially among the Union soldiers stationed in Central Park. As a young priest he supported public schools for Catholics, became a member of the Accademie (a local group of former Propagandist students who were advocating internal reforms in the Catholic church and a more open and accommodating stance toward American society), and protested against society's injustices toward the poor and unemployed.

In 1886 McGlynn became the center of an ecclesiastical and political controversy when he stumped for Henry George, who was running for mayor of New York and whose *Progress and Poverty* (1879) had awakened McGlynn and other social reformers like pastor Walter Rauschenbusch to the possibilities of George's single tax proposal. Like George, McGlynn believed that the causes of poverty were systemic and specifically related to exploitation in land ownership. Social and economic reforms like the single tax, they became convinced, were fundamental structural remedies for current economic and social injustices. A single tax on the rent of land would fairly distribute fiscal responsibility and provide economic opportunities for American workers.

In July of 1886, in the midst of a controversial mayoral campaign, Archbishop Michael Corrigan suspended McGlynn from the priesthood because he violated canonical legislation by becoming involved in partisan politics. In 1887 Rome excommunicated him for ecclesiastical disobedience. From 1887 to 1892, as founder and president of the New York Anti-Poverty Society, McGlynn continued to speak out on social reforms, drawing a large following of Catholics from his former parish, St. Stephen's, to his Sunday evening talks at Cooper Union. In 1892 McGlynn was reinstated in the church and priesthood after theologians at the Catholic University of America judged his social philosophy to be in conformity with, or at least not opposed to, the social teaching in Pope Leo's *Rerum Novarum* (1891).

Bibliography

A. "The Cross of the New Crusade," *Standard* 2 (April 1887): 2–3.
B. DAB, 7:53–54; DACB, 366; DARB, 273; DCA, 687; NCAB, 9:242–44; NCE, 9:18–19; NYT, 8 January 1900, 1; Sylvester L. Malone, *Edward McGlynn* (New York, 1918); Stephen Bell, *Rebel, Priest and Prophet: A Biography of Dr. Edward McGlynn* (New York, 1937); R. Emmett Curran, *Michael Augustine Corrigan* (New York, 1978).

McGRADY, THOMAS (16 June 1863, Lexington, KY—26 November 1907, San Francisco, CA). *Career:* ordained, 1887; pastoral work, Diocese of Galveston, TX, 1887–91; pastor, Lexington, Cynthiana, and Bellevue, KY, 1891–1903; lawyer, San Francisco, 1903–1907.

McGrady was one of the few Catholic socialists at the end of the nineteenth century. During his pastorate at Bellevue, KY, near Cincinnati, he encountered the devastating effects of industrialism upon his parishioners. The experience forced him to begin a serious study of political economy, reading Henry George's *Progress and Poverty* (1879), Edward Bellamy's *Looking Backward* (1888), Robert Blatchford's *Merrie England* (1895), and, after a trip to Europe in 1898, Karl Marx's *Kapital* (1867, 1885–95). By 1899 he considered himself a socialist and began to publish his arguments on the compatibility of Christianity and scientific socialism. "I was firmly convinced," he reported in 1902, "that the collective ownership and administration of capital for the benefit of all people was the only rational solution of the industrial problem." Such a view was in sharp contrast to Pope Leo XIII's encyclical *Rerum Novarum* (1891), but McGrady believed that that encyclical had wrongly supported the capitalist profit motive and offered no realistic solution to the problems of industrialization.

McGrady traveled throughout the country as a Catholic socialist priest and became a popular lecturer and propagandist for various Socialist Party locals. In his books and pamphlets as well as his lectures, he criticized Catholic misunderstandings of socialism and the pragmatic Catholic support for a laissez-faire capitalism that promoted social injustices. His socialist views were attacked by many Catholic clergy and the Catholic press. His own bishop, Camillus Paul Maes, considered him a poor parish administrator and absentee pastor as well as an unorthodox social thinker.

In December 1902 McGrady resigned his pastorate and left the priesthood because he interpreted Maes's criticisms of his views as forms of ecclesiastical vested interest. He also believed that American bishops like Maes had unjustly interfered with his and other priests' intellectual freedom. One year later, after preparing himself for the law, he moved to San Francisco, where he became a lawyer and where he spent the remaining years of his life. He wrote two articles the year of his death that criticized again what he considered the unjust exploitative alliance between Catholicism and capitalism, an alliance he believed would eventually destroy much of the former. Although he seems to have retained emotional and spiritual ties with Catholicism after he left the priesthood, he had separated himself from what he considered the church's institutional and political authoritarianism and seems to have lost his faith in the church's claims of supernatural authority. In 1907, after a lifetime of generally poor health, he died of chronic myocarditis.

Bibliography

A. *The Mistakes of Ingersoll* (Cincinnati, 1898); *The Two Kingdoms* (Cincinnati, 1899); *Beyond the Black Ocean* (Chicago, 1901; reprint, New York, 1971); *City of Angels: Review of Bishop Montgomery's Christian Socialism* (Terre Haute, IN, 1901); *The Clerical Capitalist: Reply to Father Mackey* (Terre Haute, IN, 1901); *Socialism and the Labor Problem: A Plea for Social Democracy* (Terre Haute, IN, 1901); "How I Became a Socialist," *Comrade* 2 (October 1902): 74–76.
B. Eugene V. Debs, "Obituary of Thomas McGrady," *Christian Socialist* (Chicago), 1 January 1908, 4–5; Toby Terrar, "Thomas McGrady, American Catholic So-

cialist," *Ecumenist* 21 (November and December, 1982): 14–16; idem, "Catholic Socialism: The Reverend Thomas McGrady," *Dialectical Anthropology* 7 (1983): 209–35; Dominic Scibilia, "Edward McGlynn, Thomas McGrady, and Peter C. Yorke: Prophets of American Social Catholicism" (Ph.D. diss., Marquette University, 1990).

McMASTER, JAMES A. (1 April 1820, Duanesburg, NY—29 December 1886, Brooklyn, NY). *Education:* studied at Union Coll. (NY), 1838–39; read law at Columbia Coll., 1840; studied for the Episcopal ministry at General Theological Sem., New York, 1840–44. *Career:* Redemptorist novice, St. Trond, Belgium, 1845; journalist, New York, 1846–48; editor and owner, *New York Freeman's Journal*, 1848–86.

James A. McMaster was born and raised in a Presbyterian family, became a participant in the Tractarian movement while he studied for the priesthood in the Protestant Episcopal church, and converted to Catholicism in 1845. Like Isaac Hecker and a number of other young men in their early twenties, he was drawn to the sacramental and magisterial tradition of the Catholic church, believing that the world in which they were living had lost a sense of religious unity and purpose and/or was bent upon a materialistic and superficial path that provided no outlet for the religious and spiritual dimensions of human existence. Catholicism seemed to offer a synthesis of spirit and matter, freedom and authority, that appealed to them in the mid-1840s. For one year after his conversion, McMaster studied for the priesthood in the Redemptorist Order in Belgium but discovered that he did not have the commitment for the vocation.

From 1846 until the end of his life McMaster became a fiery advocate for Catholicism against what he saw as the disintegrating tendencies of a Protestant Puritan tradition. As proprietor and a journalist of the *New York Freeman's Journal*, he became a lay apologist for Catholic doctrines and practices, an ultramontane advocate of papal infallibility and a strong centralized ecclesiastical authority, and a fierce critic of "liberal" Catholicism. Although generally ultramontane, he was a primary supporter of the pastoral and clerical rights movement against an arbitrary and excessive episcopal control in the American church and periodically quarreled with Bishop John Hughes over a number of ecclesiastical and civil issues. He also sympathized with Southern values and states' rights philosophy before and during the Civil War, criticized President Lincoln and the Emancipation Proclamation, and with his inflammatory editorials against the draft in 1863 insighted Irish immigrants to riot in New York. The United States government jailed him and forced him to shut down his newspaper during the Civil War because of his reputed seditious and treasonable attacks on the Lincoln administration's war policy.

Bibliography

B. DAB, 12:140; DACB, 377–78; DCA, 695; NCE, 9:41; New York *Herald*, 12 December 1886, 15; NYT, 30 December 1886, 5; Clarence A. Walworth, *The Oxford*

Movement in America (New York, 1895); Mary Augustine Kwitchen, *James Alphonsus McMaster* (Washington, D.C. 1949).

McQUAID, BERNARD J. (15 December 1823, New York, NY—18 January 1909, Rochester, NY). *Education:* studied at Chambley Coll., Montreal, 1839–43; St. Joseph's Sem., Fordham, NY, 1843–48. *Career:* rector, St. Vincent's Church, Madison, NJ, 1848–53; rector, St. Patrick's Cathedral, Newark, NJ, 1853–68; president, Seton Hall Coll., 1857, 1859–68; bishop of Rochester, NY, 1868–1909.

The son of Irish immigrants, Bernard McQuaid was orphaned by the age of ten. The New York Sisters of Charity took him into their orphanage and provided a caring home and early education for him. McQuaid spent most of his life within the protective confines of ecclesiastical structures, becoming in later life a forceful advocate of the construction of separate Catholic institutions, especially schools. Receiving his early education and early clerical experience under the watchful eye and forceful government of Bishop John Hughes, McQuaid developed an aggressive countercultural attitude toward American society—one that perceived the Catholic church as the ship of religious and social stability and protection for immigrants who were tossed about in a sea of religious diversity and civil and social hostility. Although he was a native-born American, he saw himself very much like Hughes, as the protector of poor and oppressed immigrants who needed education and religious formation to be productive Americans.

As first bishop of Rochester, NY, he became a builder of Catholic educational institutions. He brought the Sisters of St. Joseph and other women religious to his diocese to teach, and he insisted that Catholics send their children to parochial schools. He also founded in Rochester St. Andrew's Preparatory Seminary (1870), St. Bernard's Seminary (1891), a Catholic Summer Institute (1896) for training teachers and laity in general, the Nazareth Normal School (1898), and a Young Men's Catholic Institute. Although he was a strong advocate of ecclesiastical authority, he opposed the doctrine of papal infallibility during the First Vatican Council (1869–70) but affirmed it once it was promulgated as a Catholic dogma.

In the period after the Third Council of Baltimore (1884) he became allied with New York's Archbishop Michael Corrigan against the Americanist bishops. As one of the major leaders of late-nineteenth-century conservative Catholicism, he opposed the founding of the Catholic University of America, all secret societies, the appointment of a Roman Apostolic Delegate, Archbishop Ireland's Faribault-Stillwater plan, and the ecumenical activities of Bishop John Joseph Keane. He reprimanded Archbishop Ireland from the pulpit for his interference in New York State politics and was himself admonished by Rome for doing so. During the last years of his life, after the crisis of Americanism had passed, he resumed a cordial relationship with Ireland. Throughout his career, though, he remained a consistent conservative and an effective builder of immigrant Catholic institutions.

Bibliography

A. *The Letters of Archbishop Corrigan to Bishop McQuaid and Allied Documents* (Rochester, NY, 1946); Henry J. Browne, ed., "The Letters of Bishop McQuaid from the Vatican Council," *CHR* 41 (1956): 408–41.

B. DAB, 12:163–64; DACB, 380–81; DAH, 198–99; DARB, 279–80; DCA, 697; DCB, 789–90; NCAB, 12:141–42; NCE, 9:44–45; NYT, 19 January 1909, 9; *Rochester Democrat and Chronicle,* 19 January 1909, 1–2; Frederick J. Zwierlein, *The Life and Letters of Bishop McQuaid,* 3 vols. (Rome, Italy, and Louvain, Belgium, 1925–27).

MERTON, THOMAS (31 January 1915, Prades, France—10 December 1968, Bangkok, Thailand). *Education:* studied at Cambridge Univ., 1933–34; B.A., Columbia Univ., 1938; M.A., 1939. *Career:* instructor in English, St. Bonaventure Coll., 1940–41; member, Reformed Cistercians of the Strict Observance (Trappists), 1941–68; master of students, 1951–55; master of novices, 1955–65.

Like Isaac Hecker, Thomas Merton was a restless seeker throughout his life, searching for spiritual peace, social justice, and unity among the religions of the world. Born into a nominal Anglican family and orphaned when he was a teenager, Merton matriculated for a year at Cambridge University but was expelled because of a dissolute life and failure to meet academic standards. In 1935 he moved to the United States to live with his maternal grandparents and eventually enrolled at Columbia University, where he studied poetry and literature, wrote for student publications, became involved in agnostic socialist movements, and was introduced to Catholicism through the writings of the neo-Thomist Etienne Gilson and the pastor of Corpus Christi parish near Columbia. In 1938 he was received into the Catholic church.

After graduating from Columbia he taught literature at St. Bonaventure's College, and during his year of teaching he visited Catherine de Hueck's Friendship House in Harlem. He found no personal satisfaction, however, either in teaching or work for social justice, although he saw the need and benefit of both. Driven by a need for contemplation, silence, and spiritual meaning, he entered a Trappist monastery at Gethsemani, near Bardstown, KY, in 1941, where he spent the next twenty-seven years in contemplative prayer, writing nearly fifty books and several hundred articles about the interdependence of contemplation and action in the modern world, and giving spiritual advice to Catholics and others who came to the monastery for retreats. In 1948 he published his spiritual autobiography, *The Seven Storey Mountain,* which became a best-seller, resonating as it did with a yearning for peace and security in the post–World War II era. Merton also supported the efforts of the Catholic Worker movement, the liturgical movement, Catholic pacificists, and the post–Vatican II Catholic and Christian dialogues with Eastern religions. In 1968, while at an ecumenical conference of Catholic and Buddhist monks in Bangkok, he was killed by accidental electrocution.

Bibliography

A. *The Seven Storey Mountain* (New York, 1948); *The Sign of Jonas* (New York, 1953); *No Man Is an Island* (New York, 1955); *New Seeds of Contemplation* (New York, 1961); *Seeds of Destruction* (New York, 1964); *Zen and the Birds of Appetite* (New York, 1968); *Thomas Merton,* ed. Laurance Cunningham (New York, 1992).

B. DACB, 387–88; DARB, 305–306; NYT, 11 December 1968, 1; James T. Baker, *Thomas Merton: Social Critic* (Lexington, KY, 1971); John J. Higgins, *Merton's Theology of Prayer* (Spencer, MA, 1971); Dennis Q. McInerry, *Thomas Merton: The Man and His Work* (Washington, DC, 1974); Monica Furlong, *Merton: A Biography* (New York, 1980); Michael Mott, *The Seven Mountains of Thomas Merton* (Boston, 1984); James H. Forest, *Living with Wisdom: A Life of Thomas Merton* (Maryknoll, NY, 1991); William H. Shannon, *Silent Lamp: The Thomas Merton Story* (New York, 1992).

MICHEL, VIRGIL GEORGE (26 June 1890, St. Paul, MN—26 November 1938, Collegeville, MN). *Education:* B.A., St. John's Univ. (MN), 1909; Ph.B., 1912; M.A., 1913; S.T.B., Catholic Univ. of America, Washington, DC, 1917; Ph.D., 1918; studied at Sant'Anselmo, Rome, 1924; Louvain, Belgium, 1924–25. *Career:* novice, the Order of St. Benedict, St. John's Abbey, Collegeville, MN, 1909; teacher and administrator, St. John's Univ., 1918–24; founding editor, *Orate Fratres,* 1926–30, 1936–38; missionary work among the Ojibuay Indians, northern Minnesota, 1930–33; teacher and administrator, St. John's Univ., 1933–38.

Dom Virgil (née George) Michel was the foremost spokesman for the liturgical revival in American Catholicism during the early twentieth century. The son of German immigrants, Michel was a student and member of St. John's Abbey, the largest Benedictine community in the world. After receiving his education for the priesthood at St. John's, he matriculated at the Catholic University of America, where he wrote a doctoral dissertation on Orestes Brownson's literary principles in preparation for a teaching career in English at St. John's University. In 1924 and 1925 he went to Europe to study philosophy, and while there he met Dom Lambert Beauduin, the Belgium Benedictine monk of Mont-César and a liturgical reformer. When he returned from Europe in 1926 he translated Beauduin's major work on the liturgy and published it as the initial volume of his "Popular Liturgical Library."

Combining interests in sociology, economics, education, art, and philosophy with his study of liturgy, Michel developed a liturgical movement in the United States that differed significantly from its European Catholic precursor, emphasizing the liturgy's potential for social reform. The liturgy expressed a Christian community of justice as well as faith. For Michel this meant that a renewal of the social order must be tied to a revival of the liturgy, and that a revived concern for the liturgy demanded a corresponding concern for social reconstruction, since the liturgy expressed the divine ideal of communal living and provided the divine means for effectively reforming society.

Michel advanced the connection between liturgy and social reform during the Depression, shortly after the publication of Pius XI's *Quadragesimo Anno* (1931) and after Michel had served a three-year missionary experience (1930–33) among the economically depressed Indians in northern Minnesota. Michel and others established *Orate Fratres* and the Liturgical Press at St. John's to publish liturgical studies and texts and promote a renewed liturgical sense among American Catholics. Michel's pragmatic and activist-oriented liturgical movement was not popular in American Catholicism, but it did eventually contribute to the renewal of the liturgical life of the church through the reforms initiated by Vatican II.

Bibliography

A. *The Critical Principles of Orestes A. Brownson* (Washington, DC, 1918); *The Liturgical Apostolate* (Collegeville, MN, 1926); *My Sacrifice and Yours* (Collegeville, MN, 1926); with Martin B. Hellriegel, *The Liturgical Movement* (Collegeville, MN, 1930); *Philosophy of Human Conduct* (Minneapolis, 1936); *Christian Social Reconstruction* (Milwaukee, 1937); *The Liturgy of the Church* (New York, 1937); *The Christian in the World* (Collegeville, MN, 1939); *Our Life in Christ* (Collegeville, MN, 1939).

B. DAB, 22:454–56; DACB, 391; DARB, 306–7; NCE, 9:800–801; NYT, 27 November 1938, 48; Emerson Hynes, "The Social Thought of Virgil Michel, O.S.B.," *American Catholic Sociological Review* 1 (December 1940): 172–80; Paul B. Marx, *Virgil Michel and the Liturgical Movement* (Collegeville, MN, 1957); Jeremy Hall, *The Full Stature of Christ: The Ecclesiology of Dom Virgil Michel* (Collegeville, MN 1976); R. W. Franklin and Robert L. Spaeth, *Virgil Michel: American Catholic* (Collegeville, MN, 1988).

MUNDELEIN, GEORGE WILLIAM (2 July 1872, New York, NY—2 October 1939, Chicago, IL). *Education:* B.A., Manhattan Coll., 1889; studied at St. Vincent's Sem., Beatty, PA, 1889–91; Urban Coll. of Propaganda, Rome, 1891–95. *Career:* ordained, 1895; pastoral work in Diocese of Brooklyn, NY, 1895–97; diocesan chancellor, 1897–1909; auxiliary bishop of Brooklyn, 1909–15; archbishop of Chicago, 1915–39; cardinal, 1924–39.

In 1915 at the age of forty-three, George Mundelein, son of German immigrants, became the archbishop of Chicago, the largest Catholic diocese in the United States. For the next twenty-four years he helped build and manage a host of ecclesiastical institutions that helped to further the Americanization of Chicago's Catholic immigrants and his vision of the fusion of American and Catholic values. He was a fund-raiser, organizer, builder, and manager of an ecclesiastical bureaucracy that was known for its efficiency and effectiveness.

Mundelein was interested in big and ostentatious projects that manifested the growing prosperity of the Chicago Catholic community and his confidence that

Catholics would respond to his vision of making Chicago Catholicism influential in the Midwest. He encouraged the parochial schools and diocesan high schools to be instruments of Americanization. He built Quigley Preparatory College (1918) and the Seminary of St. Mary of the Lake (1921) to provide for a native clergy and to manifest, at least in the seminary's architecture, the symbolic collaboration of American and Roman styles. Because of his financial support of the Vatican, his double allegiance to the papacy and the American political system, and the growing importance of the diocese of Chicago, he was made Chicago's first cardinal in 1924. In 1926, to draw attention to Chicago's Catholic community and raise the religious fervor of his diocese, he hosted the twenty-eighth International Eucharistic Congress, which became a massive symbolic display of corporate Catholic life and its international connections.

During the Depression Mundelein became a strong supporter of President Roosevelt's New Deal, an early critic of Nazism, a promoter of the cause of labor, and an advocate for social justice. Although he made no public comments on Father Charles Coughlin's anti-Roosevelt rhetoric, he denounced Coughlin before the priests of his diocese and authorized Bishop Bernard Sheil to make opposition to Coughlin public. Mundelein stayed clear of partisan political campaigning, but he supported those local and federal politicians who he believed upheld the freedom of the church and the rights of the poor and unemployed. His primary legacy, however, was his reorganization and restructuring of diocesan administration, providing for an efficient development of twentieth-century Chicago Catholicism.

Bibliography

A. *Two Crowded Years* (Chicago, 1918); *Letters of a Bishop to His Flock* (New York, 1927).
B. DAB, 22:477–79; DACB, 407–8; DAH, 211; DCA, 783–84; DCB, 833–34; NCE, 10:70–71; NYT, 3 October 1939, 1, 16; Paul R. Martin, *The First Cardinal of the West* (Chicago, 1934); Edward Kantowicz, *Corporation Sole: Cardinal Mundelein and Chicago Catholicism* (Notre Dame, IN, 1983).

MURRAY, JOHN COURTNEY (12 September 1904, New York, NY—16 August 1967, New York, NY). *Education:* B.A., Boston Coll., 1926; M.A., 1927; S.T.L., Woodstock Sem. (MD), 1934; S.T.D., Gregorian Univ., Rome, 1937. *Career:* ordained, 1933; instructor, Ateneo de Manila, Philippines, 1927–30; professor of theology, Woodstock Sem., 1937–67; editor, *Theological Studies,* 1941–67; associate editor, *America,* 1945–46; adviser, Second Vatican Council, 1963–65.

John Courtney Murray was the principal twentieth-century American Catholic theoretician on religious liberty. His views on religious liberty not only gave American Catholics a systematic way of looking at their political experience, but also influenced the official Catholic teaching at the Second Vatican Council. The issue of religious liberty and the American experience of separation of church and state gradually arose as central theological and political problems for Murray in the immediate post–World War II era. Religious liberty evolved as a problem for two very different reasons. On the one hand, during the war, Murray saw the necessity of intercreedal political and social cooperation to meet national and international crises. Before Catholics could cooperate with other Christians and Jews in addressing issues of justice and peace, however, they had to overcome Protestant and Jewish suspicions about the supposed Catholic designs on the world order. These suspicions arose because of an official Catholic teaching on the confessional nature of the state. In this teaching, articulated by modern popes and by John A. Ryan in the United States, union and harmony between the Catholic church and the state was the ideal institutional relationship; religious liberty was at best a constitutional, historical expedient that could be allowed because it provided for the church's freedom in society.

On the other hand, after the 1947 and 1948 Supreme Court decisions on religious freedom, Murray believed that there was an increasingly secularist interpretation of the First Amendment that relegated religion to the sacristy or "private" sphere of individual conscience, thereby making religious perspectives totally irrelevant to political and social processes. These postwar circumstances made it necessary, he believed, for a new investigation of the Catholic teaching on religious liberty that would enable Catholics to cooperate with others in the social and political arena and provide legitimate grounds for the influence of religion on justice and peace in society.

In the course of a number of systematic-historical studies published after 1948, Murray developed the view that the constitutional provisions for religious liberty that had developed in the Western world for the past two centuries were consistent with an evolving Catholic teaching on the dignity and freedom of the person. Catholics should accept the constitutional developments not simply on the grounds of historical expediency and beneficial historical experience, but also on the moral ground that they provided for social peace and harmony among peoples—i.e., they fulfilled the state's ultimate purpose for existence. The state's function was to protect freedom, not to enforce or secure religious belief or ecclesiastical goals. Such a view, he argued, provided for the church's freedom as well as that of the individual, and such a view of the state's role was consistent with all that the church had struggled to achieve in its own past declarations. For him there was no such thing as an ideal relationship between church and state.

Murray's position was contrary to the prevailing view at the Vatican and at the Catholic University of America, where the theologian Joseph Fenton challenged Murray's orthodoxy. In the mid 1950s Rome and Murray's Jesuit superiors silenced him on the issue, but his position was eventually vindicated at the Second Vatican Council, where he became a primary author of the *Declaration on Religious Liberty* (*Dignitatis Humanae,* 1965).

Bibliography

A. With Edward S. Corwin, *Religion and the State; the Supreme Court as National School Board* (Durham, NC, 1949); with Walter Mills, *Foreign Policy and the Free Society* (New York, 1958); *We Hold These Truths* (New York, 1960); *The Problem of God: Yesterday and Today* (New Haven, CT, 1964); *The Problem of Religious Freedom* (Westminster, MD, 1965).

B. DACB, 413; DARB, 327–28; DCA, 785–86; NYT, 17 August 1967, 37; Thomas L. Love, *John Courtney Murray's Contemporary Church-State Theory* (Garden City, NY, 1965); Donald E. Pelotte, *John Courtney Murray: Theologian in Conflict* (New York, 1975); Walter J. Burghart, ed., *Religious Freedom 1965–1975: A Symposium on an Historical Document* (New York, 1977); J. Leon Hooper, *The Ethics of Discourse: The Social Philosophy of John Courtney Murray* (Washington, DC, 1986).

O

O'CONNELL, DENIS JOSEPH (28 January 1849, Donoughmore, Ireland—
1 January 1927, Richmond, VA). *Education:* studied at St. Charles Coll. (MD),
1868–71; D.D., Urban Coll. of Propaganda, Rome, 1877. *Career:* assistant
pastor, St. Peter's Cathedral, Richmond, 1877–83; rector, North American Coll.,
Rome, 1885–95; rector, Church of Santa Maria, Rome, 1895–1903; rector,
Catholic Univ. of America, 1903–1909; auxiliary bishop of San Francisco,
1909–12; bishop of Richmond, 1912–26; retired archbishop of Mariamne, Syria,
1926–27.

Sometime in the early 1850s the O'Connells emigrated from Ireland to Columbia, SC, and after the Civil War moved near Charlotte, NC. Denis's three
uncles, who were priests in North and South Carolina, encouraged him to attend St. Charles College in Elliott, MD, where in 1868 he met and became a
close friend of James Gibbons, the newly appointed vicar apostolic of North
Carolina. His friendship with Gibbons paved a path to ecclesiastical prominence in American Catholicism. In 1877, after a Roman education for the
priesthood, O'Connell went to the diocese of Richmond, Virginia, where Gibbons had been bishop since 1872 and where O'Connell spent the next six years
in pastoral work, maintaining throughout these years a close association with
Gibbons, who was named archbishop of Baltimore in 1877. In 1883 and 1884
Archbishop Gibbons appointed O'Connell to help prepare an agenda for the
Third Plenary Council of Baltimore.

After the Third Plenary, from 1885 to 1903, O'Connell played a major role
as Roman agent for Gibbons and the Americanist bishops (especially John Ireland and John Keane), maneuvering at the Vatican to win approval for Americanist pastoral objectives in accommodating Catholicism to late-nineteenth-century American social and political conditions. Anti-Americanist conservatives
in the church considered him a pawn in the hands of the Americanizing party

and sought to discredit his work at the North American College, where he was rector. Removed as rector of the college in 1895, he continued to articulate the Americanist program in Europe, giving a major address on the subject at the International Catholic Scientific Congress (1897) in Fribourg, Switzerland. His speech, entitled "A New Idea in the Life of Father Hecker," distinguished between political Americanism, which expressed the fundamental ideas of American government, and ecclesiastical Americanism, which expressed the pragmatic beneficial relationship between church and state in the United States. His advocacy of Americanism, however, was ineffective in turning the tide of European and American reaction against it.

Because of the support and protection of Cardinal Gibbons, O'Connell's ecclesiastical career was advanced even after Pope Leo XIII's condemnation of Americanism in 1899. In 1903, O'Connell was made rector of the Catholic University of America where he rescued the fledgling university from tentative obscurity, helped to improve the faculty, expanded the university to include undergraduates, and placed it on a firm financial footing. In 1909, he was ordained a bishop and after a short and unsatisfactory role as auxiliary bishop of San Francisco he was named bishop of Richmond where his fourteen-year episcopate was generally uneventful.

Bibliography

A. *A New Idea in the Life of Father Hecker* (Freiburg im Breisgau, 1897).

B. DACB, 433; DAH, 220–21; DARB, 338–39; DCA, 837–38; DCB, 863; NCAB 15:65; NCE 10:635–36; NYT 2 Jan. 1927, sec. 2, 9; Colman J. Barry, *The Catholic University of America, 1903–1909: The Rectorship of Denis J. O'Connell* (Washington, DC, 1950); Gerald P. Fogarty, *The Vatican and the Americanist Crisis: Denis J. O'Connell: American Agent in Rome, 1885–1903* (Rome, 1974).

O'CONNELL, WILLIAM HENRY (8 December 1859, Lowell, MA—22 April 1944, Boston, MA). *Education:* studied at St. Charles Coll., Ellicot City, MD, 1879; B.A., Boston Coll., 1881; studied at North American Coll., Rome, 1881–84. *Career:* ordained, 1884; pastoral work, Archdiocese of Boston, 1885–95; rector, North American Coll., Rome, 1895–1901; bishop of Portland, ME, 1901–1906; coadjutor archbishop of Boston, 1906–1907; archbishop of Boston, 1907–1944; cardinal, 1911–44.

William Henry O'Connell rose to ecclesiastical prominence in American Catholicism at the beginning of the Roman movements against prominent Americanist clergy and bishops. Roman-trained and -educated, he was appointed in 1895 rector of the North American College in Rome, where he replaced the Americanist Denis J. O'Connell. Throughout the remaining period of the Americanist crisis, 1895 to 1899, he continued as rector of the college and made friends with Cardinal Francesco Satolli and Archbishop Rafael Merry del Val, leaders in the Roman campaign against Americanism and later, under Pope Pius X (1903–14), against modernism.

His success in bringing stability and increasing the enrollment at the North

American College as well as his ideological identification with the anti-Americanist and anti-modernist Roman leadership made him a prime candidate in 1901 for the episcopacy of Portland, ME. As bishop of Portland he visited every parish, encouraged retreats for the clergy, and organized the Catholic youth. In 1905 he was appointed special papal envoy to Emperor Mutshito of Japan, where he surveyed the miss:ons and made a number of recommendations that were accepted by Rome, including founding a Catholic university in Tokyo.

In 1906, against the wishes of the New England bishops, O'Connell was appointed coadjutor to Archbishop John Joseph Williams of Boston, a moderate Americanist. During his thirty-eight-year reign as archbishop and cardinal of Boston, O'Connell turned away from the Americanist tendencies of his predecessor, centralized episcopal administrative control over the diocese, aligned his administrative policies with the anti-modernist and integralist stance of Pius X, and simultaneously reaffirmed Catholic allegiance and loyalty to America. He also supported missionary activity (especially the establishment of James A. Walsh and Thomas Price's Maryknoll), the lay apostolate and street preaching methods of David Goldstein and Martha Moore Avery, the lay activism inherent in the American Federation of Catholic Societies, and President Wilson's Fourteen Points. Like Pius X, he also encouraged the retreat movement, frequent communion, and lenten devotions. He was an accomplished organist, too, and created and translated numerous hymns. During his episcopate, parishes increased from 194 to 322, clergy from 600 to over 1,500, and school and seminary enrollments more than doubled. Although he was never popular among the American bishops, and although his national leadership in American Catholicism decreased after the death of Pius X in 1914, he had a significant conservative impact on the Archdiocese of Boston throughout his reign and was a forceful public figure there. His episcopal declarations commanded the attention of the press and politicians, even when they were not appreciated. From Protestants and Jews as well as Catholics he was able to raise significant funds for charitable and educational projects.

Bibliography

A. *Letters of Cardinal O'Connell, 1876–1901* (Boston, 1915); *Sermons and Addresses of His Eminence William Cardinal O'Connell, Archbishop of Boston,* 11 vols. (Boston, 1915–38); *Reminiscences of Twenty-Five Years* (Boston, 1926); *Recollections of Seventy Years* (Boston, 1934).
B. DAB, supp. 3, 568–70; DACB, 434; DAH, 221–22; DCA, 838; DCB, 863–64; NCAB, 33:11–12; NCE, 10:636–38; NYT, 23 April 1944, 1; Robert H. Lord et al., *History of the Archdiocese of Boston . . . 1604–1943,* 3 vols. (New York, 1944), 3:500–627; Dorothy G. Wayman, *Cardinal O'Connell of Boston* (New York, 1955); James O'Toole, *Militant and Triumphant: William Henry O'Connell and the Catholic Church in Boston, 1859–1944* (Notre Dame, IN, 1992).

O'HARA, EDWIN VINCENT (6 September 1881, Lanesboro, MN—11 September 1956, Milan, Italy). *Education:* studied at St. Thomas Coll. and Sem.

(MN), 1900–1905; Catholic Univ. of America, 1910; Catholic Institute, Paris, 1918. *Career:* ordained, 1905; pastoral work, Archdiocese of Portland, OR, 1905–30; archdiocesan superintendent of schools, 1907–18; pastor, St. Mary's, Eugene, OR, 1920–28; founder and chairman, National Catholic Rural Life Conference, 1921–30; instructor in sociology, Catholic Univ. of America, 1929–30; bishop of Great Falls, MT, 1930–39; bishop of Kansas City, MO, 1939–56; personal title of archbishop *(ad personam),* 1954–56.

After receiving his education for the priesthood, Edwin O'Hara became one of the new breed of activist priests who envisioned and organized a number of movements that demonstrated a Catholic confidence in its ability to influence American social, cultural, educational, and religious life in rural as well as urban areas. He was prominent and/or influential in helping to establish in Oregon the first minimum wage law for women and children (1913), a law upheld in the United States Supreme Court. He also promoted the papal social encyclicals and applied the Catholic principles of social justice to rural problems. To publicize and promote interests in rural justice and the need for religious education among rural peoples, he published in 1921 the magazine *Isidore's Plow,* which became known as *Catholic Rural Life* after 1924. In 1923 he organized the National Catholic Rural Life Conference to provide a forum for the discussion of Catholic approaches to changes in American rural life.

In Oregon, Montana, and Kansas City, MO, he became a prominent proponent of a lay-lead religious education movement. In the early years of his clerical career he analyzed the problems of religious education in the United States, and in 1933 he helped organize on a national level the Confraternity of Christian Doctrine (CCD), a canonically established program of religious instruction that had hitherto been neglected in the United States. Through this movement he was also instrumental in organizing the Catholic Biblical Association (1936), initiating the new Confraternity translation of the Bible (1941), and revising the Baltimore Catechism (1941). He promoted the liturgical movement and lay participation in church and liturgy by obtaining the first uses of English in the Roman Catholic ritual between 1947 and 1954. He died in Milan on his way to an international liturgical congress.

Bibliography

A. Trans. with John Pescheges, *At the Deathbed of Darwinism* (Burlington, OR, 1904); *Pioneer Catholic History of Oregon* (Portland, OR, 1911; reprint, Patterson, NJ, 1939); *A Living Wage by Legislation: The Oregon Experience* (Salem, OR, 1916); *The Church and the Country Community* (New York, 1927).
B. DACB, 443; DAH, 228; DARB, 339–41; DCA, 839–40; DCB, 870; NCAB, 43:26; NCE, 10:660–61; NYT 12 September 1956, 37; James G. Shaw, *Edwin Vincent O'Hara: American Prelate* (New York, 1957); Gerald P. Fogarty, *American Catholic Biblical Scholarship: A History from the Early Republic to Vatican II* (New York, 1989): 199–275; Timothy M. Dolan, *"Some Seed Fell on Good Ground": The Life of Edwin V. O'Hara* (Washington, DC, 1992).

O'REILLY, JOHN BOYLE (28 June 1844, near Drogheda, Ireland—10 August 1890, Hull, MA). *Career:* editor, *Pilot,* 1870–90.

For twenty-one years (1869–90) John Boyle O'Reilly was an articulate Irish-American lay Catholic poet, novelist, and editor who supported Irish home rule, religious toleration, and justice for industrial workers, African-Americans, and Native Americans. In 1863 he joined the Fenian revolutionary movement in Ireland and was arrested and sentenced to penal work in Australia; he escaped in 1869 and fled to the United States. In 1870 he became editor of the Boston *Pilot,* a Catholic newspaper that was, during his editorship, closely associated with Archbishop John Williams's moderate Americanizing tendencies. Throughout his twenty-one years in the United States he also published five books of poetry and a novel and was acknowledged as one of the better American Catholic writers of the late nineteenth century.

Bibliography

A. *Songs from the Southern Seas, and Other Poems* (Boston, 1873); *Songs, Legends and Ballads* (Boston, 1878); *Moondyne Joe* (New York, 1879); *Statues in the Block* (Boston, 1881); *In Bohemia* (Boston, 1886); *The Poetry and Song of Ireland* (New York, 1887).
B. DAB, 14:53–54; DARB, 343–44; NCAB, 1:428–29; NCE, 10:741; NYT, 11 August 1890, 1; James J. Roche, *Life of John Boyle O'Reilly* (New York, 1891); William G. Schofield, *Seek for a Hero* (New York, 1956); Francis G. McManamin, *The American Years of John Boyle O'Reilly* (Washington, DC, 1959, 1976); Kevin T. Shanley, "John Boyle O'Reilly: Journalist and Civil Rights Advocate" (M.A. thesis, Marquette University, 1967).

O'SULLIVAN, MARY KENNEY (8 January 1864, Hannibal, MO—18 January 1943, West Medford, MA).

Educated in convent schools and a Catholic all her life, Mary Kenney O'Sullivan became a leader in organized labor, active suffragist, prohibitionist, member of the Women's International League for Peace, wife, and mother of four. Like many single young Irish women in the late nineteenth century, she worked as a laborer, became acquainted with problems of unjust working conditions and wages, and experienced the need for cooperative labor unions. With the help of Jane Addams she organized in Chicago a cooperative enterprise where working women could share housing, food, and companionship. In 1892 Samuel Gompers appointed her the first female organizer of the American Federation of Labor. After being relieved of her AFL position five months after her appointment, she lobbied in Springfield, IL, for the passage of the state's first factory law (passed in 1893), which regulated the employment of women and children and set up a factory inspection department. In 1894 she married John F. O'Sullivan, a labor reporter for the *Boston Globe* and AFL representative, and moved to Boston, where she continued to work in organized labor.

A year after the death of her husband (1903) she cofounded the National

Women's Trade Union League. As a widowed mother of four young children, she became the sole support of the family. From 1914 until 1934 she supported them as a Massachusetts factory inspector, and throughout the period she continued to be involved in activist causes. Besides supporting organized labor and working women in particular, she pushed for women's suffrage, seeing the ballot as a means of needed social and economic reforms. She testified before a congressional committee and campaigned for women's right to vote in Illinois and Massachusetts. At one of the annual meetings of the WTUL she castigated suffrage opponents as women of leisure who "led sheltered and protected lives" and who selfishly obstructed the efforts of organized working women to obtain "full citizenship."

Bibliography

A. "The Labor War at Lawrence," *Survey* 28 (April 1912): 72–74.
B. NAW, 2:655–56; *Boston Globe,* 19 January 1843, 10; James K. Kenneally, *Women and American Trade Unions* (Montreal, 1981), 20–22, 42–44; idem, "Catholic and Feminist: A Biographical Approach," *U.S.CH* 3 (Spring 1984): 229–53.

P

PACE, EDWARD ALOYSIUS (3 July 1861, Starke, FL—26 April 1938, Washington, DC). *Education:* studied at St. Charles Coll., Ellicott, MD, 1876–80; North American Coll. and Propaganda Univ., Rome, 1880–85; S.T.D., Propaganda Univ., 1886; studied at Univ. of Louvain, Belgium, and Paris, 1888; Ph.D., Univ. of Leipzig, 1891. *Career:* ordained, 1885; curate, St. Augustine's Cathedral, St. Augustine, FL, 1885–87; professor, Catholic Univ. of America, 1891–1935; cofounder and coeditor, *Catholic Educational Review,* 1911–36; vice rector, Catholic Univ. of America, 1925–36; retired, 1936–38.

Pace was one of the progressive professors at the Catholic University of America who tried in the early twentieth century to raise the level of intellectual life in American Catholicism. Educated under the Thomist Francisco Satolli in Rome and under Wilhelm Wundt in experimental psychology at Leipzig, he became interested in the dialogue between Thomist philosophy and theology and the natural sciences. Throughout his life he believed, much like Pope Leo XIII, that Thomist philosophy was capable of being adapted to the problems of the modern world. To engage in such a project required that one possess a thorough knowledge not only of Thomist principles and conclusions, but of contemporary scientific thought and achievements. Throughout his life Pace tried to foster that dialogue on the institutional as well as intellectual level. He also believed that Thomism should inform the total Catholic educational process, and he helped to develop something of this mentality at the Catholic University and throughout the Catholic school system in the United States.

Pace became a major contributor to the intellectual revival through his work in establishing the institutions of that revival. At the Catholic University he was at first a professor of psychology (1891–94), founder and dean of the School of Philosophy (1895–1935), and collaborator in establishing the School of Education (1909). He fostered the emergence of an American Catholic intellectual tradition as a founding associate editor of the *Catholic Encyclopedia* (1907–12), as cofounder of the *Catholic Educational Review,* as first editor of *Studies in Psychology and Psychiatry* (1926), as founder and first president of the American Catholic Philosophical Association (1926), and with James Hugh Ryan, editor of the association's journal, *New Scholasticism* (1926–32).

Because he was so preoccupied with establishing the founding institutions for a Catholic intellectual renaissance, he published few major works after his doctoral dissertation, *Das Relativitaets-prinzip in Herbert Spencer's psychologischer Entwicklungslehre* (1891). He did coedit with Thomas Edward Shields, however, a series of textbooks for Catholic schools and wrote numerous scholarly articles in the *Catholic Encyclopedia, Catholic University Bulletin, New York Review, New Scholasticism, Catholic World,* and *Catholic Educational Review* on philosophy, religion, and education—articles that were characterized by originality, clarity, and precision. He was also a pioneer in experimental psychology, establishing the second psychological laboratory in the United States.

Bibliography

A. "St. Thomas and Modern Thought," *Catholic University Bulletin* 2 (1896): 188–201; "Modern Substitutes for Soul," *New York Review* 1 (1905): 541–54; with Thomas Edward Shields, *Catholic Educational Series of Primary Textbooks,* 6 vols. (Washington, DC, 1908–17); *The Mass for Every Day in the Year* (Washington, DC, 1916); "Assimilari Dei," *New Scholasticism* 2 (October 1928): 342–56.

B. DACB, 456; NCE, 10:850–85; *Aspects of the New Scholastic Philosophy* (New York, 1932); H. Misiak and V. M. Staudt, *Catholics in Psychology: A Historical Survey* (New York, 1954); J. K. Ryan, "In Memory of Edward Aloysius Pace," *New Scholasticism* 35 (1961): 141–51.

POWDERLY, TERENCE VINCENT (22 January 1849, Carbondale, PA—24 June 1924, Washington, DC). *Education:* read law and admitted to the bar, 1894. *Career:* machinist apprentice, 1866; organizer of the Industrial Brotherhood, 1874; union local organizer in Scranton, PA, 1876; mayor of Scranton, 1878; grand master workman of the Knights of Labor, 1879–93; US commissioner general of immigration, 1897–1902; special representative of the Department of Commerce and Labor and chief of the Bureau of Immigration's information division, 1906.

During his early teenage years Terence Powderly worked on the railroads, and as a young man he became involved in various movements to unionize labor. He helped organize the Knights of Labor in 1879 and became its chief spokesman between 1879 and 1893. In 1886 he tried to demonstrate for Cardinal James Gibbons the compatibility of the Knights of Labor with Catholicism, and supported the mayoral candidacy of Henry George in New York. Throughout his life he was an advocate of labor and criticized those in the Catholic church who neglected the just demands of laborers. Although he opposed systematic socialism and the violence associated with labor strikes in the late nineteenth and early twentieth centuries, he rejected those who assaulted socialism without acknowledging that it had uncovered real and tangible injustices in industrial society. For him, socialism was an effect, not a cause, of industrial unrest. By the early twentieth century Powderly moved away from institutional Catholicism, believing that the church itself had become an accomplice in industrial injustices by not speaking out more forcefully against them, by identifying with the rich and powerful, and by obscuring the simple message of Jesus, who was a toiler for the poor.

Bibliography

A. *Thirty Years of Labor* (New York, 1899); *The Path I Trod: The Autobiography of Terence V. Powderly* (New York, 1940).
B. DAB, 15:142; NCE, 11:653–54; NYT, 25 June 1924, 23; *Who's Who in America*, 1916–17, 1978; Henry J. Browne, *The Catholic Church and the Knights of Labor* (Washington, D.C. 1949), passim.

PURCELL, JOHN BAPTIST (26 February 1800, Mallow, Ireland—4 July 1883, Brown County, OH). *Education:* studied at Mount St. Mary's Coll. (MD), 1820–23; sem. of St. Suplice, Paris, 1834–27. *Career:* professor (president after 1829), Mount St. Mary's Coll., 1827–33; bishop of Cincinnati, 1833–50; archbishop of Cincinnati, 1850–83.

For fifty years John Baptist Purcell presided over the phenomenal expansion of midwestern Catholicism. During his episcopal career he saw the center of Catholic gravity shift from Bardstown, KY, to St. Louis and Cincinnati, both of which were made metropolitan sees in 1847 and 1850 respectively. Irish by birth, Sulpician by education and early clerical experience, and American by choice, Purcell had the skills of an orator, the mind of a Gallican-trained professor, and the pragmatism of an American ecclesiastical builder. He met the religious and institutional needs of midwestern German and Irish Catholic immigrants who were flooding his and other newly erected dioceses throughout the Midwest, from the Alleghenies to the Mississippi River. When he began his bishopric the diocese had 14 priests and 16 churches; when he died there were 480 priests, 510 churches, two newspapers (the *Catholic Telegraph* and *Der Wahrheitsfreund*), 3 colleges, 3 seminaries, 6 hospitals, 30 schools, and about 24 orphanages. During his episcopate, moreover, the territory north of the Ohio and east of the Mississippi River served by his diocese and that of St. Louis saw the creation of 10 new dioceses and 2 metropolitan sees (Milwaukee, 1850; Chicago, 1880).

Purcell was an apologist for Catholicism in the Midwest as well as a builder. At a time when Cincinnati itself was perceived as a key to the religious struggle to win the West (i.e., a central focus of Lyman Beecher's *Plea for the West,* Lane Theological Seminary, and Charles G. Finney's activities at Oberlin College), Purcell became a spokesman for a moderate post-Tridentine Catholicism open to American values. In a series of public religious debates with Alexander

Campbell (1836–37) and Thomas Vickers (1867), Purcell upheld the Catholic doctrinal tradition and demonstrated that Catholic leaders could promote their traditions and institutions and simultaneously contribute to the needs of the expanding Midwest without appropriating the new measures used by Protestant evangelicals. In the midst of nativist hostility during the early 1850s, he defended Archbishop Gaetano Bedini against the assaults of Cincinnati's free thinkers and the German revolutionaries of 1848. He also defended Catholic schools and periodically applied for public funds to support them, a measure that created considerable animosity in Ohio.

As a Gallican conciliarist, Sulpician-trained theologian, and archbishop, Purcell convoked two provincial councils (1855, 1858) to create legislation and adapt general conciliar legislation to the midwestern dioceses. He also attended the First Vatican Council (1869–70), where he became an opponent of the definition of papal infallibility because he believed the doctrine was not only inopportune but also inconsistent with earlier ecclesiastical tradition. Once the doctrine was defined by the council, however, he, like other American opponents, accepted it. During the Civil War he was a strong supporter of the Union side and advocated emancipation five months before President Lincoln announced it. In 1878, because of his brother Father Edward Purcell's financial mismanagement of four million dollars, the diocese of Cincinnati was bankrupted. The pressures of the financial embarrassment and ill health forced Purcell to retire from public ecclesiastical life. In 1883 he died in an Ursuline convent at St. Martin's, Ohio.

Bibliography

A. *A Debate on the Roman Catholic Religion* (Cincinnati, 1838); *The Vickers and Purcell Controversy* (Cincinnati, 1868).
B. DAB, 15:266–68; DACB, 471–72; DAH, 243; DARB, 372–73; NCAB, 5:186–88; NCE, 11:1029–30; NYT, 6 July 1883, 1; SH, 9:364; *Enquirer* (Cincinnati), 4 July 1883, 1; Mary A. McCann, *Archbishop Purcell and the Archdiocese of Cincinnati* (Washington, DC, 1918); John H. Lamott, *History of the Archdiocese of Cincinnati* (New York, 1921); M. Edmund Hussey, "The 1878 Financial Failure of Archbishop Purcell," *Cincinnati Historical Society Bulletin* 36 (Spring 1978): 7–41.

R

REPPLIER, AGNES (1 April 1855, Philadelphia, PA—15 December, 1950, Philadelphia, PA).

Agnes Repplier was one of a few late-nineteenth- and early-twentieth-century Catholic women writers. Educated in convent schools, she began writing short stories for the *Catholic World* and *Young Catholic* when she was in her late teens. By the mid 1880s she began writing for the *Atlantic Monthly* and earned a reputation as a talented essayist. Throughout the remainder of her life she published seventeen volumes of her collected essays and historical biographies. Unlike many American Catholic writers of the nineteenth century, her writings were not didactic; they advocated the basic equality of the sexes, the fundamental dynamics of spiritual commitment, and the historical and exemplary significance of the lives of certain American Catholic missionaries like Jacques Marquette and Junípero Serra.

Her Catholicism and her creed were not pressed apologetically in her works, but her characters did reveal a kind of religious life that unostentatiously came through in living humanely and for others. Although she advocated the basic human equality of the sexes, she did not support women's suffrage because she believed that women could achieve social equality without it and that many arguments for it were simply based upon emotionally charged issues like the moral superiority of women—a position that did little honest credit to the cause or to women. In fact she was a traditionalist as far as women's suffrage was concerned and supported many of the social conventions of the late nineteenth and early twentieth centuries. Traditionalist though she was, she periodically criticized the individualism and materialism in American culture and the pious inanities and superficial spirituality in segments of American Catholicism.

Bibliography

A. *Varia* (Boston, 1897); *Compromises* (Boston, 1904); *In Our Convent Days* (Boston, 1905); *Eight Decades: Essays and Episodes* (Boston, 1912); *Americans and Others* (Boston, 1913); *Counter-Currents* (Boston, 1916); *Points of Friction* (Boston, 1920); *Père Marquette* (New York, 1929); *Junípero Serra* (New York, 1933); *In Pursuit of Laughter* (Boston, 1936).

B. CA1947: 642–43; DACB, 484; NAW, 3:137–39; George S. Stokes, *Agnes Repplier: Lady of Letters* (Philadelphia, 1949).

RICHARD, GABRIEL (15 October 1767, Saintes, France—13 September 1832, Detroit, MI). *Education:* studied at St. Sulpice Sem., Angers, France, 1784–91. *Career:* ordained, 1791; missionary in IL, 1792–98; missionary in MI and WI, 1798–1801; pastor, St. Anne, Detroit, 1801–32; a founder and vice president of the Univ. of Michigan, 1817; Michigan territorial delegate to US Congress, 1823–25.

Of all the French Catholic clergy who served as missionaries and pastors in Detroit's St. Anne parish since 1701, none had as long a tenure or as great an influence as did the Sulpician Gabriel Richard. An émigré from the French Revolution, Richard came to Baltimore in 1792 with three other French clergy. Bishop John Carroll sent him immediately to the western Illinois frontier, where he served French and Indian settlements for six years. In 1788, two years after Detroit came under American political control and John Carroll's ecclesiastical administration, Richard was sent to Michigan to be a missionary and pastor among the French and Indians. As pastor of Detroit's St. Anne after 1801, Richard became an ecclesiastical builder and major contributor to the cultural as well as religious life in frontier Michigan.

In 1809 he purchased a printing press while in Baltimore and established the first newspaper in Michigan, the *Michigan Essay or Impartial Observer*. His press also published a number of religious and educational texts throughout his pastorate. An avid supporter of the American political system, he was imprisoned in Canada by the English during the War of 1812. In 1817 he helped establish the University of Michigan, became a professor in the fledgling institution, and served as vice president during the founding years. At the urging of some of his parishioners in 1823 he became a political candidate to represent Michigan territory in the House of Representatives, was elected delegate, and continued his office as pastor. During his years as delegate he was imprisoned for libel because he excommunicated one of his parishioners who had obtained a civil divorce. Although considered a candidate for the episcopacy of Detroit, he did not live long enough to see the erection of Detroit as a diocese in 1833, having died of the cholera epidemic of 1832.

Bibliography

B. DAB, 15:549–51; DACB, 487–88; NCE, 12:484–85; *Democratic Free Press and Michigan Intelligencer* (Detroit), 27 September 1832, 1; P. Guerin, *Le Martyr de la Charité ou Notice sur M. G. Richard, Missionaire* (Paris, 1850); N. E. Dionne,

Gabriel Richard, Suplicien, Curé et Second Fondateur de la Ville de Detroit (Quebec, 1911); S. M. Pagellis, *Father Gabriel Richard* (Detroit, 1950); Frank Woodward and Albert Hymna, *Gabriel Richard: Frontier Ambassador* (Detroit, 1958); Dolorita Mast, *Always the Priest: The Life of Gabriel Richard, S.S.* (Baltimore, 1965).

RIEPP, MOTHER BENEDICTA (28 June 1825, Waal, Bavaria—15 March 1862, St. Cloud, MN). *Career:* entered Benedictine Convent, Eichstätt, Bavaria, 1844; convent novice mistress, 1849–52; superior, St. Mary's Convent, St. Mary, PA, 1852–57.

In 1852 Mother Benedicta (née Maria Sybilla) established at St. Mary, PA, the first Benedictine community of nuns in the United States. By the time of her death in 1862 Benedictine nuns had developed autonomous convents in Erie, PA, Newark, NJ, Covington, KY, St. Cloud, MN, and Chicago, IL. From their beginnings in the United States the Benedictine nuns, although cloistered, became an active teaching order. Their mission flowed from the exigencies of German immigrant life, and to some extent this mission changed the way Benedictine monasteries functioned in American society. The immigrants needed teachers, but the nuns also needed the income from teaching to help support their own religious way of life. Voluntaryism influenced monasteries and convents as well as other Catholic religious institutions.

Shortly after the Benedictine nuns were settled in Pennsylvania Mother Benedicta became involved in a series of jurisdictional conflicts with the German Abbot Boniface Wimmer, O.S.B., of St. Vincent's Abbey, who had invited the nuns to teach in that state. In 1857, because of the conflicts with Wimmer and because of the need for financial support, Mother Benedicta traveled to Europe to obtain jurisdictional independence from Wimmer and to seek funds. Rome responded to the request in 1859 by placing Benedictine convents under the jurisdiction of local bishops. That decree, however, came too late for Mother Benedicta. Wimmer, considering her disobedient and undisciplined, ousted her as superior of the Benedictine nuns in 1857. Wimmer's antagonism forced her to separate herself from the Pennsylvania community and to join a group of young nuns who had gone to St. Cloud in 1857 to establish another community there. From 1857 to 1862 she continued to live as a Benedictine nun in St. Cloud, but she never regained her leadership role in the community after Wimmer summarily dismissed her.

Bibliography
B. NAW, 3:160–61; M. Grace McDonald, *With Lamps Burning* (St. Joseph, MN, 1957); M. Incarnata Girgen, *Behind the Beginnings: Benedictine Women in America* (St. Joseph, MO, 1981).

ROBINSON, CAROL JACKSON (see JACKSON, CAROL).

RUDD, DANIEL (7 August 1854, Bardstown, KY—3 December 1933, Bardstown, KY). *Career:* founder and editor, *Ohio State Tribune* (renamed *American Catholic Tribune*), Springfield, 1886–94; organizer and president, Afro-American Lay Catholic Congresses, 1889–94; member, committee of organization, Lay Catholic Congress, Baltimore, 1889; manager, lumber mill, Bolivar County, MS, c. 1910; accountant, Madison, AR, c. 1918–20; feed-store operator, Marion, AR, 1920–32.

Son of Kentucky Catholic slaves, Daniel Rudd was one of the most prominent and articulate. African-American Catholic lay journalists, lecturers, and organizers in the late nineteenth century. His *American Catholic Tribune,* the first African-American Catholic newspaper, focused on religious and social issues, emphasized the need for racial and religious solidarity, and fostered the idea that only the Catholic church possessed the doctrine and will to break down all barriers of color and treat all people equally. Rudd also promoted the church's social teachings and published a translation of Pope Leo XIII's *Rerum Novarum,* seeing it as an abolitionist document. Rudd, however, was no blind idealist, blithely waving the banner of Catholicism. He criticized other Catholic newspapers' failure to address issues of religious segregation and other racial injustices in the church. Rudd also lectured on these topics in German as well as English, not only in the diocese of Cincinnati, but throughout the United States. Moreover, in 1899 he traveled to France to meet Cardinal Lavigerie and represent African-Americans at an international congress on slavery. While in England he lectured in Cardinal Manning's St. George's Cathedral Hall in Westminister.

Aware of the Catholic congresses in Belguim and Germany, Rudd founded and organized the first of five national Catholic Afro-American Congresses (1889–94) to promote solidarity, Catholic missionary work among African-Americans, and Catholic schools for African-Americans. Rudd's national work on behalf of racial justice in church and society waned after 1894, but he continued to promote these causes on the local level in Arkansas throughout the early twentieth century. He is remembered primarily for his late-nineteenth-century efforts to raise African-American Catholic consciousness and pride.

Bibliography

A. *Three Catholic Afro-American Congresses* (Cincinnati, 1893; reprint, New York, 1978); with Theophilus Bond, *From Slavery to Wealth: The Life of Scott Bond. The Rewards of Honesty, Industry, Economy, and Perseverance* (Madison, AR, 1917).

B. David Spalding, "The Negro Catholic Congresses, 1889–1894," *CHR* 55 (April 1969): 337–57; Cyprian Davis, *The History of Black Catholics in the United States* (New York, 1990), 164–72.

RUSSELL, MOTHER MARY BAPTIST (18 April 1829, Newry, County Down, Ireland—6 August 1898, San Francisco, CA). *Career:* member, Sisters of Mercy, Kinsale, Ireland, 1848–54; mother superior, Sisters of Mercy, San Francisco, 1854–98.

In 1898 the *San Francisco Bulletin* called Mother Mary Baptist (née Katherine) of the Sisters of Mercy the "best-known charitable worker on the Pacific Coast." In 1854 the first archbishop of San Francisco, Joseph Alemany, invited the Irish Sisters of Mercy to come to his new diocese. Mother Mary Baptist led the first contingent of eight nuns and novices and immediately began to nurse the sick, one of their primary works. During the next forty years she and her sisters founded St. Mary's Hospital (1857), a night school for adults, a home for unemployed women, a reform shelter for former prostitutes, primary schools for girls and boys, and homes for the aged. They made regular visits to the city prisons, taught religion to the young, trained "wayward" girls to be self-supporting, and helped other young women find employment. Mother Mary Baptist also founded a new convent in Sacramento in 1857. To develop a common purpose and elicit common support she convoked in 1894 a meeting of Catholic schoolteachers in the San Francisco archdiocese, the first meeting of its kind in the United States.

Bibliography

B. DACB, 498; NAW, 3:213–14; Matthew Russell, *The Life of Mother Mary Baptist Russell, Sister of Mercy* (New York, 1901); Mary Aurelia McArdle, *California's Pioneer Sister of Mercy: Mother Mary Baptist Russell, 1829–1898* (Fresno, CA, 1954); Mary E. Evans, *The Spirit Is Mercy: The Story of the Sisters of Mercy in the Archdiocese of Cincinnati, 1858–1958* (Westminster, MD, 1959), 61–71.

RYAN, JOHN AUGUSTINE (25 May 1869, Vermillion, MN—16 September 1945, St. Paul, MN). *Education:* studied at St. Thomas Coll. and St. Paul's Sem. (MN), 1892–98; S.T.D., Catholic Univ. of America, 1906. *Career:* professor of moral theology, St. Paul's Sem., 1902–15; professor of political science and moral theology, Catholic Univ. of America, 1915–39; director of the Department of Social Action, National Catholic Welfare Conference, 1919–45.

During the first half of the twentieth century John A. Ryan became the foremost American Catholic social analyst and promoter of systematic social thought. Raised under the influence of Minnesota's prairie populism and Archbishop John Ireland's seminary, Ryan believed that the Catholic social ethic, as he discovered it in Pope Leo XIII's encyclical *Rerum Novarum,* had to be wedded to the empirical and theoretical study of economics. After writing his two most important theoretical works on economic justice in the industrial order, *A Living Wage* (1906) and *Distributive Justice* (1916), Ryan became an active promoter of minimum wage legislation and a lobbyist in state and federal legislatures for protective laws for workers. He also propagated Catholic social thought among clergy and laity through the activities of the National Catholic Welfare Conference's Social Action Department, his classes on moral theology at the Catholic University, the *Catholic Charities Review,* which he founded and edited (1917–20), and through lectures at summer schools of social action at various Catholic universities and colleges.

In 1919 he wrote the "Bishops' Program for Social Reconstruction," a detailed outline of progressive legislation in favor of workers and wage earners. During the 1920s he became an active member of the Catholic Association for International Peace, American Civil Liberties Union, and Federal Council of Churches, hoping to advance the cause of universal liberty and justice through these institutions. In the 1930s he supported President Roosevelt's economic initiatives and programs, earning for himself the sobriquet "Right Reverend New Dealer." He also publicly criticized the economic nostrums and anti-Semitism of the radical radio priest Charles Coughlin.

Bibliography

A. *A Living Wage: Its Ethical and Economic Aspects* (New York, 1906); *Distributive Justice: The Right and Wrong of Our Present Distribution of Wealth* (New York, 1916); *Social Reconstruction* (New York, 1920); *Declining Liberty and Other Papers* (New York, 1927); *Seven Troubled Years* (Ann Arbor, MI, 1937); *Social Doctrine in Action* (New York, 1941).

B. DAB, 23:679–82; DACB, 501–2; DARB, 388–89; NCAB, C:190; NCE, 12:767; NYT, 17 September 1945, 19; Patrick W. Gearty, *The Economic Thought of Monsignor John A. Ryan* (Washington, DC, 1953); Francis L. Broderick, *The Right Reverend New Dealer: John A. Ryan* (New York, 1963).

S

SADLIER, MARY A. MADDEN (31 December 1820, County Cavan, Ireland—5 April 1903, Montreal, Canada). *Career:* editor, *New York Tablet,* 1869–80.

After her father died in 1844, Mary Madden emigrated from Ireland to New York, where she married publisher James A. Sadlier (d. 1869) in 1846. Shortly after their marriage they moved to Montreal, where James managed a branch of the publishing firm for fourteen years and where Mary began her career as a writer. In 1860 they returned to New York, where Mary, the mother of six children including the writer Anna T. Sadlier, became a well-known popular writer who self-consciously promoted her Catholicism through almost sixty books and numerous essays in the Boston *Pilot, New York Tablet,* and other journals.

Mary Sadlier was one of the most widely read of the Catholic authors of her age and one of the most productive for her husband's publishing firm. Her writings were typical in their nineteenth-century apologetic use of literature to demonstrate the superiority of Catholic doctrines and practices over those of Protestantism. Her novel *Con O'Regan* (1864), for example, condemned Protestantism as "a mere chaos . . . dark and void, and shapeless like the original nothing from which the world was founded." She also advised immigrants to go west to avoid becoming Yankee and to avoid the poverty and miserable living conditions of urban areas. If Americanization meant one had to become a Protestant Yankee, it was better, she believed, for the immigrant to escape Americanization.

Sadlier not only wrote novels and short stories; she also collected essays for the *Young Ladies Reader* (1875), which was intended to provide young women with models of beauty and taste while it reinforced the traditional role of women in family and society. Most of her written work was meant to provide advice on the virtues of maintaining a good home. Although she attacked Yankee Protestantism, she promoted Yankee values of her own upward middle-class mobility: hard work, thrift, and sobriety. These virtues were essential, she believed, for stability and tranquility in the immigrant Irish homes for which she wrote.

Bibliography

A. *Willy Burke; or, The Irish Orphan in America* (Boston, 1850); *The Blakes and the Flanagans* (New York, 1855); *Con O'Regan; or, Emigrant Life in the New World* (New York, 1864); *Aunt Honor's Keepsakes: A Chapter from Life* (New York, 1866); *Confessions of an Apostate* (New York, 1868).
B. DACB, 505–6; NAW, 3:219–20; Willard Thorp, *Catholic Novelists in Defense of Their Faith, 1829–1865* (New York, 1978).

SERRA, JUNÍPERO (24 November 1717, Petra, Majorca, Spain—28 August 1784, near Monterey, CA). *Education:* entered the novitiate for the Order of Friars Mendicant, 1730; doctorate in theology, Lullian Univ., Palma, Majorca, 1743. *Career:* lecturer in philosophy at St. Francis Friary, Palma, 1738; professor of philosophy, Lullian Univ., 1743–49; teacher, Apostolic Coll. of San Fernando, Mexico, 1750; missionary in Sierra Gorda, 1750–58; administrator and missionary, Apostolic Coll., 1758–67; missionary in Lower CA, 1767–69; missionary in Upper CA, 1769–84.

Baptized as Miguel José and educated in Majorca, Junípero Serra became a successful student and professor in the Franciscan Order. In 1749, however, he left a promising career as a professor of theology (holding the Duns Scotus Chair of Philosophy at Lullian University in Palma) and a popular pulpit preacher to join the Franciscan missionary effort among the Native Americans in Mexico.

From 1750 until 1767 he served as instructor and administrator of the Franciscan Apostolic College of San Fernando and spent eight years among the Pames in the Sierra Gorda. His missionary apprenticeship among the Pames made him familar with Indian customs and languages, which his mind absorbed to such an extent that he was able to translate the catechism into the native tongue. Because of his administrative skills he was appointed superior of the Franciscan missionary effort in Lower California in 1767, when the Jesuits were expelled from that territory.

In 1769 he joined a Spanish expedition into Upper California and founded San Diego mission, the first of nine Indian missions he would establish between San Diego and San Francisco during his life. Under his ecclesiastical jurisdiction, which was periodically challenged by Spanish civil authorities, he sent Franciscan missionaries to the Indians, built the missions as centers of Spanish Catholic evangelization, and organized them into prosperous agricultural and farming institutions. Using religious education and at times Spanish military force and rigorous discipline, he tried to convert the Indians and make them productive members of a sedentary Spanish Catholic culture. According to his own accounts, he was responsible for 6,000 baptisms and 5,300 confirmations in Upper California. In 1934 his cause for beatification was started in Rome but was seriously challenged in the 1980s by activists for Native American cultural independence and by critics of the Spanish cultural devastation of Indian life.

Bibliography

A. *The Writings of Junípero Serra,* ed. Antonine Tibesar, 4 vols. (Washington, DC, 1955–58).

B. DAB, 16:591–92; DACB, 520–21; DARB, 404–5; NCE, 13:124–25; Omer Englebert, *The Last of the Conquistadors: Junípero Serra 1713–1784* (New York, 1956); Maynard Geiger, *The Life and Times of Fray Junípero Serra, O.F.M., Or the Man Who Never Turned Back 1713–1784: A Biography,* 2 vols. (Washington, DC, 1959); Winifred E. Wise, *Fray Junípero Serra and the California Conquest* (New York, 1967); Daniel D. Fogel, *Junípero Serra, the Vatican and Enslavement Theology* (San Francisco, 1988).

SETON, ELIZABETH ANN BAYLEY (28 August 1774, New York, NY— 4 January 1821, Emmitsburg, MD). *Career:* various teaching and boarding school projects in New York and Baltimore, 1804–1809; founder and mother superior, Sisters of Charity of St. Joseph, Emmitsburg, MD, 1809–21.

Elizabeth Ann Bayley was born into a prosperous New York family. Her father, Richard, was a distinguished surgeon and authority on yellow fever. Her mother, Catherine Charlton, who died when Elizabeth was three years old, was the daughter of the Episcopalian rector of St. Andrew's Church on Staten Island. At the age of twenty Elizabeth married William Magee Seton, a promising New York merchant. Throughout her youth and during the early years of her marriage Elizabeth had read and been influenced to some extent by Jean-Jacques Rousseau and Voltaire, but she never completely abandoned her religious life. As a young married woman she cofounded with Isabella Marshall Graham the Society for the Relief of Poor Widows with Small Children (1797) and contributed in other ways to the social and cultural life of New York. Her fortunes began to change, however, by 1800, when her husband's business and health began to fail. In 1803, on a trip to Italy to regain his health, William died of tuberculosis, leaving Elizabeth with five children, the oldest being only eight.

In the midst of this tragedy Elizabeth came under the care and influence of the families of Antonio and Filippo Filicchi, Italian Catholics who had been William's business associates. While in Italy Elizabeth became interested in the Catholic faith and religious practices. In 1805, after her return to New York, she took instructions and was received into the Catholic church. As a Catholic widow with five small children, she tried to make a living by running a boarding school in New York, but the project failed. In 1808, at the encouragement of a number of priests, she moved her family to Baltimore, a more Catholic city at the time, and opened a girls' school there. As her religious life deepened, so did her desire to live a common Christian life and serve the church through education. That desire was realized in 1809, when Elizabeth gathered around her a number of young women to live a common regulated religious life whose primary mission was the education of the young, establishing in Baltimore the Sisters of Charity of St. Joseph.

In June of 1809 Elizabeth moved her new community to Emmitsburg, MD, where they had been offered land and a house close to a newly established Catholic college for young men. During the next twelve years she raised her children, built the new convent, enlisted new members from prominent New York and Philadelphia families, and took on the additional mission of nursing the sick. By 1814 the new community had grown to such an extent that she was able to send some of her sisters to Philadelphia to establish schools and hospitals, and in 1817 she expanded to New York. Although periodically embattled with clerics over the administration of her new religious community and in the midst of personal tragedies (two of her children died in the convent) and weak health, she managed to develop a spirit of common Christian life and service among her sisters. In 1821, at the age of forty-six, she died at Emmitsburg. She was declared venerable in 1959, beatified in 1963, and in 1975 she became the first native-born American to be canonized a saint.

Bibliography

A. *Memoirs, Letters and Journal of Elizabeth Seton,* ed. Robert Seton, 2 vols. (New York, 1869); *Elizabeth Seton: Selected Writings,* ed. Ellin Kelly and Annabelle Melville (New York, 1987).
B. DAB, 16:596–97; DACB, 522; DARB, 406–7; NAW, 3:263–65; NCAB, 2:436; NCE, 13:136; Katherine Kurz Burton, *His Dear Persuasion: The Life of Elizabeth Ann Seton* (New York, 1940); Annabelle M. Melville, *Elizabeth Bayley Seton, 1774–1821* (New York, 1951); Ellin M. Kelly, *Numerous Choirs: A Chronicle of Elizabeth Bayley Seton and Her Spiritual Daughters* (Evansville, IN, 1981); Marie Celeste Cuzzolina, *Elizabeth Ann Seton, a Self-Portrait (1774–1821): A Study of Her Spirituality in Her Own Words* (Libertyville, IL, 1986).

SHEED, FRANCIS "FRANK" JOSEPH (20 March 1897, Sydney, Australia—20 November 1981, Jersey City, NJ). *Education:* B.A., LL.B., Sydney Univ., 1915–22. *Career:* member, Catholic Evidence Guild, London, 1922–33; cofounder, Sheed and Ward, London, 1927, and New York, 1933.

Born and educated in Australia, Sheed went to England in 1922 to practice law. In London he became an active member of the Catholic Evidence Guild and one of its most expert street debaters (in the Hyde Park tradition). In 1926 he married Maisie Ward, one of the guild's charter members. They founded Sheed and Ward, a Catholic publishing firm, in 1927 and expanded to New York in 1933. The firm was intended to be a form of Catholic Action.

Sheed was able to attract many of Catholicism's most outstanding minds to the publishing firm and thereby contributed to what became known in the 1920s, 1930s, and 1940s as the Catholic Literary Revival. In the United States after 1933 Frank Sheed published translations not only of leading contemporary German and French Catholic authors, but also of classical Christian texts. Notable among the latter was his own 1943 translation of Augustine's *Confessions*. In addition to publishing and translating, he became a participant in the American Catholic literary revival and a frequent speaker at various conferences and Catholic colleges and universities across the country. He also wrote a number of books that concisely synthesized major creative works in history, philosophy, and theology. His work and that of his publishing firm helped acquaint some intellectuals in American Catholicism with the theological works that led the way toward the Second Vatican Council, which Sheed supported until his death at the age of eighty-four.

Bibliography

A. *Sidelights on the Catholic Revival* (New York, 1940); *Selective Bibliography: Born Catholics* (New York, 1954); *Theology for Beginners* (New York, 1957); *God and Politics* (New York, 1960); *F. J. Sheed* (New York, 1972); *The Church and I (by) Frank Sheed* (Garden City, New York, 1974).

B. DACB, 526; NCE, 18:473–74; NYT, 21 November 1981, 19; Wilfrid Sheed, *Frank and Maisie: A Memoir with Parents* (New York, 1985).

SHEEN, FULTON J. (8 May 1895, El Paso, IL—9 December 1979, New York, NY). *Education:* B.A., M.A., St. Viator's Coll., Bourbonnais, IL, 1917; studied at St. Paul Sem. (MN), 1917–20; J.C.B., S.T.D., Catholic Univ. of America, 1920; Ph.D., Univ. of Louvain, Belgium, 1923; *agrégé* in philosophy, Louvain, 1925. *Career:* ordained, 1919; theology professor, St. Edmund's Coll., Ware, England, 1925; assistant pastor, St. Patrick's Church, Peoria, 1925–26; professor of philosophy, Catholic Univ. of America, 1926–50; NBC radio preacher, "The Catholic Hour," 1930–50; national director, Society for the Propagation of the Faith, 1950–66; auxiliary bishop of New York, 1951–66; ABC television host, "Life is Worth Living," 1952–57; bishop of Rochester, NY, 1966–69; retirement, 1969–79.

Fulton J. Sheen was perhaps the most visible representative of American Catholicism in the 1950s. His education at Catholic schools in Peoria, St. Paul, and Washington, DC—i.e., at institutions molded to a certain extent by Americanist bishops of the previous generation—gave him a sense of the compatibility of his own Catholic and American identity and a desire to engage in the dialogue between Catholicism and modern forms of thought. His doctoral dissertation, written for the University of Louvain where he went to study Thomist philosophy, was his first major attempt to demonstrate the strengths and weaknesses of contemporary understandings of God when compared to Thomist notions being propagated by Cardinal Desiré Mercier and others at the university.

The dissertation, published as *God and Intelligence in Modern Philosophy* (1925), earned for him the honor of *agrégé* at Louvain and made him a significant part of the rising twentieth-century literary and intellectual revival of Catholicism.

When he returned to the United States his bishop appointed him to a parish in Peoria and after a year sent him to teach at the Catholic University of America. Gifted with eloquence in both oral and written communication, he abandoned the pursuit of serious philosophical inquiry in the 1930s and began to popularize the Thomist intellectual revival and address issues of political and social concern in American life. His eloquence attracted attention in the 1930s when he lectured at various churches and colleges across the country, especially at St. Patrick's Cathedral in New York, where his sermons and talks drew large audiences. In the 1930s, too, he became a regular speaker on NBC's radio program "The Catholic Hour" and became one of the first television evangelists in the 1950s when he hosted ABC's "Life is Worth Living." He also published more than sixty-five books and numerous articles on Catholic views of philosophy, psychology, spirituality, politics, and social justice.

As national director of the Society for the Propagation of the Faith from 1950 to 1966, he helped raise the consciousness of American Catholics to the missionary enterprise and collected millions of dollars to support social and evangelical work in many Third World countries. His work in this office prepared him for participating in the Second Vatican Council, where he spoke out on social justice and missionary work. In 1969, moreover, he was made a member of the Vatican's Commission for Missions. Although he opposed communism and saw it as philosophically antithetical to Catholicism and Western Christian civilization, he warned Catholics that the communist criticism of social and economic injustices in modern society should not be taken lightly, and that Catholics should be in the forefront of movements to eliminate such injustices.

After the Second Vatican Council Sheen, as bishop of Rochester, tried to put his notions of social justice into action by offering the United States government a church building and church land for housing the poor and homeless. This move created a forceful public resistance from the Catholic laity and a few clergy and eventually forced Sheen to withdraw the offer and resign from his see in 1969. He spent the remaining ten years of his life writing, giving lectures, and fostering the spiritual life of diocesan priests.

Bibliography

A. *God and Intelligence in Modern Philosophy* (New York, 1925); *Religion without God* (New York, 1928); *The Mystical Body of Christ* (New York, 1935); *Freedom under God* (Milwaukee, 1940); *Preface to Religion* (New York, 1946); *Communism and the Conscience of the West* (Indianapolis, 1948); *Life is Worth Living,* 5 vols. (New York, 1953–57); *A Fulton Sheen Reader* (St. Paul, 1979); *Treasure in Clay* (Garden City, NY, 1980).

B. DACB, 526–27; DAH, 272; DCA, 1081–82; NCAB, F:466; NCE, 18:474–75; NYT, 10 December 1979, A:1, D:13; Daniel P. Noonan, *Missionary with a Mike: The Bishop Sheen Story* (New York, 1968); idem., *The Passion of Fulton Sheen* (New York, 1972); Kathleen Riley Fields, "Anti-Communism and Social Justice: the

Double-Edged Sword of Fulton Sheen," *RACHS* 96 (1986), 83–91; idem, "Bishop Fulton J. Sheen: An American Catholic Response to the Twentieth Century," (Ph.D. diss., University of Notre Dame, 1988).

SHIELDS, THOMAS EDWARD (9 May 1862, Mendota, MN—5 February 1921, Washington, DC). *Education:* studied at Coll. of St. Francis, Milwaukee, 1882–85; Sem. of St. Thomas Aquinas, 1885; M.A., St. Mary's Sem. (MD), 1892; Ph.D., Johns Hopkins Univ., 1895. *Career:* ordained, 1891; curate, St. Paul Cathedral, 1891; professor, Sem. of St. Paul (MN), 1895–1902; professor, Catholic Univ. of America, 1902–21; founding editor, *Catholic Educational Review,* 1911–21; founder, Sisters Coll., Catholic Univ. of America, 1911.

Thomas Shields—educator, author, journalist, national lecturer, and administrator—was a significant part of the progressive era in American Catholic education. Like John A. Ryan in social thought, Edward Pace in philosophy, and William Kerby in sociology, he was one of the progressive faculty members at the Catholic University who sought to develop creatively a rapprochement between Catholic theology and modern science and philosophy. Educated in theology, biology, and experimental psychology, Shields became at the Catholic University a national leader in developing a Christian view of education that was clearly influenced by the findings of biology, experimental psychology, and the child-centered approaches to education current during the progressive era. In 1907 and 1908 Shields entered into a major national debate with Father Peter Yorke of San Francisco at the Catholic Educational Association national meetings on religious education. Yorke emphasized the content of such teaching, and Shields argued for more emphasis to be placed on the method of teaching and teacher awareness of the learning readiness and psychological capacity of the student. Shields opposed the method of memorization that had been common in teaching the catechisms and wanted to correlate content with the psychological growth of the student. In 1908 such an approach was considered revolutionary.

His primary work on education, *The Philosophy of Education* (1917), incorporated the thoughts of many thinkers of his day. Like other innovators Shields wanted educators to supplant the passivity of the old educational system by activities within the normal experiences of children. Like John Dewey and others he believed that children learned best by doing, by becoming active in the pursuit of knowledge, and that they learned not only through books and lessons but also through music, signs, symbols, and liturgical activity. Education should correspond to the actual stage of the child's psychological development. Shields also believed, like Dewey, that students needed a center of correlation to link together the various subjects presented to them. Unlike Dewey, however, he believed that religion was that integrating and directive center of all education. Like Dewey he believed in developing the child according to the laws of his or her own nature, but unlike Dewey he asserted that nature itself needed the guidance of revelation and religion to provide a directive principle in the child's total development.

To propagate his revolutionary new methods of teaching, he developed a series of religion textbooks, set up his own Catholic Education Press, founded the *Catholic Educational Review,* developed summer schools and correspondence courses for sisters who taught in Catholic schools throughout the country, and established the Sisters College (1911) at the Catholic University to provide sisters with professional training and certified degrees for teaching at the elementary, secondary, and college levels. Shields was one of the prime movers in progressive era attempts to develop professionalism and certification for young teaching sisters. His support for higher education for women in general and sisters in particular was considered innovative in the early twentieth century, when many at the Catholic University of America, as elsewhere in Catholic higher education, resisted the trend.

Bibliography

A. *The Education of Our Girls* (New York, 1907); *The Teaching of Religion* (Washington, DC, 1907); with Edward A. Pace, *Catholic Educational Series of Primary Textbooks,* 6 vols. (Washington, DC, 1908–17); *The Making and the Unmaking of a Dullard* (Washington, DC, 1909); *Teachers Manual of Primary Methods* (Washington, DC, 1912); *The Philosophy of Education* (Washington, DC, 1917).

B. DACB, 531–32; NCE, 13:176; Justine Bayard Cutting Ward, *Thomas Edward Shields, Biologist, Psychologist, Educator* (New York, 1947).

SHUSTER, GEORGE NAUMAN (27 August 1894, Lancaster, WI—25 January 1977, South Bend, IN). *Education:* B.A., Univ. of Notre Dame, 1915; M.A., 1920; studied at Univ. of Poitiers, France, 1919; Hochschule für Politik, Berlin, 1930; Ph.D., Columbia Univ., 1940. *Career:* professor, Univ. of Notre Dame, 1920–24; professor, Polytechnic Institute, Brooklyn, NY, 1924–25; professor, St. Joseph's Coll., 1925–35; associate and managing editor, *Commonweal,* 1925–38; president, Hunter College, 1940–60; chairman, US War Department Historical Commission, 1945; United States land commissioner for Bavaria, 1950–51; a director, Carnegie Endowment for International Peace, 1954–64; director, Center for the Study of Man in Contemporary Society, Univ. of Notre Dame, 1961–71; retired, 1971–77.

Shuster, an educator, journalist, author, and public servant, was one of the most distinguished American Catholic laymen of the twentieth century. In his early career he published a number of works on the Catholic spirit in English and German literature, and as editor of *Commonweal* he tried to interpret Catholicism to the modern world. He argued repeatedly for a Catholic promotion of self-reliance and self-assertion within an understanding of the sacramental relation between spirit and matter. For him the link between Catholicism and American culture was not to be found in political theory, social influence, or historical contributions, but primarily in the spiritual and intellectual tradition that was behind the fundamental American ethos that transcended political culture.

Shuster's world transcended the confines of his and his church's ethnic and parochial concerns. He was part of the emerging class of second- and third-generation immigrants who participated significantly in the public life of the nation, and indeed in international affairs. Throughout his life Shuster was particularly concerned with the higher education of women, becoming at the age of forty-six the president of Hunter College, then the largest public college for women in the world. He had served as a sergeant in army intelligence during World War I, helped to create and served on the executive committee of the United Nations Educational, Scientific and Cultural Organization (1946, 1958–64), and was the United States land commissioner in post–World War II Bavaria.

He returned to Notre Dame in 1960, where he directed interdisciplinary research in the humanities and social sciences, including a major Carnegie Foundation–funded study of Catholic education. That controversial study urged major reorganization of the entire Catholic educational system and recommended a number of reforms—including abandonment of elementary schools in order to strengthen other parts of the educational endeavor, promotion of education as primarily a lay, not a clerical, mission, and the establishment of central agencies to provide for the "orderly management" of Catholic education. Shuster also directed the first population-control study under Catholic auspices, and in the early 1960s he chaired a group of American Catholic scholars who gave qualified endorsement to contraception and urged a change in the church's position on birth control.

Bibliography

A. *The Catholic Spirit in Modern English Literature* (New York, 1922); *The Catholic Spirit in America* (New York, 1927; reprint, 1978); *The English Ode from Milton to Keats* (New York, 1940); *Religion behind the Iron Curtain* (New York, 1942); "George N. Shuster," *American Spiritual Autobiographies: Fifteen Self-Portraits,* ed. Louis Finkelstein (New York, 1948), 25–38; *The Ground I Walked On: Reflections of a College President* (New York, 1961); *Catholic Education in a Changing World* (New York, 1967).
B. DACB, 532–33; NCE, 17:609–10; NCAB, 61:69–71; NYT, 26 January 1977, B:6; *On the Side of Truth: George N. Shuster, an Evaluation with Readings,* ed. Vincent P. Lannie (Notre Dame, IN, 1974).

SLATTERY, JOHN (16 July 1851, New York, NY—1926, Monte Carlo, Monaco). *Education:* studied at City Coll. of New York, 1863–65; St. Charles Coll. (MD), 1865–66; Columbia Coll. School of Law, 1873; St. Joseph's (Society of the Sacred Heart for Foreign Missions) Missionary Coll., Mill Hill, London, 1873–77. *Career:* ordained, 1877; logic teacher, St. Joseph's Coll., 1877; rector, St. Francis Xavier Church, Baltimore, 1877–83; American provincial of St. Joseph's Society, 1878–83; rector, Josephite mission, Richmond,

VA, 1884–88; founder and president, St. Joseph's Sem., Baltimore, 1888–93; superior general, American Josephites, 1893–1904; resigned from Josephites and publicly renounced Catholicism, 1906; admitted, California Bar, 1916.

John R. Slattery was the first superior general of the American branch of the Society of St. Joseph of the Sacred Heart for Foreign Missions (Josephites) after their separation from the English branch organized by Herbert Vaughan at Mill Hill, London. In 1872, after hearing Vaughan preach on the Catholic mission to Africans at St. Paul's Church in New York, Slattery decided to join his English Josephites and dedicate himself to the evangelization and service of African-Americans. After education for the priesthood he returned to Baltimore in 1877, at the end of Reconstruction, to begin a twenty-seven year effort as a Josephite priest to create an American Catholic mission to African-Americans, develop an African-American clergy, and raise the consciousness of white Catholics to the needs of African-Americans. In this endeavor he became identified with the Americanist and later modernist wings of American Catholicism, numbering among his ideological compatriots the Paulists, Baltimore Sulpicians, more liberal faculty of the Catholic University, Archbishops Gibbons and Ireland, Bishop Keane, and Father Denis O'Connell.

As a young priest of twenty-seven he became the provincial of the American branch of the English Josephites but was voted out of office in 1883 because of opposition from his own priests, who considered him insensitive to their needs. After four years of pastoral work among African-American Catholics in Richmond, VA, during which time he published numerous articles on evangelization, he conceived of and helped establish in 1888 St. Joseph's Seminary for the training of African-American as well as white Josephite priests. In 1889 he also established Epiphany Apostolic College as a preparatory school for African-Americans interested in the priesthood. Although he had many prejudices against African-Americans, he was convinced that only an African-American clergy could be an effective instrument of evangelization and pastoral work. The establishment of these schools was an initial step in the separation of the American from the English Josephites, which took place in 1893 when Slattery was made the first American superior of the newly independent American Josephites.

Although Slattery initiated the movement toward an African-American clergy, he eventually became disillusioned with that project and with the anti-modernist and anti-Americanist tendencies in late nineteenth- and early-twentieth-century Catholicism. In 1904 he resigned as superior general of the Josephites, and in 1906 he renounced Catholicism. He married, became a lawyer, and lived in comfort as the result of a large fortune inherited from his father. He died in Monte Carlo, where he had moved to live in retirement.

Bibliography

A. "The Present and Future of the Negro in the United States," *Catholic World* 40 (December 1884): 294; "An Apostolic College," *Catholic World* 49 (July 1889):

526–31; "The Congress of Negro Catholics," *Donahoe's Monthly Magazine* 24 (September 1890): 271; "The Josephites and Their Work for the Negroes," *Catholic World* 51 (April 1890): 102–3; "How My Priesthood Dropped from Me," *Independent* 61 (6 September 1906): 565–71.

B. NYT, 15 June 1927, 48; William L. Portier, "John R. Slattery's Vision for the Evangelization of American Blacks," *U.S.CH* 5, (1986): 19–44; idem, "Modernism in the United States: The Case of John R. Slattery," in *Varieties of Modernism*, ed. Ronald Burke, Gary Lease, and George Gilmore (Mobile, AL, 1986), 77–97; Jamie T. Phelps, "John R. Slattery's Missionary Strategies," *U.S.CH* 7 (Spring/Summer 1988): 201–14; Stephen J. Ochs, *Desegregating the Altar: The Josephites and the Struggle for Black Priests, 1871–1960* (Baton Rouge, LA, 1990).

SPALDING, JOHN LANCASTER (2 June 1840, Lebanon, KY—25 August 1916, Peoria, IL). *Education:* studied at St. Mary's Coll. (KY), 1855–57; Mount St. Mary's Coll. (MD), 1857–58; B.A., Mount St. Mary's of the West (OH), 1859; S.T.B., American Coll., Louvain, Belgium, 1862; lic. theology, Louvain, 1864; studied in Rome, 1864–65. *Career:* secretary to the bishop of Louisville, KY, 1865–71; chancellor, Diocese of Louisville, 1871–73; curate at St. Michael's Church, New York, 1873–76; bishop, Diocese of Peoria, 1877–1908; retirement, 1908–16.

After studying for the priesthood in the United States and Belgium, where he was exposed to ontologism, John Lancaster Spalding served in various pastoral and administrative capacities in his native diocese of Louisville. During the early post–Civil War years he supported the ontologism of the Louvain school while the orthodoxy of that position was being debated in American Catholic circles and being condemned in Rome. Although he eventually abandoned his public support for ontologism, he never completely abandoned the idea that human knowledge of God was basically intuitive and that individuals were made more explicitly open to the divine through poetry, liturgy, and art than through rational investigation or speculation. This perspective, which he articulated in numerous well-written essays and books on education and other social topics, was a departure from the more common scholastic perspective of the American Catholic clergy and bishops.

Ten years after he returned from Europe he was made the first bishop of Peoria, an office he served for thirty-two years. Although the new diocese did not have the influence of the more established and much larger dioceses, Spalding had a significant impact on the larger American church through his literary efforts to bring American Catholicism in tune with modern developments in thought and literature. He was also responsible for conceiving of and promoting the idea of a Catholic University in the United States to prepare clergy to dialogue with modern patterns of thought and utilize the empirical sciences to respond to social and cultural problems. He championed, too, the causes of prohibition, women's higher education, the franchise for women, and a just wage for workers. Although aligned with many of the Americanists in his general orientation to society, he opposed Archbishop John Ireland's Faribault-Stillwater education plan and his endorsement of a Roman apostolic delegate, Americanist hostility to German preservationists, and the second-generation Irish-American tendency to identify uncritically with American values. Because of personal entanglements with the Caldwell sisters, benefactors of the Catholic University, and his public criticism of the sending of a Roman apostolic delegate, he came under a cloud of ecclesiastical suspicion in Rome and was never promoted to a large episcopal see.

During his episcopacy in Peoria he supervised the building of 140 churches, 58 schools, a new cathedral, and many charitable institutions. In 1902 and 1903 he was a member of President Roosevelt's Anthracite Coal Strike Commission and helped end the strike. He suffered a paralyzing stroke in 1905, resigned his bishopric in 1908, was consequently appointed a titular archbishop, and retired from 1908 to 1916.

Bibliography

A. *Essays and Reviews* (New York, 1877); *Religious Mission of the Irish People and Catholic Colonization* (New York, 1880); *Education and the Higher Life* (Chicago, 1890); *Things of the Mind* (Chicago, 1894); *Means and Ends of Education* (Chicago, 1895); *Thoughts and Theories of Life and Education* (Chicago, 1897); *Opportunity, and Other Essays* (Chicago, 1900); *Religion and Art and Other Essays* (Chicago, 1901); *Religion, Agnosticism and Education* (Chicago, 1902); *Socialism and Labor and Other Arguments* (Chicago, 1902).
B. DAB, 17:422–23; DACB, 542–43; DAH, 275; DARB, 416–17; DCA, 1117; NCAB, 10:44; NCE, 13:515–16; NYT, 26 August 1916, 7; *Chicago Daily Tribune* 26, 27 August 1916, 1, 13; John T. Ellis, *John Lancaster Spalding: First Bishop of Peoria; American Educator* (Milwaukee, 1961); David F. Sweeney, *The Life of John Lancaster Spalding* (New York, 1965).

SPALDING, MARTIN JOHN (23 May 1810, Rolling Fork, KY—7 February 1872, Baltimore, MD). *Education:* B.A., St. Mary's Coll. (KY), 1826; B.D., St. Thomas Sem. (KY), 1830; Urban College of Propaganda, Rome, 1834. *Career:* rector, St. Joseph's Church, Bardstown, KY, 1834–38, 1841–44; president, St. Joseph's Coll. (KY), 1838–40; rector, Lexington, KY, 1840–41; vicar general, Diocese of Louisville, KY, 1844–48; auxiliary bishop and bishop, Louisville, 1848–64; archbishop of Baltimore, 1864–72.

Martin J. Spalding was a native Kentuckian and a member of a family that had a long history on American soil. After a seminary education in Kentucky and Rome he became a forceful clerical and episcopal apologist for Catholicism in his native diocese of Bardstown (transferred to Louisville in 1841) for thirty years, a period when nativism was becoming a potent force in American life and a threat to American Catholic identity and institutions. As editor of the newly established *Catholic Advocate* (1836–49), popular lecturer, debater, and preacher, and prolific writer of apologetic and historical tracts and books, he gained a national reputation as an articulate defender of the faith. Like many of the apologists of his day, he emphasized the historical continuity and unity of the church, the centrality of the papal office, and the authority of the church in the propagation and preservation of Western culture and advancement of civil and religious liberty. His romantic and idealized version of ecclesiastical history served his purpose of providing the Catholic community with a sense of continuity and unity in a period torn apart by the winds of revolution, rebellion, reform, and hostility toward the institutional Catholic church.

As the seventh archbishop of Baltimore, Spalding became the most visible and influential episcopal representative of Catholicism in the United States between 1864 and 1872. During that period he continued, as he had in Louisville, to emphasize Catholic education on the parochial level, but he also became a prime supporter of the establishment of the North American College in Rome and the American College in Louvain, Belgium, and of the notion that a major Catholic university ought to be erected in the United States. During the Civil War his sympathies were with the South, but he was adamant that the church should take no stand on either side of the conflict. After the war he convoked the Second Plenary Council of Baltimore (1866) to demonstrate a united Catholicism and elicit from the nation's bishops plans for evangelizing African-Americans in the postwar South, but no plans were forthcoming. Like most other American bishops, he supported the conciliar approach to national ecclesiastical legislation, having previously participated in the First Plenary Council of Baltimore (1852) and three previous provincial synods (Cincinnati, 1855, 1858, 1861). At the Vatican Council (1869–70) he became a moderate proponent of papal infallibility, seeing the definition of this doctrine as a timely antedote to various forms of Gallicanism. After the council he tried to demonstrate how the religious doctrine was not a threat to American civil and political values. Although Spalding was a native American and cherished American values, he lived at a time when he felt called upon to reinforce the internal support systems within the Catholic tradition, build up the ecclesiastical institutions, and develop a religious perspective that delineated and emphasized the differences between Catholicism and Protestantism.

Bibliography

A. *D'Aubigne's "History of the Great Reformation in Germany and Switzerland"* Reviewed (Baltimore, 1844); *Lectures in the General Evidences of Catholicity* (Louisville, 1847, and subsequent editions); *Sketches of the Life, Times, and Character of the Right Reverend Benedict Joseph Flaget* (Louisville, 1852; reprint, New York, 1969); *Miscellanea* (Louisville, 1855, and subsequent editions); *The History of the Protestant Reformation*, 2 vols. (Louisville, 1860).

B. DAB, 17:424–26; DACB, 543–44; DAH, 275–76; DARB, 417–19; DCA, 1117–18; NCAB, 1:486; NCE, 13:517–19; NYT, 8 February 1872, 5; SH, 11:33; John L. Spalding, *The Life of the Most Reverend Martin John Spalding, D.D., Archbishop of Baltimore* (New York, 1873); Adam A. Micek, *The Apologetics of Martin John Spalding* (Washington, DC, 1951); Thomas W. Spalding, *Martin John Spalding: American Churchman* (Washington, DC, 1973); David Schimpf, "Martin Spalding's 'Apocalyptical' Use of History in the Social Setting of the Mid-Nineteenth-Century American Catholic Community," *RACHS* 96 (March-December 1986): 19–34.

SPELLMAN, FRANCIS JOSEPH (4 May 1889, Whitman, MA—2 December 1967, New York, NY). *Education:* B.A., Fordham Univ., 1911; S.T.D., North American Coll., Rome, 1916. *Career:* curate, Roxbury, MA, 1916–18; staff, Cathedral of the Holy Cross, Boston, 1918–22; vice-chancellor, Diocese of Boston, 1922–25; attaché, Secretariate of State, Rome, 1925–32; auxiliary bishop, Boston, 1932–39; archbishop of New York, 1939–67; military vicar for the army and navy, 1940–67; cardinal, 1946–67.

Cardinal Francis Spellman was perhaps the most influential episcopal representative of Catholicism in the United States between 1939 and the end of the Second Vatican Council. Like many other pre–Vatican II, postmodernist, big-city bishops, he was thoroughly American yet utterly Roman in his allegiances. A second generation Irish-American, he was educated in the United States and Rome during the days of Pope Pius X's anti-modernism. He rose to ecclesiastical leadership in the dioceses of Boston and New York because of the influence of Cardinal Eugenio Pacelli, the Vatican secretary of state (1929–39), for whom he worked in Rome between 1925 and 1932. When Cardinal Pacelli was elected Pope Pius XII in 1939, Spellman was made archbishop of New York, where he rose rapidly to national ecclesiastical prominence through his office as military vicar for the United States Army and Navy.

Prior to and during World War II Spellman cultivated the friendship of prominent and influential Americans like Joseph P. Kennedy and President Roosevelt and was an important diplomatic link between the Vatican and the Roosevelt government, helping to pave the way for Roosevelt's 1939 appointment of Myron Taylor as the president's personal representative to Pius XII. Spellman repeatedly reinforced the links between Catholicism and American governmental policies during World War II and throughout the cold war years through his yearly trips as military ordinary to the armed forces overseas. No other postwar American prelate, with the exception of Bishop Fulton J. Sheen, traveled as extensively throughout the world, making Catholic and American influence a part of the new postwar world order.

In the United States Spellman became a voice for cold war Catholic anticommunism, aligning himself with Senator Joseph McCarthy. Like other American prelates, he was also a forceful voice against what he considered the growing licentiousness and pornography of popular literature and motion pictures. His battles with prominent Americans like Eleanor Roosevelt over the issue of governmental aid to parochial schools furthermore made him a national symbol of cold war Catholic aggressiveness in the minds of many Americans.

Because of his influence at the Vatican, he had an impact on the appointment of numerous bishops in the United States, particularly on the East Coast. Within his own diocese he was a capable builder of numerous educational institutions and an efficient administrator who encouraged and collected an enormous amount of funds for charitable institutes.

Although he was himself a theological and social conservative and not well acquainted with postwar theological developments taking place in Europe and other places, he gave his episcopal protection to Catholic biblical scholars in the 1950s and to John Courtney Murray's themes of religious liberty during the Second Vatican Council. He opposed a number of new measures, especially in the liturgy, at the council, but he used his influence there to organize the American bishops in favor of a declaration on religious liberty. In fact, he made more oral and written interventions (131) than any other American bishop, was one of the presidents of the council, and was considered the titular leader of the American hierarchy there.

After the council Spellman continued his advocacy of American governmental policies and militant objectives, supporting the war in Vietnam in his Christmas message to the troops there in 1966, at a time when the Berrigan brothers and a few other Catholics were protesting against the war. To the end of his life he gave his wholehearted allegiance to the American government and saw this support as consistent with his Roman anticommunist stance, but that kind of support was increasingly called into question in the late 1960s.

Bibiliography

A. *The Word of God* (Boston, 1920); *In the Footsteps of the Master* (Boston, 1924); *The Road to Victory* (New York, 1942); *Action This Day* (New York, 1943); *No Greater Love: The Story of Our Soldiers* (New York, 1945).
B. DACB, 545–46; DAH, 276; DARB, 421–23; DCA, 1120; NCAB, F:220–21; NYT, 3 December 1967, 1; Robert I. Gannon, *The Cardinal Spellman Story* (New York, 1962); John Cooney, *The American Pope: The Life and Times of Francis Cardinal Spellman* (New York, 1984); Gerald P. Fogarty, "Francis J. Spellman: American and Roman," in *Patterns of Episcopal Leadership,* ed. Gerald P. Fogarty (New York, 1989), 216–34.

STARR, ELLEN GATES (19 March 1859, near Laona, IL—10 February 1940, Suffern, NY). *Education:* studied at Rockford Female Sem. (IL), 1877–78. *Career:* schoolteacher, Mount Morris, IL, 1878–79; instructor, private girls' school, Chicago, 1879–88; social worker, Chicago, 1889–1929; retirement in convent, Suffern, NY, 1930–40.

Ellen Gates Starr was a nominal Unitarian as a child, became an Episcopalian in 1884, and in 1920, after the 1919 publication of the American Catholic "Bishops' Program of Social Reconstruction," converted to Catholicism. Starr was a progressive-era social activist prominent in the social settlement movement, member of the Socialist Labor Party, promoter of organized labor, and a founder and first president (1894) of the Chicago Public School Art Society. In 1897 she and her Rockford classmate Jane Addams founded Hull House in Chicago to provide aid to the poor and dispossessed immigrants on the city's west side. For more than thirty years she was the primary coordinator of Hull

House's cultural activities. Influenced by the writings of John Ruskin and Thomas Carlyle, she sought to use art as a means of raising the human spirit. She was especially concerned about the needs of immigrants, taught them English and the principles of democracy, and joined organized labor's effort to improve workers' living and working conditions, being arrested numerous times for leading strikes.

Influenced by the religious life of the immigrants she served and by increasing social concern among some American Catholics, she joined the Catholic church in 1920. Her conversion deepened her devotion to the poor, and although Hull House was criticized in some Chicago Catholic circles as a bastion of liberalism and secularism, she continued to work there until a spinal operation in 1929 incapacitated her for the remainder of her life. She spent her last years confined to a bed in the Convent of the Holy Child in Suffern, NY.

Bibliography

A. "A Bypath into the Great Roadway," *Catholic World* 119 (May 1924): 177–90; (June 1924): 358–73.
B. DARB, 425–26; NAW, 3:351–53; NYT 11 February 1940, 49.

SULLIVAN, MOTHER KATHRYN (17 May 1905, New York, NY—). *Education:* B.A., Manhattanville Coll., 1926; M.A., Univ. of Pennsylvania, 1927; Ph.D., 1935. *Career:* entered Religious of the Sacred Heart, 1928; professor, Manhattanville Coll., 1938–70; member, Catholic Biblical Association, 1947–; a founding editor, the *Bible Today,* 1962–72; professor, San Anselmo, Anglicum, and North American Coll., Rome, 1967–; professor, St. Joseph's Sem. (NY), 1970–78; national and international lecture tours, 1971–.

Mother Kathryn Sullivan, R.S.C.J., was the first American Catholic woman to become a recognized biblical scholar and the first to become an active member of the Catholic Biblical Association, which was until 1947 an exclusively clerical enterprise. As a professor of biblical studies at her religious order's Manhattanville College and as a publishing scholar, she became a significant part of the biblical revival during the 1940s, 1950s, and 1960s. With Msgr. John E. Steinmueller of Brooklyn she prepared the first extensive series of Catholic biblical textbooks for use in seminaries and colleges. She was also instrumental in 1962 in establishing the *Bible Today,* a popular periodical intended to develop a biblical-based spirituality for clergy, religious, and laity, and to inform them on the latest research in biblical studies. After the Second Vatican Council she edited a series of biblical commentaries for the Liturgical Press, taught in various Roman schools, and lectured on biblical topics and spirituality in renewal programs for women religious throughout the nation and around the world.

Bibliography

A. *A Companion to the New Testament* (New York, 1944, 1954); *A Companion to the Old Testament* (New York, 1946); with John Steinmueller, *Catholic Biblical En-*

cyclopedia, 2 vol. (New York, 1950, 1956); *God's Word and Work: The Message of the Old Testament Historical Books* (Collegeville, MN, 1958); *The Captivity Epistles* (Collegeville, MN, 1960); *The Book of Daniel. The Book of Jonah. Introduction and Commentary* (Collegeville, MN, 1975).
B. *The American Catholic Who's Who 1952–53,* 467; *The American Catholic Who's Who 1976–1977,* 519.

SULLIVAN, WILLIAM L. (15 November 1872, East Braintree, MA—5 October 1935, Germantown, PA). *Education:* B.A., St. John's Sem., Brighton, MA, 1896; S.T.B., Catholic Univ. of America, 1899; S.T.L., 1900. *Career:* joined Paulists, 1897; ordained, 1899; Paulist missionary work, 1899–1901; professor, Paulist Coll., Washington, DC, 1901–1908; pastor, Austin, TX, 1908–1909; joined Unitarian Church, 1911; Unitarian minister, New York, Schenectady, NY, St. Louis, and Germantown, PA, 1912–35.

As a Paulist William Sullivan was one of a small number of American Catholics who were trying in the early twentieth century, prior to the encyclical *Pascendi* (1908) condemning modernism, to develop a rapprochement between American political and social institutions and Catholicism and between the new historical and critical sciences and Catholic theology. He was linked with the Americanists as well as with the incipient modernists. To a certain extent his intellectual journey was almost the exact opposite of that of Orestes Brownson. He started within the American Catholic church, trying to reconcile Catholicism and liberty, and when he believed that that effort was doomed to utter failure because of the papal anti-modernist mentality and condemnations, he left Catholicism for Unitarianism, where he found the unrestricted freedom he unsuccessfully yearned for as a Catholic. As a Catholic he pleaded for an intellectual renaissance and wanted to develop an apologetic for Catholicism that would take into account modern philosophical and scientific work. After *Pascendi* he published a series of polemical *Letters to His Holiness Pope Pius X* (1910), which attacked Catholic scandals, historical practices, and the ideology that had supported them. The publication was an apology for his separation from Catholicism. As a Unitarian Sullivan continued to preach missions in various Unitarian parishes and continued to do research and write historical and theological essays as well as spiritual meditations and prayers.

Bibliography

A. "Catholicity and Some Elements in our National Life," *New York Review* 1 (1905): 259–67; *Letters to His Holiness, Pope Pius X* (Chicago, 1910); *The Priest: A Tale of Modernism in New England* (Boston, 1914); *From the Gospel to the Creeds: Studies in the Early History of the Christian Church* (Boston, 1919); *Under Orders: The Autobiography of William L. Sullivan* (Boston, 1944); *The Flaming Spirit: Meditations and Prayers of William L. Sullivan* (New York, 1961).
B. NYT, 7 October 1935, 15; John Ratte, *Three Modernists: Alfred Loisy, George Tyrrell, and William L. Sullivan* (London, 1966), 257–337; Warren E. Duclos, "Crisis of an American Catholic Modernist: Toward the Moral Absolutism of Wil-

liam L. Sullivan,'' *CH* 41 (1972): 369–84; Michael B. McGarry, ''Modernism in the United States: William Laurence Sullivan, 1872–1935,'' *RACHS* 90 (March-December 1979): 33–52; R. Scott Appleby, *''Church and Age Unite!'' The Modernist Impulse in American Catholicism* (Notre Dame, IN, 1992), 169–206.

T

TALBOT, FRANCIS XAVIER (25 January 1889, Philadelphia, PA—3 December 1953, Washington, DC). *Education:* studied at St. Joseph's Coll. (PA), 1904–1906; St. Andrew-on-the-Hudson (NY), 1906–10; M.A., Woodstock Coll. (MD), 1913; studied at Woodstock Coll., 1918–23. *Career:* entered Jesuits, 1906; teacher, Loyola School, New York, 1913–16; professor, Boston Coll., 1917–18; ordained, 1921; literary editor and editor in chief, *America,* 1923–44; editor, *Thought,* 1936–44; president, Loyola Coll., Baltimore, 1947–50; pastor, St. Aloysius and Holy Trinity, Washington, DC, 1950–53.

Francis Talbot entered the Jesuits just before the papal anti-modernist crusade and, like other Jesuits of the period, was influenced by that ideology throughout his life. His anti-modernist mentality became a major motivating force in his crusades to transform the world according to Catholic principles of faith and justice. He saw the press and school as the primary agents for this transformation in American society. In addition to editing *America,* he helped organize the Catholic Book Club (1928), Catholic Poetry Society (1930), and Spiritual Book Associates (1932). He wrote a number of articles on Catholicism and the Jesuits for the *Encyclopedia Britannica* and published a number of books, among them the lives of Isaac Jogues and Jean Brébeuf, to promote Catholic spirituality. Throughout his life he tried to raise the cultural and intellectual life of American Catholicism, participating actively in the Catholic literary revival of the 1930s and 1940s. Through *America* and through Catholic colleges he promoted Catholic literary achievement and tried to draw attention to contemporary Catholic authors. This self-promotion of Catholic literary achievement was in part a response to the charge that Catholicism in the United States had produced no scholars and made no cultural contribution in society.

Bibliography

A. *Jesuit Education in Philadelphia* (Philadelphia, 1927); *Shining in Darkness* (New York, 1932); *Saint among Savages: The Life of Isaac Jogues* (New York, 1935);

"Catholicism in America," in Harold E. Stearns, ed., *America Now: An Inquiry into Civilization in the United States* (New York, 1938), 528–42; *Saint among the Hurons: The Life of Jean de Brébeuf* (New York, 1949).
B. CA1947: 726–28; DAB, supp. 5: 677–78; DACB, 555–56; NCE, 13:918; NYT, 10 December 1953, 47; "Francis X. Talbot and the Catholic Literary Emergence," in Arnold Sparr, *To Promote, to Defend, to Redeem* (New York, 1990), 15–30.

TANEY, ROGER BROOKE (17 March 1777, Calvert County, MD—12 October 1864, Washington, DC). *Education:* studied at Dickinson Coll., 1792–95; read law in the office of Judge Jeremiah Townley Chase in MD, 1796–99. *Career:* entered law practice, 1799; state legislator, MD, 1799–1800; state senator, 1816; attorney general of MD, 1827–31; attorney general of the United States, 1831–32; interim secretary of the treasury, 1833–36; chief justice of the Supreme Court, 1836–64.

Educated in the postrevolutionary period, Roger B. Taney was one of a small number of prominent Maryland Catholic laymen who were significantly involved in American political life. He was a practicing lawyer after 1799, and in 1811 he came to public attention when he successfully defended General James Wilkinson, commander in chief of the army, who was charged with being an accomplice in Aaron Burr's "western conspiracy." He also participated in federalist politics at both the state and national levels and held a number of positions in both legislatures. As President Jackson's attorney general he was involved in the charter renewal fight of the Bank of the United States. He served under the same president as secretary of state and secretary of the treasury. He was nominated for the Supreme Court and was twice rejected by the Senate largely for political reasons, but in 1836 his nomination was confirmed, and he served as the first Catholic chief justice for the next twenty-eight years. As chief justice he sustained states' rights and in this vein wrote the majority opinion in the Dred Scott decision (1857), which held that no African-American slave or descendant of a slave could be a citizen of the United States, that Congress had no right to prohibit slavery in the territories, and that the Missouri Compromise (1820) had been null and void from the day of its enactment.

Bibliography
B. DAB, 18:289–94; DACB, 556–57; NCAB, 1:27–28; NCE, 13:931–32; NYT, 14 October 1864, 4; *Daily Intelligencer* (Washington, DC) 13, 14 Oct 1864, 7, 4; Bernard C. Steiner, *Life of Roger Brooke Taney: Chief Justice of the United States Supreme Court* (Baltimore, 1922); Lewis Walker, *Without Fear or Favor: A Biography of Chief Justice Roger Brooke Taney* (Boston, 1965); John T. Noonan, "The Catholic Justices of the United States Supreme Court," *CHR* 67 (July 1981): 369–85.

TEKAKWITHA, CATHERINE (1656?, Gandahouhague, Mohawk territory—17 April 1680, La Prairie de la Madeleine, Canada).

Catherine Tekakwitha's short, twenty-four-year biography reads like the lives of some early converts to primitive Christianity, with the exception that her conversion story and her four-year life as a Christian are conditioned by seventeenth-century French Catholic piety. Catherine was born in a Mohawk village in present-day upstate New York. A smallpox epidemic disfigured her when she was four and took the lives of her parents. Although she met French Jesuits as a child, she was not instructed in Christianity until she reached her late teens and was baptized on Easter, 1676, at the age of about twenty.

Her conversion to Catholicism and her own particular austere appropriation of it alienated her from her former traditions, and her own family and tribe ostracized her. In 1677, therefore, shortly after her baptism, she abandoned her tribe and went to live in an Indian village in Sault St. Louis in Upper Canada, where she received her first communion and continued a regular routine of prayer, fasting, and self-flagellation. She also kept a private vow of chastity and refused to marry. Her austere Christian life was admired by the Jesuits as well as the new converts in Canada, and the Jesuits in particular spread the stories of her remarkable holiness and steadfastness in the faith. Although she was about to begin a small convent in 1679, she did not live long enough to direct it. Almost immediately upon her death in 1680 her tomb became a pilgrimage site. In 1932 she was nominated for beatification, and in 1980 she was declared "Blessed," the first stage in the process toward canonization.

Bibliography

B. DACB, 558–59; DARB, 456–57; NAW, 3:436–37; NCE, 13:978–79; Ellen Walworth, *The Life and Times of Kateri Tekakwitha* (Buffalo, NY, 1891); Edouard Lecompte, *An Iroquois Virgin: Catherine Tekakwitha* (New York, 1932); Daniel Sargeant, *Catherine Tekakwitha* (New York, 1936); Marie C. Buhrle, *Kateri of the Mohawks* (Milwaukee, 1954); Ron Zellinger, *Kateri Tekakwitha* (Chamberlain, SD, 1985).

TOLTON, AUGUSTUS (1854, Ralls County, MO—9 July 1897, Chicago, IL). *Education:* private tutoring, St. Boniface Church, Quincy, IL, 1873–78; special student, Quincy Coll., 1878–80; studied at Urban Coll. of Propaganda, Rome, 1880–86. *Career:* ordained, 1886; parish priest, St. Joseph's, Quincy, 1886–89; pastor, St. Augustine's, Chicago, 1889–94; retirement, 1894–97.

Born to Missouri Catholic slaves, Augustus Tolton escaped from slavery with his mother when he was a small child during the Civil War. Moving to Quincy, IL, a city full of refugee slaves, he was soon enrolled in Catholic schools and during his youth developed a vocation to the priesthood. In 1880 he went to Rome to study for the priesthood because he could find no American seminary to educate him. Ordained in 1886, he became the first fully African-American Catholic priest in the United States.

After ordination he became the pastor of St. Joseph's, Quincy, IL (1886), a small African-American congregation, but he also attracted many whites to his services, which angered some of the white priests in the diocese. Many priests were openly racist in their comments to him, and one priest actively campaigned against him. The lack of other African-American priests heightened the effect of his alienation from the clerical leadership. He became discouraged at the lack of support from priests and his own bishop and therefore requested a transfer to Chicago in 1889, where he served as pastor of St. Augustine's, an African-American congregation which met in the basement of St. Mary's Church. Between 1891 and 1893 he supervised the construction of St. Monica's Church and remained there until he retired in 1894 for health reasons.

Tolton was active in the first Afro-American Congresses from 1889 to 1894 and became a national symbol of rising African-American Catholic leadership. His first masses drew large congregations shortly after he was ordained, and his lectures throughout the country drew some attention. But he was periodically criticized for his lack of aggressiveness in articulating African-American Catholic grievances within the church. His responsibility for representing his race in a predominantly immigrant church was a heavy burden, and his priesthood was judged not simply by the standards of common human strength and frailty, but by criteria that demanded more of him because of his race. Never in good health, he died of a stroke at the age of forty-three.

Bibliography

A. *Three African-American Congresses* (Cincinnati, 1893; reprint, New York, 1978), 18.

B. "Rev. Augustus Tolton," *St. Joseph's Advocate* 4 (1886): 185–87; 5 (1887): 202–4, 245–46, 322–23, 326, 360; Caroline Hemesath, *From Slave to Priest: A Biography of the Rev. Augustine Tolton (1854–1897), First Afro-American Priest of the United States* (Chicago, 1973); Cyprian Davis, *The History of Black Catholics in the United States* (New York, 1990); Stephen Ochs, *Desegregating the Altar* (Baton Rouge, LA, 1990).

TURNER, THOMAS WYATT (16 March 1877, Hughesville, Charles County, MD—21 April 1978, Washington, DC). *Education:* A.B., Howard Univ., 1901; studied at Univ. of Rochester, 1903; M.A., biology, Cold Springs Biological Laboratory, Howard Univ., 1905; studied at John Hopkins Univ., 1905–1906; Columbia Univ., 1913; Ph.D., Cornell Univ., 1921. *Career:* teacher, Tuskegee Institute, 1901–1902; Baltimore High and Training School, 1902–10, 1911–13; and St. Louis High School, 1910–11; founding member, NAACP, 1909; professor of biology, Howard Univ., 1913–24; acting dean, School of Education, Howard Univ., 1914–1920; teacher, Hampton Institute, 1914; agent, National Security League of New York, 1916–17; organizer, Committee Against the Extension of Race Prejudice in the Church, 1917 (name changed to Committee for the Advancement of Colored Catholics in 1919 and to Federated Colored Catholics of the United States from 1925–58); cytologist, US Dept. of Agriculture, and potato field investigator, Presque Isle, ME, 1918–19; department head, Biological Sciences, Hampton Institute, 1924–45; retired from Hampton Institute, 1945; consultant, Florida Normal Coll., St. Augustine, 1947–48; consultant to president, organizer of biology department, professor of biology, Texas Southern Univ., 1949–50.

Thomas Wyatt Turner was born to African-American Catholic sharecroppers in a heavily Catholic-populated county of southern Maryland. When Thomas was eight years old his father died and his mother was left to raise a family of nine children. Although he lacked financial resources, he was given a good elementary education by Episcopalians and eventually received a doctorate in biology from Cornell University. None of his education came from Catholic institutions, most of which were segregated.

As a result of increasing discrimination against African-Americans in the early twentieth century, Turner became an active participant in the NAACP in Baltimore and Washington. Because Catholic institutions like the Knights of Columbus, Catholic University of America, and Josephite seminary of Baltimore refused to accept African-American Catholics, Turner and others from St. Augustine's parish in Washington, DC, organized a movement in 1919, eventually called the Federation of Colored Catholics, to protest against racism in the church, develop African-American Catholic solidarity, and increase their educational, social, and health-care opportunities within Catholic institutions. In 1919, as chairman of the federation, Turner wrote that African-American Catholics were "without voice anywhere in the Church." He and his movement intended to change that situation. The federation became active after World War I as race hatred and murders of African-Americans became almost epidemic.

From 1927 to 1932 Turner convoked national meetings of the federation and after each one wrote to the national hierarchy demanding more active episcopal promotion of racial justice and opportunity within Catholic institutions. In 1933, however, the movement split because of differing perceptions of the goals it should pursue. Turner and his faction emphasized racial solidarity, but the white Jesuits William Markoe and John LaFarge, participants in the federation, wanted the group to emphasize interracial Catholic activities. The Turner group remained under the title of Federated Colored Catholics until 1958, but after 1933 the group lacked the focus and strength it had had in the earlier period. Turner continued to speak out on racial justice, but he would not be a central voice in the movement. When he was ninety-nine years old in 1976, he received an honorary degree from the Catholic University of America, a school he could not enter in the early 1900s, for his work in raising Catholic consciousness on racial justice.

Bibliography

A. "After the Parish School, What?—For the Colored Catholic Child," *Missionary* (November 1915), 651–53; "Actual Condition of Catholic Education among the

Colored Laymen,'' *Catholic Educational Association Bulletin* 16 (November 1919): 431–40; ''Experiences of a Colored Catholic,'' *Fortnightly Review* (1 April 1926), 143–45; ''The Spirit of the Federated Colored Catholics,'' *Chronicle* (May 1932), 92.

B. DACB, 568–69; NCAB, 61:10–11; NCE, 17:670–71; NYT, 25 April 1978, 40; ''Journey of a Black Catholic,'' *America* 135 (July 1976): 6–8; Marilyn W. Nickels et al., ''NOBC Pioneer Dies in 102nd Year,'' *Impact!* 8 (April–May 1978): 2–3; Marilyn W. Nickels, *Black Catholic Protest and the Federated Colored Catholics, 1917–1933: Three Perspectives on Racial Justice* (New York, 1988); idem, ''Thomas Wyatt Turner and the Federated Colored Catholics,'' *U.S.CH* 7 (Spring/ Summer 1988): 215–32.

V

VARELA, FÉLIX (20 November 1788, Havana, Cuba—25 February 1853, St. Augustine, FL). *Education:* B.A., San Carlos Coll. (Havana), 1806; S.T.B., 1808. *Career:* ordained, 1811; professor of philosophy, San Carlos Coll., 1812–21; elected Cuban delegate, Spanish Cortes, Madrid, 1821–23; assistant pastor, St. Peter's Church, New York, 1825–27; pastor, Christ Church, 1827–36, and Transfiguration Church, New York, 1836–50; retired, 1850–53, St. Augustine, FL.

As a priest, philosopher, political activist, and apologist, Varela tried to create a rapprochement between Catholicism and the age of Enlightenment. As a young philosopher in Cuba he wrote a number of works that eclectically incorporated much of the thought of Descartes, Bacon, and Locke into his own system which departed significantly from the decadent scholasticism of the day. In 1821 he was elected a delegate to the Spanish Cortes, where, until the French Army entered Spain in 1823, he supported Cuban political autonomy, Spanish recognition of the South American republics, and the abolition of slavery. After the demise of the Cortes, Varela escaped to Gibraltar, and from there he emigrated to New York because he believed he and his views would no longer be safe in Cuba.

In the United States he continued to write in favor of a peaceable Cuban political independence from Spain, but he was never able to return to Cuba. After a brief year in Philadelphia where he edited a Spanish republican magazine for Cuban independence, he returned to New York where he became a pastor to the polyglot immigrants, founding editor and contributor to a number of Catholic newspapers and magazines (e.g., *New York Weekly Register and Catholic Diary,* the *Catholic Expositor, Young Catholic Magazine, Children's Catholic Magazine*), and apologist for an enlightened Catholicism, believing that "Christianity and freedom are inseparable." With other New York City

Catholic pastors he responded to the attacks of William Craig Brownlee, a New York Protestant pastor, and the New York Protestant Association in the 1830s, and helped to organize Catholics to obtain public aid for Catholic schools from the New York Public School Society in the early 1840s. He also wrote a number of philosophical and apologetic books and tracts that revealed his love for political and cultural freedom, democratic forms of government, separation of church and state, and religious liberty. In one of his more famous works, *Cartas a Elpidio* (*Letters to Elpidio,* 1835–36), he advised young Cubans of the need for a religion of love as the basis for a just society and a positive barrier against ignorance, prejudice, and fanaticism. Within American Catholicism he was a pastor and a productive publishing apologist who repeatedly tried to demonstrate the reasonableness of the Catholic tradition.

Bibliography

A. *Institutiones Philosophiae Eclecticae Ad Usum Studiosae Iuventutis* (Havana, 1812); *Lecciónes de Filosofía,* 3 vols. (Havana, 1818–19); *Apuntes Filosón del Espíritu Humano* (Havana, 1824); *Manual de práctica parlamenteria para el uso del Senado de los Estados Unidos, traducido del inglés y anotado por Félix Varela* (New York, 1826); *The Protestant's Abridger and Annotator,* 3 vols. (New York, 1830–33); *Letters to Elpidio* (1835–36; reprint, New York, 1989).

B. DAB, 19:224–25; NCE, 14:439; José Ignacio Rodríguez, *Vida del Presbítero Don Félix Varela* (Havana, 1878); Joseph and Helen McCadden, *Father Félix Varela: Cuban Catholic Apologist in the United States, 1823–1853* (New York, 1969); Felipe J. Estévez, "Introduction," *Félix Varela: Letters to Elpidio* (New York, 1989), 1–19; *El Padre Varela: Pensador, Sacerdote, Patriota,* ed. Roberto Esquenaza-Mayo (Washington, DC, 1992).

VEROT, JEAN-PIERRE AUGUSTIN MARCELLIN (23 May 1805, Le Puy, France—10 June 1876, St. Augustine, FL). *Education:* studied at Sulpician Sem., Issy, France, 1821–28. *Career:* lecturer, Issy sem., 1828–30; professor of mathematics and science, St. Mary's Coll. (MD), 1830–52; pastor, Ellicott's Mills, MD, and surrounding chapels, 1852–58; vicar apostolic of Florida, 1858–70; bishop of Savannah, GA, 1861–70; bishop of St. Augustine, FL, 1870–76.

Verot was one of a number of French émigré Sulpicians who provided episcopal leadership in nineteenth-century American Catholicism. As a young seminarian he was influenced to some extent by Félicité de Lamennais. After ordination and emigration to Baltimore he became an apologist for the Catholic faith during the antebellum phase of nativism. In 1858, after twenty-eight years as a professor and pastor in Maryland, he was made a bishop and spent the next eighteen years serving in Florida and Georgia. Although he was a French émigré Catholic, he identified with Southern culture, and at the outset of the Civil War he published a sermon, *Slavery and Abolition,* which supported slavery, attacked its abuses, and became a widely distributed Confederate tract. After the Civil War he tried to construct or reconstruct Catholic institutions in

Georgia, especially Catholic schools, but the lack of financial resources and numerous Catholics in the state impeded any progress in this regard.

During the First Vatican Council (1866–70) he earned for himself the title of "enfant terrible" because his oral interventions at the council seemed to some bishops to be comic or ridiculous. At the council he criticized the church and its theologians for impeding the progress of science, called for an acknowledgment of free scientific investigation, defended the essential dignity of African-Americans and advocated the publication of a conciliar statement on African-American equality, and argued that there was "no foundation in tradition" for the doctrine of papal infallibility and that its promulgation would unnecessarily aggravate the already tense relations between Protestants and Catholics. Throughout the council he sided with the opponents of the doctrine and refused to attend the final vote out of respect for the pope. After the doctrine was promulgated, however, he accepted it.

Bibliography

A. *The Comet: A Tract for the Times* (Baltimore, 1843); *A Just Judgment on the Catholic Doctrine* (Baltimore, 1843); *A Tract for the Times. Slavery and Abolitionism,* . . . (Baltimore, 1861); *Sacrorum Conciliorum Nova et amplissima Collectio* (Leipzig, 1923–27), 50:163–69, 539–49, 735; 52:289–302, 585–91; 53:1009.
B. DAB, 19:252–53; DACB, 574; DAH, 289–90; DARB, 485–86; NCAB, 12:535; NCE, 14:626; Michael V. Gannon, *Rebel Bishop: The Life and Era of Augustin Verot* (Milwaukee, 1964).

W

WALSH, JAMES ANTHONY (24 February 1867, Boston, MA—14 April 1936, Maryknoll, NY). *Education:* studied at Boston Coll., 1884–85; Harvard Univ., 1885–86; St. John's Sem., Brighton, MA, 1886–92. *Career:* ordained, 1892; curate, St. Patrick's Parish, Roxbury, MA, 1892–1903; director, Society for the Propagation of the Faith, Boston, 1903–11; cofounder of the Catholic Missions Bureau, 1906; editor, the *Field Afar,* 1907; cofounder with Thomas F. Price, Catholic Foreign Missions Society of America (Maryknoll), 1911; superior general, Maryknoll, 1929–33; titular bishop of Syene, 1933–36.

James A. Walsh is significant in American Catholicism for his work in raising the missionary consciousness of the American Catholic people and for cofounding Maryknoll. As a seminarian and young cleric, Walsh had an abiding interest in spreading the gospel to foreign lands and in awakening American Catholics to this dimension of a mature Christian life. In 1903, after he became the director of the Boston branch of the Society for the Propagation of the Faith, he successfully began to raise funds for and disseminate information on Catholic missionary work in foreign lands. In 1906 he collaborated with Joseph M. Bruneau, S.S., James F. Stanton, and John I. Lane in founding the Catholic Missions Bureau, and in 1907 they began to publish the *Field Afar.* The purpose of both the bureau and the journal was to provide means to generate interest in domestic as well as foreign missions.

Walsh, like the Paulists Walter Elliott and Alexander P. Doyle and the North Carolina diocesan priest Thomas F. Price, was interested in a home missionary movement that would encourage Catholic evangelical efforts among non-Catholics in the United States. Out of his association with these like-minded men, especially Price, he began to develop the idea for a new religious order that would be an American Catholic contribution to foreign missions. In 1911 he and Price won the approval of the American hierarchy and Pope Pius X to establish the Maryknoll Fathers as a religious society of diocesan priests dedicated exclusively to foreign missionary work. That same year the two began to build a seminary for the new work, and in 1917 they sent the first five Maryknoll priests to Yeungkong, China. Walsh was elected the first superior general of the new order and between 1917 and 1930 toured the rapidly growing mission fields in the Orient, where Maryknoll sisters as well as priests were active. In recognition of his missionary work Walsh was made a titular bishop of Syene in 1933, but his failing health caused his retirement in 1934 and his death in 1936.

Bibliography

A. *A Modern Martyr* (New York, 1905); *Observations in the Orient* (New York, 1919); *In the Home of Martyrs* (New York, 1922).
B. DAB, 22:691–93; DACB, 583; DAH, 291; NCE, 14:781–82; NYT, 15 April 1936, 21; George C. Powers, *The Maryknoll Movement* (New York, 1926); Daniel Sargent, *All the Day Long* (New York, 1941); Raymond A. Lane, *The Early Days of Maryknoll* (New York, 1951); Albert J. Nevins, *The Meaning of Maryknoll* (New York, 1959); Glenn D. Kittler, *The Maryknoll Fathers* (New York, 1961).

WALSH, ROBERT (30 August 1784, Baltimore, MD—7 February 1859, Paris, France). *Education:* studied at Georgetown Coll., 1797–1800; B.A., M.A., St. Mary's Sem., Baltimore, 1806; read law under Robert Goodloe Harper, 1806–8. *Career:* writer for the French and British press, 1806–1809; editor, *American Review of History and Politics,* 1811; cofounder with William Fry, the *National Gazette and Literary Register,* 1820; worked at the *American Quarterly Review,* 1827; foreign correspondent for the *National Intelligencer and Journal of Commerce,* 1837–59; US consul general, Paris, 1844–51.

Robert Walsh was a prominent American Catholic layman who had what Benjamin Franklin called a zeal for the public good. Educated in Maryland Catholic institutions and tutored under Robert Goodloe Harper, he was, like many late-eighteenth- and early-nineteenth-century Maryland Catholics, a Federalist and ardent opponent of President Madison's administration during the War of 1812. Walsh was also a prolific writer who tried between 1809 and the early 1830s to foster in Philadelphia a movement to develop indigenous American literary works. To this purpose he founded and/or edited the *American Register* (1809–10), *American Review of History and Politics* (1811–12), *National Gazette and Literary Register* (1820–36), *Museum of Foreign Literature and Science* (1824–30), and the *American Quarterly Review* (1827). He also edited the last twenty-eight volumes of *The Works of the British Poets* and wrote several of his own works as well. He taught English at the University of Pennsylvania (1823–33) and became a trustee. In 1837 he retired from the university due to ill health and left for Paris. While there he was a foreign correspondent for American newspapers and the American consul general.

Bibliography

A. *A Letter on the Genius and Disposition of the French Government* (Philadelphia,
   1810); *An Appeal from the Judgements of Great Britian Respecting the United
   States of America* (Philadelphia, 1815; reprint, New York, 1969); *Didactics: Social, Literary and Political* (Philadelphia, 1836).
B. DAB, 19:391–92; DACB, 586; NCE, 14:783–84; *New York Tribune* 1 March 1859,
   7; Henry C. Walsh, "Robert Walsh," *United States Catholic Historical Magazine*
   2 (1889): 301–13; Joseph Cyrillus Walsh, "Robert Walsh, 1784–1859," *Journal
   of the American Irish Historical Society* 26 (1927): 207–27; Mary Frederick Lo-
   chemes, *Robert Walsh: His Story* (New York, 1941).

WALWORTH, CLARENCE AUGUSTUS (30 May 1820, Plattsburg, NY—
19 September 1900, Albany, NY). *Education:* B.A., Union Coll., 1838; studied at General Theological Sem. (NY), 1842–44; St. Trond Coll., Belgium,
1846–48. *Career:* ordained as Redemptorist, 1848; missionary in eastern United
States, 1848–58; diocesan pastor, St. Peter's, Troy, NY, 1858–61; Paulist missionary, 1861–65; pastor, St. Mary's, Albany, NY, 1866–1900.

Walworth had a mercurial temperament and a vacillating career as a Catholic
priest. Born into a distinguished upstate New York Presbyterian family, he
became a Catholic in 1845 after a brief period of ministerial education at the
Episcopalian General Theological Seminary, which was in the midst of an Anglo-Catholic Romantic movement. In 1846 he joined the German-American
Congregation of the Most Holy Redeemer (i.e., the Redemptorists) and was
sent to Belgium to study for the priesthood. After ordination in 1848 he returned to the United States, where together with Isaac Hecker and other young
Redemptorist converts he led a series of parish missions for a decade. In 1858
he left the Redemptorists because of a belief that the German-dominated order
could not adequately adapt to American ways. After a brief period as a parish
pastor he joined fellow ex-Redemptorists who had formed the Paulist order. In
1865, however, because of some disagreements with Hecker, the founder of
the Paulists, and because of his own unsettled understanding of his vocational
aptitude, he left the Paulists and again became a parish pastor.

As a pastor in Albany, NY, for the remainder of his life, he became known
as an emotionally forceful and intelligent preacher, an active advocate for temperance and social justice, and an opponent of industrial abuses, poor working
conditions, and political corruption. He also worked to improve living conditions on the St. Regis Indian Reservation outside of Albany. Throughout his
career as a Catholic priest he was a writer, historian, and apologist for the
Catholic tradition. After 1865 he wrote frequently for the *Catholic World*, a
Paulist-published journal of opinion on social as well as religious issues. Like
a number of other Anglo-American converts to Catholicism, he provided an
intellectual leadership in the Catholic community that it did not possess prior
to the mid-1840s. He had a strong sense of the need for community and authority in reaction to what he perceived to be the disintegrating effects of indi-

vidualism in American religious, political, and economic life. For him, Catholicism was the antidote to the disease of individualism. In the postwar period he saw Catholicism as a corrective to the growing threat of historical relativism, atheistic evolutionism, socialism, and secularism.

Bibliography

A. ed., *Gentile Skeptic* (New York, 1863); *The Doctrine of Hell* (New York, 1873);
   Andiatorocte and Other Poems (New York, 1888); *Early Ritualism in America*
   (New York, 1893); *Reminiscences of Edgar P. Wadhams* (New York, 1893); *The
   Oxford Movement in America* (New York, 1895); *The Walworths of America* (Albany, NY, 1897).
B. DAB, 19:405–6; DACB, 588; NCAB, 3:97; NCE, 14:793–94; Walter Elliott, "Father Walworth: A Character Sketch," *Catholic World* 73 (1901): 320–37; Ellen
   Walworth, *Life Sketches of Father Walworth* (Albany, NY, 1907); Joseph McSorley, *Father Hecker and His Friends* (St. Louis, 1953).

WARD, MAISIE (4 January 1889, Shanklin, Isle of Wight, England—28 January 1975, New York, NY). *Career:* charter member, Catholic Evidence Guild, 1919; cofounder, Sheed and Ward, London, 1927, New York, 1933.

Maisie Ward was the granddaughter of William George Ward and the daughter of Wilfred Ward, two intellectuals who had been at the center of British Catholic intellectual and literary life since the early 1840s, when the Anglican theologian William George converted to Catholicism. Maisie herself became one of the leaders of the twentieth-century Catholic revival in England and the United States. From an early age she was interested and involved in a variety of social causes. During World War I she served as a nurse's assistant, helping the wounded in military hospitals. In 1919 she became a charter member of the Catholic Evidence Guild, a movement to propagate through street lecturing the fundamental tenets of Catholicism. Seven years later she married Frank Sheed, whom she had met through the guild.

A year after they were married they founded what was to become a major force in the Catholic intellectual and literary revival, the publishing firm of Sheed and Ward. In 1933 the firm opened a branch in New York. Like her husband, Frank, she was not only a publisher but also a writer, lecturer, and social activist. She wrote a number of historical essays and biographies, particularly on the figures of the Oxford Movement, on her friend Gilbert Chesterton, and on Robert Browning. In the 1930s she also became involved in Dorothy Day's Catholic Worker movement and the French worker-priests movement. She campaigned to provide better social services in India, improve low-cost housing in both England and the United States, and publicize Catholic lay efforts in the social apostolate. Throughout a very active career she upheld by word and example the quality and integrity of family life. Her work and that of her husband helped prepare the way for the Second Vatican Council, which she supported until her death at the age of eighty-six.

Bibliography

A. *Catholic Evidence Training Outlines* (New York, 1934); *The Wilfrid Wards and the Transition* (New York, 1934); *Insurrection Versus Resurrection* (New York, 1937); *Gilbert Keith Chesterton* (New York, 1943); *Young Mr. Newman* (London, 1948); *Return to Chesterton* (New York, 1952); *Be Not Solicitous* (New York, 1953); *Unfinished Business* (New York, 1964); *Robert Browning and His World,* 2 vols. (New York, 1968); *To and Fro on the Earth: The Sequel to an Autobiography* (New York, 1973).

B. CA1947: 774–75; DACB, 589; NCE, 17:702–3; NYT, 29 January 1975, 38; Walter Romig, *The Book of Catholic Authors,* 4th ser. (Grosse Pointe, MI, [1948?]), 324–30; Charles Moritz, ed., *Current Biography Yearbook, 1966* (New York, 1967), 423–26; Wilfred Sheed, *Frank and Maisie: A Memoir with Parents* (New York, 1985).

WARDE, MARY FRANCIS (? 1810, Abbeyleix, County Queens, Ireland— 17 September 1884, Manchester, NH). *Career:* member, Sisters of Mercy, Dublin, 1832; founding superior, Sisters of Mercy, Carlow (1837), Naas (1839), Wexford (1840), and Westport (1842), Ireland; founding superior, Sisters of Mercy, USA, 1843–84.

Mother Mary Francis Warde (née Mary Xavier) founded more convents during her lifetime than St. Teresa of Avila and traveled more widely than St. Paul. As a young woman she joined Mother Catherine McAuley's newly established Sisters of Mercy in Dublin. The primary purpose of the new order of women religious was the education, care, and support of the sick and the poor. After founding a number of convents in Ireland, Mother Warde was invited by Bishop Michael O'Connor to establish the new order in Pittsburgh. In 1843 she came to Pittsburgh with six other Sisters of Mercy to build a convent and boarding school for girls. Almost immediately, however, the sisters also began to care for orphans and the sick. In the first three years of its existence the Pittsburgh convent grew so rapidly that it was able to send out sisters to build convents throughout the United States.

Mother Warde in particular was indefatigable in personally directing or establishing convents in Chicago (1846), Loretto, PA (1848), Providence (1850), Newport, RI (1854), Rochester, NY (1857), Buffalo, NY (1857), Portland, ME (1858), Manchester, NH (1858), Philadelphia (1861), Omaha, NB (1864), Bangor, ME (1865), Eureka, CA (1871), North Whitefield, ME (1871), Jersey City, NJ (1872), Princeton, NJ (1872), and St. Johnsbury, VT (1872). By the time of her death she was responsible for bringing the new order to the service of thousands of immigrants across the United States. By the end of the century the Sisters of Mercy had grown to over two thousand and had established numerous convents, schools, hospitals, orphanages, and soup kitchens in fifty-eight American dioceses. Mother Warde was an activist who lived a community life and whose religious devotion endeared her to her followers and the people she served.

Bibliography

B. DACB, 589–90; DARB, 490–91; NCE 14:810; M. Catherine Garety, *Rev. Mother M. Xavier Warde* (Boston, 1902); Kathleen Healy, *Frances Warde: American Founder of the Sisters of Mercy* (New York, 1973).

WEIGEL, GUSTAVE (15 January 1906, Buffalo, NY—3 January 1964, New York, NY). *Education:* B.A., Woodstock Coll. (MD), 1928; S.T.D., Gregorian Univ., Rome, 1938. *Career:* ordained, 1933; professor of dogmatic theology, Catholic Univ. of Chile, 1937–38; professor of ecclesiology, Woodstock Coll., 1949–64; special advisor, Secretariat for the Promotion of Christian Unity, 1960; liason officer for non-Catholic observers at Vatican II, 1962–64.

Gustave Weigel was a pioneer ecumenist during the 1950s. He tried to awaken American Catholics to the significance of the movement toward Christian unity, which he saw as "the most striking ecclesiological event since the sixteenth century." He introduced many articulate Catholics to the ecumenical movement through his numerous books, pamphlets, and articles, and he encouraged them to study Protestant traditions from Protestant sources, a tactic he hoped would contribute to mutual understanding. He was engaged in a number of dialogues with Protestant theologians, most notably with Paul Tillich, and was an observer at the Oberlin Conference on Faith and Order (1957) and other ecumenical gatherings. He was pessimistic, though, about the immediate possibilities of Christian unity and believed that his attitude was well grounded in a realistic evaluation of American circumstances. Numerous historical, cultural, and theological differences and an apparent lack of concern for doctrinal unity within the Protestant ecumenical movement made Christian union extremely difficult, he believed. Weigel called himself a "middle generation" Catholic ecumenist. He stood between those Catholics who refused to engage in any theological discussions with Protestants and those who would in the future take up the chore of furthering Christian union.

In 1960, prior to the Second Vatican Council, he was appointed a consultor to the Vatican's new Secretariat for the Promotion of Christian Unity—a commission to help members of other religious traditions follow the council's work, assist council members in understanding other Christian bodies, mediate Protestant observers' suggestions, and guide the council on those pastoral and theological matters that bore directly and indirectly on the problem of Christian unity. Although Weigel did not contribute much to the secretariat's preparatory work, he proved invaluable once the council began in 1962, guiding journalists and Protestant observers through the daily developments and conflicting theological battles on the council floor. Although his pre-Vatican scholastic and juridical ecclesiology prevented him from acknowledging the ecclesial dimensions of Protestant Christianity and from developing a more ecumenical ecclesiology, his personal openness to Protestants made him an effective pioneer of a changing mentality in Catholicism and helped to break down some of the historical and cultural walls that had separated American Protestants and Catholics for generations.

Bibliography

A. *A Survey of Protestant Theology in Our Times* (Westminster, MD, 1954); *A Catholic Primer on the Ecumenical Movement* (Westminster, MD, 1957); *Faith and Understanding in America* (New York, 1959); with Robert M. Brown, *An American Dialogue: A Protestant Looks at Catholicism and a Catholic Looks at Protestantism* (New York, 1961); *Catholic Theology in Dialogue* (New York, 1961); *Churches in North America* (Baltimore, 1961); *The Modern God: Faith in a Secular Culture* (New York, 1963).

B. DACB, 592; DARB, 495–96; NCE, 14:843–44; NYT, 4 January 1964, 1; Patrick W. Collins, *Gustave Weigel: A Pioneer of Reform* (Collegeville, MN, 1991).

WHITE, ANDREW (1579, London, England—27 December 1656, near London, England). *Education:* studied at St. Alban's Coll., Valladolid, Spain, and at Seville, Spain, and Douai, Flanders, before 1605. *Career:* entered Jesuit novitiate, 1607; missionary in England and professor of scripture, languages, and theology in Lisbon and Louvain and Liège, Belgium, 1610–33; missionary in Maryland, 1634–45; missionary in England, 1645–56.

Born and baptized as a Catholic in Elizabethan England, Andrew White was forced to obtain his education on the Continent, where he studied for the priesthood. After ordination he returned to England and became involved or implicated in the so-called Gunpowder Plot (1605) against the government of James I. Banished from England he sailed for the Continent again, and this time he became a Jesuit and taught in their colleges at Lisbon, Louvain and Liège, Belgium, for twenty-three years.

In 1634 at the age of fifty-five, he responded to Cecil Calvert's invitation to the Jesuits to join his colonization efforts in his new land-grant colony of Maryland. White, together with fellow Jesuit priest John Altham and lay brother Thomas Gervase, boarded the *Ark* and sailed to Maryland, where in March of 1634 they began to establish the first British colonial Catholic church, ran a colonial farming enterprise for their own sustenance, and by the late 1630s evangelized the Patuxents and Piscataways. Living among these Native Americans, White learned their culture and language, wrote a grammar and dictionary, and translated a Catholic catechism into their language. The missionary efforts among the Indians did not last, however, because it was not supported by the colonists and because anti-Catholic Virginians, under the leadership of William Claiborne, invaded Maryland in 1645, captured White, and sent him back to England in chains. Charged with treason, he was acquitted in an English court but banished again from the country, only to return secretly from the Continent a short time afterward to provide religious services to English Catholics during the last decade of his life.

Bibliography

A. E. A. Dalrymple, ed., *Relatio Itineris in Marylandiam* (Baltimore, 1874).
B. DAB, 20:87–88; DACB, 595; DARB, 502–3; NCE, 14:892; Bernard C. Steiner, *Beginnings of Maryland, 1631–39* (Baltimore, 1903); Clayton Coleman Hall, *Narratives of Early Maryland, 1633–1684* (New York, 1910).

WILLIAMS, MICHAEL (5 February 1877, Halifax, Nova Scotia—12 October 1950, Westport, CT). *Career:* city editor, San Francisco *Examiner,* 1906; founder and editor, *Commonweal,* 1924–37.

Michael Williams was one of the leading Catholic laity during and immediately after World War I. Born and educated in Canada, he left college and the church when his father died and led a vagabond existence for a few years. Moving to Boston as a young man, he made a living as a writer of verse and stories. Eventually through his contact with Philip Hale of the *Boston Journal* he became a reporter for the *Boston Post* and the New York *World* and *Evening Telegram.* He moved to San Francisco as city editor of the *Examiner* in 1906, the year of the devastating earthquake and fire. After a brief stay in San Francisco, he went to Englewood, NJ, where he joined Upton Sinclair's utopian colony and collaborated with him in publishing *Good Health* (1909). Unsatisfied with his life in the colony, he moved to Carmel, CA, and there he had a religious conversion, was led back into the Catholic church in 1912, and reported his experience in *The Book of High Romance* (1918).

The Paulist John Burke was impressed with Williams's *High Romance* and his abilities as a journalist and invited him to be the assistant director of the press department of the National Catholic War Council during the first World War. Williams became acquainted with other leading Catholic clerics, bishops, and laity through his work publicizing Catholic efforts during the war. After the war the bishops commissioned him to write *American Catholics in the War* (1921), an apologetic attempt to make a case for Catholic patriotism. Through these experiences, Williams became convinced of the need for a lay-edited intellectual Catholic weekly analogous to the influential *New Republic* and *Nation.* In the early 1920s he moved to New York, organized a group of Catholic laymen called the Calvert Association, and in 1924 established *Commonweal,* a journal by and for lay Catholic intellectuals.

From 1924 to 1937 he edited the journal, presenting a Catholic view on the major issues of his day (e.g., evolution and theology, the candidacy of Al Smith, New Deal programs, the Calles' persecution of Catholics in Mexico, the rise of Nazi Germany, and the Spanish Civil War). Although his own positions were marked by his understanding of the papal social encyclical tradition, his support for Generalissimo Franco during the Spanish Civil War was not agreeable to his fellow editors, and in 1937 he gave up the editorship to a new generation of young Catholic intellectuals who were anti-Franco as well as anticommunist in their approach to Spain. After he left the editorship he continued to contribute a column, "Views and Reviews," but for all practical purposes his national influence on developments in American Catholicism ceased.

Bibliography

A. *The Book of High Romance: a Spiritual Autobiography* (New York: 1918; rev. ed., 1926); *American Catholics in the War* (New York, 1921); *Little Brother Francis of Assisi* (New York, 1926); *The Little Flower of Carmel* (New York, 1926); *Catholicism and the Modern Mind* (New York, 1928); *The Present Position of Catholics in the United States* (New York, 1928); *The Shadow of the Pope* (New York, 1932); *Anthology of Christian Literature* (New York, 1933); *The Book of Christian Classics* (New York, 1933); *The Catholic Church in Action* (New York, 1934).
B. DACB, 600; NCE, 14:943–44; NYT, 13 October 1950, 29; S. J. Kunitz and H. Haycraft, eds., *Twentieth Century Authors* (New York, 1942), 1523; George N. Schuster, "Michael Williams," *Catholic Press Annual* (1964), 19–22; Rodger Van Allen, *The Commonweal and American Catholicism* (Philadelphia, 1974); Martin J. Bredeck, *Imperfect Apostles: Catholic Laity, 1924–1976* (New York, 1988).

WIMMER, BONIFACE (née SEBASTIAN) (4 January 1809, Thalmassing, Bavaria—8 December 1887, Latrobe, PA). *Education:* studied at Univ. of Munich, 1827–30; Regensburg Sem., Germany, 1830–31. *Career:* ordained, 1831; curate, Marian Shrine, Altotting, Germany, 1831–32; Benedictine vows, Bavaria, 1833; professor at Metten, Augsburg, and Munich, Germany, 1833–46; founder, St. Vincent's Benedictine Abbey, Latrobe, PA, 1846; abbot, St. Vincent's, 1855–83; archabbot, St. Vincent's, 1883–87.

Sebastian Wimmer was born during the Napoleonic wars and at a time when German Catholic life in general and Benedictine monasticism in particular were undergoing a Romantic revival. Ordained as a Regensburg diocesan priest, Sebastian became a member of the newly (1827) restored Benedictine monastery at Metten, Bavaria, in 1832, taking the name of Boniface. In 1845 he met a German priest, Peter Lemke, who had been serving German immigrants in Pennsylvania since 1834. Lemke offered Boniface some land in western Pennsylvania if he would establish a monastery there. In 1846, after some initial reluctance on the part of his religious superiors, he was allowed to go with four postulants and fourteen young laymen to establish a Benedictine mission at Carrolltown, PA.

By 1852, under Boniface's forceful direction, the small Benedictine community had enlarged itself with new recruits from Metten, built a college, seminary, and brewery at Latrobe, PA (where the community had moved in 1847), and brought Benedictine nuns to the United States to aid the religious mission to German Catholics. In 1855 the monastic community had grown to 150 members; Pope Pius IX elevated it to the status of abbey, and Boniface was named abbot.

Boniface was an activist, not a contemplative monk, who believed that building and extending monastic institutions and providing active missionary work was a way of preserving German traditions, ethnic solidarity, and religious integrity in a pluralistic country where disintegration and the centrifugal forces of religious and ideological pluralism were constant threats to German immigrants. By his death in 1887 Boniface had helped develop fledgling Benedictine houses at St. John's in Minnesota (1856), Newark, NJ (1857), Atchison, KS (1857), Covington, KY (1858), Texas (1859), Alabama (1875), and North Carolina (1876), and had sent Benedictine missionaries into twenty-five states as well as into Canada and Ecuador.

Bibliography

A. Conrad Zimmerman et al., "Wimmer Letters," *The Scriptorium* (St. John's Abbey, MN) 17 (1958): 53–64; 18 (1959): 67–82; 19 (1960): 61–83; Warren Murrman, "The Wimmer Correspondence: A Collection and a Project," *Benedictine Confluence* 6 (1972): 16–24.
B. DACB, 602; NCE, 14:953–54; NYT, 9 December 1887, 5; Oswald Moosmüller, *St. Vincenz in Pennsylvanien* (New York, 1873); obituary in *Studien und Mittheilungen aus dem Benedictiner und dem Cisterciener Orden* 11 (1888, 15); Oswald Moosmüller, *Erzabt Bonifaz Wimmer* (New York, 1891); Jerome Oetgen, *An American Abbot: Boniface Wimmer, O.S.B., 1809–1887* (Latrobe, PA, 1976); Joel Rippinger, *The Benedictine Order in the United States: An Interpretative History* (Collegeville, MN, 1990).

WOLFF, MARY MADELEVA (24 May 1877, Cumberland, WI—25 July 1964, Boston, MA). *Education:* studied at Univ. of WI, Madison, 1905; B.A., St. Mary's Coll., Notre Dame, IN, 1909; M.A., English, Univ. of Notre Dame, 1918; Ph.D., English, Univ. of CA, Berkeley, 1925; studied at Oxford Univ., 1933–34; *Career:* entered novitiate of the Sisters of the Holy Cross, 1908; English teacher and department chairperson, St. Mary's Coll., 1912–19; principal, Sacred Heart Academy, Ogden, UT, 1919–22; principal, Holy Rosary Academy, Woodland, CA, 1922–25; president, St. Mary-of-the-Wasatch Coll., Salt Lake City, 1926–33; president, St. Mary's Coll., 1934–61.

Mother Madeleva (née Mary Evaline) Wolff was the only daughter and second of three children born to August Frederick and Lucy Arntz Wolff, German immigrants. After entering the Sisters of the Holy Cross and taking the name of Madeleva, she became best known as a poet, author, and educator. As president of St. Mary's College (a small college for women at Notre Dame, IN) between 1934 and 1961, she made a number of major contributions to higher education for women. Under her presidency, the enrollment at St. Mary's increased from three hundred to one thousand, and she helped to develop the curriculum and student achievement goals. In the mid-1940s she established the world's first graduate school in theology explicitly for Catholic lay and religious women. Throughout the 1940s and 1950s she was acknowledged as an authority on higher education of women, and her *Education of Sister Lucy* (1949) was considered a benchmark in promoting a systematic program for the higher education of women religious. She traveled and lectured extensively throughout the nation, was at one time the Indiana director of the National

Conference of Christians and Jews, and became president of the Catholic Poetry Society of America (1942–47). Throughout a busy life of administration she published critical essays and books on Chaucer and medieval literature and poetry, her own poems, and a number of provocative essays in, among others, the *New Republic, Commonweal,* the *New York Times, Thought,* and the *Saturday Review.*

Bibliography

A. *Knights Errant, and Other Poems* (New York, 1923); *Chaucer's Nuns and Other Essays* (New York, 1925); *Pearl: A Study in Spiritual Dryness* (New York, 1925); *Penelope and Other Poems* (New York, 1927); *The Education of Sister Lucy* (Philadelphia, 1949); *A Lost Language and Other Essays on Chaucer* (New York, 1951); *Theology and the Teacher* (Notre Dame, IN, 1953); *The Four Last Things: Collected Poems* (New York, 1959); *My First Seventy Years* (New York, 1959); *Conversations with Cassandra* (New York, 1961).

B. DACB, 338–39; NAW, 4:741–42; NCAB, 51:202; NYT, 26 July 1964, 57; NCE, 9:48; *Current Biography* (New York, 1942), 556–57; C. Jencks, *The Sister Madeleva Story* (Notre Dame, IN, 1961); Maria Concepta McDermott, *The Making of a Sister Teacher* (Notre Dame, IN, 1965); Mary Immaculate Creek, *A Panorama: 1844–1977* (Notre Dame, IN, 1977); Mary Ellen Klein, "Sister M. Madeleva Wolff, C.S.C., Saint Mary's College, Notre Dame, Indiana: A Study of Presidential Leadership 1934–1961" (Ph.D. diss., Kent State University, 1983).

WYNNE, JOHN JOSEPH (30 September 1859, New York, NY—30 November 1948, New York, NY). *Education:* B.A., St. Francis Xavier Coll. (NY), 1876; studied at Woodstock Coll. (MD), 1879–82, 1887–90. *Career:* entered Jesuits, 1876; professor, St. Francis Xavier Coll., 1882–86; professor, Boston Coll., 1886–87; ordained, 1890; editor, *Messenger of the Sacred Heart,* 1891–1908; founding editor, *America,* 1908–1909; associate editor, *The Catholic Encyclopedia,* 1905–12.

John Wynne was one of the prominent early-twentieth-century Jesuits who emerged from the confines of local ecclesiastical interests to become actively engaged in projects for the transformation of American society according to Catholic principles. Wynne continued the late-nineteenth-century Jesuit anti-modernist tendency into the twentieth century, but he also confidently believed that Catholic anti-modernist intellectual principles and teachings should be promulgated effectively and applied judiciously to social and cultural problems in the United States.

Wynne founded two organs, *The Catholic Encyclopedia* and *America* magazine, to promote Catholic thought and apply it to modern cultural and political issues. In 1905 he helped form an editorial board (consisting of Fathers Thomas J. Shahan and Edward A. Pace of the Catholic University of America; Dr. Charles Herbermann, Latin professor and librarian at the City College of New York; and Condé Pallen, former editor of *Church Progress and Catholic World*) for the new encyclopedia that he hoped would present the best current Catholic thought on a whole range of political, religious, cultural, and historical issues—demonstrating in particular Catholic contributions to Western intellectual life and culture. He thought a specific Catholic encyclopedia was needed to counter the false or inaccurate assertions that were made about Catholic life and doctrine in some secular encyclopedias. By 1912 the editors had produced fifteen volumes written by a host of Catholics from throughout the world. *The Catholic Encyclopedia* was the most significant Catholic intellectual achievement of the early twentieth century. Wynne also published *America* to carry out Pope Pius X's directive to bring the world to Christ and edited a collection of Pope Leo XIII's encyclicals and a *New Catholic Dictionary* to serve the same functions as the *Encyclopedia* and *America*.

Wynne's nineteenth-century interests, as editor of the *Messenger of the Sacred Heart,* in reviving the spiritual life among American Catholics also continued into the twentieth century. He was a major leader, for example, in the Apostleship of Prayer, the Holy Hour movement, and the Holy Name Society. He was prominent, too, in promoting the beatification and canonization of the North American martyrs, especially Catherine Tekakwitha. In 1946 he was instrumental in erecting near Lake George, New York, a statue of St. Isaac Jogues, whose canonization he had promoted and saw realized in 1929.

Bibliography

A. ed., *The Great Encyclical Letters of Pope Leo XIII* (New York, 1903); *The Jesuit Martyrs of North America* (New York, 1925); ed., *The New Catholic Dictionary* (New York, 1929).

B. CA1947: 807–8; DACB, 606; NCE, 14:1053; NYT, 2 December 1948, 29; Xavier Alumni Sodality, *Fifty Years in Conflict and Triumph* (New York, 1927).

Y

YORKE, PETER CHRISTOPHER (15 August 1864, Galway, Ireland—5 April 1925, San Francisco, CA). *Education:* studied at St. Patrick's Coll., Maynooth, Ireland, 1882–86; St. Mary's Sem., Baltimore, 1886–87; S.T.B., Catholic Univ. of America, 1890; S.T.L., 1891. *Career:* ordained, 1887; curate, St. Mary's Cathedral, San Francisco, 1887–89; editor, *Monitor,* 1894–99; chancellor, Archdiocese of San Francisco, 1894–99; curate, St. Mary's, mission district, San Francisco, 1899–1903; founder, the *Leader,* 1902; pastor, St. Anthony's, Oakland, CA, 1903–13; pastor, St. Peter's, San Francisco, 1913–25.

After his ordination Peter Yorke earned a reputation in San Francisco as a forceful and effective advocate for labor, an Irish nationalist, and early educational and liturgical reformer. In 1889 San Francisco's Archbishop Patrick William Riordan—a sympathizer with other Americanist bishops who supported the establishment of the Catholic University of America in Washington, DC—sent Yorke, whom he considered a brilliant young priest, to the new university to obtain a doctorate and provide his diocese with a new level of intellectual leadership. Yorke did not, however, obtain the doctorate (the Vatican awarded him an honorary one in theology in 1906); instead, he retired from academic life after receiving a licentiate in theology and returned to San Francisco in 1891, where he became an activist advocate for various causes. Influenced by *Rerum Novarum,* Yorke supported labor in the bitter fights that disturbed San Francisco in the late nineteenth and early twentieth centuries. In 1901 he successfully obtained the aid of the governor of California to assist the labor unions in their struggles against their employers and established the *Leader* in 1902 to counteract the anti-union press in the city. Unlike John Ryan, whose writings he quoted periodically after 1907, Yorke did not see legislation as an adequate means to social reform. He emphasized, much more than Ryan, the necessity of a religious conversion as the primary means of social regeneration.

Throughout his career as a pastor in San Francisco, Yorke became involved in the development of Catholic schools, which he saw as an instrumental means for preserving Catholic identity and socially uplifting Catholic immigrants. To this end, he wrote and published a number of religion texts for use in Catholic schools and became an active and leading participant in the newly formed National Catholic Educational Association. During the reign of Pope Pius X (1903–14) he became interested in liturgical renewal, long before the establishment of the liturgical movement in the United States, and wrote a number of books and pamphlets to promote more intelligent participation in the liturgy. Yorke was also an ardent Irish nationalist, which made him a favorite among the other numerous Irish immigrants in San Francisco, but his controversial public stands and activism alienated him from episcopal leadership, rising middle-class Catholics, and the political powers in San Franciso.

Bibliography

A. *Father Yorke to Mr. Maguire* (San Francisco, 1898); *Father Yorke to Mr. Phelan* (San Francisco, 1898); ed., *Text Books of Religion* 5 vols. (San Francisco, 1901); *Roman Liturgy* (San Francisco, 1903); *Altar and Priest* (San Francisco, 1913); *The Ghosts of Bigotry* (San Francisco, 1913); *Sermons by Rev. P. C. Yorke,* 2 vols. (San Francisco, 1931).

B. DACB, 607; NCE, 14:1075; *San Francisco Call,* 7 April 1925, 7; *San Francisco Examiner,* 10 April 1925, 10; Bernard C. Cronin, *Father Yorke and the Labor Movement in San Francisco, 1900–1910* (Washington, DC, 1944); Joseph S. Brusher, *The Consecrated Thunderbolt: Father Yorke of San Francisco* (San Francisco, 1973); Timothy Sarbaugh, ''Father Yorke and the San Francisco Waterfront, 1910–1916,'' *Pacific Historian* 28 (1981): 28–35; Dominic P. Scibilia, ''Edward McGlynn, Thomas McGrady, and Peter C. Yorke: Prophets of American Social Catholicism'' (Ph.D. diss., Marquette University, 1990).

Z

ZAHM, JOHN AUGUSTINE (14 June 1851, New Lexington, OH—10 November 1921, Munich, Germany). *Education:* B.A., Univ. of Notre Dame, 1871; studied at Notre Dame Sem. (IN), 1871–75. *Career:* ordained, 1875; professor of chemistry and physics, Univ. of Notre Dame, 1875–92; visiting lecturer in NY, WI, CA, Belgium, and Switzerland, 1893–97; US provincial, Congregation of the Holy Cross, 1898–1905; traveler, lecturer, and author, 1906–21.

John Augustine Zahm was an ordained member of the Congregation of the Holy Cross and a science professor at the Congregation's University of Notre Dame. He was one of the first American Catholic intellectuals during the late nineteenth century to develop a Catholic understanding of evolution. Steering a path between special creationism and naturalistic evolutionism, he developed a view he and others called theistic evolutionism. He opposed what he considered the unscientific literalism of those who maintained that God was immediately and directly responsible for the creation of all species and all forms of life as well as the dogmatism of those scientists who ruled God out of creation and attributed all creation to the laws of evolution. According to Zahm, a theistic theory of evolution was compatible with a properly understood biblical account of creation and with Christian and Catholic teachings.

Zahm's position, maturely articulated in his *Evolution and Dogma* (1896), was welcomed by the Americanists and liberal Catholics of the late nineteenth century but severely criticized by the conservatives within American Catholicism. The conservatives pressured Rome to have Zahm's book condemned; rather than condemning the book publicly, however, Rome requested that Zahm withdraw it from publication in 1898. This censure was one part of the growing Roman anti-Americanist sentiment prior to Leo XIII's condemnation of Americanism in 1899. After 1898 Zahm ceased publishing anything relating to the dialogue between science and religion, became provincial of his religious order, and thereafter traveled extensively until his death in 1921.

Bibliography

A. *Catholic Science and Catholic Scientists* (Philadelphia, 1893); *Bible, Science and Faith* (Baltimore, 1894); *Evolution and Dogma* (Chicago, 1896); *Science and the Church* (Chicago, 1896); *Scientific Theory and Doctrine* (Chicago, 1896).

B. DAB, 20:641–42; DACB, 609–10; DARB, 539–40; NCAB 9:274; NCE, 14:1109; NYT, 12 November 1921, 13; Ralph E. Weber, *Notre Dame's John Zahm: American Catholic Apologist and Educator* (Notre Dame, IN, 1961).

CHRONOLOGY

1492   Christopher Columbus's first voyage to America.

1542   Fray Juan de Padilla, proto-martyr of the United States, murdered by Indians on the plains of Kansas.

1565   First Catholic parish of the United States founded at St. Augustine, Florida.

1609   Founding of Santa Fe, future headquarters of the missions of New Mexico.

1611   Pierre Biard, S.J., and Ennémond Massé, S.J., open missionary efforts among the Indians of Maine.

1622   Pope Gregory XV establishes Congregation de Propaganda Fide, under whose jurisdiction American Catholics would remain until 1908.

1634   The *Ark* and the *Dove* reach Maryland with first settlers.

1646   Isaac Jogues, S.J., murdered by the Iroquois near Auriesville, New York.

1649   Maryland's general assembly passes an act of religious toleration for all Christians.

1654   Puritan regime repeals the act of religious toleration in Maryland.

1671   Sieur de Lusson and Claude Allouez, S.J., at Mackinac Island take possession of the western country for France.

1673   Louis Jollet and Jacques Marquette, S.J., conduct an expedition down the Mississippi River.

1680   Indian rebellion destroys the missions of New Mexico.

1687   Eusebio Francisco Kino, S.J., enters Pimeria Alta to inaugurate the missions of Arizona.

1692   Church of England established by law in Maryland; De Vargas reconquers New Mexico, and the friars return to reopen the missions.

1704   Destruction of Florida's northern missions by Governor James Moore of South Carolina.

1716   Antonio Margil, O.F.M., launches his missionary career in Texas.

1718   Disfranchisement of Catholics in Maryland.

1727   Ursuline Sisters arrive from France to open first Catholic school in New Orleans.

1763   Jesuits banished from Louisiana and the Illinois Country; Spain cedes Florida to England, and the latter gains all lands east of Mississippi River from France.

1769   Junipero Serra, O.F.M., founds the first of the California missions at San Diego.

1773   Charles Carroll of Carrollton publishes "First Citizen" letters against Daniel Dulany and the royal government in Maryland; Society of Jesus suppressed by Pope Clement XIV.

1774   Quebec Act passes the British Parliament.

1775   Continental Congress denounces Catholicism to George III and the British people; Washington suppresses the army's celebration of Guy Fawkes Day.

1776   Charles Carroll appointed with Benjamin Franklin and Samuel Chase as commission of Congress to seek Canadian aid, with Father John Carroll accompanying the commissioners; Virginia the first state to vote full religious freedom in its bill of rights, followed by religious freedom for Christians in Pennsylvania and Maryland; Charles Carroll signs the Declaration of Independence.

1784   Vatican appoints John Carroll as superior of the American Catholic missions.

1787   Daniel Carroll of Maryland and Thomas FitzSimons of Pennsylvania sign the Constitution of the United States.

1789   Pope Pius VI erects the Diocese of Baltimore and names John Carroll as first bishop.

1791   French Sulpicians open first seminary in the United States, St. Mary's in Baltimore; Georgetown Academy begins classes; Bishop Carroll convokes first synod of his clergy; Bill of Rights ratified.

1808   Baltimore made first metropolitan see of the United States, with Bardstown (KY), Boston, New York, and Philadelphia as first suffragan sees.

1809   Mother Elizabeth Bayley Seton establishes first native American sisterhood at Emmitsburg, MD.

1822   Bishop John England founds the *United States Catholic Miscellany,* the first Catholic newspaper in the country; Society for the Propagation of the Faith founded in France.

1829   First Provincial Council of Baltimore convoked; Elizabeth Lange, Marie Balas, Rosine Boegue, and Almeide Duchemin Maxis begin religious life in Baltimore as the Oblate Sisters of Providence, the first African-American congregation of women religious in the United States.

1834   Ursuline Convent at Charlestown, MA, burned by a nativist mob.

1836   Publication of Maria Monk's *Awful Disclosures of the Hotel Dieu Nunnery of Montreal;* President Jackson nominates Roger Brooke Taney as chief justice of the Supreme Court.

1839   Pope Gregory XVI condemns slave trade in *In Supremo Apostolatus.*

1842   Henriette Delille and Juliette Gaudin begin the Sisters of the Holy Family in New Orleans, the second African-American order of women religious.

1844   Philadelphia rioters burn two Catholic churches and kill thirteen persons; Orestes A. Brownson received into Catholic church; establishment of *Brownson's Quarterly Review.*

1845   Isaac Hecker received into Catholic church; beginning of potato famine in Ireland.

1846   Establishment of first Benedictine priory (PA).

1848   Establishment of first permanent American Trappist foundation (KY).

1852   First Plenary Council of Baltimore.

1855   Founding of the German Catholic Central Verein.

1857   Opening of American College at Louvain, Belgium.

1858   Founding of the Paulists, the first native religious community for men.

1859   North American College opens in Rome.

1865   Founding of *Catholic World.*

1866   Second Plenary Council of Baltimore.

1869   American bishops attend the First Vatican Council in Rome.

1871   Arrival of Mill Hill Fathers (Josephites) in Baltimore.

1875   Archbishop John McCloskey of New York becomes first American cardinal; James Augustine Healy named the first African-American (mulatto) bishop (for Portland, ME).

1876   Founding of the *American Catholic Quarterly Review;* publication of James Gibbons's *Faith of Our Fathers.*

1884   Third Plenary Council of Baltimore.

1886   Archbishop James Gibbons of Baltimore named the second American cardinal; Augustus Tolton ordained the first African-American priest.

1889   Opening of the Catholic University of America; first African-American Catholic lay congress in Washington, DC (others held in Cincinnati, 1890; Philadelphia, 1892; Chicago, 1893; and Baltimore, 1894).

1890   Archbishop Ireland's address on public and private schools before the National Education Association in St. Paul.

1891   Mother Katharine Drexel founds the Sisters of the Blessed Sacrament for Indians and Colored People.

1893   Apostolic Delegation established in Washington, DC; opening of College of Notre Dame of Maryland, first Catholic college for women.

1899   Pope Leo XIII publishes *Testem Benevolentiae.*

1904   Founding of the National Catholic Education Association.

1905   Founding of the Catholic Church Extension Society for home missions.

1907   Publication of the first volume of the *Catholic Encyclopedia.*

1908   Pope Pius X publishes *Pascendi Domini Gregis* against modernism; American Catholicism removed from jurisdiction of the Congregation de Propaganda Fide; William O'Connell becomes bishop of Boston.

1911   Establishment of Catholic Foreign Mission Society of America (Maryknoll).

1917   Founding of the National Catholic War Council.

1919   Publication of the *Bishops' Program of Social Reconstruction;* founding of the National Catholic Welfare Council.

1924   Federated Colored Catholics of the United States established.

1925   Supreme Court declares Oregon school law unconstitutional.

1926   Twenty-eighth International Eucharistic Congress held in Chicago.

1934   John LaFarge, S.J., founds first Catholic Interracial Council in New York.

1939   Myron C. Taylor named personal representative of President Roosevelt to Pope Pius XII.

1948   Protestants and Other Americans for Separation of Church and State (POAU) organized.

1951   President Truman nominates General Mark Clark as American ambassador to Vatican City.

1954   Establishment of the Sister Formation Conference.

1955   Publication of John Tracy Ellis's "American Catholics and the Intellectual Life."

1958   Christopher Dawson named first occupant of the Chauney Stillman Chair of Roman Catholic Studies in the Divinity School of Harvard University.

1959   Pope John XXIII announces convocation of the Second Vatican Council.

1960   John F. Kennedy becomes the first Catholic president.

1962   Opening of the Second Vatican Council; Vatican appoints Gustave Weigel, S.J., as one of five Catholic observers at the third general assembly of the World Council of Churches at New Delhi; Archbishop Joseph F. Rummel of New Orleans announces integration of Catholic schools; organization of National Farm Workers Association.

1963   Catholic University of America prohibits Godfrey Diekmann, O.S.B., Hans Kung, John Courtney Murray, S.J., and Gustave Weigel, S.J., from speaking there; Elizabeth Seton becomes first American to be beatified; widespread discussion of Dr. John Rock's pill and birth-control methods; President Kennedy assassinated.

1965   March on Selma, Alabama; visit of Pope Paul VI to United Nations; Gommar A. De Pauw organizes Catholic Traditionalist movement; academic freedom debates at St. John's University, Jamaica, NY; Roger LaPorte immolated before United Nations Building.

1966   Organization of the National Conference of Catholic Bishops and the United States Catholic Conference; Harold Perry, S.V.D., becomes second African-American to be ordained a bishop.

1967   Land O' Lakes Statement; beginning of Catholic Charismatic movement.

1968   Pope Paul VI publishes *Humanae Vitae* against artificial means of birth control; Richard Nixon elected president; formation of the National Black Catholic Clergy Caucus, National Black Sisters' Conference, National Black Catholic Seminarians Association, and National Federation of Priests' Council;
        Catonsville Trial.

1969   Organization of Priests Associated for Religious, Educational, and Social Rights
        (PADRES); formation of Dignity.

1970   Patricio Flores becomes first contemporary Hispanic to be ordained a bishop.

1971   Establishment of Leadership Conference of Women Religious (formerly the
        Conference of Major Superiors of Women, 1956), *Consortium Perfectae Caritatis,* Las Hermanas, and Network.

1972   Harrisburg Trial.

1973   *Roe v. Wade.*

1975   Organization of first Catholic Women's Ordination Conference (Detroit).

1976   Convocation of "Call to Action" Conference (Detroit).

1979   Pope John Paul II visits the United States.

1983   Publication of NCCB's *Challenge of Peace.*

1985   Vatican disciplines Seattle's Archbishop Raymond Hunthausen.

1986   Publication of NCCB's *Economic Justice For All;* Vatican removes Father
        Charles Curran from teaching theology at the Catholic University of America.

1987   Pope John Paul II's second visit to the United States; convocation of the National Black Catholic Congress (Washington, DC).

1989   Separation of Father George Stallings from Catholic church and his ordination
        as bishop and archbishop of schismatic African-American Catholic Church.

1991   Gulf War; breakup of the Soviet Union.

BIBLIOGRAPHIC ESSAY

Although there is no general directory for unpublished manuscripts relating to American Catholicism in the various foreign and American ecclesiastical archives, Finbar Kenneally *United States Documents in the Propaganda Fide Archives: A Calendar,* 11 vols. (Washington, DC: Academy of American Franciscan History, 1966–90) provides a serviceable guide to published as well as unpublished resources from the seventeenth to the late nineteenth centuries. James M. O'Toole, *A Guide to the Archives of the Archdiocese of Boston* (Boston: Archdiocese of Boston, 1982) and Evangeline Thomas, ed., *Women Religious History Sources: A Guide to Archives and Manuscript Collections in the United States* (New York: R. R. Bowker, 1983) are useful directories for specific collections, but the most general guide remains the *Directory of Archives and Manuscript Repositories in the United States* (Washington, DC: National Historical Publications and Records Commission, 1978; 2d ed., Phoenix: Oryx Press, 1988).

The standard and most useful annotated guide to bibliographic sources remains John T. Ellis and Robert Trisco, *A Guide to American Catholic History,* 2d ed., rev. and enl. (Santa Barbara, CA: ABC-Clio, 1982), but it needs to be updated with James J. Hennesey, *American Catholic Bibliography 1970–1982* (ser. 12, no. 1, Notre Dame Cushwa Center Working Papers Series, Fall 1982), his *Supplement to American Catholic Bibliography 1970–1982* (ser. 14, no. 1, Notre Dame Cushwa Center Working Papers Series, Fall 1983), and the numerous book reviews since 1982 in the *Catholic Historical Review* and listings of recently published works in the *American Catholic Studies Newsletter* (Notre Dame, IN, 1975–). This bibliographic essay focuses primarily on those works published since Ellis and Trisco's 1982 guide.

The Catholic Encyclopedia, 16 vols. (New York: Robert Appleton, 1907–12) and the *New Catholic Encyclopedia,* 15 vols. (New York: McGraw-Hill, 1967), vols. 16–18, *Supplements* (Washington, DC: Publishers Guild, 1974–88) contain a wealth of information on American Catholic history and represent the best scholarship in the early and mid-twentieth centuries. Other standard reference works include Joseph Bernard Code, *Dictionary of the American Hierarchy, 1789–1964* (New York: Joseph F. Wagner, 1964) and his pamphlet "American Catholic Bishops, 1964–1970," (St. Louis: Wexford, 1970), *The Official Catholic Directory* (New York: P. J. Kennedy, 1913–) and its many previous titles, and *The Directory of Women Religious in the United States* (Wilmington, DE: Michael Glazier, 1985). Edwin S. Gaustad, *Historical Atlas of Religion in the American Churches*, rev. ed. (New York: Harper and Row, 1976) also contains much information on the geographical and numerical distribution of Catholics in the United States.

Collections of published documents relating to the history of Catholicism in the United States include Claudia Carlen, *The Papal Encyclicals*, 5 vols. (Wilmington, NC: McGrath, 1981), Reuben Gold Thwaites, ed., *The Jesuit Relations and Allied Documents, 1610–1791*, 73 vols. (Cleveland: Burrows, 1896–1901), Hugh J. Nolan, ed., *Pastoral Letters of the United States Catholic Bishops*, 5 vols. (Washington, DC: National Conference of Catholic Bishops/United States Catholic Conference, 1984–89), John T. Ellis, ed., *Documents of American Catholic History*, 3 vols. (Wilmington, DE: Michael Glazier, 1987), Aaron I. Abell, ed., *American Catholic Thought on Social Questions* (Indianapolis: Bobbs-Merrill, 1968), Patrick W. Carey, ed., *American Catholic Religious Thought* (New York: Paulist Press, 1987), Donald C. Shearer, ed., *Pontificia Americana: A Documentary History of the Catholic Church in the United States 1784–1884* (Washington, DC: Catholic University of America Press, 1933), and Vincent A. Yzermans, ed., *American Participation in the Second Vatican Council* (New York: Sheed and Ward, 1967).

The conciliar activity and legislation of the American Catholic bishops is published in a number of collections: e.g., *Concilia Provincialia, Baltimori Habita ab anno 1829 usque ad annum 1849* (Baltimore: John Murphy, 1851), *Concilium Plenarium Totius Americae Septentrionalis Foederatae, Baltimori Habitum Anno 1852* (Baltimore: John Murphy, 1853), *Concilii Plenarii Baltimorensis II., in Ecclesia Metropolitana Baltimorensi, ad Die VII. ad Diem XXI. Octobris, A.D. MDCCCLXVI., Habiti, et a Sede Apostolica Recogniti, Acta et Decreta* (Baltimore: John Murphy, 1868), and *Acta et Decreta Concilii Plenarii Baltimorensis Tertii: A.D. MDCCCLXXXIV* (Baltimore: John Murphy, 1886). For the documents of and American episcopal participation in the two Vatican councils, see *Collectio Lacensis: Acta et decreta sacrorum conciliorum recentiorum usque ad annum 1870*, ed. G. Schneemann and T. Granderath, 7 vols. (Freiburg im Breisgau, Germany, 1870–92), John F. Broderick, ed., *Documents of Vatican I, 1869–1870* (Collegeville, MN: Liturgical Press, 1971), and Walter M. Abbott, *Documents of Vatican II* (New York: America Press, 1966).

The most complete collections of American Catholic newspapers and published pamphlets are found in the libraries of the Catholic University of America, the University of Notre Dame, and the Catholic Historical Society of Philadelphia, located at St. Charles Seminary, Overbrook, Philadelphia. Charlotte Ames has compiled a valuable guide to Notre Dame's collections in *Directory of Roman Catholic Newspapers on Microfilm: United States* (Notre Dame, IN: Memorial Library, University of Notre Dame, 1982), and Joseph J. Casino has done a similar task for the Philadelphia archives in "Ryan Memorial Archives and Historical Collections," *American Catholic Studies Newsletter* 14 (Fall 1987): 11–15. Also valuable in locating pamphlets, newspapers, and other serials are Charlotte Ames, "Catholic Pamphlets and Pamphleteers: A Guide to Indexes and Collections," *Records of the American Historical Society of Pennsylvania* 103 (Spring 1992): 1–16, and Eugene P. Willging and Herta Hatzfeld, *Catholic Serials of the Nineteenth Century in the United States: A Descriptive Bibliography and Union List*, 15 vols. (Washington, DC: Catholic University of America Press, 1959–68).

A serviceable guide to the numerous twentieth-century American Catholic journals of thought and opinion is the *Catholic Periodical Index* (New York and Washington, DC: Catholic Library Association, 1930–33; 1939–). *Records of the American Catholic Historical Society of Pennsylvania* (1887–), *Historical Records and Studies* (New York: Records of the United States Catholic Historical Society, 1899–1964), the *Catholic Historical Review* (1915–), *Church History* (1932–), *Review of Politics* (1939–), and the *U.S. Catholic Historian* (1980–) are the standard journals of scholarly research in American Catholic history.

The most comprehensive history of the Catholic church, which contains recent scholarship by a team of European and American historians and places American Catholicism within the context of worldwide historical developments, is the *History of the Church,* ed. Hubert Jedin and John Dolan, 10 vols. (New York: Seabury Press, 1980), a translation of *Handbuch der Kirchengeschichte,* ed. Hubert Jedin, 7 vols. (Freiburg, Germany: Herder, 1962–79). The first major attempt to write a separate history of American Catholicism was Henry DeCourcy and John Gilmary Shea, *The Catholic Church in the United States* (New York: Edward Dunigan, 1856), a text based primarily on a foreign observer's popular report of institutional developments within American Catholicism. John Gilmary Shea, *The History of the Catholic Church in the United States,* 4 vols. (New York: John G. Shea, 1886–92) was the first scientific history, based on archival documents but also reflective of a providential view of history that glorified Catholic growth and presence in the United States to the year 1866. Shea's work was condensed and brought up to the end of the nineteenth century by Thomas O'Gorman, *A History of the Roman Catholic Church in the United States* (New York: Charles Scribner's, 1907), which was volume 9 of the *American Church History Series,* ed. Philip Schaff. In the 1920s Peter Guilday's lives of bishops John Carroll and John England and his many other historical studies based on extensive documentary evidence advanced the scientific study of American history but still within an apologetical posture, placing significant emphasis on the compatibility of fundamental American and Catholic values. Influenced by social history and the progressive historians, John T. Ellis, *American Catholicism* (Chicago: University of Chicago Press, 1956; 2d ed., rev., 1969) and his many other works presented Catholicism within the general American political and social movements. Ellis used his histories to advance the need for moderate reforms within the church. Thomas McAvoy, *A History of the Catholic Church in the United States* (Notre Dame, IN: University of Notre Dame Press, 1969), also influenced by social and progressive historians, advanced the thesis of cultural conflict to explain the development of what he called the American Catholic minority.

Like a number of other Catholic historians of the 1960s, David J. O'Brien, "American Catholic Historiography: A Post-Conciliar Evaluation," *CH* 37 (March 1968): 80–94, has criticized these pre–Vatican II histories because of their overly institutional approach. Henry Warner Bowden, "John Gilmary Shea: A Study of Method and Goals in Historiography," *CHR* 54 (July 1968): 235–60, and his "Catholic Historiography" in his *Church History in the Age of Science: Historiographical Patterns in the United States, 1876–1918* (Chapel Hill: University of North Carolina Press, 1971), 69–93, provide a balanced critical assessment of Shea's scientific and providential approach within the context of historical writing in the late nineteenth century. David O'Brien has also made a similar assessment of the work of Peter Guilday in "Peter Guilday: The Catholic Intellectual in the Post-Modernist Church," in *Studies in Catholic History in Honor of John Tracy Ellis,* ed. Nelson H. Minnich, Robert B. Eno, and Robert Trisco (Wilmington, DE: M. Glazier, 1985), 260–306. The most comprehensive examination of the historical writing of Shea, Guilday, McAvoy, Theodore Maynard, and Ellis is found in Jack Douglas Thomas, "Interpretations of American Catholic Church History: A Comparative Analysis of Representative Catholic Historians, 1875–1975," (Ph.D. diss., Baylor University, 1976) and in the more recent collection of essays "Reflections on Catholic Historiography," *U.S.CH* 6 (Winter 1987), which also provide a helpful bibliography of unpublished theses and dissertations. Another excellent general assessment of twentieth-century Catholic as well as Protestant historiography is Henry Warner Bowden, *Church History in an Age of Uncertainty: Historiographical Patterns in the United States, 1906–1990* (Carbondale and Edwardsville: Southern Illinois University Press, 1991).

In the period after the Second Vatican Council (1962–65) the history of American Catholicism received a considerable amount of attention, but a notable shift of interests occurred, reflecting increased attention to the social history of the "People of God," emphasizing the roles of the laity and especially of women in that history, the diverse religious and cultural experiences of various immigrant groups and racial minorities, and the development of spirituality and religious thought—themes that had been by and large neglected in earlier histories. The two most important studies reflecting these new concerns were James Hennesey, *American Catholics: A History of the Roman Catholic Community in the United States* (New York: Oxford University Press, 1981) and Jay P. Dolan, *The American Catholic Experience: A History from Colonial Times to the Present* (Garden City, NY: Doubleday and Co., 1985). The readable and always insightful Martin Marty, relying upon the studies of Hennesey and Dolan, published *An Invitation to American Catholic History* (Chicago: Thomas More Press, 1986), which reflected his view of the historical emergence from a "Catholic ghetto" into American pluralism in the post–Vatican II period.

In the late 1980s a team of historians under the general editorship of Christopher J. Kauffman and sponsorship of the National Conference of Catholic Bishops produced a six-volume history of American Catholicism, *Makers of the Catholic Community,* that also reflected the new historical interests of the post-Vatican II church: Gerald P. Fogarty, ed., *Patterns of Episcopal Leadership;* Joseph P. Chinnici, *Living Stones: The History and Structure of Catholic Spiritual Life in the United States;* Margaret Mary Reher, *Catholic Intellectual Life in America: A Historical Study of Persons and Movements;* Dolores Liptak, *Immigrants and Their Church;* David O'Brien, *Public Catholicism;* and Karen Kennelly, ed., *American Catholic Women: A Historical Exploration* (all, New York: Macmillan, 1989).

The neglect of women, African-Americans, and Hispanics in pre–Vatican II histories was also addressed by a number of new studies: Mary Jo Weaver, *New Catholic Women: A Contemporary Challenge to Traditional Religious Authority* (San Francisco: Harper and Row, 1985); James K. Kenneally, *The History of American Catholic Women* (New York: Crossroad, 1990); "Women in the Catholic Community," *U.S.CH* 5 (Summer/Fall 1986); Cyprian Davis, *The History of Black Catholics in the United States* (New York: Crossroad, 1990); Stephen J. Ochs, *Desegrating the Altar: The Josephites and the Struggle for Black Priests, 1871–1960* (Baton Rouge: Louisiana State University Press, 1990); "The Black Catholic Experience," *U.S.CH* 5 (1986); "The Black Catholic Community, 1880–1987," *U.S.CH* 7 (Spring/Summer 1988); Julian Samora, *A History of the Mexican-American People,* rev. and exp. (Notre Dame, IN: University of Notre Dame Press, 1992); Moises Sandoval, ed., *Fronteras: A History of the Latin American Church in the USA Since 1513* (San Antonio, Texas: Mexican American Cultural Center, 1983); his *On the Move: A History of the Hispanic Church in the United States* (Maryknoll, NY: Orbis Books, 1990); and "Hispanic Catholics: Historical Explorations and Cultural Analysis," *U.S.CH* 9 (Winter/Spring 1990).

The post–Vatican II study of American Catholicism has been greatly advanced by the publication of multivolume historical studies. Arno Press, under an advisory editorial board of Jay P. Dolan, Paul Messbarger, and Michael Novak, published a fifty-volume series of previously unpublished dissertations, reprints, and newly edited collections of resources entitled "The American Catholic Tradition" (New York, 1978). Garland Press, under the general editorship of Timothy Walch, published a twenty-eight-volume series, "The Heritage of American Catholicism" (New York, 1988), which contains twenty volumes of previously unpublished dissertations and eight of previously published articles.

Some very good diocesan, parish, and regional studies have also emerged since 1982. Three of the most insightful diocesan histories, reflecting post–Vatican II interests in the church as the "People of God" and the church's interaction with political and social conditions in American society, are Thomas Spalding, *The Premier See: A History of the Archdiocese of Baltimore, 1789–1989* (Baltimore: Johns Hopkins University Press, 1989); Clyde F. Crews, *An American Holy Land: A History of the Archdiocese of Louisville* (Wilmington, DE: Michael Glazier, 1984); and Leslie Tentler, *Seasons of Grace: A History of the Catholic Archdiocese of Detroit* (Detroit: Wayne State University Press, 1990). Though not a comprehensive diocesan history, Steven M. Avella, *This Confident Church: Catholic Leadership and Life in Chicago, 1940–1965* (Notre Dame, IN: University of Notre Dame Press, 1992) provides insight and careful historical analysis of the immediate pre–Vatican II American church in the nation's largest Catholic diocese. Jay P. Dolan has edited *The American Catholic Parish: A History from 1850 to the Present*, 2 vols. (New York: Paulist Press, 1987), which reflects the new emphasis on social history and demonstrates the regional variations in parish life and structures. The regional variation in American Catholicism is evident, too, in *Catholics in the Old South: Essays on Church and Culture*, ed. Randall M. Miller and Jon L. Wakelyn (Macon, GA: Mercer University Press, 1983) and in a number of essays in David J. Alvarez and Carl Guarneri, eds., *Religion and Society in the American West* (Lanham, MD: University Press of America, 1987).

American Catholic education and educational institutions have also received a new critical assessment. Joseph M. White, *The Diocesan Seminary in the United States: A History from the 1780s to the Present* (Notre Dame, IN: University of Notre Dame Press, 1989) is the first comprehensive survey of the spiritual formation and theological education of the American diocesan clergy. William P. Leahy, *Adapting to America: Catholics, Jesuits, and Higher Education in the Twentieth Century* (Washington, DC: Georgetown University Press, 1991) is a major study of how the twenty-two Jesuit colleges and universities have adapted themselves to American culture and the patterns of higher education in the United States. Other particular historical and critical essays and assessments are found in "Catholic Higher Education," *U.S.CH* 7 (Fall 1988). The most insightful studies of Catholic higher education, however, have been done by Philip Gleason in a number of published articles, one of the most recent being "Changing and Remaining the Same," in *Perspectives on the American Catholic Church, 1789–1989*, ed. Stephen J. Vicchio and Sister Virginia Geiger (Westminster, MD: Christian Classics, 1989), 223–30. The fruit of Gleason's more than twenty-five years of study of Catholic higher education is expected to be published in a major monograph in the near future. The history of attempts to provide Catholic education and spiritual guidance at major non-Catholic schools of higher education is the subject of John Whitney Evans, *The Newman Movement: Roman Catholics in American Higher Education, 1883–1971* (Notre Dame, IN: University of Notre Dame Press, 1980). Except for Andrew M. Greeley, *Catholic High Schools and Minority Students* (New Brunswick, NJ: Transaction Books, 1982), which is a sociological study of the quality of Catholic schools in black and Hispanic communities, there have unfortunately been no systematic historical and cultural studies of Catholic primary and secondary education since 1982.

The roles of the various religious orders of men and women have likewise received some attention since 1982. Christopher J. Kauffman's excellent *Tradition and Transformation in Catholic Culture: The Priests of Saint Sulpice in the United States from 1791 to the Present* (New York: Macmillan, 1988) is particularly valuable, not only as a history of the Sulpicians, but also as a general cultural history of American Catholicism. The Sulpicians set the standards for the spiritual and theological formation of diocesan clergy and became the primary ecclesiastical advisors to the archbishops of Baltimore. An understanding of the monastic life and its interaction with American culture is the subject of Joel Rippinger, *The Benedictine Order in the United States: An Interpretive History* (Collegeville, MN: Liturgical Press, 1990). There has been a veritable flood of published research on religious orders of women. Patricia Byrne, "Sisters of St. Joseph: The Americanization of a French Tradition," *U.S.CH* 5 (1986): 241–72, is indicative of the theme of Americanization that many of the new histories follow. Margaret Susan Thompson, who is working on a general history of religious orders of women in the United States, has also published a survey analysis of the role of women religious in "Discovering Foremothers: Sisters, Society, and the American Catholic Experience," *U.S.CH* 5 (1986): 273–90. "Women Religious: Historical Explorations," *U.S.CH* 10 (1992) also demonstrates the various new methodologies used in studies on women religious in recent years.

The specific roles of religious and lay women have also been examined in Alden V. Brown, *The Grail Movement and American Catholicism 1940–1975* (Notre Dame, IN: University of Notre Dame Press, 1989). Margaret M. McGuinness has contributed to the expanding historical analysis of women's participation in the social apostolate with her "Response to Reform: The History of the Catholic Social Settlement Movement, 1897–1915" (Ph.D. diss., Union Theological Seminary, New York, 1985) and "A Puzzle with Missing Pieces: Catholic Women and the Social Settlement Movement, 1897–1915" (Charles and Margaret Hall Cushwa Center Working Paper Series 22, Spring 1990).

The role of the laity in the institutional church and in American society has received increased historical attention during the post–Vatican II years. Patrick Carey has examined antebellum lay trusteeism in *People, Priests, and Prelates: Ecclesiastical Democracy and the Tensions of Trusteeism* (Notre Dame, IN: University of Notre Dame Press, 1987) and surveyed elite "Lay Catholic Leadership in the United States," *U.S.CH* 9 (Summer 1990): 223–47. Christopher Kauffman, *Faith and Fraternalism: The History of the Knights of Columbus 1882–1982* (New York: Harper and Row, 1982) is a model history of the interaction of lay voluntaryism and associationism within the dynamic currents in American social life. Alfred J. Ede, *The Lay Crusade for a Christian America: A Study of the American Federation of Catholic Societies, 1900–1919* (New York: Garland, 1988) demonstrates the influence of progressivism upon middle-class lay leaders in the early twentieth-century struggle for reform and justice in society.

African-American lay Catholic leadership is analyzed in Marilyn Wenzke Nickels, *Black Catholic Protest and the Federated Colored Catholics 1917–1933* (New York: Garland, 1988). Since her "David Goldstein and the Lay Catholic Street Apostolate 1917–41" (Ph.D. diss., Boston University, 1982), Debra Campbell has published a number of significant path-breaking studies on the laity's role in pre–Vatican II twentieth-century American Catholicism: e.g., "A Catholic Salvation Army: David Goldstein, Pioneer Lay Evangelist," *CH* 52 (September 1983): 322–32; "Catholic Lay Evangelism in the 1930s: Four Models," *RACHS* 95 (March–December 1984): 5–15; "David Goldstein and the Rise of the Catholic Campaigners for Christ," *CHR* 72 (1986): 33–50; and "Part-Time Female Evangelists of the Thirties and Forties: The Rosary College Evidence Guild," *U.S.CH* 5 (Summer/Fall 1986): 371–83. Twentieth-century elite lay intellectuals and their perceptions of the laity's roles in church and American society are the subject of Martin J. Bredeck, *Imperfect Apostles: The Commonweal and the American Catholic Laity, 1924–1976* (New York: Garland, 1988). Patrick Allitt has examined the rise of conservative Catholic lay intellectuals in "American Catholics and the New Conservatives of the 1950s," *U.S.CH* 7 (Winter 1988): 15–37. Two issues of *U.S.CH* 9, Summer 1990 and Fall 1990, have focused on a variety of historical analyses of labor and lay movements throughout American history. A helpful sociological and historical examination of some of the elite American Catholic lay and clerical leadership between 1973 and 1983 is Joseph A. Varacalli, *Toward the Establishment of Liberal Catholicism in America* (Washington, DC: University Press of America, 1983).

The study of various immigrant social and religious traditions has been a major part of the new history that is clearly manifested in Jay P. Dolan's general history and Dolores Liptak's specific analysis, both previously mentioned. The general story of immigrant Catholic interaction with American culture and other immigrant Catholics is also the subject of James S. Olson, *Catholic Immigrants in America* (Chicago: Nelson-Hall, 1987). Dolores Liptak, *European Immigrants and the Catholic Church in Connecticut, 1870–1920* (New York: Center for Migration Studies, 1987) is an excellent specific study of how diocesan policies and ethnic parishes combined to incorporate immigrants into the Catholic church. The best single social and cultural analysis of the popular religion and spirituality of an immigrant group is Robert Anthony Orsi, *The Madonna of 115th Street: Faith and Community in Italian Harlem, 1880–1950* (New Haven, CT: Yale University Press, 1985).

Conflict, community, and leadership are the themes of numerous other studies of immigrant traditions in American Catholicism. Representative studies would have to include the following: Joseph Fitzpatrick, "Cultural Change or Cultural Continuity: Pluralism and Hispanic Americans," in *Hispanics in New York: Religious, Cultural, and Social Experiences* (New York: Archdiocese of New York, Offices of Pastoral Research, 1982); Henry B. Leonard, "Ethnic Tensions, Episcopal Leadership, and the Emergence of the Twentieth-Century American Catholic Church: The Cleveland Experience," *CHR* 71 (July 1985): 394–412; "The Italian American Community," *U.S.CH* 6 (Fall 1987); and "Hispanic Catholics: Historical Explorations and Cultural Analysis," *U.S.CH* 9 (Winter/Spring 1990). The most insightful analysis of the scholarly discourse on ethnicity and religion is Philip Gleason's collection of essays entitled *Speaking of Diversity: Essays on the Language of Ethnicity* (Baltimore: Johns Hopkins University Press, 1992).

The examination of American Catholic scholarship and the interaction of the Catholic mind with the currents of American and European intellectual developments is the subject of a number of recent studies, some of which are included in Margaret Mary Re-her's general study, mentioned above. Patrick Carey's introduction to his *American Catholic Religious Thought* (New York: Paulist Press, 1987) and his "Catholic Religious Thought in the U.S.A.," in *Perspectives on the American Catholic Church, 1789–1989*, 143–66, survey the history of Catholic apologetical and theological perspectives. Gerald P. Fogarty, *American Catholic Biblical Scholarship: A History from the Early Republic to Vatican II* (San Francisco: Harper and Row, 1989) is the first analysis of the conflicts over and developments of biblical scholarship. The history of the immediate pre– and post–Vatican II liturgical movement is the subject of Kathleen Hughes, *The Monk's Tale: A Biography of Godfrey Diekmann, O.S.B.* (Collegeville, MN: Liturgical Press, 1991).

A more general history of the last fifty years of theology is contained in a number of survey essays in the fiftieth anniversary volumes of *Theological Studies* (March, June, September, and December 1989). Scott Appleby, *"Church and Age Unite!" The Modernist Impulse in American Catholicism* (Notre Dame, IN: University of Notre Dame Press, 1992) is a first-rate specific study of the religious conflict over modernism. Two specific and very different studies of the intellectual climate in the immediate pre–Vatican II period are also worthy of note: Arnold Sparr, *To Promote, Defend, and Redeem: The Catholic Literary Revival and the Cultural Transformation of American Catholicism, 1920–1960* (New York: Greenwood Press, 1990) and James Terence Fisher, *The Catholic Counterculture in America, 1933–1962* (Chapel Hill: University of North Carolina Press, 1989). More general assessments of "Catholics and the Intellectual Life" are published in *U.S.CH* 4 (1985). Perhaps the most provocative analyses of the intellectual issues facing Catholic attempts to adapt to American culture and the inherent conflicts between continuity and change are found in Philip Gleason's excellent collection of essays *Keeping the Faith: American Catholicism Past and Present* (Notre Dame, IN: University of Notre Dame Press, 1987).

In addition to David O'Brien's *Public Catholicism*, there have continued to be since 1982 a number of focused studies of American Catholic social and economic thought. Charles E. Curran, *American Catholic Social Ethics: Twentieth-Century Approaches* (Notre Dame, IN: University of Notre Dame Press, 1982) is a general historical and critical assessment of American Catholic developments. Another general study of prominent Catholic thinkers from Orestes Brownson to Cesar Chavez is John J. Mitchell, *Critical Voices in American Catholic Economic Thought* (New York: Paulist Press, 1989). Mel Piehl's brief but perceptive essay "American Catholics and Social Reform, 1789–1989," in *Perspectives on the American Catholic Church, 1789–1989*, 317–40, is also a general introduction to the dynamics of Catholic movements toward social justice, as are a number of essays in "American Catholic Social Thought," *U.S.CH* 5 (1986). Three historical studies of specific periods and movements are also worthy of note: Joseph McShane, *"Sufficiently Radical": Catholicism, Progressivism, and the Bishops' Program of 1919* (Washington, DC: Catholic University of America Press, 1986); Thomas E. Blantz, *A Priest in Public Service: Francis J. Haas and the New Deal* (Notre Dame, IN: University of Notre Dame Press, 1982); and Mel Piehl, *Breaking Bread: The Catholic Worker and the Origin of Catholic Radicalism in America* (Philadelphia: Temple University Press, 1982).

Historical study of American Catholic spirituality, devotionalism, and popular religion has significantly increased since 1982. Paulist Press has continued to make a major contribution by publishing a series of anthologies and reprints of the *Classics of Western*

Spirituality and *Sources in American Spirituality,* both edited until recently by John Farina. The *American Spirituality* collection, for example, includes texts and historical introductions to works on devotion to the Holy Spirit (1985), Jesuit spirituality (1988), and the writings of Elizabeth Seton (1987), Isaac Hecker (1988), Félix Varela (1989), Orestes A. Brownson (1991), and Thomas Merton (1992), among others. The beginnings of a general history of American Catholic spirituality have appeared in Joseph Chinnici's *Living Stones* (already mentioned) and "Spirituality, Devotionalism, and Popular Religion" *U.S.CH* 8 (Winter/Spring 1989). Ann Taves, *The Household of Faith: Roman Catholic Devotions in Mid-Nineteenth-Century America* (Notre Dame, IN: University of Notre Dame Press, 1986) is an excellent example of the use of devotional texts as an entrée into the devotional spirituality of American Catholics. Allan Deck, "The Spirituality of the United States Hispanics: An Introductory Essay," *U.S.CH* 9 (Winter/Spring 1990): 137–46, and Cyprian Davis, "Black Spirituality" *U.S.CH* 8 (Winter/Spring 1989): 39–46 give brief overviews of ethnically and racially conditioned manifestations of Catholic spirituality. Mary Jo Weaver has also outlined some of the more recent attempts to create a "Roman Catholic Feminist Spirituality" in her *New Catholic Women,* 180–214.

The social and demographic characteristics of American Catholics, especially in the post–Vatican II era, have been the subject of a number of studies. One of the more useful summaries of recent sociological analyses of actual American Catholic beliefs and practices is George Gallup, Jr., and Jim Castelli, *The American Catholic People: Their Beliefs, Practices, and Values* (Garden City, NY: Doubleday and Co., 1987). Their *People's Religion: American Faith in the 90s* (New York: Macmillan, 1989) is more general in scope but also beneficial for placing Catholics in the wider context of current trends in American religious denominations. Andrew M. Greeley, *American Catholics since the Council: An Unauthorized Report* (Chicago: Thomas More Press, 1985) also summarizes much of the data collected by the National Opinion Research Center on American Catholic opinions, practices, and institutional affiliations. The most provocative sociological analysis, which helps to place the experiences of American Catholics in the context of wider religious trends in post–World War II America, is Robert Wuthnow, *The Restructuring of American Religion: Society and Faith Since World War II* (Princeton, NJ: Princeton University Press, 1988).

INDEX

About the Author

PATRICK W. CAREY is Associate Professor of Theology at Marquette University. He is an authority on the history of American religious life and thought. He has authored or edited 5 books, and his articles have appeared in journals such as the *Catholic Historical Review* and *Church History*.